ORIENTALISM AND WAR

CRITICAL WAR STUDIES SERIES

Series Editors, Tarak Barkawi & Shane Brighton

War transforms the social and political orders in which we live, just as it obliterates our precious certainties. Nowhere is this more obvious than in the fate of truths offered about war itself. War regularly undermines expectations, strategies and theories, and along with them the credibility of those in public life and the academy presumed to speak with authority about it. A fundamental reason for this is the frequently narrow and impoverished intellectual resources that dominate the study of war. Critical War Studies begins with the recognition that the unsettling character of war is a profound opportunity for scholarship. Accordingly, the series welcomes submissions from across the academy as well as from reflective practitioners. It provides an open forum for critical scholarship concerned with war and armed forces and seeks to foster and develop the nascent encounter between war and contemporary approaches to society, history, politics and philosophy. It is a vehicle to reconcile the field of war studies, expand the sites where war is studies, and open the field to new voices.

TARAK BARKAWI and KEITH STANSKI

(*Editors*)

Orientalism and War

Columbia University Press
New York

Columbia University Press
Publishers Since 1893
New York
cup.columbia.edu
© Tarak Barkawi and Keith Stanski, 2012
All rights reserved

Library of Congress Cataloging-in-Publication Data

Orientalism and war / Tarak Barkawi and Keith Stanski, editors.
    p. cm.
"[B]ased on a conference held at the University of Oxford, June 17/19,
2010"—Introd.
Includes bibliographical references and index.
ISBN 978-0-231-70356-7 (alk. paper)
    1. Orientalism—Philosophy—Congresses. 2. War and civilization—Orient—
Congresses. 3. War and civilization—Western countries—Congresses. 4. Orient—
History, Military—Congresses. 5. East and West—Congresses. I. Barkawi, Tarak.
II. Stanski, Keith, 1981–

DS61.85.O7526 2012
303.6'6095—dc23

                            2012029146

Columbia University Press books are printed on permanent and durable acid-free paper.
This book is printed on paper with recycled content.
Printed in India

c 10 9 8 7 6 5 4 3 2 1

References to Internet Web sites (URLs) were accurate at the time of writing. Neither
the author nor Columbia University Press is responsible for URLs that may have expired
or changed since the manuscript was prepared.

CONTENTS

v

CONTENTS

ACKNOWLEDGEMENTS

This project began with a hurried conversation in a San Francisco hotel lobby more than four years ago. Since then we have accumulated numerous debts in producing this volume. Richard Caplan, Andrew Hurrell, and Kalypso Nicolaïdis supported the initial proposal. A timely intervention by Alia Brahimi and Patrick Porter helped bring the project to fruition. We are also grateful to Martin Coward for his generous endorsement.

This volume is based on a conference held at the University of Oxford, June 17–19, 2010. What insights it contains is entirely due to the willingness and generosity of conference participants to share their ideas. Andrea Baumann, Christopher Bickerton, Christine Cheng, Alexander Evans, and Patricia Owens ensured the conference proceedings moved along. Presenters and the audience alike benefited from the reflections of the discussants, to whom we owe special thanks: Josef Teboho Ansorge, Shane Brighton, Tina Mai Chen, James Der Derian, Bud Duvall, Laleh Khalili, John Mowitt, Iver Neumann, Harry Sidebottom, and Hew Strachan. We are especially grateful to our paper presenters, especially those whose contributions could not for various reasons be included in the volume: Katherine Brown, Douglas Bulloch, Tina Mai Chen, Faisal Devji, Omar El-Khairy, Robert Johnson, Craig Jones, Darryl Li, Kwong Chi Man, Daniel Neep, and Simon Philpott.

The conference would not have been possible without the assistance of Sundas Ali. Her talents, enthusiasm, and dedication are second to none. Kate Candy, Sarah Travis, and their colleagues also helped ensure that the conference was a success. A special thanks is due to Michael Dwyer and the Hurst staff for helping assemble the volume. An anonymous reviewer offered measured criticisms and helpful suggestions.

ACKNOWLEDGEMENTS

Several institutions supported the project at various stages. The generous assistance of the British Academy's Small Research Grant allowed the project to convene such talented participants from various corners. The University of Oxford's Department of Politics and International Relations and Centre on International Studies were instrumental in hosting the event. Nuffield College and the Nuffield College Politics Group shared their facilities and financial largesse with the project.

To all we are very thankful. Any errors and misjudgements which remain in the pages to follow are our responsibility.

LIST OF FIGURES

ABOUT THE CONTRIBUTORS

Josef Teboho Ansorge, J.D. Candidate, Yale Law School.

Tarak Barkawi, Associate Professor, Department of Politics, New School for Social Research.

Arjun Chowdhury, Assistant Professor, Political Science, University of British Columbia, Vancouver.

Bruce Cumings, Professor, History, University of Chicago.

Derek Gregory, Peter Wall Distinguished Professor, University of British Columbia, Vancouver.

Hugh Gusterson, Professor, Cultural Studies and Anthropology, George Mason University.

Susan Jeffords, Professor, English and Women Studies, and Vice Chancellor, University of Washington.

Maria Mälksoo, Senior Researcher, Institute of Government and Politics, University of Tartu.

Margaret A. Mills, Professor, Near Eastern Languages and Cultures, Ohio State University.

John Mowitt, Professor, Cultural Studies and Comparative Literature, University of Minnesota.

Himadeep R. Muppidi, Associate Professor, Political Science, Vassar College.

ABOUT THE CONTRIBUTORS

Quỳnh N. Phạm, Ph.D. Candidate, Political Science, University of Minnesota.

Patrick Porter, Reader in Strategic Studies, University of Reading.

Patricia Owens, Reader in International Relations, University of Sussex.

Keith Stanski, Senior Program Officer, NYU Center on International Cooperation.

1

INTRODUCTION

ORIENTALISM AND WAR

Tarak Barkawi and *Keith Stanski**

'Fucking savages!'
Colonel Kilgore[1]

If ever there was a topic whose time has come, it is orientalism and war. The public discourses of the War on Terror are suffused with orientalism. Law abiding, Christian and Western civilization is threatened by 'mad mullahs' who hail from an East ever-resistant to modernity and who use violence in ways that violate the most fundamental ethical protocols of armed conflict.

* In many respects, this introduction reflects the combined wisdom of the participants at the Orientalism at War Workshop, held at the University of Oxford on June 17–19, 2010. We are very grateful for their willingness to share and debate ideas. We would like especially to thank Josef Teboho Ansorge, Shane Brighton, Tina Mai Chen, James Der Derian, Bud Duvall, Susan Jeffords, Laleh Khalili, John Mowitt, Iver Neumann, Patrick Porter and an anonymous reviewer for their comments and thoughts. This introduction draws in places on Barkawi and Brighton, 'Powers of War.'

These themes and their many cousins can be found in newspapers and other media, in government documents and pronouncements, and in the texts of academics and policy experts. They are in significant respects constitutive of the War on Terror, which is unimaginable without the orientalist imagery invoked daily to reproduce its practices and dynamics. But what does it mean to think through the relations between these two concepts? What is the place of orientalism in war, and of war in orientalism?

Notably, the idea of a West at war with an East conceived as radically other is pervasive and longstanding. Edward Said's seminal statement focused largely on a specific scholarly tradition that arose in the eighteenth and nineteenth centuries, but orientalist tropes and themes have since proliferated to many sites and contexts. They are used to frame interpretations of conflicts as far back as the Greek and Persian Wars. Notable examples include the Crusades, European wars with the Ottomans, imperial 'small wars' in Latin America, Asia and Africa, efforts to define Germany as non-Western in the World Wars, the Cold War and the idea of the Soviet Union as an 'oriental despotism,' and the 'humanitarian' wars of the post-Cold War period fought against 'ethnic barbarians.' In such instances, recognizably Western and Eastern characters and categorizations populate interpretations and representations of conflicts in various media. This mode of thinking shapes the actions of those making war, and informs the opinions and beliefs of people far removed in time and place from the fighting.

Representations of self and other are certainly the most evident sign of the ways orientalism participates in war and shapes our understandings of it. They make up a major theme of this volume, and the first set of papers is devoted to it. However, the pervasiveness of the associations between orientalism and war, of violent conflict as a site of, and an incitement for, orientalist discourse, suggests the connections run deeper. While the 'war on terror' may be unimaginable without orientalism, it would seem that orientalism is also not thinkable without war. In fact, war and the processes of othering it entails, may be more important to orientalism than the Orient. As is widely recognized, you need not be 'Oriental'—however that term is understood—to be orientalized.[2] Despite the blond hair under many of their helmets, Kaiser Wilhelm II's soldiers were characterized as 'Huns,' a horse tribe from the depths of Asia. In the Cold War, communists of many nations and races were widely constructed in orientalist terms, as a species of devious barbarian arrayed in the order of an ant colony. War appears to play a constitutive role in orientalism, generating new orientalisms. For Colonel Kilgore, as for many fictional and real soldiers of his era, the violence of Vietnamese peasants and revolutionaries seemed obviously 'savage,' while their own was 'rational' and 'limited.' It is in and through violent conflict that various Western and Eastern identities are defined and come to be taken for granted, as truths about the essential nature of peoples. The second set of papers below looks at some of the ways in which this is so.

If war makes orientalisms, what, precisely, does orientalism do for war? How does orientalism come to play a role in war? What is its 'weapons system' as it were? The third set of papers in this collection explores how orientalism participates in war through interpretation, by providing an account of the meaning of a war and the identities of the parties involved in it. Inherent in the idea of war is a conflict of interpretation, of opposing views between and among groups of people, friends and enemies. War might be said to be a difference of opinion pursued through violent means. Orientalism, through interpretation, produces and shapes opinion and belief. For example, various 'experts' provide interpretations to the public and to government about the War on Terror. For these experts, and for many in their audiences, their interpretations are not just interpretations, they are truths, authorized and legitimated by their own expertise. This is orientalism as 'orientalists,' a community of experts that functions as an interpretive machine producing, authorizing, and disseminating truths about some object, such as terrorism, in ways which rely on and reproduce East/West categories and distinctions. It was precisely one such community of 'orientalists' that was the object of Said's initial statement. Orientalists fight war at the level of meaning, over which account of reality dominates opinion. As John Mowitt emphasizes in Chapter 11, this 'war of opinion' is fought as much within as between the warring sides. In defining the meaning of a conflict in ways which require the self to violently struggle against an enemy understood as radically other, orientalism becomes a constitutive moment in war.

Having set the stage with these broad sweeps—orientalist representation in war; war as a constitutive moment in orientalism; orientalism as a constitutive moment in war—the remainder of this introduction provides some further background on orientalism, on war and on thinking the two together, before closing with a description of the papers to follow.

Orientalism

In a variety of sites and contexts, Westerners define themselves against an inferior, orientalized other, shaping dominant identities and ideologies in diverse ways. As discourse, orientalism posits two putatively separate worlds, the West and the East. In producing an idea of the East it also elaborates a vision of what is understood as West. However, perhaps more striking than the supposedly stark difference between these two realms is the inherent inequality between them. Regardless of the context, the East is consistently cast as inferior to the West, as possessing clear deficiencies that only affirm its counterpart's presumed superiority. Said's influential work on this subject has given rise to diverse literatures critiquing and developing his ideas, as well as exploring his themes in a variety of literary, scholarly, and popular sites.[3] While much of this work touches upon armed conflict, war is rarely the central theme in scholarship on orientalism.[4] Orientalism is figured primarily as a cultural 'style,' a form of 'intellectual authority' over the East.[5]

Loose uses of the term see orientalism at work in any form of bias or condescending representation. But not all forms of identifying the self through relations of othering are orientalist in character. Friend/enemy and self/other relations are diverse. Orientalist discourses are those that produce categories of 'East' and 'West' and imagine the world can be meaningfully categorized and analyzed in terms of distinctions of this kind. Once one is thinking in terms of an East that has a set of attributes and a West that has a contrasting set of attributes, one is already operating in a world defined by orientalism. These cultural distinctions can be drawn across a range of referents, whether communities of people, governments, or other types of political actors. Crucially, it is not the actual, geographic East and West (wherever located) that is at issue. If that were so it would be difficult to understand how people and ideas in the West can be orientalized. Rather, whatever its specific object, an orientalist discourse is one that draws from the pool of cultural materials associated with and defined by East/West distinctions.

The contributors to this volume take their cue from, but are not limited to, Said's original focus in *Orientalism*. Said was concerned with an institutionalized interpretive community, scholars of the Orient. On the basis of their authority as a community of experts, these scholars offered authoritative accounts of their subject matter. They produced a regime of truth in and through which distinctions between East and West were constituted. As Said argued, 'Orientalism…is not an airy European fantasy about the

Orient, but a created body of theory and practice in which, for many generations, there has been a considerable material investment.'[6] Thus for us, in the first instance, orientalism concerns the institutionalized production of expertise. It is about who is empowered to represent with authority, who is seen to speak knowledgeably. A community of experts is specifically orientalist when they produce and reproduce distinctions between East and West. In contexts of conflict and imperialism, the West is imagined as a site of modernity and order and the East as one of tradition and disorder. A contemporary example of an institutionalized community of experts who are liable to think in these kinds of terms is that of 'terrorism studies.'[7]

Several themes emerge from this focus on orientalism as an institutionalized community of experts. One concerns the way in which experts in various sites are trained and credentialed. How does one become authorized to represent with authority in government, the academy, the media, and the military? The role of technology in the ways these communities of experts gather, interpret and display data about the East—and by extension the West—also figures prominently here. Another issue is the self-referential character of orientalist expertise. The views of experts are validated by the community of experts in and through their shared orientalist discourse, often by citing longstanding cultural arguments about the East and the West. This does not mean there is a unitary 'party line.' There is usually plenty of scope for debate between and among any given community of experts. The orientalist scholars Said focused on disagreed about many things, and had sustained debates and conversations over crucial matters. But ultimately what counts as a legitimate view, and a legitimate object of debate and contestation, is decided by reference to the community of experts, as opposed to an outside arbiter. In this way the community of experts polices boundaries between itself and those who are not authorized to represent with authority, while also internally constraining topics of discussion. Finally, and perhaps most importantly, an orientalist community of experts denies that it offers merely 'an interpretation' of some phenomenon. On their own account, such experts deal in the currency of truth, they are 'telling it like it is.'

For us, this focus on orientalism as an institutionalized community of experts is crucial. Orientalism is not mere bias against Easterners; it is a regime of truth.[8] Views that in fact amount to grotesque misrepresentation come to be accepted by the authorized experts and by those they communicate with. One such misrepresentation that sits at the core of historical and contemporary orientalisms concerns the East as a site of disorder and the West as that which brings order to disorder. An example is the idea that 'insurgents' in Iraq and Afghanistan are the source of disorder, and that the occupying Coalition forces are sources of order.[9] In diverse and longstanding ways, intervention by outside powers has shaped the political and social character of these two countries, most recently in invasions which destroyed their governing regimes. The claim that the source of 'destabilization' in these countries is insurgents and insurgency thus requires a great deal of forgetting and misrepresentation. Similarly, considerable work must be done to affirm the supposed success of such interventions in delivering appropriate and durable forms of order to these otherwise troubled lands. Yet these claims are broadly accepted and reproduced by a community of experts in the media, in government, the military, and elsewhere. How does this come to be so, and with what effects?

War

Much writing on war concerns questions of strategy and histories of armed forces and military operations. Given the significance of war for politics and society, there is remarkably little attention to it in the major traditions in the social sciences and humanities, critical or otherwise. As Michael Mann observes, 'From the Enlightenment to Durkheim most major sociologists omitted war from their central problematic' believing 'future society would be pacific and transnational.'[10] Yet, for Clausewitz, and the thin line of major thinkers who have tackled war as their centerpiece, a key dimension of war is its socially generative properties.[11] War consumes and reworks social and political orders. Clausewitz repeatedly emphasizes war's capacity to unmake certainties, in chaotic and unpredictable ways.[12] This was in part a reflection of his own experience of a period of violent social transformation occasioned by the Napoleonic way of war.

The 'war and society' tradition in sociology and history has sought to make good on these kinds of insights, and offers a hook for thinking through the relations between war and orientalism.[13] The basic idea is that war and society are entwined in mutually constitutive relations. War shapes society; society shapes war. War conjoins not only opposing military forces but also their societies and leaderships in a thick web of social and political interaction.[14] War, as it were, exceeds 'war' as the clash of arms and is related to a whole range of social phenomena on and off the battlefield, not least the numerous sites where it is memorialized and represented.[15] From this perspective, war's enormous consequences—over and above human and material destruction—come into view. War has been central to the rise and course of the modern state; it has shaped technological and scientific developments; it is fundamental for gender relations and for economies; and all these social domains react back on war, shaping it.[16] It is here that we would locate the role of war, in the form of conflicts interpreted in East/West terms, in shaping the identity politics we know as orientalism.

In this vein, war has been central for culture and cultural change. In his seminal analysis of the literary experience of the First World War, Paul Fussell looks at 'the way the dynamics and iconography of the Great War have proved crucial political, rhetorical, and artistic determinants on subsequent life.' As the same time as the making of the war relied on pre-existing ideas and myths, 'it was generating new myth, and that myth is part of the fiber of our own lives.'[17] The violence war does to bodies and things often compels attention, obscuring the violence done to meaning. War not only annihilates people but also interrupts their continuity, their identity, making them play roles—killer, soldier, victim, bystander, spectator—in which they no longer recognize themselves. As Emmanuel Levinas remarks, war is a 'casting into movement of beings hitherto anchored in their identity…by an objective order from which there is no escape.'[18] War entails a cycle of the unmaking and remaking of truths of all kinds, for the individuals directly involved and for the societies they return to.

These socially and culturally generative powers of war tend to disappear in the standard understandings of the concept, especially the notion that 'war' and 'peace' are discrete categories, where one ends the other begins. Clausewitz is often taken to have 'defined' war as the 'continuation of policy by other means,' namely violence.[19] Although he can be quoted in this way, Clausewitz's conception of war vastly exceeds such an instrumental approach. At a minimum there is the matter of the variable relations between his trinities of people, government, and army and their attendant characteristics of passion, reason, and technique.[20] The so-called definition of war is in fact a strategic appropriation of war, a plea for the rational direction of war from the standpoint of policy. This is necessary because, on Clausewitz's account, war tends to exceed the purposes for which it is fought, serving itself rather than policy.[21] It is within this 'excess' that the social productivity of war initially is to be found. But in reducing war to strategy, to the instrumentally rational relation between military means and political ends, a space is created for a policy science, and along with it overlapping communities of experts authorized to speak in government and in the public sphere on strategy and matters related to it.

Accordingly, what terrorism 'experts' mostly debate are policy responses: what to do about 'terror'? How to stop 'terror'? How to defend against it? As with any strategic debate, answers to these questions potentially involve nearly every aspect of a state's foreign and domestic policies. Such debates concern how a political community survives and flourishes in a world of competing armed powers. They take place amid contestation over interest and identity, and are shaped by power/knowledge and regimes of truth. Patriotism, nationalism, and ideology inform views, while the material interests at stake shape the realm of acceptable thought in diverse ways. In addition to academics and other experts, these debates are conducted by state executives, ministries, militaries, legislatures, political parties, non-governmental organizations, and their combined public relations operations. A host of political investments, commitments, and powers are regularly at stake in such matters of 'national security,' both in councils of state and in civil society.

When the communities of experts involved in debates over strategic and foreign policy invoke orientalist categories and characterizations, in the face of war or the possibility of war, they bring orientalism and war into orbit with one another.

Orientalism and War

Political authority must always appear to be in efficacious and legitimate command of armed force, most especially so in times of war and other violence. In the highly mediated public sphere of the contemporary world, with its many voices, technologies, and sources of information, this is no easy matter. War adds additional challenges, for it produces events that have an uncanny capacity to overturn received wisdom of all kinds. Wars and military operations rarely turn out as expected. When they go awry they can undermine the claims and reputations of those who initiated them. More fundamentally, narratives regarding the authoritative and legitimate command of force undergird political identities. These, too, are vulnerable to the contingencies of war. For the defeated as for the victors, war can disrupt, undermine, and transform orders of public reason and the political identities they define.

The fate of the Bush and Blair administrations in Iraq offers an example. In initiating military operations against Iraq, among other arguments, they invoked the need to act against Saddam's regime as an extension of armed struggle against tyranny, for which the defeat of Nazi Germany stood as an exemplary precedent. They positioned their actions within a narrative of emancipatory violence rooted in an interpretation of the meaning of World War II. Both leaders suffered serious loss of legitimacy as their conduct of the war foundered, and the narratives within which they positioned their political project ran aground in the complexities and uncertainties of the fighting in Iraq. Desperate attempts to recover the strategic, political and moral purpose of this mission, whether by inflating supposed successes or recasting its origins, only further undermined both leaders' political standing at home and abroad.

A dynamic arises between efforts to speak truth about war, and war's repeated undoing of these certainties.[22] Within this cauldron of war and meaning, new and old identities and politics can be asserted and institutionalized, as the parties to the conflict seek to define through various media who they are, who they are fighting and why. In the era of satellite TV, the Internet, and drone surveillance, mediation has become even more central to the conduct and course of war, as well as to its historical memory. Experts offer advice to governments and the public, instantiating their visions of self and other. Interpretations follow on interpretations, and here is where orientalism's interpretive machines intersect with war. Orientalism provides a rich pool of resources by which to represent events and their authors. New enemies offer opportunities to rework orientalist themes and apply them to new fronts, creating new orientalisms. And, as ever, war requires the continual othering of those constituted as a threat, providing orientalism its constitutive moment in the hostilities of war.

In many respects, orientalist constructions are profoundly vulnerable to war's contingencies, which perhaps explains why war is such an incitement to orientalist discourse. Orientalism, as Said argues, is always and everywhere about Western superiority: it 'puts the Westerner in a whole series of possible relationships with the Orient without ever losing him the relative upper hand.' The Orient offers 'very little resistance' to this imagined world.[23] In any given scholarly or literary text, such a self/other relation can be held relatively stable. But a war characterized as occurring between East and West always threatens to blow up categories of meaning. Its events are likely to challenge and destabilize even the most adroit and flexible frames of interpretation, both during the violent confrontation of war and after the fighting subsides. A particular problem is that war preys upon the relational character of identity constructions. A self that presents itself as strong suddenly faces a problem when it loses a battle to those it has identified as weak. The dependence of the definition of the self on that of the other is a key vulnerability exploited by such battlefield upsets. Likewise, encounters with violent Eastern others can evoke enduring anxieties and uncertainties, as when these struggles with supposedly inferior enemies come to resemble past defeats and failures. Other problems of this kind concern the appearance of Western soldiers as savages, as torturers, as bearers of violent urges and unacceptable desires normally associated with the East. In yet other cases, the supposed victims of war exercise a degree of agency otherwise denied the apparently helpless and voiceless. Such reversals are common to the 'small wars' generated by historical and contemporary imperialisms, and which are so often sites of orientalist discourse.

These are only some of the ways in which war and orientalism are entwined, and these introductory comments have sought to provide a basic framework by which to begin to approach their mutual implication. The papers that follow explore various themes in the generative encounter between these two concepts, and expand upon the beginnings made here.

Guide to the chapters

The contributions to this volume bring orientalism and war under the same analytical frame to explore how truths are made (and unmade) through violent conflict. They are grouped into three sections, each of which develops a dimension of the relationship between orientalism and war. The first considers representations of self and other that are based upon East/West distinctions. Such representations pervade interpretations of violent conflict across various settings. More than simply describing these constructions, the chapters put them in motion by examining the dynamics that ensue when policy is conceived, made, and interpreted in orientalist terms.

Arjun Chowdhury opens by asking why, despite its authoritative nature and constitutive effects, orientalism does not aim to provide accurate representations of the Orient? As a system of knowing the self and the other, Chowdhury argues, orientalism refuses to acknowledge the desire of this other where it departs from that of the self. This unwillingness has immediate consequences in war: the regimes of truth produced by orientalist thought deny the potential for enmity to exist between the self and the other. Such denial refuses the political nature of conflict between East and West. Drawing on elite British accounts of the 'Indian Mutiny' (1857), the chapter examines how this dynamic leads to a feeling of shock when Easterners use force to resist Western dominance. Instead of abandoning—or even revising—these essentialized understandings, Chowdhury argues that war reinforces orientalist constructions, as the occupier searches for ways to understand and act upon the 'natives.' These deepening forms of orientalism extend beyond the realm of ideas and representations to affect occupiers' basic attempts to forge relations with 'traditional leaders' seen as able to command the loyalty of violent 'natives.'

Moving to another site of repeated Western military intervention, Bruce Cumings examines the ways orientalism constituted an authoritative grammar through which American military officials, policymakers and academics historically conceived and dealt with Korea. Beginning with nineteenth century attempts to acquire Asian trade partners, Cumings traces how, decades later, academics and political elites in the United States formed a particular brand of 'American Orientalism.' The extent to which this authoritative worldview locked the United States in a war against an orientalized other was evident not only in the massacres and bombing attacks perpetrated by American forces against a dehumanized Communist enemy during the Korean War. Back in the United States, amid McCarthyite witch-hunts, this American Orientalism framed an interpretive community at war with itself, as the same scholars and policy leaders who formulated the original orientalist accounts of Asia a generation earlier were recast as 'internal foreigners' or 'American Others.' The lasting influence of these formative accounts of East and West, Cumings concludes, can be seen in continued stereotyping and demonization of North Korea in contemporary American popular culture.

As noted above, stark visions of the East and the West are at the core of the U.S.-led War on Terror. In Chapter 4 Susan Jeffords revisits the role of such orientalist representations by focusing on the pivotal figure in the Bush administration's construct of War on Terror: the 'Terrorist.' For Jeffords, this figure also gave rise to its other, the 'not terrorist,' in the form of George W. Bush's own 'imperial presidency.' Emboldened by the fear provoked by the terrorist, Bush used the self-referential nature of orientalist thought to remake the executive branch, claiming extraordinary institutional powers and, perhaps more importantly, authority over who was considered a terrorist. The chapter concludes by examining how these visions informed popular culture, producing 'heroes' such as Jack Bauer on *24* and Mitch Rapp in the Vince Flynn novels. They served to assuage the very fears and anxieties stoked by Bush's vision of the 'terrorist' in the American psyche.

The final chapters in the first section turn to Afghanistan as a principal site of American encounters with violent oriental others. Hugh Gusterson begins Chapter 5 by examining the essential but under-scrutinized place of the 'insurgent' in the ongoing 'American war project.' This essentialized figure is vital to affirming the United States' self-image of bringing order to Afghanistan. Gusterson shows how, in media representations, the insurgent never leaves the chaos of the battlefield to appear in full view and never amounts to more than an ideologically vacuous caricature. Fundamental questions are raised about whether—to borrow from Gayatri Spivak's classic formulation—the insurgent can speak and if so what s/he can reveal about the origins, nature and course of the protracted war. In looking beyond the expert communities who regularly appear in 'mainstream' American media to more 'alternative' outlets which eschew US official accounts to provide glimpses of Taliban forces, Gusterson shows how it is possible to take tentative steps beyond the orientalist terms in which the insurgent is cast to render more human, more real the prolonged war in Afghanistan. This reluctance to allow the Afghan insurgent to speak is a reflection of American fears about what he would say (or not say) following more than a decade of inconclusive fighting.

In Chapter 6 Quỳnh N. Phạm and Himadeep R. Muppidi examine the colonial anxieties provoked by the war in Afghanistan. The U.S. military's inability to force their oriental enemies to admit defeat or submit to superior force conjures up the specter of American defeat in Vietnam, and with it lingering doubts about the possibility of ever convincing the oriental other of his/her inferior condition. These enduring, self-referential frustrations manifest in the interplay between order and disorder that permeates elite US accounts of Afghanistan. Failed attempts to reduce American casualties, impose new governance institutions and defeat a persistent enemy reveal how the colonial self becomes captive to the disorder of the oriental other.

The second set of chapters examines the ways war constitutes many of the cultural, social and political standpoints that characterize orientalist thought. It is often in and through war that recognizably Eastern and Western identities are defined. These chapters underscore the role of war as a site for establishing supposedly essential truths about the nature of peoples, creating accounts and categories that are taken for granted. As several authors conclude, war accounts in no small measure for the emergence of a variety of orientalisms.

Josef Teboho Ansorge begins by examining the interpretive machine of orientalism as developed within the visual apparatus of the war machine. This convergence, particularly as played out in surveillance drones and video games, raises questions about what happens when data collection and spatial representation appear to reach a technical capacity that allows for the oriental other to be continuously and potentially panoptically observed by the West. The answer, Ansorge argues, lies in the 'network.' The dependence on additional machines to interpret, project, and represent the overwhelming data reveals how it is in the network, that is, the technological and analytical inter-linkages that conjoin these machines, that the oriental and its essential truths comes to exist in the modern military visuality. The inundation of information about the East provides further evidence of how the tactical and strategic promise of the panopticon is never quite realized.

Next, Derek Gregory elaborates on the limited scope, but far-reaching consequences, of this military visualization of the oriental other. Following Ansorge's account of surveillance and representation of the Orient, Gregory examines how 'scopic regimes,' the variable fields that structure what is seen, have long mediated the ways notions of self and other develop in the context of war. During Napoleon's occupation of Egypt, Cairo was mapped according to the cognitive space of European reason. Similarly, contemporary neo-orientalist scopic regimes can be seen at work in the U.S. counterinsurgency campaigns in Iraq and Afghanistan. Gregory surveys different interpretive communities at the center of the late modern war machine, such as those associated with military doctrine, networked technologies, and command and control structures. He highlights how their mapping and surveillance machinery rendered more knowable and, by extension, more orderly, the increasingly violent and expansive territories in which operations were being conducted. The effect was the construction of 'an exhibitionary order' in Iraq and Afghanistan that propelled and made possible the 'intimacy of contemporary counterinsurgency' with which Americans have become accustomed.

Maria Mälksoo examines in Chapter 9 a different form of war, the memory wars over the remembrance of the Second World War. These have produced new varieties of orientalism in Russia and its former satellites across Eastern Europe. Drawing on Milica Bakiç-Hayden's notion of 'nesting Orientalisms,' Mälksoo shows how mutable hierarchies of 'easternness' and 'otherness' developed among the very political communities that others have dismissed as irredeemably 'Eastern.' The significance of this mutual orientalization extends to these states' very identity, and informs their relations with the moral order and legal regime of the wider European community. By examining this 'mnemonical confrontation' it is possible to understand how the legacy of the Second World War has undermined efforts to foster and consolidate normative solidarity across Europe.

Chapter 10 concludes the section with a discussion of the fate of notions of self/other produced through war. Through a close reading of recent war memoirs published for audiences beyond Afghanistan, Margaret A. Mills probes how several Afghan women exercised a degree of agency and literary voice rarely ascribed to orientalized victims of armed conflict. Mills reveals the 'double-voiced' qualities of these texts, which advance distinct messages for mass audiences rooted in western social opinions and for an alternate audience exposed to Afghan viewpoints and experiences. This overlooked complexity demonstrates how, as an interpretive community, the memoirists co-opt audiences with the promise of insights into the true life of an exotic, female other. The limits of this agency, as well as the authority characteristic of orientalist thought, become apparent in the slippage between intent and reception in this literary genre. In detailing the brutality of war in the East, Mills concludes, these memoirs inadvertently give new urgency to longstanding Western colonial conclusions about the need to 'rescue' the women from the men that repress them.

The third section turns to the role of orientalism as a constitutive moment in war. John Mowitt begins in Chapter 11 with a reading of Said's notion of orientalism. Focusing on *Covering Islam*, Mowitt stresses how Said understood orientalism as an interpretive community, an institutionalized way of understanding the Orient. This interpretive community was a particularly fraught one, as it refused to acknowledge its interpretive character. Orientalism, Mowitt goes on to argue, is best understood as an interpretive machine at war with itself. To explicate the nature of this war within orientalism an analogue is found in Franz Fanon's writing about the use of radio as an interpretive weapon in the Algerian war for independence, the '*guerre des ondes*' (war of the airwaves). Fanon's essay brings to the forefront how, despite the recognition of its importance, Said lacked a theory of war that could account for the conflicted nature of orientalism. What emerges from Mowitt's discussion is a distinction between orientalism and the concept of orientalism. With respect to the latter, othering is more central than the Orient. In this way, Mowitt maps out how to understand the constitutive role of orientalism (as concept) in war.

The interpretive powers of orientalism in war are especially evident in how the body becomes a site of imperial conquest. Focusing on recent debates over American detention practices, Patricia Owens challenges the tendency to reduce the influence of orientalism in the torture of Arab and Muslim prisoners to functional terms. Orientalism was more than an authoritative inspiration for gendered and sexualized acts designed to humiliate captives' supposed vulnerabilities. Instead, Owens argues that, just as the East at war is produced in the Western imaginary, as seen in Jefford's discussion of the 'Terrorist' in Bush's 'war on terror,' the sexually repressed Muslim male body was produced in American torture in Abu Ghraib and other American prison sites. The capacity for orientalism to authorize truths in war becomes more apparent by locating Orientalist notions of 'Muslim sexuality' and sexual identity within the wider history of European ideas about the binary distinction between hetero- and homo-sexuality that developed throughout nineteenth century colonial history. It is within this older history, Owens concludes, that it is possible to appreciate how crude orientalist assumptions about the deviant sexuality of those being tortured, as well as the moral fortitude of those torturing, came to be confirmed through repeated and violent acts of confession orchestrated by American captors.

One of the only military historians to seriously engage with the idea of orientalism, Patrick Porter, closes the volume with an afterword. In reviewing the contributions, he draws out the tensions between orientalism as an account of Western superiority, on the one hand, and the Western anxieties, doubts and fears that are often expressed in orientalist idiom. Indeed, Porter points out that one prominent strain of military orientalism encourages Western soldiers to be more like their tough and wily Asian opponents. Equally, orientalist constructions, as in the idea of 'Balkan ghosts,' are often invoked as a caution against Western imperialism, and not only as invitations for 'white man's burden.' Porter sees a fault line between those scholars inclined to focus on orientalism as a site of Western ambivalence, and those who see it as necessarily expressive of a racist hierarchy between superior Western selves and their inferior oriental others. He closes with a call for a research agenda on orientalism and war focused around questions of agency and power; on change and continuity in orientalist traditions; and on a commitment to avoid reducing either the East or the West to essentialized categories.

PART 1

REPRESENTATIONS OF SELF AND OTHER

2

SHOCKED BY WAR

THE NON-POLITICS OF ORIENTALISM

*Arjun Chowdhury**

It is not saying much, perhaps, but there are few countries and few histories about which the English know less than they do about India...in a word, it is British India that we know—India in her British aspect, as coming in contact with a bold, resolute, and persevering race, and falling gradually into subjection to her lord and master.[1]

One of Edward Said's central claims is that orientalism is not an accurate representation of its object, the Orient. He goes further: 'we need not look for correspondence between the language used to depict the Orient and the Orient itself, not so much because the language is inaccurate *but because it is not even trying to be accurate.*'[2] Given that European powers seek to rule the Orient, one might expect accurate, 'actionable' knowledge to be the primary goal of orientalism. That it is not, at least in Said's estimation,

* I thank Tarak Barkawi, Patrick Porter, and Keith Stanski for their kind invitation; Rogers Smith and the Penn DCC Program for supporting my research; Bud Duvall, Murad Idris, and conference participants for feedback.

suggests we might start the inquiry into orientalism and war with the question: why is orientalism, a system of representation, 'not even trying' to accurately represent the Orient?

I answer that orientalism is a system of representing and knowing the Oriental Other that regulates a relationship of desire that is prior to, and hence compromises, the accumulation of knowledge. It is a historically specific relationship where the desire of the Other is expected to either coincide with the desire of the Self (the Other wants what the Self has to give her), or is at least not in opposition to the Self's desire (the Other does not want to kill the Self). Orientalism marks an unwillingness to recognize the desire of the Other where it departs from that of the Self. The politically significant aspect of this unwillingness is that the Self cannot recognize a declaration of enmity from the Other. Orientalism depoliticizes conflict, and misrecognizes enmity between Self and Other, even though orientalism works to represent and manage a relationship of conflict between Self and Other.

However, colonial Others are often violently recalcitrant, and so the Self's reaction illuminates the role of orientalism in war. Historically, colonial occupiers have responded to the natives' recalcitrance with a sense of shock: 'why do they hate us' is a contemporary manifestation of a hoary theme. One might expect that as one's initial (Orientalist) understanding of the natives, namely that they are passive and welcoming, is proven mistaken, the colonial enterprise would be revised, even rejected. This does not happen. Rather, the shock at native recalcitrance pushes the occupier back into Orientalist discourses to better understand and act on the natives. The consequence is to reinforce Orientalist tropes. Specifically, the natives are understood as backward and rejecting the forces of modernization. Such reinforcement does not function solely at the level of ideas, but animates strategies of alliance with local forces: occupiers support 'traditional leaders' because they perceive the latter as commanding the loyalty of backward natives.

The argument is illustrated through reference to a historical episode—the Indian Mutiny of 1857—through newspaper coverage in the London *Times*, contemporaneous narratives, and secondary accounts. The Mutiny began with isolated protests of Indian soldiers of the East India Company in January 1857, spread to the population in summer, was largely subdued by January 1858, when the revolt's symbolic leader, Bahadur Shah Zafar was tried, and conclusively ended in November 1858, with India coming under direct rule. Over two years, narratives from India were widely publicized in Britain, fascinating audiences with stories of gore and bravado. One might have expected, as the scale of the rebellion evidenced the unpopularity of British rule, that the viability of empire be questioned, at least debated, in these public realms. But, rather than a debate about the viability of empire, observers blamed the East India Company for poor governance and demanded reconquest, leading to the imposition of direct rule in 1858. Between 1857 and 1858, public discourse in England encountered, rationalized, and dismissed native recalcitrance at an existentially threatening level. This was a process of misrecognizing the enmity between colonizer and colonized, enabling the expansion of empire where it might have been withdrawn.

The paper contains four subsequent sections. The second section offers a theorization of orientalism as a relationship of desire. The third section explains how orientalism cannot admit conflict within the relationship of Self and Other. The fourth section analyzes the sense of shock when the Other does rebel. A fifth section describes the political effects.

Two systems of representation

Orientalism is a system of representation that regulates the interaction between two identities, the Occident and the Orient. Being 'a technique of establishing one's identity over and in terms of another,' orientalism imbricates power and knowledge.[3] Said emphasizes the element of power by suggesting orientalism be understood as a 'systematic discipline of *accumulation*…far from being exclusively an intellectual or theoretical feature, it made orientalism fatally tend towards the systematic accumulation of human beings and territories.'[4] The power/knowledge nexus can be best understood by theorizing orientalism in terms of a relationship of desire.

Said seems to theorize orientalism as a relationship of knowledge rather than a relationship of desire. He defines orientalism as 'a style of thought based upon an ontological and epistemological distinction made between "the Orient" and (most of the time) "the Occident,"' and 'Orientalism is the discipline by which the Orient was (and is) approached systematically, as a topic of learning, discovery, and practice.'[5] Yet, two crucial phenomena contradict the idea of orientalism as a relationship of knowledge. First, the Other is conceptualized exclusively in terms of the Self: being merely the opposite or absence of the Self, she has no positive content.[6] Second, the representation of the Orient is not one of correspondence, of approximating the object in a veridical sense. Therefore, orientalism cannot represent the

Orient; it produces the Orient.[7] Aware of this, Said uses terms like 'radical realism' and 'imaginative geography' to describe Orientalist discourses.[8] But if orientalism is not a relationship of veridical knowledge, what is its status? What motivates it, or more crudely, where does it come from?

An obvious answer suggests itself: orientalism is a relationship of power, meant to declare and maintain the dominance of Occident over Orient.[9] Insofar as orientalism manifests itself in and through practices of knowledge, these practices are in the service of governing the natives effectively and legitimating colonial rule. But there are two objections to this. First, if orientalism is not an accurate representation of the Orient, it cannot provide 'actionable' information through which to govern. If the Self only sees what he wants to see in the Other, governance becomes harder, not easier. As the historian of the East India Company J.M. Kaye retrospectively observed: 'we saw everything as we wished to see it…we saw contentment in submission, loyalty in quiescence.'[10] Second, even though orientalism expresses a hierarchy within which the Self is manifestly dominant, the shifting and malleable nature of Orientalist discourses suggests a profound anxiety of power. For example, Orientalist discourses stress the deceitfulness and treachery of the natives, and the threat of sexual mixing. These fears articulate in broader concerns about the decline of civilization, where empire simultaneously spreads civilization and compromises it through racial intermixing and procreation.[11] Such anxieties suggest that the maintenance of hierarchies is never entirely realized: orientalism is a performance aiming at domination, not a statement of it.

Recognizing this, Said associates the anxiety of power with the inability of orientalism to represent the Orient: 'psychologically, orientalism is a form of paranoia, knowledge of another kind, say, from ordinary historical knowledge.'[12] The problem of power, the anxiety at the insecurity of one's rule, cannot be understood unless it is seen in relation to the problem of knowledge, of orientalism not representing the Other *qua* Other. Orientalism is not knowledge of the Orient but a projection of the Occident.[13] Therefore, Orientalist knowledge does not invest the Self with the serene confidence of knowing one's object, but instead generates paranoia about the extent of the Self's power. The 'knowledge' that is orientalism is knowledge within the context of, and regulating, a fraught encounter between Occident and Orient.

Of this fraught encounter, two aspects require elaboration. First, the encounter is not a meeting between two already existing entities, but a meeting through which these entities are constituted. The encounter is ontological: through becoming conscious of each other, the Self and the Other become conscious of themselves, they become as they are recognized by the Other: 'man's desire finds its meaning in the desire of the other, not so much because the other holds the key to the object of desire, as because *the first object of desire is to be recognized by the other.*'[14] If the constitution of the Self is conditional on the recognition of the Other, what if the Other does not desire to recognize the Self? If recognition is withheld, the Self cannot constitute itself. To manage this risk and ensure recognition, the Self must master the Other, overcome the Other's desire to not recognize the Self, and compel recognition through the risk of death. By placing itself at mortal risk, the Self becomes through recognizing and negating the Other's desire. The path to self-consciousness is through mastery of the Other.[15]

Second, although the initial act of recognition is compelled through mastering the Other and her desire, to extend this process through force alone is impossible. As a French officer in Algeria noted, establishing political authority involved 'captur(ing) their minds after we have captured their bodies.'[16] To 'capture their minds' the Self must shape the Other's desire so that the Other desires to recognize the Self. For this task, force is insufficient; the Self must know the Other. Only through knowing the Other can the Self can train her until her world is that of the Self. Ultimately, the Other's desire must be made the same as the Self's, and this can only happen through knowing the Other.

But while knowledge of the Other is essential for transforming the latter's desire, the relationship between desire and knowledge is a contradictory one. Most generally, if knowledge of an object is the effect of desire, that knowledge can degenerate into a narcissistic process of self-deception, for the Self will only see in and of the Other what he wants to see, and ignore what he does not wish to see.[17] In Lacanian terms, this is a risk prevalent in all situations of desire: desire always misses its object because what one desires is not a concrete object or person but a certain fantasmatic structure unavailable in the 'real' world, what Lacan calls 'object a.' This 'object a' can induce dissatisfaction and failure when it comes to relations with concrete objects of desire. For example, John Ruskin, whose 'object a' was modeled on Greco-Roman sculpture, was so shocked to find pubic hair on his wife on their wedding night that he became impotent![18] The desire for an unavailable or impossible object poses a general problem for knowing and interacting with the concrete object of desire, a problem exacerbated when the Self-Other relationship is one of asymmetric power. In such situations, like the Occident-Orient relationship, not only does the Self not know the Other, the Other may actively be trying to deny the Self information. The question of being recognized by the Other becomes complicated when one cannot know the Other in a relationship of desire, and the Other cannot be relied upon to generate information about herself.

Orientalism functions as a particular historical solution to the general problem of transforming conquest into manageable, 'sustainable' rule. Orientalism is a regulative framework for the relationship of desire between Self and Other, where the challenge for the Self is not just to force the Other to recognize him, but to shape the Other's desire in a way that the Other *wants* to recognize the Self. Orientalism is caught between two modes of relating to the Other. On the one hand, there is a political relationship with the Other, where the Other is an equal, an enemy capable of dominating the Self. Here the Self battles for survival and self-consciousness. On the other hand is a tutelary relationship with the Other, where the Other is not equal, but can come of age and become the Self. Here the dimension of irreducible difference and antagonism is absent. The Oriental Other occupies neither position fully: she is not an equal, and hence can never be an enemy.[19] At the same time, she can never become the Self, because the native is always behind the Self in temporal terms.[20]

Colonial functionaries were aware that their power operated through the behavior of the natives and not just through force. As news of the Mutiny broke, 'Miles' bemoaned the 'centralization' of power which had

deprived both the commissioned and non-commissioned officers of the Indian army, European and native, of the respect of the masses whom they are expected to command, *and in whose hands, as has been so terribly shown, the real power lies. A sense of interest and a sense of fear form the groundwork of respect in common minds; without respect on the one side moral influence on the other cannot exist.*[21]

Here we can see the precarious status of colonial power, and how that power is only maintained through the recognition of the natives. The natives do not automatically obey, but 'the sipahis have always obeyed a master who knows how to command...they will not obey a lay figure.'[22]

We can better understand the relationship between power and knowledge in orientalism by paying attention to (or placing primacy on) the dimension of desire. This is not to say that orientalism is not a system of thought, with its own consistency and recurring motifs. It is rather to say that because orientalism is knowledge that manages a relationship of desire between unequals, it can never adequately represent the Other in a veridical sense. Or, as Said put it, its raison d'être is not to represent the Other at all. Rather, we can think of orientalism as 'a discourse of intimidation,' 'a language intended to bring about a coincidence between norms and facts, and to give a cynical reality the guarantee of a noble morality.'[23] In bringing about this coincidence, veridical knowledge of the Other is the casualty.

The conflict vanishes

We can now elaborate the fundamental paradox orientalism inhabits. On the one hand, as the colonial relationship is grounded, in the last instance, by violence, it is too much to expect the Other's desire to coincide exactly with what the Self plans for her. On the other hand, the Self cannot understand the Other's desire as fundamentally opposed to that of the Self. Consequently, even though the colonial relationship is one of violence, the Other is not understood as an enemy. By contrast, European Others were recognized as enemies: Europeans might misjudge the duration and outcome of intra-European wars, but that there would be war was not in doubt.[24] The native Other is denied that political status where war is always possible, and where she would be recognized as an equal under the laws of war.

The paradox is exemplified by the contrast in two accounts of the Mutiny. In 1853, Kaye had remarked that British knowledge of India was much improved.[25] The Mutiny therefore came as surprise and bitter disappointment. Kaye explained it as a failure of intelligence and knowledge. The British officer had 'seen no indications of anything to disturb his settled faith in the fidelity of the native soldier.'[26] The Mutiny revealed that 'we know so little of Native Indian society beyond its merest externals' like skin tone and architecture.[27] Indian sentiment had been fundamentally misinterpreted because the British had no means to peer below the surface and access the underlying rumors and conspiracies behind the Mutiny.

By contrast, the clergyman Alexander Duff argued the British had willfully ignored evidence of local 'hatred': 'there ever was *anything like affection* or *loyal attachment*, in any true sense of these terms, on the part of any considerable proportion of the native population towards the British power, is what no one who really knows them could honestly aver.'[28] In Duff's view, the lower classes might have initially welcomed British rule, because it freed them from the depredations of native tyrannies, but over time they chafed under the imposition of the consistent demands of the colonial state, demands they could not avoid like they avoided the capricious rule of native tyrants. Refuting accounts in England representing the violence as an intra-military revolt, he described the entire Bengal army as 'our deadliest enemy.'[29] Yet, though the native's hatred was implacable, Duff did not suggest empire be rethought. Rather, he argued for intensified evangelization, to be conducted by the colonial state.[30]

That Duff does not question empire reveals that, like Kaye, he understands the problem to be one of knowledge. For Kaye, intelligence gathering failed; for Duff, the people in the know, those with proximity to the natives, were not the ones making decisions. The conclusion is that empire is sustainable, if better information were to be collected and acted on. The hatred natives bear towards the colonizer is manageable, if the colonizer knew the native better. Put otherwise, the native's hatred need not be recognized as a political issue, and it does not constitute an impossible hurdle for colonial rule. As Ranajit Guha has shown, despite the multiplicity of peasant insurrections, the British did not see deeper political mobilization, and relegated the causes of the insurrections to irrational, spontaneous outbursts.[31]

We should understand this inability to recognize political mobilization as an effect of the structure of the Self-Other relationship in Orientalist discourses. That is, the very idea that the peasants might desire something other than what the British intended for them, and thus could perceive the British as enemies, was inconceivable, creating a blind spot when it comes to recognizing the political content of insurrections. But it is also more than that. Viewed through this optic, the evidence of resistance could be understood as making colonial rule seem more viable! For example, a *Times* editorial reviewed the record of (numerous) insurgencies in India to argue that their failure revealed the superiority and sustainability of empire:

Within a very few years we have witnessed several occasions on which our Indian fellow-subjects, had they thought themselves oppressed, had they been united and ready to co-operate, and had they felt the least wish of hope for independence, had all the opportunity that fortune could possibly offer. Our reverses in Affghanistan, the attempted invasion of the Sikhs, the long conflict between the Mahomedans and the Hindoos in the kingdom of Oude, and the Santal rebellion, all supplied the brand for a general conflagration, had India been the magazine of mischief that some have described her.[32]

That there was violence in India indicated merely that India had 'relapsed to her old, natural, and what is called normal condition,' the brutish state which British intervention had rescued her from.[33] The failure of the

Mutiny indicated that such violence was not truly political, and Indians as a whole did not back revolution. A later editorial extrapolated to say 'if the rebellion in Bengal had represented the insurrection of a nation on behalf of independence and freedom, the revolters, notwithstanding the predilection of this country for its Indian empire, would probably have found sympathizers among us'.[34]

The notion that a revolution was unthinkable or its success impossible might seem surprising, because the English had recently lost a certain colony through just that means. But few drew parallels between India and America. In a nice irony, a *Washington Union* editorial stressed the lack of commensurability: 'we do not believe that the rebellion in India will eventuate in successful revolution…Asiatic nations have, with few exceptions, been easily conquered by Europeans, however great the disparity in numbers.'[35] The civilizational difference between Occident and Orient figured as more salient than the structural similarity of being a colony.

In denying the possibility of a revolution, writers invoked Indian passivity, as when an officer reported that it was only the unification of the divided Indians into an army by the British that created a revolt, for 'the people have neither the will nor the power to rise.'[36] Others, like a director of the East India Company, acknowledged that a revolution would have had dire consequences for British rule, but this was not a revolution: 'I see no indication of its being a general movement on the part of a people rising against misgovernment, oppression, and wrong; if so, I should despair of a speedy restoration of peace and tranquility…but I see many indications that it is not a national struggle for independence.'[37] There is obviously a strategic explanation for describing the Mutiny as a Mutiny and not a revolution. There was much tongue-twisting over this definition, as when a judge at Agra explained, 'that we have in many parts of the country drifted from mutiny into *rebellion*, is all too true, but I repeat my assertion, that we have to deal now with a *revolt* caused by a mutiny, not with a mutiny growing out of a national discontent.'[38] However, that a broad array of people immediately, almost reflexively, denied that the Mutiny could be a revolution indicates a deeper source for this sentiment than cynical, strategic calculation. More specifically, if the representation of the Mutiny as mutiny and not rebellion was purely cynical, we would expect to see some evidence of a gap between private information[39] about the rebellion and public representations of it. While one cannot conclusively establish the content of private information, there is no reason to believe that private information and public rhetoric deviated from each other in this instance. This points us towards a psychical explanation for the reaction to the Mutiny, rather than a cynical-strategic one.

Shocked by war

Have you found in any one instance a national or even the symptom of a national rising? Has not the whole country, with very few exceptions, been perfectly tranquil and quiescent?[40]

In early 1857, most accounts of India described it as 'profoundly tranquil.'[41] The conflict that irrupted in the coming months came, as the Anglo-Indian *Calcutta Review* put it, as an 'electric shock.'[42] Others noted the surprise of the Mutiny: even though it had been compared to a volcano, 'it differs most materially from that, because volcanic explosions are always preceded with some warning.'[43] Right 'up to the very outbreak of the Mutiny at Mirath, no one, from highest to lowest, believed in the possibility of a general combination.'[44] In its unexpected irruption, the Mutiny was a crisis of knowledge. Dire consequences had issued from not knowing the natives, especially native soldiers. How was such an unexpected event understood? Interestingly, an event that indicated both widespread dissatisfaction with British rule and a clear misunderstanding of native behavior did not lead to a questioning of the imperial project, rather, it led to the expansion of empire.

When Dalhousie handed over power to Canning in 1856, 'he placed upon record an opinion that the condition of the Native soldiery left nothing to be desired.'[45] Subsequent events were therefore experienced as a profound betrayal: 'if the calamity had come upon us from some foreign foe it would have been bad enough; but coming from our own subjects, our old familiar friends, it is doubly hard to bear.'[46] Occasionally, the dimension of desire, of wanting to know the natives as one wanted them to be, not as they were, was noted. Malleson commented

One of the most remarkable features of the great rebellion was the supreme confidence which officers of the native army reposed to the last in their own men. This confidence was not shaken when the regiments around them would rise in revolt. Every officer argued, *and sincerely believed that*, whatever other sipahis might do, the men of his regiment would remain true.[47]

This confidence proved misplaced, to which Frederick Roberts (later Field Marshall Roberts) referred to angrily in a letter: 'our Officers have had only too much faith and confidence in their men, and many a gallant fellow has gone to his last home from this feeling, *almost amounting to infatuation.*'[48] This 'infatuation' intensified the sense of betrayal; it did not suggest a fundamental miscalculation of the natives.

The intensity of the violence imposed a further shock. Even for those observers claiming prior knowledge of the parlous condition of the native army, 'no one could have contemplated the actual manner of (the Mutiny)… no one could have imagined the possibility of its being accompanied with such fiendish ferocity.'[49] An officer in Calcutta could not fathom the events, writing 'goodness knows what has come over the Sepoys, hitherto so obedient, so patient, and so orderly.'[50] His explanation was striking. The Sepoys had been caught up by religious feeling, but they were not responsible for all the atrocities, which had also been committed by 'two or three peculiar castes of tribes, something similar to our gypsies, only holding human life at less value.'[51] The motives behind violent mobilization were not political, rather they stemmed from religious divides or criminal behavior.

Arguments as to why the revolt was inexplicable and could not have been anticipated took several forms. First, the natives had no reason for dissatisfaction, as they were treated well.[52] Their behavior was a treasonous betrayal: 'the Sepoys all thought so faithful and true, nasty scoundrels…they have shown themselves at heart to be worse than even our enemies.'[53] Second, there had been mismanagement on the part of either the central government, who had weakened the authority of the officers by demanding greater centralization, or of British officers who had grown lax in their interaction with their sepoys. Neither of these admitted a fundamental political conflict between colonizer and colonized. But even if they explained the lack of forewarning, they did not explain the intensity of the revolt.

And it was the intensity of the revolt, particularly the stories of the violation of women, which transfixed producers and consumers of Mutiny narratives alike. Among many lurid tales, one might note Ball's accounts of mutineers forcing children 'to witness the expired agonies of their murdered parents, and even to drink their blood!' and feeding parents the flesh of their children.[54] Stories of vampires and cannibals were accompanied by numerous accounts of the rape of white women.[55] To explain this departure from the norms of conflict, observers mostly ascribed religious motives, either explicitly or through the use of adjectives like 'fanatical.'[56] Religious motives placed the rebels beyond the realm of reason, and made compromise impossible. In Barrackpore, Malleson wrote, the sepoys rebelled despite there being no change in the cartridges issued to them.[57] These sepoys had no reason to revolt, but they did so anyway for 'fanaticism never reasons…the Hindus were fanatics for caste…they had been told that their religion was to be attempted by means of the cartridges, and their minds being, for the reasons already given, in an excited and suspicious condition, they accepted the tale without inquiry.'[58] Other accounts of the Bengal army stressed that 'everything…turned upon caste…high-caste men almost exclusively were enlisted, and they were permitted to set their caste and its requirements above every consideration of discipline or duty.'[59] Insofar as the British were at fault, it was for their tolerance of these 'prejudices most obnoxious to civilization.'

Eventually, however, Indian Muslims would bear the brunt of the blame for the Mutiny.[60] A correspondent disputing this charge still observed that 'the most obvious, popular, and pressing theory is that the Mahomedans have rebelled… that the Mahomedans are our enemies, and must be put down.'[61] As evidence of Muslim perfidy, a 'Commissioner on Special Duty' submitted to the *Times* a translated 'letter' from 'the rebel Nawab of Bareilly' to 'Hindoo chieftains.' The provenance of this letter is unimportant, but its logic is illustrative. The purported writer, the seditious Nawab, advocates Hindus ally with Muslims against the English who are 'bent on destroying the Hindoo religion.'[62] Citing recent legislation suspending sati, or widow-burning, and the imposition of conversion, the 'Nawab' promised the Rajahs that Muslims will, by contrast, respect the Hindu faith, and desist from eating beef. The 'letter' testified to both the presumed centrality of religion, and the perfidy of the Muslims. Disgruntled at their loss of power, Muslims were said to have conned the otherwise faithful and pliant Hindus into reluctantly backing their revolt.[63] If the Hindus went along, they did so because they erroneously believed that their faith was threatened. As such, the violence of the revolt did not stem from recognizable political grievances stemming from occupation, but symbolized India's backwardness.

The significance of these arguments lies in how they manage the cognitive dissonance occasioned by the inability of Orientalist discourse to accurately represent the behavior of the Orientals. The sepoys, well-treated by the English, would never have rebelled if not for a minority of royal conspirators, disgruntled by their loss of power, who spread rumors about the cartridges, thus sparking religious, rather than political, sentiments, for 'sentiment goes much further than logic with Asiatics.'[64] An oft-repeated implication of this argument was that the revolt was restricted to the sepoys and had not spread to the population as a whole, in which event the rebellion would become unmanageable.[65]

The process of learning from the 'disaster' is therefore instructive. Almost no observer suggested there was a fundamental conflict between colonizer and colonized. This despite the intensity of the rebellion, which might have occasioned arguments that perhaps empire should be reconsidered or even ended.[66] A more critical view (not printed in England) came from Karl Marx: 'however infamous the conduct of the sepoys, it is only the reflex, in a concentrated form, of England's own conduct in India...there is something in human history like retribution; and it is a rule of historical retribution that its instrument be forged not by the offended, but by the offender himself.'[67] Marx suggested that the revolt issued from the sepoys, the 'offenders' of British rule, not from the peasants who were the true 'offended' in the colonial enterprise. This is ironic: as Guha and others have shown, there were multiple peasant insurrections.[68] Even Marx, critic of empire, was caught in its presuppositions: the Indians could not revolt without exposure to British influence, and the revolt would be restricted to Indians influenced by the British. Indeed, Marx's argument shares the structure of a British officer's observation that the sepoys, expected to 'put down insurrection among their fellow-countrymen, are the first to set them the example, and have so wofully [sic] failed in their attempt, chiefly, if not solely, because these very turbulent 180,000,000 of our Indian subjects refuse to support them.'[69]

If a critic like Marx was caught in Orientalist representations of Indian rebels, what of the advocates of empire? Metropolitan observers and colonial functionaries alike demanded revenge, what John Lawrence predicted would be 'a war of races.'[70] A colonel proposed laws be rewritten to allow flaying, impalement, and burning for 'the idea of simply hanging the perpetrators of such atrocities is maddening.'[71] In demanding revenge for atrocities against women and children, a writer charged that 'these bloodthirsty fiends have placed themselves in the same relation to their fellow man as that of a rabid dog to his kind... nothing but extermination will cure the malady and preserve the race.'[72] Another drew the following lessons: '1. That (Europeans) were engaged in a war *a l'outrance* with the military caste throughout India...2. That that class must be destroyed, and the predominance of the European finally established.'[73] The call was for reconquering India, and doing it right this time.[74]

Hypothetically, there could have been three responses to the violence. First, the rebellion may have been read as evidence of a fundamental conflict between natives and colonizers, and empire been placed in question. Second, the rebellion may have been read as evidence of a fundamental conflict between natives and colonizers, and observers, though advocating the maintenance of empire, warned of a long, continuing struggle to hold on to it. Third, the violence, not defined as rebellion, could have been read as anomalous actions of sections of the population, and once subdued, empire could be strengthened. The final narrative dominated. An editorial asserted, 'we have now to reconquer India, and we shall do it… we have lost ground, slipped, and fallen; but we have no doubt India will soon be ours in a sense in which it has never been before.'[75] Beyond revenge, the reconquest had two goals. First, inseparable from retribution, was to send a signal of potency to the natives, to display through the overwhelming defeat of the sepoys that resistance was futile.[76] Second, such a policy was to be 'animated by one single idea—the complete subjugation of the native mind.'[77]

To achieve this, observers demanded that India be brought under direct rule.[78] Insofar as there were objections to the justice of imperial rule, the injustice derived not from the fact of foreign rule, but from the 'divided' or 'dual' government of the East India Company.[79] A representative argument read

We may say that as a nation that India is ours. Its government has long been our affair, and it has been administered in effect by the CROWN and the Parliament of this country. The second government of the India-house [East India Company] is an effete tradition; its own action, as far as it was left to itself, an avoidance of responsibility.[80]

To address this, a resolution prefiguring the 1858 India Bill read, 'it is expedient that there be established for India a responsible form of Government in the name of the Crown.'[81] This was indeed what happened: on November 1, 1858, the East India Company was dissolved, and India came under the 'undivided' rule of the Crown.

The establishment of direct rule marked a culmination of the process wherein a revolt by Indian subjects ultimately would have little to do with those subjects. Rather, as Palmerston emphasized, the Bill was purely an internal matter for Britain: 'again, as regards our interests in India, I may state at once that the Bill which I am about to propose to the House *is confined entirely and solely to a change in the administrative organization at home, and that we do not intend to make any alteration in the existing arrangements in India.*'[82] Thirty years previously, James Mill had described the history of precolonial India as 'an entire, and highly interesting, portion of the British history.'[83] In 1858, the Mutiny could similarly be reduced to 'portions' of British history; it need have nothing to do with Indians as autonomous subjects. Kaye articulated this circularity: 'because we were too English, the great crisis arose; but it was only because we were too English that, when it arose, it did not utterly overwhelm us.'[84] The Indians revolted because the British had 'permitted' them to revolt, by uniting and educating them in military units, but British courage had proved adequate to the challenge.[85] The revolt had begun and ended with the British.

The return to, or intensification of, the previous order testifies to the self-referential nature of orientalism. Unanticipated violence is not understood as falsifying a discourse that stressed the lack of enmity between colonizer and passive colonized; it is resolved within the discourse itself. Disconfirming evidence is ultimately assimilated to verifying the terms of the discourse, as when the failure of the revolt indicated the historical inability of Indians to ever rebel effectively. Orientalist understandings structured the British response to the Mutiny in three steps. First, initial revolts were greeted with incredulity that the natives were rebelling at all: the colonizers were 'shocked by war.' Second, the revolts were coded as issuing from unreasonable religious or criminal motives—such a 'secondary revision'[86] was consistent both with Orientalist arguments that the interests of the colonizer and colonized were not at odds and with the fact of widespread violence—and reconquest deemed necessary. Third, the British had to reassert their rule but avoid the pitfalls that had led to the Mutiny: 'in the years after the Mutiny, and in large measure in response to it, the British set out to create a more efficient government that could more effectively master, and so control, their most valuable dependency.'[87] It is to how they would do so that I now turn.

Losing and regaining their orientalism

Orientalist arguments are malleable because they have to manage cognitive dissonance between ideas of how Orientals behave, and evidence of how they do behave. This follows from Said's claim that orientalism not only did not function as a veridical discourse, it never even tried to be one. I conclude by identifying two consequences for imperial rule: first, managing this cognitive dissonance involved a political process of shifting alliances; second, it was through this political process that the Orient was produced.

The British faced a challenge: how to expand empire in an India far more backward and recalcitrant that initially assumed? The recalcitrance was unexpected at first blush, but explicable within Orientalist representations of India. The British had underestimated the Indian's backwardness; they had not misunderstood their nature altogether. Updating to the Indian's 'true' level of superstition suggested the following conclusion: the British had to scale back efforts at liberal reform, rule through alliances with 'traditional' elites, and understand Indians through their traditional markings of caste, tribe, and religion.

Summarizing this process, Kaye suggested that the bonds between British officers and sepoys had frayed due to a creeping 'Englishism.'[88] As centralization reduced his relationship with his soldiers, and immigrating Englishwomen became available as wives, reducing his liaisons with native women, the 'Sepoy officer shook out the loose folds of his Orientalism.'[89] Consequently, sepoys lost faith in their officers, exacerbating a broader problem. The Dalhousie administration had accelerated a process of reform, including women's rights, for which Indians were unprepared. This 'Englishism' fell on infertile soil: the natives could not appreciate it, and it alienated existing authorities, particularly the Brahmins, who felt their grip over their passive underclass threatened.[90] However, Kaye did not prescribe a policy of alliance with the underclass to depose native authorities. Rather, he argued that broad reformist goals were impossible, and the best that could be achieved was a sort of pacification through shoring up native authorities who had not rebelled.[91] This was because the underclass, despite having much to gain from reform, could not countenance the loss of their caste, perceived to be under attack by the British.[92] Here, again, the difference between Occident and Orient proves more salient than strategic calculation. An alliance between the British and the underclass may not have been sufficient to overthrow existing rulers, but the idea was not even entertained, because the evidence of the Mutiny revealed the underclass to be backward warriors protecting ancient institutions of caste and religion, not rational actors demanding the end of their subjugation. Consequently, colonial officials like Charles Wood argued that, 'we ought to adopt and improve what we find in existence and avail ourselves as far as possible of the existing institutions of the country.'[93] Queen Victoria defined two elements of this strategy in her Proclamation 'to the Princes, Chiefs, and People of India: committing to 'respect the Rights, Dignity, and Honour of Native Princes as Our own,' and promising that 'in framing and administering the Law, due regard be paid to the ancient Rights, Usage, and Customs of India.'[94]

We can represent this process in the following schema:

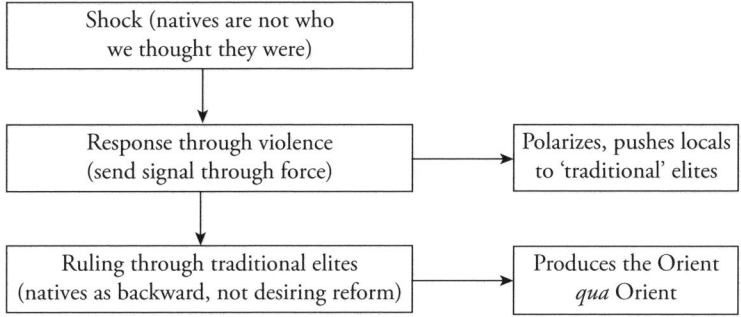

Figure 2.1: Process of shock-escalation-retraditionalization.

The Mutiny suggests orientalism is not a static discourse, but is shaped by political events, even events, like conflict, that it did not predict. Conflict widens the divide between Occident and Orient, as the colonizer recognizes and forges alliances with 'traditional' authorities. This process is not unique to the Mutiny. Contemporary counterinsurgency doctrine, forged in the wake of the (unexpected) civil war in Iraq and struggles in Afghanistan, stresses the need to engage local authorities, whether sectarian leaders in Iraq, or 'tribal chieftains' in Afghanistan. For example, the U.S. Army *Counterinsurgency Field Manual* distinguishes between three types of authority: rational-legal, associated with 'developed, Western societies,' charismatic, and traditional, a 'common type of authority in non-Western societies,' associated with tribal and religious forms of organization, much like the British depicted India.[95] 'Traditional' authorities are represented as either the source of the insurgency, or targets for co-optation to defeat it.[96] David Kilcullen, a counterinsurgency intellectual, writes of his military experience in East Timor that 'in this society, which was honor-based, placed great emphasis on reciprocity, exchange, and kinship, and was extremely warlike (despite media stereotypes of 'peace-loving Timorese'), *achieved* authority based on personal actions and reputation was important, but *ascribed* authority, deriving from position in a traditional hierarchy or a ladder of tribal endorsements, was essential.'[97] 'Tradition,' 'hierarchy,' 'tribe' are identified as markers—how natives are to be known and acted on—for potential allies (if also potentially threats), Western soldiers are encouraged to adopt 'traditional' mores like taking tea,[98] and other actors are mostly ignored. The irony is that a project initially justified as reformist ultimately produces precisely the backwardness it aims to combat: the reformer winds up on the side of tradition because of his understanding of the native.[99] I have described orientalism as a system of knowledge that seeks to regulate a relationship of desire. The primacy of desire detrimentally affects the quality of knowledge, diminishing the ability to recognize enmity and anticipate conflict. In diminishing the quality of knowledge in general, and misrecognizing enmity in particular, the strategic interaction between Self and Other functions less than optimally, from the point of view of the Self.[100] There are two implications for orientalism as a regulative framework.

First, the collection of information is not the same as knowledge of the Other. Bayly has suggested that the empire in India be understood as a set of networks through which the British collected information.[101] Yet, as he notes, despite there being no dearth of information, this impressive apparatus did not predict the Mutiny. The dimension of desire can explain how the exhaustive collection of information missed its mark. The British were not trying to understand the Other *qua* Other, but trying to grasp a figure produced by their own desires, indeed fantasies. They were therefore not in a position to collect accurate information, or process it in a way that would have predicted events accurately. In other words, orientalism motivated and structured the relationship with the Other, but also obscured understanding the Other. Further, the colonial relationship meant that the natives had little to gain by disclosing useful or accurate information about themselves. The oft-noted duplicity of the natives may be a function of, indeed a strategic response to, the colonial situation, and not a feature of the natives' character.[102] Faced by a lack of useful information, and duplicitous natives, the colonizer often becomes bewildered and cannot exert authority effectively.

Second, orientalism is inseparable from colonial governance. More precisely, salient categories of orientalism, such as the backward, sectarian nature of the natives, are produced through practices of governance. These practices of governance are not neutral. They are projections of Orientalist notions that originate in desire, even fantasy. Though misrecognized as immutable and timeless, Orientalist categories are changing political identities. For example, it is only because the Mutiny was understood as a Muslim uprising that the British allied with Hindu landowners, thus solidifying ethnic divisions. It was because their violence identified the Indian peasants as subject to 'traditional' mores that British authorities cultivated ties with 'traditional' authorities. One cannot talk of orientalism outside of practices of governance that mark subjects as Orientals, as members of castes, tribes, and religions. But at the same time, while orientalism only comes into being through these practices of governance, it also necessarily pre-exists them: colonial functionaries always seek to impose a sense of order that they believe has always characterized the Orient. This order is orientalism, the historically invariant, but veridically inaccurate, nature of the Orient. In imposing this order, colonial rule brings the Orient into being through and as categories and practices of governance. As Said points out, this order is not what the Orient necessarily was, but speedily becomes what it is.

3

AMERICAN ORIENTALISM AT WAR IN KOREA AND THE UNITED STATES

A HEGEMONY OF RACISM, REPRESSION, AND AMNESIA

Bruce Cumings

Korea is typically called 'the Forgotten War' in the United States, without much probing as to why it disappeared from the American memory. A key reason is the stark repression of the McCarthy era in the early 1950s, a war of movement at home that made a many-sided inquiry into the war dangerous; I.F. Stone had his *Hidden History of the Korean War* rejected by more than two dozen publishers before the independent Marxist Monthly Review Press had the courage to bring it out. Thus a war never really known in the first place easily slips into a realm of amnesia and oblivion. A second reason is the longstanding segregation and rank stereotyping of people of color throughout the country, which predisposed white Americans toward racism and orientalism in Korea and helped to make it such a dirty war, a 'Vietnam Before Vietnam' in the words of the late Callum Macdonald; for those who saw this war up close, the famous line that a colleague whispers into Jack Nicholson's ear at the end of an unforgettable film is apt: 'Forget it Jake—it's *Chinatown*.' Third, the American media habitually pillories and stereotypes North Korea (which also does quite enough of its own self-parodies), while doing exceedingly little honest, balanced investigative journalism; most people take the images they see today as representative of the regime during the war, when in fact Pyongyang was by far the strongest and most formidable of the two Koreas in the 1950s. The result is a kind of hegemony of repression (McCarthyite and Freudian), amnesia, forgetting and orientalism wrapped around American involvement in a war that, in fact, has never ended.

The outline of my support for these assertions proceeds as follows: a compact history of American attitudes toward the Asian Other before the Pacific and Korean wars; how elites, usually academics, provided theories of racism and orientalism; the manner in which a veritable handful of American experts on East Asia, who might have helped Americans grasp the nature of the Korean conflict, were themselves scorned, exoticized and then ostracized; the critical outcome of a general American habit of not being able to take Koreans seriously as human beings, namely, the absolutely atrocious nature of this war, which had its most sustained implementation in the saturation bombing of North Korea, evincing not the slightest concern for civilian casualties; and finally, the persistence of orientalism in American popular culture, symbolized best by contemporary images of North Korea.[1]

A brief genealogy of American Orientalism

In my 1998 book, *Parallax Visions*, I sought to show how disputes about trade and interstate conflict lay at the bottom of sharp swings of American opinion about Japan and China, as a residual orientalism seemed to lie fallow, or lie in wait, 'to leap from the wings to the center stage' (in Nietzsche's words) at times of crisis to shape a dyadic, either-or image of the Oriental object of attention. Thus periodic bouts of euphoria (Ezra Vogel's *Japan as Number One*, 1979) and fear (*The Coming War with Japan*, 1991) swept public opinion, beginning with the elites; then after Japan's real estate bubble burst the agitation subsided, and Japan returned to its usual status of good boy and dutiful U.S. ally, but no longer very interesting. Today Americans are caught between excitement and apprehension about China, symbolized by the ubiquitous trope, 'the Rise of China.' If trade or interstate disputes reach a crisis between the U.S. and China, we can expect a full-blown orientalism to emerge again. But orientalism and racism have a long history in the U.S., and deeply shaped how both the Pacific War and the Korean War were fought.

After Commodore Matthew Perry returned home from his mission to 'open' Japan, he produced a book-of-the-mission in 1856 that made him—however temporarily—a national hero.[2] In so doing he established a stereotype of Japan and the Japanese that, in various forms, continued down to the 1930s (when it was sharply reversed), and then started up again after 1945: of all the nations in the Orient, Japan is the best. This large book has a particular fascination in recounting American reactions to the various peoples encountered on the Perry Mission's voyage—blacks in Capetown, Portuguese and Arabs in Macao, Chinese in Canton and Shanghai—who by and large were seen through the condescending and often venomous lenses of race. And then come the Japanese, who make a startling and unexpected impression in their impeccably good manners, their decorous rituals, their overweening curiosity in spite of themselves about Americans and the mechanical wizardry they deployed (a miniature train set got all the officials hoping for a ride), and their intelligence and cleanliness. Cleanliness was not next to Godliness in the nineteenth century, with states like Kentucky having to pass laws requiring people to take a bath at least once a year, but it was impressive when located among the non-white races who were thought to be unhygienic (unlike Kentuckians). The Japanese scrubbed themselves squeaky clean, albeit in communal baths with both sexes mingling together stark naked. There were perhaps signs of poverty in the country 'but no evidence of public beggary,' the men of all classes 'were exceedingly courteous,' and the women were prim with no hint of 'wantonness and license.' Japanese homes were plain and simple 'but always scrupulously clean and neat.' *Plus ça change, plus c'est la même chose.* Perry and his men decided that Japan was 'the most moral and refined of all eastern nations,' a judgment that would color American perceptions for nearly a century, until a different stereotype arrived in the 1930s.

For the next century racism and orientalism provided a vocabulary and a grammar to understand the world, and as usual the experts led the charge. Books like Lothrop Stoddard's *The Rising Tide of Colour Against White World Supremacy* (1920) took it for granted that world politics revolved around an axis of race relations. For this Harvard Ph.D. and the biologist who introduced the book (Madison Grant, Chairman of the New York Zoological Society), 'science' had proved the superiority of whites and the inferiority of the red, yellow, brown, and black peoples. Dr. Grant did not stop just at colors: there were also nasty 'Semites,' and the 'Mediterranean race'—'swarthy-skinned' and 'long-skulled.' True, their skull shape had an inexplicable affinity with the head-shape of 'the great Nordic race,' but most other races were round-skulled (technically the 'brachycephalic' skull type, found in 'the Asiatic Mongols' among others). The just-concluded Great War, Grant thought, was mere prelude to the coming assault on Western Europe by 'Bolshevism with Semitic leadership and Chinese executioners.' Stoddard, however, was more worried about the pollution of white America by immigrants. The white world—which, we remember, still controlled most of Asia and Africa—stood 'at the crossroads of life and death' because of the global march of colored peoples: 'Fifty millions of our race wherewith to conquer and possess the earth!...China is our steed! Far shall we ride upon her!'[3]

These were not crackpot views, but representative of American leaders from Benjamin Franklin to Woodrow Wilson's well-known racism to Berkeley professor R. L. Adams who in 1921 classified various ethnicities into 'an absurdly retentive, racialized bestiary' that ranked their suitability for agricultural labor in California, and to Jack London who thought 'the menace to the Western world' lay in 'the little brown man' (the Japanese) undertaking to manage 'the four hundred millions of yellow men' in China. London's writings were tremendously influential, imparting an image of an intelligent, efficient, clean but dangerous Japan and a dirty slumbering Chinese giant, hard-working under proper leadership and therefore also dangerous (but otherwise indolent). London's paranoid fears of organized Orientals are all too evident in 'The Unparalleled Invasion' (1907), which imagines China's teeming population spilling over into white colonies in Southeast Asia, whereupon Western armies cordon off all escape from China and then bombard it with deadly germ projectiles cooked up by an American scientist. China, now happily empty of the Chinese, is fumigated and then resettled by people of other nationalities under a 'democratic American program.'[4] It is as if China were forcibly returned to the condition of New World natives after smallpox and other European diseases had run their course.

The 1924 exclusion of 'Orientals' marked a change, however, from the harebrained science of race, focusing on head shape and the like, to an official racism emphasizing 'cultural, national, and physical *difference*,' in Mae Ngai's words. For the first time numerical limits were placed on immigrants, and the U.S. established 'a *global* racial and national hierarchy that favored some immigrants over others.' The disfavored were those thought to be unassimilable—'that our white race will readily intermix with the yellow strains of Asia,' California governor William Stephens wrote in 1920, 'and that out of this interrelationship shall be born a new composite human being is manifestly impossible.' Likewise the Asiatic Exclusion League of North America argued that Asians were 'incongruous and non-assimilable.' Between the white American and the Asian, 'there is no common tie whatever. There is no community of thought, nor of feeling, nor of sympathy,' just a vast Pacific void. A genuine Caucasian, Bhagat Singh Thind, argued that he was white and should be naturalized, but the Supreme Court ruled that whites were those deemed white by the common man—and so South Asians were not white. The American Federation of Labor's *Clarion* backed Asian exclusion, while sounding like the ladies of the *Social Register*: 'this great Caucasian club of ours must vote out people who are not clubbable.' Unfortunately dictums about the unassimilability of Asians were widespread, long lasting and convincing, even to progressive historians like Charles Beard.[5]

America's little brown brothers in the Philippines fared little better. In 1934 Franklin Roosevelt pushed through Congress the Tydings-McDuffie Act, transforming the Philippine colony into a semi-autonomous commonwealth, pending independence that was scheduled for 1946. This gift from one hand was instantly nulled by the other: the bill deprived Filipinos of American citizenship and cut their immigration quota back to fifty per year. Dr. George Clements, a publicist for big agriculture, wrote in the *Pacific Rural Press* in 1936 that the Filipino was 'the most worthless, unscrupulous, shiftless, diseased, semi-barbarian that has ever come to our shores.'[6] (Clearly the California *latifundistas* had no more need for Filipino labor, as whites emptied out of dustbowl Oklahoma.)

With Japan's attack at Pearl Harbor, of course, its increasingly tough image of the 1930s turned into one of pure racism. As *Life* said in December 1941, 'The whole cartoon aspect of the Jap changed overnight. Before that sudden Sunday the Jap was an oily little man, amiable but untrustworthy, more funny than dangerous.' *Time's* issue of the same day featured Pearl Harbor attack architect and Harvard graduate Admiral Yamamoto Isoroku on the cover, his face polished in the hue of a moldering lemon, and gave readers instructions on how to tell 'Japs' from 'Chinamen.' By 1943, most of the characteristics that previous observers had admired were being used to explain why the Japanese were aggressors: the strong group life, the all-powerful state and 'mindless' subordination to authority.[7]

Orientalism and racism finally led the U.S. Air Force to have no hesitation in razing Japanese cities with incendiary and atomic bombs, on the grounds that they are savages so we can treat them savagely (the same rationale was used in destroying native Americans), and that they do not value human life, so why should we value theirs? On August 9, 1945, Samuel McCrea Cavert, head of the Federal Council of the Church of Christ, wrote to President Truman condemning the 'indiscriminate' killing at Hiroshima. Two days later Truman responded,

Nobody is more disturbed over the use of the Atomic bombs than I am but I was greatly disturbed over the unwarranted attack by the Japanese on Pearl Harbor and their murder of our prisoners of war. The only language they seem to understand is the one we have been using to bombard them. When you have to deal with a beast you have to treat him as a beast. It is most regrettable but nevertheless true.[8]

Here is the reasoning: Japanese naval and air units attacked our naval and air outposts in what was effectively an American colony, and some of their soldiers killed our captured soldiers. Therefore the Japanese are beasts. To deal with beasts you must become a beast, however regrettable. Now compare Kaiser Wilhelm II in World War I:

My soul is torn, but everything must be put to fire and sword; men, women, and children and old men must be slaughtered and not a tree or a house be left standing. With these methods of terrorism, which are alone capable of affecting a people as degenerate as the French, the war will be over in two months, whereas if I admit considerations of humanity it will be prolonged for years.[9]

It is painfully apparent that even Truman could not rise above the racism inherent in American attitudes toward Japan, which made no distinction between leadership by fanatical militarists and the Japanese people, or between combatants and innocent civilians. Barton Bernstein comments cogently, 'which group—American leaders or ordinary citizens—was more willing to kill the Japanese in vast numbers, including non-combatants? Is not the process of trying to reach an answer, as well as the answer itself, profoundly troubling?' To say that Tojo or Hitler or Stalin would have used the bomb had it been available to them is no doubt true, but those who use this argument (and it was a stock rationale during the Cold War balance of terror) do not seem to understand that they thereby place American leaders on a plane with monsters of the twentieth century. It is just another stupidity, bereft of clear thinking. But this thinking continued on uninterrupted, into the mindless carnage of the Korean War.

The Asian Other in Korea

Korea was at its modern nadir during the war, yet this is where most of the millions of Americans who served in Korea got their impressions—ones that often depended on where the eye chose to fall. Foreigners and GIs saw dirt and mud and squalor, but Reginald Thompson, the most observant war correspondent in Korea, saw villages 'of pure enchantment, the tiles of the roofs upcurled at eaves and corners…the women [in] bright colors, crimson and the pale pink of watermelon flesh, and vivid emerald green, their bodies wrapped tightly to give them a tubular appearance.' Thompson had been all over the world; most GIs had never been out of their country, or perhaps their home towns. What his vantage point in 1950 told him, in effect, was this: here was the Vietnam War we came to know before Vietnam—gooks, napalm, rapes, whores, an unreliable ally, a cunning enemy, fundamentally untrained GIs fighting a war their top generals barely understood, fragging of officers,[10] contempt for the know-nothing civilians back home, devilish battles indescribable even to loved ones, press handouts from Gen. Douglas MacArthur's headquarters apparently scripted by comedians or lunatics, an ostensible vision of bringing freedom and liberty to a sordid dictatorship run by servants of Japanese imperialism.

Thompson's *Cry Korea* is the only Western book of the Korean War that can be compared to the classics of the Chinese civil war like Graham Peck's *Two Kinds of Time* or Jack Belden's *China Shakes the World*. In it he wrote that war correspondents found the campaign for the South in the summer of 1950 'strangely disturbing,' different from World War II in its guerrilla and popular aspect. 'There were few who dared to write the truth of things as they saw them.' G.I.s 'never spoke of the enemy as though they were people, but as one might speak of apes.' Even among correspondents, 'every man's dearest wish was to kill a Korean. 'Today…I'll get me a gook.' G.I.s called Koreans gooks, he thought, because 'otherwise these essentially kind and generous Americans would not have been able to kill them indiscriminately or smash up their homes and poor belongings.'[11]

Contempt for Koreans began at the top. American officers had no idea that they would be fighting against truly effective troops, a disastrous misjudgment of the Korean enemy that started the day the war began. 'I can handle it with one arm tied behind my back,' Gen. Douglas MacArthur said; the next day he remarked to John Foster Dulles that if he could only put the First Cavalry Division into Korea, 'why, heavens, you'd see these fellows scuttle up to the Manchurian border so quick, you would see no more of them.' At first MacArthur wanted an American regimental combat team, then two divisions. Within a week, however, he cabled Washington that only a quarter of South Korean troops could even be located, and that the Korean People's Army was 'operating under excellent top level guidance and had demonstrated superior command of strategic and tactical principles.' By the beginning of July he wanted a minimum of 30,000 American combat soldiers, meaning more than four infantry divisions, three tank battalions, and assorted artillery; a week later he asked for eight divisions.[12]

Such misjudgments grew out of the ubiquitous racism of whites coming from a segregated American society, where Koreans were 'people of color' subjected to apartheid-like restrictions (they drank from 'colored' fountains in Virginia, could not marry Caucasians in other southern states, and could not own property in many Western states). Consider the judgment of the respected military editor of the *New York Times*, Hanson Baldwin, three weeks after the war began:

We are facing an army of barbarians in Korea, but they are barbarians as trained, as relentless, as reckless of life, and as skilled in the tactics of the kind of war they fight as the hordes of Genghis Khan…They have taken a leaf from the Nazi book of blitzkrieg and are employing all the weapons of fear and terror.

Chinese communists were reported to have joined the fighting, he erred in saying, and not far behind might be 'Mongolians, Soviet Asiatics and a variety of races'—some of 'the most primitive of peoples.' Elsewhere Baldwin likened the Koreans to invading locusts; he ended by recommending that Americans be given 'more realistic training to meet the barbarian discipline of the armored horde.'[13]

A few days later Baldwin remarked that to the Korean, life is cheap: 'behind him stand the hordes of Asia. Ahead of him lies the hope of loot.' What else 'brings him shrieking on,' what else explains his 'fanatical determination?'[14] Mongolians, Asiatics, Nazis, locusts, primitives, hordes, thieves—one would think Baldwin exhausted his kitbag of bigotry to capture a people invading their homeland and defending it against the world's most powerful army. But he came up with another way to deal with 'the problem of the convinced fanatic':

In their extensive war against Russian partisans, the Germans found that the only answer to guerrillas… was 'to win friends and influence people' among the civilian population. The actual pacification of the country means just that.

Seeking analogies with Nazi counterinsurgency did not make Baldwin uncomfortable, but he was discomfited by North Korean indignation about 'women and children slain by American bombs.' So he went on to say that Koreans must understand that 'we do not come merely to bring devastation.' Americans must convince 'these simple, primitive, and barbaric peoples... that we—not the Communists—are their friends.'[15] Now hear the chief counsel for war crimes at the Nuremberg Trials, Telford Taylor:

The traditions and practices of warfare in the Orient are not identical with those that have developed in the Occident...individual lives are not valued so highly in Eastern mores. And it is totally unrealistic of us to expect the individual Korean soldier...to follow our most elevated precepts of warfare.[16]

Simple massacres

These most elevated precepts included a series of American slaughters of civilians in Korea, the most famous of which became the massacre at Nogun village in July 1950. In the summer of 2000, and for every summer of the previous half century, a soldier named Art Hunter had awakened in the middle of the night with cold sweats, imagining the faces of two old people, a man and a woman, hovering above his bed. These two weathered faces had made his life 'a living hell,' and when they haunted him he would arise, get his hunting rifle, go sit on the porch, and smoke a cigarette. In 1991 soldier Hunter finally got the U.S. Government to give him full disability pay for his severe Post-Traumatic Stress Disorder, but the nightmares still came to him in his home in the foothills of Virginia's Blue Ridge Mountains.[17]

On September 30, 1999, a woman named Chon Chun-ja appeared on the front page of the *New York Times*, dressed as if she were yet another middle-aged and middle-class Korean housewife going shopping. Instead she stood at the mouth of a tall tunnel in Nogun village and pointed to a hill where, she alleged, in July 1950 'American soldiers machine-gunned hundreds of helpless civilians under a railroad bridge.' She and other survivors went on to say that they had been petitioning their government and the American government for years, seeking compensation for this massacre; they had been completely stonewalled in both Seoul and Washington. Meanwhile the article also carried the testimony of American soldiers who did the firing, who said that their commander had ordered them to fire on civilians.[18] Art Hunter was one of those soldiers, shooting into a white-clad mass of women, children and elderly people gathered under the railroad bridge.

The *Times* did not produce this story, but rather front-paged an Associated Press account of the massacre. In subsequent days and weeks it did no follow-up reporting, to my knowledge, except periodically to up-date its readership on what the Associated Press was saying about the reaction in the Pentagon, or Seoul, the announcement of an investigation into the survivor's claims, and the like. Two months after this story broke, Doug Struck, a reporter for the *Washington Post*, learned that civilians were huddled in the railroad tunnel for as much as three days, while American soldiers repeatedly returned: Chong Ku-hun, then seventeen years of age, told Struck that 'They were checking every wounded person and shooting them if they moved. Other soldiers climbed down toward a drainage pipe where dozens of villagers had taken shelter and began shooting into families, according to the accounts of other survivors.' Yang Hae-suk, then a girl of thirteen, was also in the tunnel: 'Suddenly there were planes and bombs. My uncle covered his child, and I heard him say, "Oh, my God." I looked and saw his intestines had come out. The bullet had passed through his back and killed his daughter.' A few moments later the young teenager also got hit and lost her left eye. Mr. Struck said investigators 'face the delicate task of measuring a dirty war by standards that officials here say were violated by all sides during the three-year conflict.'[19] This account carried the story a very troubling step further: not only were the American G.I.s ordered to shoot at civilians, they returned again and again to make sure they were all dead. This suggests, of course, that they wanted to assure themselves that there would be no survivors to tell the tale of Nogun-ri.

In 1950 the people in 'white pajamas' (peasants wore white raiment) and what they provoked in Americans was as accessible as the neighborhood barbershop reading table. For example John Osborne wrote in the August 21, 1950 issue of *Life* magazine that American officers had ordered G.I.s to fire on clusters of civilians; a soldier said, 'it's gone too far when we are shooting children.' It was a new kind of war, Osborne wrote, 'blotting out of villages where the enemy *may* be hiding; the shelling of refugees who *may* include North Koreans.' As I.F. Stone put it, the air raids and the sanitized reports issued to the press 'reflected not the pity which human feeling called for, but a kind of gay moral imbecility, utterly devoid of imagination—as if the flyers were playing in a bowling alley, with villages for pins.'[20]

Military historian Walter Karig, writing in *Collier's*, likened the fighting to 'the days of Indian warfare' (a common analogy); he also thought Korea might be like the Spanish Civil War—a testing ground for a new type of conflict, which might be found later in places like Indochina and the Middle East. 'Our Red foe scorns all rules of civilized warfare,' Karig wrote, 'hid[ing] behind women's skirts'; he then presented the following colloquy:

The young pilot drained his cup of coffee and said, 'Hell's fire, you can't shoot people when they stand there waving at you.' 'Shoot 'em,' he was told firmly. 'They're troops.' 'But, hell, they've all got on those white pajama things and 'they're straggling down the road'…'See any women or children?' 'Women? I wouldn't know.' 'The women wear pants, too, don't they?' 'But no kids, no, sir.' 'They're troops. Shoot 'em.'[21]

Americans still seem to have difficulty looking with open eyes on the record of the Korean War. Why did the *New York Times* and other papers find massacre stories fit to print in 1999, but not fit to print at any point after 1950? In one sense it is a 'forgotten war.' U.S. reporters of the first rank often know nothing about it. Forgotten, unknown, never-known: and thus Nogun-ri becomes interesting and salient, even famous for a time, because it suggests to journalists of the younger generation not Korea but the Vietnam War and the My Lai Massacre—and we thought things like that happened only in Vietnam (and really, only once). So, in this curious American lexicon, civilian massacres—about which one could read in *Life* magazine in the summer of 1950—disappear into oblivion because of a false construction of the nature of the Korean War; they get lost for a sufficiently long time, such that when they resurface they appear to contradict much of the received wisdom on this war.

Art Hunter surely knew the truth of what happened in Nogun village so many years ago, but why did it haunt him? I think it is because a young man on the giving end of a rifle intuits a fundamental human truth about warfare, that the soldier is there to kill, but also to save and protect:

The soldier, be he friend or foe, is charged with the protection of the weak and unarmed. It is the very essence and reason for his being. When he violates this sacred trust he not only profanes his entire culture but threatens the very fabric of international society.

The author of this moving statement went on to say that 'the traditions of fighting men are long and honorable, based upon the noblest of human traits—sacrifice.' He was General of the Army Douglas MacArthur.[22] But by coming forward and telling their stories, survivors like Chon Chun-ja did something wonderful for Art Hunter: they sought him out and discussed what had happened at Nogun-ri, and thus made it possible for him to begin purging himself of a terrible guilt.

Internal foreigners, or, the 'Othering' of Americans

As the year 1950 got going, Senator Joseph McCarthy remarked to a reporter, 'I've got a sock full of shit and I know how to use it.' Soon he rose to denounce 205, or 57, or, as it happened, a handful of vulnerable liberals in the State Department and elsewhere as 'Communists and queers who have sold 400,000,000 Asiatic people into atheistic slavery,'[23] thus beginning an internecine war among elites that has never really ended. McCarthy exemplified a destructive ideological era where labels stood in place of arguments and evidence made next to no difference. If the same phenomenon can be sampled today on our TV shouting matches, Tailgunner Joe and his allies dramatically wrenched the American political spectrum rightward, interrogating, castigating, and nearly burying the progressive forces of the 1930s. Their bludgeon was an undeniable global crisis detonated by the Soviet atomic bomb and the Chinese revolution, which seemed to spread red ink across half of the globe and jolted Americans, basking in their grand victory in 1945 but still remarkably unworldly, into thinking a handful of internal foreigners—traitors—had caused it all. On the very day McCarthy first rose in the Senate to denounce communism in government, Senator Homer Capehart of Indiana exclaimed,

How much more are we going to have to take? Fuchs and Acheson and Hiss and hydrogen bombs *threatening outside* and New Dealism eating away at the vitals of the nation! In the name of Heaven, is this the best America can do?[24]

For Americans who lived in a segregated society where all non-whites were 'colored' and had to be told what a communist looked like,[25] McCarthy supplied plausible models: mainly Eastern establishment blue bloods, but also Foggy Bottom scribblers, tweedy professors, closet-bound homosexuals, and China experts who had been abroad too long—anyone who might be identified as an internal foreigner, alien to the American heartland. (*The Freeman* once said that Red propaganda appealed only to 'Asian coolies and Harvard professors.') Almost anybody with a good education might qualify; thus the bane of the liberal in the 1950s was the threat of mistaken identity. A nihilist himself, McCarthy nonetheless succeeded in placing distinct outer limits on the spectrum of 'responsible' foreign policy discourse which persist to this day. McCarthy took as his prime targets a few Americans who had lived in East Asia for many years, those few with any real expertise to contribute to American policies and debates; as it happened, however broad the political spectrum among them might have been—and it was wide—they all knew each other, because so few Americans had sought to come to grips with the revolutions then sweeping East Asia.[26]

McCarthy was supplied documentation on alleged subversives, most of it classified, by FBI director Edgar Hoover, General Charles Willoughby (MacArthur's intelligence chief), and even Walter Bedell Smith of the CIA. Willoughby had begun McCarthy-style investigations of his own in 1947, especially of scholars working for 'the extremely leftist' Institute for Pacific Relations. His first case was Andrew Grajdanzev, author in 1944 of what remains today one of the best English-language accounts of Japanese rule in Korea, *Korea Today*. Willoughby had him tailed, read his mail, and determined that he might be 'a long-range Soviet agent'—the evidence being that Owen Lattimore, a professor at Johns Hopkins University, had written a recommendation for him, and that he wanted to purge Japanese leaders with unsavory pre-1945 records whom MacArthur and Willoughby supported. Willoughby fingered crafty subversives like Anna Louise Strong and Agnes Smedley who somehow, despite their blanketed obscurity, brought Mao to power by remote control. In a letter of May 1950 to the head of the House Un-American Activities Committee, Willoughby said that 'American Communist brains planned the communization of China,' fellow-traveling people who have 'an inexplicable fanaticism for an alien cause, the Communist "Jehad" of pan-Slavism for the subjugation of the Western world.' Willoughby paid particular attention to names and birthplaces that might indicate Jewish origin.[27]

Owen Lattimore's cardinal sin was that he had been in East Asia for too long, rendering him alien to the incubating anti-communist hysteria, and that in the late 1940s published books arguing that Asian communism had a large inflection of anti-colonial nationalism, and that the U.S. should try not to go into opposition against it. His experience says much about McCarthyism, the China Lobby, and its relationship to Korea. It is forgotten that McCarthy began his attacks well before the Korean War, that Lattimore's views on Korea were one of McCarthy's central subjects, and that by June 1950 McCarthyism seemed to be losing its momentum—its capacity to establish 'China' as an issue in American politics. McCarthy first attacked Lattimore indirectly on March 13, 1950, alleged a week later that he had found a 'chief Russian spy,' and finally named Lattimore when information leaked from his committee. Beyond Lattimore stood Philip Jessup, 'a dangerously efficient Lattimore front' (he was a professor of international law at Columbia then in the State Department), but ultimately his object was Secretary of State Dean Acheson, whom McCarthy termed 'the voice for the mind of Lattimore.'[28] Acheson was his final target: why? In part because by the spring of 1950 he was the last high official (besides Truman himself), standing between Chiang Kai-shek and the American backing he desperately needed to survive an impending communist invasion.

In early April McCarthy claimed to have a document incriminating Lattimore as a Soviet agent, prompting Lattimore to release it to the press—a memorandum he wrote for the State Department in August 1949, arguing that 'the U.S. should disembarrass itself as quickly as possible of its entanglements in South Korea.' Lattimore saw Korea as 'little China,' and Syngman Rhee as another Chiang: if we could not win with Chiang, he said, how could we win with 'a scattering of "little Chiang Kai-sheks" in China or elsewhere in Asia.'[29] In mid-May 1950 McCarthy again attacked the 'Acheson Lattimore axis' (or, the 'pied pipers of the Politburo') on Korea policy, saying Lattimore's plans for Korea would deliver millions to 'Communist slavery.' Taking direct aim at the Nationalists' principal antagonist, Acheson, he blared, 'fire the headmaster who betrays us in Asia.'[30]

Lattimore's fuller views on Korea were given in the fall of 1949 when the State Department called in experts to consult with them on a new Asian policy. Generally speaking, liberal scholars such as Lattimore, Cora DuBois, and John K. Fairbank tried to point out that the revolution sweeping much of East Asia was indigenous, the culmination of a century of Western and imperial impact. Conservative scholars like William Colegrove, David Nelson Rowe, and Bernard Brodie sought instead to argue that Soviet machinations were behind Asian communism. Liberals were dominant within scholarly circles, however, and in these meetings a consensus emerged looking forward to the establishment of diplomatic relations with the People's Republic of China.

The U.S. should stand with progressive and liberal forces in Asia where they existed, Lattimore said, but should not place itself in the path of changes that were already *fait accompli*, such as the Chinese revolution, which would be self-defeating and stupid. Meanwhile, 'Korea appears to be of such minor importance that it tends to get overlooked, but Korea may turn out to be a country that has more effect upon the situation than its apparent weight would indicate.' After this prophetic mouthful, he argued that the Republic of Korea politically was 'an increasing embarrassment,' an 'extremely unsavory police state' where the

chief power is concentrated in the hands of people who were collaborators of Japan…Southern Korea, under the present regime, could not resume close economic relations with Japan without a complete reinfiltration of the old Japanese control and associations…the kind of regime that exists in southern Korea is a terrible discouragement to would-be democrats throughout Asia…Korea stands as a terrible warning of what can happen.

Once the war began, however, Lattimore expressed his support for the American intervention.[31]

In spite of the obviously political and mendacious nature of McCarthy's witchhunt against Lattimore, within a few weeks major organs of opinion were already giving the classic formulation that enabled them to escape McCarthy's gunsights: supporting Lattimore's right to his opinions, but condemning them as irresponsible or extreme. In mid-April the *New York Times* singled out his 'unsound' position on Korea; it found Lattimore's view 'quite shocking,' saying that the State Department had 'rejected flatly Mr. Lattimore's advice to cut and run in Korea.'[32] Historian Mary McAuliffe is right to say

One of the major ironies of the period was the unexpected role which liberals played, first in constructing a new liberalism which rejected the American left, and then in accepting some of the basic assumptions and tactics of the Red Scare itself.[33]

In the atmosphere of McCarthyism, British author Godfrey Hodgson wrote, 'liberals were almost always more concerned about distinguishing themselves from the Left than about distinguishing themselves from conservatives.' Thus they joined 'the citadel of…a conservative liberalism.' If the fear of being investigated had shown the intellectuals 'the stick' in the early 1950s, 'the hope of being consulted had shown them the carrot' thereafter. Being an influential client meant accepting the confines of one's patronage.[34]

Orient, occident, and repression: how the experts create stereotypes

'Influential clients' also existed among intellectuals who, somewhat like Lothrop Stoddard, patronized political charlatans like McCarthy with orientalist claptrap. The primary academic McCarthyite was Karl Wittfogel, who had a strange trajectory to America: he was the leading ideologue of the German Communist Party in the early 1930s, and the leading proponent of Karl Marx's theory of 'the Asiatic Mode of Production.' Stalin purged him for reasons that are not entirely clear, and Wittfogel came to the United States and established himself as a scholar with his magnum opus,

Oriental Despotism.[35] Marx's theory appraised Asia by reference to what it lacked when set against the standard-issue European model of development: in the West, feudalism, the rise of the bourgeoisie, capitalism; in the East, a brutal satrap presided over a semi-arid environment, running armies of bureaucrats and soldiers, regulating the paths of great rivers, and employing vast amounts of slave labor in gigantic public works projects (like China's Great Wall). The despot above and the cringing mass below prevented the emergence of anything resembling a modern middle class. The broadest distinction, between static or indolent East and dynamic, progressive West, of course, goes all the way back to Herodotus and Aristotle.

Marx never really investigated East Asia, but learned enough to know that if China fitted his theory, Japan with its feudalism (and 'petite culture') clearly did not. Wittfogel, however, applied his notions of Oriental despotism to every dynasty with a river running through it—China, Tsarist Russia, Persia, Mesopotamia, Egypt, the Incas, even the Hopi Indians of Arizona. By this time he had done a full-fledged, high-wire *tenko* (Japanese for a political flip-flop), reemerging as an organic reactionary and trying to reproduce himself in, of all places, Seattle—the most thoroughly middle class city in America. Wittfogel wrote for many extreme right-wing publications and played a critical role in the purges of China scholars and Foreign Service officers during the McCarthy period. Hardly any scholars would testify against Owen Lattimore, McCarthy's prime professorial target, but the University of Washington furnished three: Wittfogel, Nikolas Poppe (a Soviet expert on Mongolia who had defected to the Nazis in 1943), and George Taylor, a British scholar/journalist.[36]

This early 1950s episode tore apart the American field of East Asian studies. People wouldn't speak to each other for years—or ever, in the case of Lattimore and Taylor. But China was now 'Red China,' and the government needed experts. In the late 1950s the Ford Foundation provided funds through the Social Science Research Council for a committee to develop scholarship on contemporary China. John King Fairbank of Harvard joined George Taylor on this committee, and a few years later the Central Intelligence Agency provided a subvention for the publication of a new scholarly journal, *The China Quarterly* (still the preeminent journal of the field). Its inaugural issue featured a debate about Wittfogel's theories. Taylor and Wittfogel were back in the fold; out in the cold were the many scholars of Asia who had their careers ruined or their character assassinated in the 1950s. This new, Cold War-shaped spectrum also greeted young people like myself, when I first enrolled at Columbia University in 1968. Its most notable feature was the open support (or more often the deafening silence) by leading scholars of East Asia for the war then tearing both Vietnam and America apart. By and large they presented themselves as objective and non-partisan, even as some ran off to Washington to tell the CIA how to defeat the Vietcong; it was the opponents of the war and American policy who were naïve and biased.

After teaching in the Philadelphia area in the mid-1970s—where I was pleased to meet Olga Lang, Wittfogel's first wife ('Why did you divorce?,' I asked. 'Irreconcilable political differences,' she answered)—I wound up at the University of Washington, which has one of the oldest East Asian programs in the U.S. Around that time Perry Anderson published *Lineages of the Absolutist State*. At the end of this magisterial book rests an 87-page 'Note' on the theory of the Asiatic mode of production,[37] where Anderson shows that Marx's views on Asia differed little from those of Hegel, Montesquieu, Adam Smith, and a host of other worthies; they were all peering through the wrong end of a telescope, or in a mirror, weighing a smattering of knowledge about Asia against their understanding of how the West developed—in other words it was vintage, if early, orientalism. Nor did Marx ever take the 'Asiatic mode' very seriously; he was always interested in one thing, really, and that was capitalism (even when it came to communism). Anderson called Wittfogel a 'vulgar charivari' and recommended giving this theory an unceremonious burial, concluding that 'in the night of our ignorance… all alien shapes take on the same hue.' I eagerly recommended his book to my colleagues: a good friend said, 'He doesn't know any Chinese.' Another responded, 'Isn't he a Marxist?' (Anderson—not Wittfogel).

The theory never really got a proper burial, though, it just reappears in less conspicuous forms. It isn't politically correct to say 'Oriental' or 'Asiatic' anymore (even if some haven't gotten the message). Stalin is long dead, but Stalinism is apparently not, and it's still okay to say almost anything about Stalinism. Furthermore, lo and behold, one set of 'Orientals' has kept it alive: journalists use the term time and again to describe North Korea, without any hint of qualifying or questioning their position. The idea that the Democratic People's Republic of Korea (DPRK) is a pure form of 'Stalinism in the East'[38] goes back to the 1940s, and was constantly reinforced by Berkeley's Robert Scalapino, a Cold War scholar who came along in the late 1950s and benefited as much as anyone from the post-McCarthy accommodation between the right and the middle.

Hollywood, of course, was not to be caught lagging behind the orientalism of the academic experts. Thus their answer to McCarthyism was a film that mocked McCarthy while perpetuating the worst stereotypes of Asians. It took more than a decade before Hollywood began to unlock any serious Korean War history in films (and in truth it never did); nearly all the films of the 1950s run the war on a World War II narrative (*The Bridges at Tokori*), or as a mysterious, enigmatic conflict (*Pork Chop Hill*, which anticipated the—mysterious, enigmatic—Korean War Memorial in Washington, D.C.). The singular classic film of the Korean War is *The Manchurian Candidate*, appearing in 1962 only to disappear for decades after it seemed to anticipate Kennedy's assassination. An odd mix of terror and high camp, its genius was to wrap the orientalism and communist-hating of the 1950s in the black humor of the 1960s, amid the self-congratulatory pillorying of the McCarthy character (presented as a henpecked fool and knave); the film allows one to be chic in one's prejudices. The battle itself is fleeting, haphazardly staged on a backlot. Yen Lo, the evil Oriental, superbly portrayed by Khigh Dhiegh, became a stunning media signifier for demonic Orientals thereafter. Dhiegh had a long career in similar Hollywood roles ('Wo Fat,' 'Four Finger Wu,' 'King Chou Lai,' aka Chou En-lai; in his first film, *Time Limit*, he played Col. Kim, a nasty interrogator of American POWs in Korea), but was otherwise known as Kenneth Dickerson—born in Spring Lake, New Jersey, of Syrian and Egyptian ancestry. *Candidate* is the one Korean War film of lasting significance, but it mostly reinforces stereotypes about Asian communists and what the war was about.

The Air War in Korea: burning out cities and, incidentally, people

If Yen Lo was an 'evil Oriental' valuing life so little that he had POWs murdered for the sport of it, you can't blame American mass bombing of civilians on the corresponding value placed on Asian lives, because it was perfected on innocent German civilians. After much experimentation and scientific study by Germany, Britain and the U.S., by 1943 it became clear that 'a city was easier to burn down than to blow up.' Combinations of incendiaries and conventional explosives, followed up by delayed detonation bombs to keep firefighters at bay, could destroy large sections of a city, whereas conventional bombs had a much more limited impact. Magnesium-alloy thermite sticks, manufactured by the million and bundled together, did the trick; when supplemented by mixtures of benzol, rubber, resins, gels, and phosphorus, they formed unprecedentedly destructive blockbuster flaming bombs that could wipe out cities in a matter of minutes (seventeen in the case of the attack on Wurzburg, March 16, 1945). The creation of urban 'annihilation zones' destroyed masses of civilian lives, an outcome accepted by all sides in the war—and 'by the people, parliaments, and armed forces.' And with that, in Jörg Friedrich's words, 'modernity gave itself up to a new, incalculable, and uncontrollable fate.'

In favorable atmospheric conditions these bombs ignited firestorms that razed Darmstadt, Heilbronn, Pforzheim, Wurzburg and, of course, Hamburg (40,000 deaths), Dresden (12,000), and Tokyo (88,000). Or in Winston Churchill's words, 'we will make Germany a desert, yes, a desert' through the power of incendiary bombing—only 'an absolutely devastating, exterminating attack by very heavy bombers' would finally bring Hitler to his knees. The goal was to destroy the morale of the enemy and the people, a horizon that receded even as the attacks intensified.[39] The postwar *U.S. Strategic Bombing Survey* demonstrated that enemy morale was mostly unaffected by the bombing, but also that the actual level of civilian deaths was less than predicted—that is, 'far removed from the generally anticipated total of several millions.' Morale was not broken, and even the harvest of blackened, scorched, blasted, or asphyxiated human beings was anticlimactic (not even several millions). Furthermore both countries were democracies, so some rose up to criticize mass attacks against civilians (Bishop George Bell told the House of Lords that 'to obliterate a whole town' because it may have some industrial targets violated 'a fair balance between the means employed and the purpose achieved').[40]

Top Air Force officers decided to repeat 'the fire' in Korea, a wildly disproportionate scheme in that North Korea had no pretense or possibility of a similar city-busting capability. Whereas German fighter planes and anti-aircraft batteries made allied bombing runs harrowing, with high loss of life among British and American pilots and crew, American pilots in North Korea had virtual free-fire zones until later in the war, when formidable Soviet MIGs were deployed. Curtis LeMay subsequently said that he had wanted to burn North Korea's big cities down at the inception of the war, but the Pentagon refused—'it's too horrible.' So over a period of three years, he went on, 'we burned down *every* [sic] town in North Korea and South Korea, too....Now, over a period of three years this is palatable, but to kill a few people to stop this from happening—a lot of people can't stomach it.'[41] To take just one example of these 'limited' raids, on July 11, 1952 an 'all-out assault' on Pyongyang involved 1,254 air sorties by day and fifty-four B-29 assaults by night, the prelude to bombing thirty other cities and industrial objectives under 'operation PRESSURE PUMP.' Highly-concentrated incendiary bombs were followed up with delayed demolition explosives.

By 1968 the Dow Chemical Company, a major manufacturer of napalm, could not enter most college campuses to recruit employees because of its use in Vietnam, but oceans of napalm were dropped on Korea silently or without notice in America, with much more devastating effect, since the DPRK had many more populous cities and urban industrial installations than did Vietnam. Furthermore the U.S. Air Force loved this infernal jelly, their 'wonder weapon,' as attested to by many articles in 'trade' journals of the time.[42] One day Pfc. James Ransome, Jr.'s unit suffered a 'friendly' hit of this wonder weapon: his men rolled in the snow in agony and begged him to shoot them, as their skin burned to a crisp and peeled back 'like fried potato chips.' Reporters saw case after case of civilians drenched in napalm—the whole body 'covered with a hard, black crust sprinkled with yellow pus.'[43]

Korea recapitulated the Air Force's mantra from World War II, that firebombing would erode enemy morale and end the war sooner, but the interior intent was to destroy Korean society down to the individual constituent. Gen. Ridgway, who at times deplored the free fire zones he saw, nonetheless wanted bigger and better napalm bombs (1,000-lb versions to be dropped from B-29s) in early 1951, thus to 'wipe out all life in tactical locality and save the lives of our soldiers.' 'If we keep on tearing the place apart,' Secretary of Defense Robert Lovett said, 'we can make it a most unpopular affair for the North Koreans. We ought to go right ahead.' (Lovett had advised in 1944 that the Royal Air Force had no restrictions on attacks against enemy territory, so the American bombers should 'wipe out the town as the RAF does.')[44]

Another irony of the air war against Germany and Japan is that the worst civilian losses came after Arthur Harris, RAF Bomber Command chief, and Carl Spaatz, commander of U.S. Army Air Forces, had run out of targets—months before the most destructive incendiary attacks in March 1945. Cities were razed 'because the bombing offensive had long ago become an end in itself, with its own momentum, its own purpose, devoid of tactical or strategic value, indifferent to the needless suffering and destruction it caused.'[45] Within months few big targets remained in Korea, either; in late 1951 the Air Force judged that there were no remaining targets worthy of using the 'Tarzon,' its largest conventional bomb at 12,000 lbs which had been used in December 1950 to try and decapitate DPRK leaders in deep bunkers. Twenty-eight of them had been used in the war.[46]

The opening of North Korean dams was another carryover from World War II. In May 1943 when the water level was highest (as in Korea), 'Operation Chastise' attacked two dams on the Ruhr; the Moehne dam had a height of 130 feet and was 112 feet thick at its base; the Eder River dam held seven billion cubic feet of water. 'A tidal wave of 160 million tons of water, with a vertex thirty feet high,' inundated five towns. The Royal Air Force considered this to be their 'most brilliant action ever carried out.' Friedrich concluded that total war consumes human beings entirely—'and their sense of humanity is the first thing to go.'[47]

Air Force plans for attacks on North Korea's large dams originally envisioned hitting twenty of them, thus to destroy 250,000 tons of rice that would soon be harvested.

In the event bombers hit three dams in mid-May 1953, just as the rice was newly planted: Toksan, Chasan, and Kuwonga. Shortly thereafter two more were attacked, at Namsi and Taechon. These are usually called 'irrigation dams' in the literature, but they were major dams akin to many large dams in the U.S. The great Suiho dam on the Yalu River was second in the world only to Hoover Dam, and was first bombed in May 1952 (although never demolished, for fear of provoking Beijing and Moscow). The Pujon River dam was designed to hold 670 million cubic meters of water, it had a pressure gradient of 999 Pa/m; its power station generated 200,000 kilowatts from the water.[48] According to the official U.S. Air Force history, when fifty-nine F-84 Thunderjets breached the high containing wall of Toksan on May 13, 1953, the onrushing flood destroyed six miles of railway, five bridges, two miles of highway, and five square miles of rice paddies. The first breach at Toksan 'scooped clean' twenty-seven miles of river valley, and sent water rushing even into Pyongyang. After the war it took 200,000 man-days of labor to reconstruct the reservoir. But as with so many aspects of the war, no one seemed to notice back home: only the very fine print of *New York Times* daily war reports mentioned the dam hits, with no commentary.[49]

Violet ashes

After his release from North Korean custody General William F. Dean wrote, 'the town of Huichon amazed me. The city I'd seen before—two-storied buildings, a prominent main street—wasn't there any more.' He encountered the 'unoccupied shells' of town after town, and villages where rubble or 'snowy open spaces' were all that remained.[50] The Hungarian writer Tibor Meray had been a correspondent in North Korea during the war, and left Budapest for Paris after his participation in the 1956 rebellion against communist rule. When a Thames Television team interviewed him, he said that however brutal Koreans on either side might have been in this war, 'I saw destruction and horrible things committed by the American forces':

Everything which moved in North Korea was a military target, peasants in the fields often were machine gunned by pilots who, this was my impression, amused themselves to shoot the targets which moved.

Meray had arrived in August 1951 and witnessed 'a complete devastation between the Yalu River and the capital,' Pyongyang. There were simply 'no more cities in North Korea.' The incessant, indiscriminate bombing forced his party always to drive by night:

We traveled in moonlight, so my impression was that I am traveling on the moon, because there was only devastation…every city was a collection of chimneys. I don't know why houses collapsed and chimneys did not, but I went through a city of 200,000 inhabitants and I saw thousands of chimneys and that—that was all.[51]

A British reporter found communities where nothing was left but 'a low, wide mound of violet ashes.' At 10:00 p.m. on July 27 the air attacks finally ceased, as a B-26 dropped its radar-guided bomb load some twenty-four minutes before the armistice ending the war went into effect.[52] For months thereafter, North Korean authorities had difficulty convincing their citizens living in caves or hiding in the countryside, that it was safe to return to the cities.

In the end the scale of urban destruction quite exceeded that in Germany and Japan, according to U.S. Air Force studies. Friedrich estimated that the RAF dropped 657,000 tons of bombs on Germany from 1942–1945, and the total tonnage dropped by the UK and the U.S. at 1.2 million tons. The U.S. dropped 635,000 tons of bombs in Korea (not counting 32,557 tons of napalm), compared to 503,000 tons in the entire Pacific theater in World War II. Whereas sixty Japanese cities were destroyed to an average of forty-three percent, estimates of the destruction of towns and cities in North Korea 'ranged from forty to ninety percent;' at least fifty percent of eighteen out of the North's twenty-two major cities were obliterated. A partial table looks like this:[53]

Pyongyang, 75%
Chongjin,   65%
Hamhung,   80%
Hungnam,   85%
Sariwon,   95%
Sinanju,   100%
Wonsan,   80%

As another official American history put it,

So, we killed civilians, friendly civilians, and bombed their homes; fired whole villages with the occupants—women and children and ten times as many hidden Communist soldiers—under showers of napalm, and the pilots came back to their ships stinking of vomit twisted from their vitals by the shock of what they had to do.

Then the authors ask, was this any worse than 'killing thousands of invisible civilians with the blockbusters and atomic bombs…?' Not really, they say, because the enemy's 'savagery toward the people' was even worse than 'the Nazis' campaign of terror in Poland and the Ukraine.'[54] Apart from this astonishing distortion, note the logic: they are savages, so that gives us the right to shower napalm on innocents. It is also the terrible result of decades (if not centuries) of orientalism: white Americans believed that 'Orientals' do not value human life—so why should they?

After the war the Air Force convinced many that its saturation bombing forced the communists to conclude the war. Air Force General Otto Weyland determined that 'the panic and civil disorder' created in the North by round-the-clock bombing was 'the most compelling factor' in reaching the armistice.[55] He was wrong, just as he had been in World War II, but that did not stop the Air Force from repeating the same mindless and purposeless destruction in Vietnam. Saturation bombing was not conclusive in either war—just unimaginably destructive.

The United Nation's Genocide Convention defined the term as acts committed 'with intent to destroy, in whole or in part, a national, ethnical, racial or religious group.' This would include 'deliberately inflicting on the group conditions of life calculated to bring about its physical destruction in whole or in part.' It was approved in 1948 and entered into force in 1951—just as the USAF was inflicting genocide, under this definition and under the aegis of the United Nations Command, on the citizens of North Korea. Others note that area bombing of enemy cities was not illegal in World War II, but only became so after the Red Cross Convention on the Protection of Civilians in Wartime, signed in Stockholm in August 1948.[56] Neither measure had the slightest impact on this air war, which operated with a mindless and implacable automaticity.

The North Korean other

North Korean political practice is reprehensible, but we are not responsible for it. More disturbing is the incessant stereotyping and demonizing of this regime in the U.S., which continues undaunted today. When Kim Il-sung died in 1994, *Newsweek* ran a cover story entitled 'The Headless Beast.' Assertions that Kim Jong-il was simply crazy abound, but when they enter the thinking of fine analysts like Steven Coll in *The New Yorker*,[57] a magazine with a venerable tradition of fact-checking, you might ask which psychiatrist diagnosed Kim? Another expert recently wrote, as if everyone knows this, that North Korea is 'a hybrid of Stalinism and oriental despotism.'[58]

Kim Jong-il, of course, specialized in do-it-yourself stereotyping, masquerading as the Maximum Leader of a communist *opera buffe* in elevator shoes and 1970s double-knit pants suit, fattening himself while the masses starve, which makes it hard to argue that 'Oriental despotism' was not the name of his fossilized politics. But there is no evidence in the North Korean experience of the mass violence against whole classes of people or the wholesale 'purge' that so clearly characterized Stalinism, and that was particularly noteworthy in the scale of deaths in the land reform campaigns in China and North Vietnam and the purges of the Cultural Revolution. Nonetheless North Korea remains everyone's example of worst-case socialism and (until 1991) Soviet stoogery, leading American observers whether at the time or since to deem it impossible for the DPRK to have had any capacity for independent action in 1950.

In fact Kim and his late father, and the ideologues around them, continue ancient monarchical practices in East and West of 'the king's two bodies,' 'a body politic' and a 'body natural.' The latter is an ordinary, frail human being who happens to be king, who will go to his death like anyone else: Kim Jong-il, in short, with the dyspeptic, cynical, irritated face of a man who, from birth, had no chance of living up to his father—yet he has to be king. The other is a superhuman presence, an absolutely perfect body representing the God-king, maintained through the centuries as an archetype of the exquisite leader. (And with this you get North Korean inanities like Kim Jong-il scoring eagles on his first golf round.) In death the body natural disappears, but the soul of the God-king passes on to the next king. In Pyongyang this translated into Kim Il-sung's 'seed' bringing forth his first son, Jong-il, and now the grandson King Jong-un, continuing the perfect 'blood lines' that his scribes never tire of applauding. The family line thus becomes immortal, explaining why Kim Il-sung was not just president-for-life, but remained president of the DPRK in his afterlife.

North Korea is thus a modern form of monarchy, realized in a highly nationalistic, post-colonial state. 'The social unity expressed in the "body of the despot,"' Fredric Jameson wrote, is political, but also analogous to various religious practices. That the favored modern practice of such regimes should be organic nationalism (the leader's body, the body politic, the national body) is also entirely predictable. But the Western Left (let alone liberals) utterly fails to understand 'the immense Utopian appeal of nationalism.' Its morbid qualities are easily grasped, but its healthy qualities for the collective and for the tight unity that post-colonial leaders crave, are denied.[59] When you add to post-colonial nationalism Korea's centuries of royal succession and Neo-Confucian philosophy, it might be possible to understand North Korea as an unusual but predictable combination of monarchy, nationalism, and Korean political culture.

Conclusion

We who live in Western liberal society have our subconscious automatically (if imperfectly) produced from birth and we take for granted the relatively stable societies that we join as adults, so that we do what is expected without necessarily thinking about it. Civil society is thus internalized and reproduced, as an outcome of centuries of Western political practice. The creation of such habits, however, the spontaneous production of good citizens and good workers, loyal subjects who are also afforded the opportunity of disloyalty, appears as an opaque mystery where it does not exist—how can social exchange be so open, so fluid, so simultaneously orderly and threatening even to the powers, and yet so stable? 'The ways by which people advance toward dignity and enlightenment in government,' George F. Kennan wrote, 'are things that constitute the deepest and most intimate processes of national life. There is nothing less understandable to foreigners, nothing in which foreign influence can do less good.'[60] It is our blindness, our hidden complex of unexamined assumptions, that constitutes the core of hatred for North Koreans—what makes them simultaneously so laughable, so impudent, and so outrageous; we revile them, while they thumb their noses at us and our values—and get away with it. We have proved over seven decades that we do not understand North Korea and that we cannot do anything about it, however much we would like to. We can do something about our prejudices, and perhaps we ought to do it quickly.

Soon we may have a more daunting 'Oriental' enemy—'Red China,' as right-wing Republicans still call this communist-capitalist hybrid. It would not surprise in the least if, in a grave crisis, the full complex of North Korea-hating were reconfigured and rejiggered to fit the People's Republic of China. If that day comes—if 'China' leaps from the wings to the center of the American stage—for the first time since the country's founding, Americans will have fielded a formidable and astute adversary.

4

TERROR, THE IMPERIAL PRESIDENCY, AND AMERICAN HEROISM

Susan Jeffords

Where have all the good men gone
And where are all the gods
Where's the street-wise Hercules
To fight against the odds
Isn't there a white knight upon a fiery steed
Late at night I toss and I turn and I dream of what I need
I need a hero

Bonnie Tyler, 1984

In May 2010, shortly after the attempted bombing of Times Square by Faisal Shahzad, Senator Joseph Lieberman and his cosponsors introduced the Terrorist Expatriation Act, a bill that proposed to revoke the U.S. citizenship of any American citizen who affiliates with a foreign terrorist organization or who fights against the United States.[1] Lieberman explained the purpose of the bill to a group of reporters: 'If you've joined an enemy of the United States in attacking the United States and trying to kill Americans, I think you should sacrifice your rights of citizenship.'[2]

ORIENTALISM AND WAR

What the proposed Terrorist Expatriation Act points to is the simultaneous uncertainty and certainty of the War on Terror: uncertainty in that one's national identity can be removed, placing the citizen in the netherworld of non-citizenship (i.e., the accused terrorist doesn't automatically become a citizen elsewhere)[3]; certainty in the determination that one is now an identified terrorist. Part of the force working behind the proposed legislation was to remove accused terrorists from the rights to being arraigned and tried in the U.S. legal system. In the spring of 2010 after the Times Square bombing attempt, there was much outcry in the United States that accused terrorists were being read their Miranda rights. Senator John McCain, among others, led the charge that reading Miranda rights to Faisal Shahzad was a 'serious mistake.' He went on to say on a morning radio program, 'Don't give this guy his Miranda rights until we find out what it's all about.'[4] The paradox here, of course, is that Miranda rights are intended to prevent accused from falsely incriminating themselves during arrest and detainment. So the very right to protect oneself from mistreatment in the U.S. justice system—the right to defend oneself against false accusation—is removed from someone who is identified—perhaps falsely—as a terrorist. It is as if the category of 'terrorist' is so 'self'-evident that one can be accused and convicted in one action.

What is important about the Lieberman legislation is that it reveals the uneasy slippage that is required to make a coherent argument about terrorism. Falling quickly, comfortably, and menacingly into the orientalist definitions of self and others that underlie U.S. thinking about 'Muslim terrorists,' this legislation points to the hidden operations begun under the Bush administration of the dynamics of 'knowing' terrorists—that the label of 'terrorist' is an act of simultaneous creation and de-creation. The 'terrorist' becomes known only by unknowing his previous identity and, by back-formation, recreating past actions as inevitable propulsions towards 'becoming terrorist.' The Terrorist[5] is therefore not only no longer a citizen but is now (and by the logic of this narrative, always was becoming) a different kind of individual—without state, without history, and without future. This is the muddy consequence of what passes for the precise logic of orientalist thinking in the Global War on Terror (GWOT): that the Terrorist becomes an amorphous category shaped in response to the definitions required to bolster U.S. confidence, citizenship, and allegiance.

This is, perversely, precisely the logic that underlay the Bush/Cheney policy of creating 'enemy combatants,'[6] individuals who are accused of terrorism and, in the act of accusation, are confirmed as terrorists and therefore as individuals who have no rights to not being a terrorist. By removing all processes of evidence, review, and defense, the Bush administration created the category of Terrorist as a catchall for those accused of being so. It is the same logic of orientalism that Patricia Owens points to in this volume as justifying torture tactics that employ accusations of homosexuality as a strategy, 'producing,' as she points out, 'what they seek to regulate.' 'The torturers were seeking to produce the subject of torture through gendered practices, to reveal the repressed and sexually perverse Muslim sexual subject that is said to have informed Pentagon torture techniques in the first place.'[7] In the most extreme cases, this logic yields the continued affirmation of terrorism even after evidence to the contrary has been produced.[8] The case of Khaled el-Masri is an example. El-Masri was detained by the CIA under the belief that he was a wanted al-Qaeda leader. His legal German passport was dismissed by the CIA as a fabrication, and he was rendered to Afghanistan and tortured. In spite of evidence of his German citizenship and his mistaken detainment, a CIA officer continued to insist on his detention and interrogation because she had, according to a colleague, 'a gut feeling he's bad.'[9] The category of 'terrorist' or, in government parlance, the 'enemy combatant,' is therefore a category of uncreation of the individual, the space in which one becomes purely and only an 'other' and from which it is almost impossible—both categorically and physically—to return.

In his essay in this volume, John Mowitt comments that, 'to grasp the concept of orientalism, one must recognize its status as an interpretive machine.'[10] He goes on to say that, indeed, 'orientalism is inconceivable in the absence of such a machine.' It is this 'interpretive machine' that is at work in the production of the concept of the 'terrorist' as the fundamental operational logic of the interpretive war machine that has come to be called the GWOT. As Mowitt continues to explain, participation in these interpretive machines assumes an acceptance of a logic in which the 'truths' of interpretation are perceived as non-interpretive, in other words, dare I say, as self-evident. Mowitt captures precisely the character of the Bush administration in its approach to 'terrorism': 'It operates in denial of what makes it possible.'

After the photographs of torture in Abu Ghraib became public, the Bush administration defended the prison system of terrorism by severing the involved military personnel from the actions of the U.S. government, declaring that the abuses were committed by a few 'bad apples' and not a result of military policy. Lest we make the same mistake of individualizing the creation of terrorists (i.e., it is the fault of Bush/Cheney) it is important to recognize the underlying dynamic of the terrorism narrative in its linkage to the self/other logic of orientalism—that the creation of terrorists and the uncreation of individuals is also the simultaneous co-creation of the terrorist's accuser.

In its uneasy slippage, the U.S. narrative of terrorism under the GWOT reveals that its role is to create the space for 'knowing' the Terrorist. In this chapter, I want to discuss two aspects of the U.S. terror narrative that have dynamic relations to the creation of the space of the Terrorist: first, in the self/other paradigm that underlies orientalist thinking, that this space is used reflectively to affirm the role of the one who is 'not terrorist' (even if the 'not terrorist' is committing acts that might otherwise be associated with terrorism). In the U.S. GWOT, this plays out principally as 'Muslim terrorists' and 'American citizens.' As focal points for this logic, I will look at how the Terrorist other of Saddam Hussein enables the development of the imperial presidency of George Bush. Second, the consistent slippage created by the necessary impermanence of the space of the Terrorist requires mechanisms to ease the anxieties created both by what comes to be called 'fear' and by the uncertainties of the Terrorist category. In the second part of this chapter, I turn to how the logic of the naming of the other in the GWOT disrupts time, creating proleptic spaces that defy stability. The anxieties created by this disruption may be stabilized in a number of ways—assurances of authority, consumerism, anger, violence, and more. One of the most comfortable popular culture mechanisms is through the role of the 'hero' as illusory anchor in this disruption.

Slippery terrorism

There is widespread recognition of the compulsion of the security state to identify Arabs as terrorists and as enemies. George Kateb explains the logic most cogently:

The demise of the Soviet Union was the loss of the enemy that organized American life. That loss made American global hegemony possible, but the establishment demands that the national security system survive the loss. To do so, the system must have a clearly defined main enemy. A worldwide mass-cultural hegemony without a menacing enemy would not be adequate for the exercise of domination... for terrorism to be adequate to the project of imperialism, for imperialism to be sustainable publicly and rhetorically, terrorism must be falsely associated with Arabs and Muslims everywhere. For this idea to take hold, ordinary people have to refuse to make distinctions among Arabs and Muslims.[11]

As Anne McClintock puts it: 'The enemy is the object of empire: the rejected from which we cannot part.'[12] Nikhil Singh goes further: 'the barbarian and the terrorist are specters haunting the liberal-democratic imagination: it is what we are not, what we cannot trust, and therefore what we must subjugate.'[13]

What then is the 'self' that is being created simultaneously in opposition to the Terrorist—in fact the self that requires the Terrorist in order to be created? It is, as Kateb states, the self that inhabits the imperial state. But more importantly, it is also the security state, the national system that projects external threats for purposes of militarism and internal control of dissent. Kateb makes explicit the link to terrorism: 'The gift of terrorism to American imperialism, to the overarching aim of maintaining the national security state and economy, is that the terrorists killed American civilians on American soil.'[14] Terrorism is itself defined by the creation of public fear as a means to achieving a political endpoint. The naming of Terrorists is then a product of the fear that terrorism is designed to produce and the consequent desire for security, which Kateb recognizes, rightly, is 'insatiable.'[15] 'Fear of' becomes the generative force that propels the U.S. narratives of terror, producing the Terrorist—the one who produces fear—and, most importantly, the 'unterrified self.' However, once a Terrorist has been named, it is impossible to remove fear, since the very act of naming a Terrorist is an act of producing the fear that is the defining feature of the Terrorist. And, in turn, the activation of fear produces the need to name a Terrorist. This is precisely why the desire for security—for being 'unterrified'—is 'insatiable'—the naming of the Terrorist feeds the desire for security, which in turn feeds a continued desire to name the source of the fear as Terrorist, a naming that produces more fear, and so on.

Edward Said noted that the element of fear is among the early defining features of orientalism. In the classic Greek theater, he notes that 'there is the motif of the Orient as insinuating danger.'[16] As the vocabulary of orientalism became embedded in European history and culture, it was more pointedly Islam that became the source of fear:

Not for nothing did Islam come to symbolize terror, devastation, the demonic, hordes of hated barbarians. For Europe, Islam was a lasting trauma. Until the end of the seventeenth century the 'Ottoman peril' lurked alongside Europe to represent for the whole of Christian civilization a constant danger, and in time European civilization incorporated that peril and its lore, its great events, figures, virtues, and vices, as something woven into the fabric of life.[17]

With this history of 'constant danger' from Islam, it is a small step to see how the fear generated by the 'gift of terrorism' could be named so easily as 'Islam.'

The dance of 'naming' and 'fearing' that has become terrorism is one whose steps are familiar, known, and comfortable. These steps are what Sara Ahmed refers to as 'truth making,' confirming 'how we know the world as it already exists.' As Ahmed asserts, 'a world comes into existence through the repeated acts of defense against injury and loss' where '"what is" is presented as at risk from others who, in being "not like us," have "given up" on "the truth" and hence "life itself."'[18] It is then in the naming of the Terrorist as one who has 'given up on the truth' that the terrorist is identified and can then, by being 'known,' be stopped.

Ahmed talks also of fear, and its relation to world making, explaining that it is precisely through responses to fear—to the 'repeated acts of defense against injury and loss'—that the world as 'what is' is known. In this way, the 'world' as knowable cannot be known without fear, without 'establishing objects from which the subject, in fearing, can stand apart, objects which become "the not" from which the subject appears to flee.'[19] Ahmed speaks of fear as 'that which is approaching, as the not quite here, but getting closer,'[20] placing fear in a future orientation of looking towards that which may come.

However, there is more to the time of fear than this. While the object of fear—the Terrorist—is always approaching and therefore cause for the security apparatus that is justified by fear of the Terrorist, the case of Faisal Shahzad shows that fear also has a relation to the past, to the world that was 'known' and which the Terrorist is trying to destroy. Faisal's U.S. neighbors saw him as non-descript—'On weekends, Mr. Shahzad hosted barbecues, mowed his lawn and played badminton in the yard.'[21] The blog, *The Pakistan Update*, which was 'established to cut through the fog of mis-and disinformation about the crucial relationship between Pakistan and the United States and clarify misperceptions Pakistanis have of Americans and vice versa' even describes Faisal in terms of one of reality television's most popular characters: 'when he arrived to begin his studies in the US he was just another South Asian guy with a cheesy wardrobe and a fondness for booze and girls—the Pakistani equivalent of *The Situation*.'[22] However, as the *New*

York Times headline for its story on Faisal explained, these 'neighborly' behaviors masked 'long roots of discontent' that culminated in Faisal becoming a Terrorist. Jessica Vaughn, former U.S. Consulate officer writing for the conservative Center for Immigration Studies, argues that Faisal's 'history…reveals a familiar pattern of a terrorist easily taking advantage of weak spots in America's immigration system. Shahzad was admitted long before 9/11, but the openings he exploited are still in place today. Until policymakers move to shrink them, they offer a sobering guarantee of job security for counter-terrorism and security personnel for the foreseeable future.'[23]

It is in this way that the GWOT further disrupts and disorients the space of narrative. The fear of 'that which is approaching'—the future—causes defensive actions in the present—those 'repeated acts of defense against injury and loss'—that in turn require rewritings of the past in order to secure 'what is.' Into this shifting timeline fall the categories, not just of Terrorist but also of 'citizen,' 'homeland,' 'neighbor.' This distemporal logic—what Nikhil Singh calls in another context 'the past-present that is these United states'—insists that the naming of terrorism is a result of the terrorist's behavior, a behavior that in turn 'causes' the one who is terrorized to respond, perhaps even in ways that exceed the terrorist act.[24]

It is precisely this slippery relationship between time, definition, and 'what is' that compels the intensity of fervor behind the desire to 'know' the Terrorist, to identify a fixed location from which other definitions—the self, the enemy, the nation—can emanate. In what Ahmed calls the 'ontology of insecurity…It *must be* presumed that things are not secured, in and of themselves, in order to justify the imperative *to make things secure.*'[25] If the need for security that is insatiable compels the identification of the Terrorist and terror as 'Islam,' then so too is the desire for the creation of the self as non-terrorist insatiable. The self can never be 'safe enough.' While this logic informs many aspects of U.S. culture today—from childrearing to immigration policy to tourism to the increase in the security industry—perhaps its most important manifestation has been in buttressing the formation of the imperial presidency. This is the logic that informs the imperial presidency—the 'commander in chief' who quells 'fear of' by naming and eliminating the one who causes fear.

The imperial presidency

Much has been written about the Bush presidency as an 'imperial presidency.'[26] The Bush administration produced the most powerful presidency in the history of the United States, instituting policies and practices of surveillance, imprisonment, torture, and murder, much of which was done without the review and scrutiny of the other two branches of the government. Presidential scholar Michael Genovese explains that President Bush has been 'unwilling to place himself within the rule of law. He exercised extra-constitutional power and claimed that his acts were not reviewable by Congress or the courts. Such a bold interpretation of the president's powers is unsupportable in law or history.'[27] In what they call his 'go-it-alone' policy, political scientists Byron Daynes and Glen Sussman tie the imperial presidency explicitly to fear:

Bush has challenged checks and balances through the use of fear—The president has done all he could to isolate his Administration from oversight from the Congress, the Court, from the press and from public debate... He has used fear to convince us all to follow his unquestioned lead in Iraq. He has repeatedly warned the American people that 'another attack is immanent [sic].'[28]

Insatiable desires for security, coupled with a knowable target, yielded an insatiable presidency.

George Bush's own Christian religious beliefs certainly encouraged his comfort with the narrative of Islam as danger and supported his belief in an imperial presidency. Stephen Wayne explains: 'Bush had personalized the challenge the country faced, a challenge that assumed almost divine proportions for him. He seemed to relish his role as a wartime president, as protector and defender of the American people, as the nation's father figure. The divine connection elevated the struggle, justifying the battle and the loss of life that would inevitably result from it; that connection clearly distinguished right and wrong for him.'[29] However, while his personal religious impulses informed his own habitation of the role, the systematic implementation of the role was grounded legally in the work of one of the most influential figures in the development of the imperial presidency, John Yoo.

Yoo served as Deputy Assistant Attorney General in the Office of Legal Counsel from 2001–2003, the critical years for the establishment of the imperial presidency. He was author of some of the most damaging legal authorizations of torture, rendition, imprisonment without review, and surveillance that underlay the Bush policies in the GWOT. Yoo's arguments depended upon his assertion that the presidential powers outlined in the Constitution are 'more general and open-ended than other powers,' with 'the bulk of executive power rest[ing] in foreign affairs and national security.'[30] In a series of books that he has written since his service in the government, Yoo develops a historically nuanced account of the Framers' intentions in creating the role of president as they did, specifically pointing to the presumed authority over foreign affairs and national security, in response to precedents in England. By Yoo's account, the powers he ascribes to the president were always implicit in the Constitution; it is just that the roles of foreign affairs and national security played less part in the president's activities during the first century of American growth. It was, according to Yoo, the Cold War that required that these two facets of the president's responsibilities—foreign affairs and national security—became full-time preoccupations. Responding directly to claims that he abetted the creation of an imperial presidency, he quips, 'it was not the Presidency that became imperial, it was the United States that became an empire.'[31]

The important point to make about Yoo's argument is that he grounds his justification of presidential powers in the historical context that was faced by the authors of the Constitution—witnessing the actions of the King during the British wars of the eighteenth century, wars in which the King acted independently of parliament to declare wars and conscript armies. Yoo's point is precisely that the defining characteristic of the president is that he must be able to act; his actions are checked by the Congress's authority to fund military engagements. As Yoo states, the president may have power to deploy troops, but Congress may choose not to provide funds to enact that decision. At the same time, Yoo argues that the Framers were influenced by the perceived failures of the Continental Congress. The loose confederation of states that had no single leader was able to authorize expenditures but could not decide on how to do so, or, if a decision was made, it was made after an extended time of deliberation, a time that was seen to be too long for matters of urgent foreign policy or military engagement. In Yoo's history, the Framers wished precisely for the president to be able to be a 'decider,' someone who was able to take swift action in the best interests of the country. If the Congress judged a president's decision to be flawed, it could choose not to provide funds for the military action or could choose not to ratify a treaty that the president had signed, but, most importantly, it was not the Framers' intention that Congress inhibit the president from acting decisively.

John Yoo's legal memos provided the mechanism for legitimating the naming of the Terrorist: with the United States having been the target of terrorism in the 9/11 attacks, Bush could assume the right to name the terrorists who had conducted the attacks. What became increasingly important over the course of his presidency was that in turn, by naming terrorists, the Bush administration could name itself as the one that had been terrorized. Because, as Kateb reminds us, this is a state of being that is 'insatiable,' Bush was required throughout his presidency to name and re-name terrorists and to affirm and re-affirm the state of fear that legitimized his ability to do so. What Ruth Blakeley says of the relationship between the torturer and the tortured is a microcosm of the relationship between the Terrorist and the one who names the terrorist/the one who feels terror:

> The identities that they [those arguing for the legitimacy of torture] seek to assign provide the basis for their arguments that torture is justified, and that they… are legitimated to use it. Establishing identities in this way is not a one-time process. Rather it has to be repeated over and over in the face of resistance. The identities only exist in their reassertion, and each time those identities are challenged, they have to be reasserted. The right to torture is claimed in an attempt to secure and fix… identities. It is thus a two-way performative process.

The authority that Yoo articulated became the bedrock for Bush's approval of torture, secret imprisonment, rendition, and surveillance. In a 2008 editorial column, the *New York Times* called Yoo's memos 'the twisted legal reasoning…that justify President Bush's decision to ignore federal law and international treaties.'[32] However, Bush's authority was itself reliant on Yoo's. In the same way that expertise was fundamental to the narrative of orientalism (the field of Oriental Studies, for example), the team of legal 'experts' whose tortured arguments granted permission for torture was fundamental to the propagation of torture and of the GWOT that justified it. 'Bush's legal team,' Jane Mayer summarizes, 'was arguing that the President not only had power to defend the nation as he saw fit in ways that were not limited by any laws, he also had the power to override existing laws that Congress had specifically designed to curb him.' Republican legal activist Bruce Fein accused Bush of making 'claims that are really quite alarming. He's said that there are no restraints on his ability, as he sees it, to collect intelligence, to open mail, to commit torture, and to use electronic surveillance…His war powers allow him to declare anyone an illegal combatant. All the world's a battlefield.' In the symbiotic and self-referential logic of presidential powers that relied on Yoo's 'expert' arguments, the voices of those accused of terrorism became equally proportionally silenced as Bush's presidential authority increased.

For the Bush administration, the performance of terror came to be embodied in its ability to name Terrorists. Bush's most famous pronouncement about terrorism was in the January 29, 2002 State of the Union address, in which he declared Iraq, Iran, and North Korea to be the 'Axis of Evil' as states that sponsored terrorism and sought to develop weapons of mass destruction through which to enact terror. More destructively, Bush also reserved the right to decide who was to be identified as a 'terrorist.' He wore the mantle of this power through his self-characterization as the 'decider': 'I listen to all voices, but mine is the final decision... I'm the decider, and I decide what is best.'[33] Through the performance of terror, Bush was able to affirm his 'right to decide' and his role as 'commander in chief.' His very persona as president, the 'deciding' president that Yoo believes the Constitution intended, thus rested upon his naming of Terrorists.

What the role of 'decider' requires, of course, is something to decide. And though the persona of 'decider' became one of Bush's hallmarks (and the target of much satire) for all of his actions, it was terrorism that enabled the creation of this persona and terrorism that sustained it. Consequently, for Bush to present himself as the role he desired and the role that Yoo's memos rationalized, he had to continue to create terrorist threats. While the 'Axis of Evil' narrative was one piece of this, it was difficult for the U.S. public to feel sustained personal fear over a possible North Korean or Iranian nuclear weapon. It required terrorists who wished to attack Americans in the United States—the 'gift' of 9/11—to create the fear watch that would sustain permission for Bush's role as decider. It is thus this dynamic that led to the almost 800 individuals who have been imprisoned in Guantanamo and the thousands who have been imprisoned in other facilities around the world. This continual naming and enumeration of terrorists was the bedrock of Bush's authority as president and the foundation upon which resided the neoconservative policies that his administration enacted.

Bush's authority as president was tied equally to the power assigned to the Terrorist, with his claim to power linked to his characterization of the potential or actual power of the terrorist enemy. Osama Bin Laden became the chief oppositional figure against whom he would declare the need to have his authority as president augmented, undeterred by the temporizing he attributed to Congress, a relationship that James Der Derian characterized as a 'mimetic struggle.'[34] While the majority of those imprisoned in Guantanamo and other U.S. affiliated prisons have been assessed by external evaluators as relatively minor participants in terrorist activities, with many wrongly accused or identified as parts of bounty schemes where others were encouraged to turn over terrorists to the United States in return for reward money, the high profile detainees are assigned significant attributes that support their potential for causing terror. In what has become one of the most famous lines, General Richard Myers described a group of detainees in Guantanamo as 'people who would chew through a hydraulic cable to bring a C-17 down.'

In Der Derian's mimetic framing, the more powerful the Terrorist, the more powerful the president. Michael Ignatieff uses the phrase 'superempowered' to describe terrorists who have access to weapons of mass destruction.[35] Weapons of mass destruction became a key part of the increasing presidential authority acquired by the Bush administration. The Bush administration used these 'superempowered terrorists' to justify the 'superempowered' presidency. To feed and sustain the insatiability of fear, weapons of mass destruction are the most effective trigger to activate fear among the U.S. population, since such weapons have the potential to impact the largest number of people and create the most widespread disruption and devastation. In the framework whereby Bush's presidential authority for all of the policies of his administration rests upon the naming of terrorists, the identification of the 'superempowered' terrorist becomes an essential declaration.

There have been many speculations about why George Bush chose, after September 11, to target Saddam Hussein for military action rather than Osama bin Laden, chief among them a psychologizing of his desire to redeem the act his father 'failed' to do after the first Gulf War. This argument is best summed up in the following:

Resentment naturally contaminated Bush's efforts to prove himself to his father and receive his father's approval. The contradictory mix showed up in his compulsion to re-fight his father's war against Iraq, but this time winning the duel some thought his father failed to win with Saddam. He could at once emulate his father, show his contempt for him, and redeem him. But beneath this son-father struggle lies a far more significant issue for Bush—a question about his own competence, adequacy and autonomy as a human being.[36]

Such arguments, while attractive and comfortably explanatory, ignore the larger dynamic of the terrorism narratives that I have been outlining here and enable the continuation of narratives that individualize the performative structures of terrorism and orientalism.

In contrast to such an individually psychologized narrative, the narratives of terrorism encourage us instead to recognize that Saddam Hussein became for George Bush the embodiment of a 'superempowered terrorist,' but also, most appropriately, an equally powerful single figure against whom Bush could be defined. If we accept the argument that Bush's desire for increased authority depended upon the identification of an equally 'decisive' opponent, then Saddam Hussein, an authoritarian, secretive, territorially-defined, and demagogic president, fits the bill better than Osama bin Laden, a curiously reclusive, amorphously defined, and territorially diffuse leader. Attributing the possession of weapons of mass destruction to Saddam Hussein enabled the narrative to move forward under the heading of terrorism.

For Bush, Saddam Hussein is 'he who is the same and other,' the understandable and identifiable enemy. As a nation-state led by a domineering president, Iraq could be the exemplar opposite of the imperial U.S. president and nation struggling with self-definition. The war in Iraq affirmed and validated the nation-state as the currency of global relations, defining the opposition between the 'good state' (democratic) and the 'bad state' (undemocratic). There is the added dynamic of what Nikhil Singh points to as the 'condescending tutelary discourse about Iraqi capacity for freedom and democracy (good Muslim)' and the 'Orientalist suspicion of menace and disability (bad Muslim).'[37] In this discourse, the 'good Muslim' is open to democratic tutelage but, more implicitly and importantly, recognizes the nation-state as the location for debate. The 'bad Muslim' is one who appears to discard democracy and, consequently, the nation-state, favoring a world in which national boundaries give way to religious ones. Again, this dynamic is lost in the psychologized paternalism narrative of Bush's reasons for targeting Saddam Hussein instead of Osama bin Laden as the embodiment of the terrorist threat. For Bush, targeting Saddam Hussein was not a 'mistake' but an entirely logical reinforcement that rationalized his imperial presidency.

Heroism and anxiety

If we go back to the Terrorist Expatriation Act, we can see one of the chief dilemmas of this performance of terror—its metaleptic necessity and therefore the temporal contradiction that is its secret. The authors of the Terrorist Expatriation Act wish to take away American citizenship from those named as 'terrorists,' even without conviction in a trial. They are named—proleptically—as a terrorist presumably because of an action they have taken against the United States in the past. In their naming, their status as U.S. citizen is called into question—'no one who is a citizen would act against the nation.' In so doing, their rights as a citizen are withdrawn, thereby recreating their past citizenship as an act of deception, a 'performance of citizenship,' as it were, that was not real, thereby invalidating their past status and justifying its negation (negating that which never was). In the days after the attempted bombing of Times Square, Faisal Shahzad's 'life' was examined in detail as the media sought for explanations for his actions, i.e., for signs of his pre-being as a 'terrorist.'

What the media's treatment of Faisal shows is that the 'two-way performance' of terror is not only a simultaneous creation of the terrorist and the 'one in terror,' but also a simultaneous creation of past narratives that accompany and justify each role. Hardt and Negri recognize this metaleptic move in their discussion of the large-scale violence of imperial war: 'violence is legitimated most effectively today, it seems to us, not on any a priori framework, moral or legal, but only a posteriori, based on its results…the reinforcement or reestablishment of the current global order is what retroactively legitimates the use of violence.'[38] Matthew Hannah expands to say that 'the counterpart and response to the ubiquitous possibility of terrorist violence anywhere in the U.S. territory is an equally ubiquitous possibility of violent U.S. intervention anywhere around the globe, whether in the form of manhunts and extraordinary rendering, or of military invasion.'[39] But what the Bush administration had shown—and what the activation of the Iraq War was based upon—is that the prevention of terrorism 'requires' the identification of terrorists before the terrorism has been enacted, thereby making the 'cause' of the response itself a projection of the fear of the terrorized.

And this is what makes the GWOT different. While history's truism that 'the victors write the history books' has long acknowledged that the past gets rewritten to justify the actions and authorities of the present, the GWOT has added the proleptic dimension of projecting future actions to justify determinations in the present, all of which then are invoked to rewrite the past: the Terrorist is one who will commit a terrorist act in the future, thereby justifying imprisonment in the present, with investigations in the past that 'show' how the future actions are inevitable. In such an amorphous and slippery space, expertise and authority become even more important, as the only linkage between these time shifts is the expert who has access to 'evidence' (that citizens do not have access to) and the authority who acts on the expert's information.

This contradictory and unstable space incites an aggressive maintenance of the authority of the one who names the Terrorist, but it is a space of simultaneous affirmation—'I am the one who has been terrorized'—and denial—'I am not the one who is terrorizing.' It is the Zizekian liminal space of terrorism and torture.[40] However, Zizek's 'in-between' space can be paralyzing. What is the 'right' decision regarding terror? How does an American citizen balance the desire to be without terror—a desire that can lead to the preemptive imprisonment of potential terrorists—with the desire to sustain the rights that have defined the principles of American citizenship—to be presumed innocent until proven guilty, to have an open trial, and to be protected from unlawful detention. Pat Buchanan summarized this seeming contradiction in American political culture by concluding that 'the left may be right on the law, but the people seem to be standing by Bush.'

How to find a point of rest among these contradictory and uncertain desires? As the definition of Terrorist gets played out over the bodies of people accused of terrorism, so the bodies of those who are 'not terrorists' are presented as points of stability in this madness. The most common 'not terrorist' body was identified soon after 9/11: the hero. Whether firefighters, police officers, soldiers, or airplane passengers, the idea of heroism was resuscitated in the aftermath of 9/11. The hero is one who, by definition, is the quintessential American citizen—one who embodies American values and defends the nation. The hero is also, by definition, one who provides security in the face of fear, who protects those who are vulnerable from attacks by enemies. In this way, the ambivalence that is generated by the apparent contradiction between security and citizenship is resolved in the figure of the hero who acts to provide security for citizens. Ahmed describes an economy of emotions in which they 'stick and slide, they move us in surprising and unexpected ways, but they do not inhabit any body or any thing.' And while Ahmed argues persuasively elsewhere that this 'stickiness' can be the source of an alternate way of listening to 'other others,' it is also this stickiness that enables the space of heroism, the figure who stabilizes the metonymic slide between fear and 'what is.'

Since September 11, 2001, fictional narratives about terrorism have become among the most popular in the United States. *24*, the narrative that takes the 'ticking time bomb' terrorist scenario as its raison d'être, ran for eight seasons and surpassed *Mission Impossible* and *The Avengers* as the longest running espionage television series. Averaging between 10–13 million viewers per show in the United States, *24* was winner of numerous awards including multiple Emmys and Golden Globes. Shown in multiple countries outside the United States,[41] *24* became not only one of the most popular U.S. television programs but also a global export. Emblematic of its impact on American culture is the focus of the program on torture scenes and the overall increase in scenes of torture on television: according to Michael Jones, 'before the show premiered… there was an average of only four torture scenes on the tube per year, across all networks. After *24*… That number shot up to more than 100. Torture became so popular across television networks, particularly *24*, that military professionals from West Point actually flew out to California to meet with producers of *24*, to kindly ask them to tone the torture scenes down. The reason? Because U.S. soldiers were starting to mimic what they saw on TV.'[42]

In addition to *24*, there are numerous bestselling novelists who have taken terrorism as their theme, ranging from Nelson DeMille to John Updike. Among the most popular is Vince Flynn, author of eleven suspense thriller novels that have sold over ten million copies. It is said that 'what Tom Clancy did for the Cold War, Vince Flynn is doing for the war on terror.' The *Washington Times* calls Flynn's protagonist, Mitch Rapp, a 'Rambo perfectly suited to the war on terror.' It is reported that Joe Hagin, George Bush's long-time friend and White House Deputy Chief of Staff, brought copies of Flynn's 1999 novel, *Transfer of Power*, to the White House Situation Room in the months after 9/11, because the plot centers around terrorists infiltrating the White House. According to Flynn himself, 'Heads of foreign intelligence agencies read these books. The King of Bahrain, King Abdullah of Jordan, and Prime Minister Brown. It floors me that all these people are reading them. They walk away saying "Hmm, this guy knows a lot."'[43]

Mitch Rapp, Jack Bauer, and the heroes like them stand in the liminal space that would be unacceptable to most U.S. citizens—the space of terrorizing in response to terror—but which many American citizens now believe is a necessary space to insure their ability to be 'free from terror.' It is also a space of theater, of the perverse desire to 'see' that which we wish to deny and yet which we already know. John Beverley says of Flynn's novels that 'something normally hidden from sight in the regime of juridical modernity is not only presented explicitly, but presented so as to elicit a peculiar kind of voyeuristic fascination.'[44] He argues that 'the proliferation of representations of torture in contemporary American popular culture… might be seen as a way of making explicit a state of affairs that we believe exists but that we are not allowed to confront directly because of the state's inevitable hypocrisy about what is going on.'[45] I disagree. It is not that we are 'not allowed' to confront the state of affairs that is torture because of government secrecy. It is that we have accepted the ambivalent in-between state of fear that balances the desire to be free from terror against the desire not to be seen as terrorizing. In this in-between state, we turn to individuals we label as 'heroic' precisely because they are explicit about that which remains unsaid—that we place our desire to be free from fear over commitments to values that are attributed to Americans. As *National Review* editor Jonah Goldberg explains, 'is abuse justified in getting a prisoner to reveal the location of a bomb that would kill many when detonated? We understand that in such a situation, Americans would expect to be protected.'[46]

And this is where the self/other dynamic of orientalism returns, for it enables the act of terrorizing to appear to be very American after all. Vince Flynn explains how Mitch Rapp, the hero of his novels,

held no illusions about who he was, or what he did. He'd been at war with radical Islam a good ten years before the country even knew there was a war. He'd threatened, beaten, tortured, and killed so many men it was hopeless to even attempt a tally. During all of that, though, he'd clung to the conviction that he was very different from the enemy. As strange as it would seem to many in a civilized society, he was able to live with what he did because of whom he did it to. Unlike the people he hunted, Rapp made every effort to make sure noncombatants stayed exactly that. Women and children were strictly off-limits. Thankfully, in the chauvinistic world of radical Islam, this was far easier to accomplish than one would think. In fact, they sought out the innocent to amplify their terror.[47]

Flynn's explanation absolves Americans from anxiety about betraying American values in torture and imprisonment by characterizing the 'people he hunted' as so morally inferior that Rapp's actions can be excused.

In *Extreme Measures*, Rapp is called to testify before the House Judiciary Committee about his reputed involvement in torture. He articulates the sentiment that Joe Lieberman would argue two years later, in describing Mohammad al-Haq: he 'is not an American citizen. He is a terrorist.'[48] He warns the collected legislators: 'I remember after nine-eleven, when the pain of that day was still fresh, many of you came to me and asked if we were doing enough to make these terrorists talk after they were captured. You didn't think we were being aggressive enough, and then Abu Ghraib hit and we went right back to fighting each other.'[49] He goes on to state the threat that haunted the Bush administration: 'Think of how the American people will react when they find out that this committee and its members were more concerned with protecting the debatable rights of a couple of bigoted, sadistic terrorists than they were in protecting their own citizens.'[50] After a terrorist bombing of a Washington, D.C. restaurant in which the Senate Chair's aide was killed, the senator states, 'I've seen the light…I want you to hunt this Karim and these other two men down, and anyone else who helped him…And I want you to kill them.'[51]

There is a direct line between the imperial presidency and the heroes of terror narratives. It is articulated in Flynn's most recent novel, *American Assassin*, in which the narrator describes the decision process of its hero, Mitch Rapp: 'After a day of watching the very people who said they would handle the situation do nothing, Rapp decided to look for a solution on his own.'[52] Action, decision-making, violence: these are the features that tie the Bush imperial presidency—the 'decider'—and the heroes of U.S. terror narratives. They are the stoppage points that give temporary halt to the Orientalist insecurities of terrorism.

But those stoppage points—what are called 'heroes' here but may also take other shapes—are ephemeral. Their very instability requires the constant repetition of the Terrorism narrative as its echoes fade and anxieties return. The very narrative of terrorism belies the proleptic nature of telling the tale of the Terrorist—s/he who is known in the present by predictions of her future behavior justified by past actions that can only be seen as part of the narrative once the story has been told and the characters have been named. The Terrorism interpretive machine both tells this tale and disrupts it, as time and narrative become victims of the naming of the GWOT.

5

CAN THE INSURGENT SPEAK?

Hugh Gusterson *

The first time one sees a member of the Vietcong there is a sharp sense of disappointment. He is not, it turns out, very different: he is simply another Vietnamese. Generally when you see him he is either kneeling and firing at you, or he has just been captured, or, more often than not, he is dead. The bodies of enemy dead are always lined up, feet all in an orderly row. The guerilla wears little, perhaps a simple peasant pajama suit, perhaps only shorts. He is slim and wiry, and his face could be that of your interpreter or of the taxi driver who drove you to My Tho. Only the haircut is different, very thin along the sides and very long on top and in front. It is a bad haircut and, like the frailness of the uniform and the wallet with only a few pictures of some peasant woman, it makes the enemy human. But one's sympathy does not last long; this is the same face which has been seen by the outnumbered defenders of some small outpost before it was overrun.

David Halberstam, 1965.[1]

* Thanks to all the participants in the 'Orientalism at War' conference at the University of Oxford in summer 2010 for their feedback on an earlier version of this chapter, and special thanks to Tarak Barkawi and Keith Stanski for their patience and encouragement as this chapter was redrafted. My thanks also for a close reading of a draft of this article by the students in my Media and War class: John Baker, Jacey Eckhart, Ariella Horwitz, Lewis Levenberg, and David Rheams. Thanks also to a journalist who wishes to remain anonymous for her detailed comments in response to an earlier draft.

ORIENTALISM AND WAR

David Halberstam was writing about Vietnam, not Iraq or Afghanistan, but, as we shall see, there are strong continuities linking American media coverage of Vietnam and current U.S. counterinsurgency wars in the Muslim world. For Halberstam the oriental enemy was largely unseen. But when he is finally seen, he has a generic quality: apparently all guerillas are 'slim and wiry,' and they are hard to distinguish from taxi drivers and other of their countrymen. Even face to face with the enemy, Halberstam, who would emerge as one of the sharpest journalistic critics of the Vietnam War, struggles to recognize the enemy's individuality and humanity. Things have not changed much for Halberstam's successors at the *New York Times* and other mainstream media outlets today.

If we ask what academics know about American media coverage of war, in recent years a sizeable body of literature has emerged in critical international relations theory, media studies and cultural studies on the deformed shape of war reporting in the American mass media.[2] This literature has focused on the ownership of mass media outlets by corporations that profit from war; on the excessive deference reporters show to official U.S. spokespersons; on media sanitization of the United States' motives in going to war; on the ways in which the embedding of journalists in American military units fosters ideological compliance among reporters; on media silences about the suffering of civilians killed and maimed by American weaponry; on Hollywood's masculinist stylizations of Americans' wars; on media complicity with official narratives of American innocence and victimhood; and on a more general erasure in mainstream reportage of America's history of military imperialism in various regions of the globe. Surprisingly, there is relatively little critique in this burgeoning literature of the diffuse orientalism that permeates much mainstream media coverage of the wars in Iraq and Afghanistan,[3] and there is even less critique of the ways in which the insurgents who are fighting American troops are figured, or erased, in this coverage. Indeed, it would not be much of an exaggeration to say that these insurgents have been doubly erased—first by mainstream media accounts, then by academic critiques of these accounts.

Yet insurgents are essential to the contemporary American war project. Without them, there would be no war in Iraq and Afghanistan. In the operational sphere, U.S. military and intelligence institutions devote considerable resources to the understanding of insurgents: who they are, how they recruit, what they want, how they interface with established institutions and networks in their host societies, how they train, what tactics they use, and how these tactics evolve. Mainstream media have made only the most tepid attempts to ask the same questions.

In the symbolic sphere, insurgents play a key role in securing American identity.[4] National identity tends to be imagined dialectically, and there is nothing like an enemy to sharpen the practice of dialectical imagination. In the Republic's earlier years Americans used as their foil the Indians, imagined as savage and backward, whom they fought and often liquidated in the frontier wars that were morphological antecedents of America's current counterinsurgency wars. More recently, entering the global arena and committing itself to what turned out to be mobilization for permanent war, World War II provided a larger canvass on which the United States was able to depict itself as a global power dedicated to freedom and democracy and to a Manichean struggle against totalitarianism. In the long Cold War the Nazis were replaced by Soviet communists, but the U.S. continued in its imagined role as the champion of freedom and modernity in a global Manichean struggle.[5] Following the loss of the Cold War errand, the war on terror and its ancillary wars in Iraq and Afghanistan offer a new defining context in which the United States has reimagined itself as the deliverer of modernity, democracy, women's rights, and development.[6] In the context of these conflicts insurgents—figured as medieval, brutal, fanatical, tyrannical and misogynistic—have provided the new foil for American identity. And yet there is a paradox here: although insurgents are essential to the war project and the process of national self-imagining with which it is inextricably imbricated, it seems also to be essential to the American war project that insurgents be present in public representations of American wars in only the most derealized forms. While providing the *casus belli* and embodying the nemesis of Western civilization, they are almost invariably hidden, or just over the horizon, or out of focus, or in disguise, or masked and veiled, or anonymous, or in caricature. In a profound sense, these people toward whose extirpation the United States is dedicating so much of its national treasure, are fundamentally unknowable and must be so. (In their essential invisibility, guerillas are a little different from many of Edward Said's classic orientalist subjects, which were constituted by their rich availability to the Western gaze, even if they still remained marked by mystery). Afghan and Iraqi guerillas perform their essential function of anchoring American mission and identity, then, as much through phantomlike absence as through their active presence in the increasingly diffuse theater of battle. If their physical presence is required for these wars, so is their absence, or at least their ideological and existential evacuation. What instability, one wonders, might they inflict on the American errand if they could come out of hiding, take off their masks and speak to us?

In a practical sense, the evacuated quality of insurgents in mainstream media figurations is surely a by-product of the form of war forced upon them by a strategic situation in which they are fighting an enemy that has the advantage of overwhelming military superiority in any conventional confrontation. Faced with overwhelming American firepower, but enjoying a more intimate knowledge of the human and physical terrain, the insurgents have made the obvious choice of operating from the shadows, and this asymmetrical reality profoundly shapes their availability for media representation. But if American journalists wanted to badly enough, they could, as a few reporters for the alternative press and as mainstream British journalists such as Robert Fisk have demonstrated, go and find insurgents and talk to them. They have not done so in part because American[7] mainstream media representations of insurgents in Iraq and Afghanistan are also deeply shaped by a chosen practice and by an inherited discursive tradition. The chosen practice is embedding. If in the Vietnam War American reporters roamed where they pleased, in Iraq and Afghanistan they have donned American uniforms and embedded themselves in American (and allied) military units. In so doing, they have chosen to see the war, including the insurgents fighting on the other side, from an American point of view. There is an inherent tension between their official ideology of journalistic objectivity and their embodied location within U.S. military units. By virtue of this embodied location, they see the terrain of battle through the eyes of the American soldiers around them, not from some Archimedean third point, and they absorb by cultural osmosis the attitudes of the soldiers who protect them and with whom they are attacked by insurgents.

The discursive tradition that shapes American journalism is orientalism. While the orientalism of a contemporary *New York Times* reporter is subtle and discreet compared to the kinds of florid prejudice from the nineteenth century anatomized by Edward Said, it is no less powerful for that. In his book, *Military Orientalism*, Patrick Porter enumerates the orientalist prejudices he has seen at work in both journalistic and military representations of the Taliban. He argues that these deformed representations, whatever essential ideological purpose they may perform, are hobbling the allied war effort, which surely requires an accurate perception of the enemy and its capabilities. Among the tropes he identifies are a figuration of insurgents as medieval or archaic, as the embodiments of an eternal and unchanging refusal of modernity; as irrational; as tribal; as sneaky; as enslaved to a code of honor and revenge; and as enamored of martyrdom and death.[8] In the absence of real, direct knowledge of insurgents, and in the presence of unspoken taboos against trying to acquire such knowledge, the orientalist code has provided a repertoire on which journalists have drawn, consciously or unconsciously, in their portrayals of the insurgent other.[9]

Constructing insurgents

Over the last nine years, whenever there has been a suicide bombing, IED attack or firefight in Iraq or Afghanistan, mainstream media have been quick to document where the incident took place, the time of day it occurred, the numbers of bodies it produced and the kinds of injuries inflicted, as well as the reactions of U.S. soldiers and innocent civilians. But the insurgents themselves—the agents of the carnage—tend to be a blank space at the center of the picture, known mainly by their acts.

It is well known that under President George W. Bush the U.S. military went to great lengths to keep images of U.S. soldiers' coffins out of the media. Less well known are U.S. attempts to obstruct images of insurgents—attempts that only compound the mysterious invisibility of these figures. Pulitzer Prize-winning AP photographer Bilal Hussein, one of the few journalists able to photograph insurgents in Iraq, was detained by the U.S. military in April 2006 on the grounds that only an insurgent, or an insurgent sympathizer, would have been able to take such pictures.[10] He was held without trial for two years until he was finally released in 2008 following pressure from AP, the Committee to Protect Journalists, and the Iraqi government. His detention led Tom Curley, President of the Associated Press, to say in 2006, 'after more than five months of trying to bring Bilal's case into the daylight, AP is now convinced the Army doesn't care whether Bilal is or isn't an insurgent....He is no longer free to circulate in his native Fallujah or Ramadi, taking photographs that coalition commanders would prefer not to see published.'[11]

And yet Bilal's oeuvre hardly puts a human face on the insurgents. In his photographs the insurgents carry huge grenade launchers or Kalashnikovs, with which their bodies appear melded, and their faces are completely wrapped in khaffiyehs.[12] In a way, then, these supposedly subversive images are trapped within the logic of anonymity that characterizes dominant con-

Figure 5.1: Photo of insurgents by Bilal Hussein.

Figure 5.2: Photo by Bilal Hussein.

ventions for portraying insurgents. And, as Judith Butler says, 'those who remain faceless…authorize us to become senseless before those whose lives we have eradicated, and whose grievability is indefinitely postponed.'[13]

Still, the narrative conventions for writing insurgents in mainstream media accounts do not so much depict them as masked bodies but as absences, shadows, disembodied voices or tantalizing traces. 'The insurgents are ghosts,' says one *New York Times* reporter.[14] The *Los Angeles Times* says, 'ragtag yet ferocious, they were so spectrally elusive that the Soviet forces called them *dukhi*, or ghosts.'[15] Here is an account, emphasizing their elusiveness, of Iraqi insurgents' tactics from *Washington Post* reporter Thomas Ricks:

As the last vehicles in the convoy crossed the river, a parachute flare shot up across the moonless night sky, then descended slowly, a white ball high to the right of the convoy. Fourhman tensed. Flares often were used by Iraqi fighters to signal comrades lying in wait for the approach of U.S. troops. A minute later, another one shot up. Then two orange flares arced up and slowly descended. Four minutes after the last flare, a flash of light and a huge noise hit the middle of the convoy.[16]

The insurgents are shadowy figures on rooftops, in alleys, in caves, in palm groves and in tunnels, shape-shifters who hide their weapons and melt into the general population, invisible actors known by the IEDs they leave behind, or a scattered set of mangled body parts in the aftermath of a suicide bombing. They are the omnipresent menace that permeates the whole picture, and yet they never quite come into focus. The military resources of a superpower are mobilized for their elimination and yet, at the level of representation, they do not fully exist. In these circumstances the narrative tactics forced by necessity upon reporters who must describe an enemy that uses techniques of evasion, disguise and ambush meld with the narrative conventions of orientalism with their emphasis on the mystery of the oriental other.

In a situation where the Taliban are, in the words of one *New York Times* article, 'a canny but mostly unseen force…a persistent and cunning presence,'[17] a sort of diffuse paranoia grows that everyone is a potential insurgent, a paranoia that can feed off traditional orientalist tropes of the Muslim as inscrutable, treacherous and deceptive. 'This is a country where during the day they speak like they are great friends and at night they become the Taliban movement,' a diplomat in Afghanistan tells Farah Stockman of the *Boston Globe*.[18] The *New York Times* speaks of 'elders who smiled in the morning and were host to insurgents in the evening.'[19] In both of these quotes the insurgents, like vampires, only take on their true form at night. For these spectral figures the dark of night is a natural medium.[20]

Insurgents also find a natural hiding place in urban markets—a long-standing icon of the Middle East in orientalist imagery, and one that is often identified not only with a mysterious impenetrability to the Westerner but with criminality. Thus one Associated Press story tells us that 'after an attack...the insurgents slip into alleys too narrow for military vehicles. Within this enclave of eight square miles (20 square kilometers) are Mosul's wholesale and retail markets, magnets for extortion, smuggling and business serving as cover for insurgents.'[21] The identification of the insurgents with criminality is pervasive in Western media accounts, which repeatedly emphasize the Taliban's involvement with opium trafficking and their shadowy connections with warlords who have made overnight fortunes through corruption and the black market.

Insurgents are often referred to as hiding in 'strongholds,' 'safe havens,' and 'sanctuaries.' In such contexts they are often metaphorically likened to animals. The *New York Times* refers to Pakistan's 'tribal areas' as 'a breeding ground' for the Taliban, and as a 'lair' where they hide out.[22] The *Washington Post*, likewise, refers to a notorious Afghan prison as 'a Taliban breeding ground.'[23] It also headlined one story, 'militant den is penetrated by Pakistan.'[24] And it quoted the Governor of Marja as saying it was hard to estimate the number of Taliban because 'it's like looking into an ant hole....When you look into an ant hole, who knows how many ants there are?'[25] In another article the same newspaper quoted a U.S. official saying 'they are like bees. How many do you have to kill to get them all?'[26] The *Washington Post* speaks of 'a nest of insurgents'[27] and 'a government campaign to tame the Taliban insurgency.'[28] One of its opinion columnists, metaphorizing the Taliban as vermin, referred to 'Taliban-infested belts around the city' of Kandahar.[29]

Given the spectral and concealed nature of the insurgents, media accounts that evoke them often work with fragments or traces, making these shards stand in metonymically for a more complete representation of the individual or social body of insurgency. 'Soon they [the Marines] were finding signs of the Taliban,' says the *New York Times*. These traces are often weapons, which are a popular metonymic device for representing insurgents in the same way that, for example, a crown might represent a king. These weapons might be IEDs, buried in the dark, abandoned rifles, or crude explosive devices in the making: 'A sweep of one compound turned up twelve sacks of fertilizer used to make explosives and a batch of new cooking pots, which insurgents have used as the shells of bombs.'[30] In another account, in the *New York Times*, the reporters say, 'the insurgents were invisible, hidden behind the thick mud walls of the compounds. Their rifles poking through narrow slits.'[31]

Or the traces might be mysterious pinpricks of light in the darkness: 'I'm just so tired of seeing muzzle flashes at 800 yards,' said Gunnery sergeant Daniel McKernan, who trains and advises the Afghan Army here. 'This is like Vietnam. Hike around these mountains and you never see them. But they are always out there. And they always attack you.'[32] Or take this story from the *Washington Post*:

After the firefight had died down, some of Harrison's troops spotted flashlights moving around a ridgeline. The Afghan compound had taken fire from the same area…'These guys aren't so dumb as to use flashlights when they are in the middle of a firefight,' argued Staff Sgt. Richard Ehardt, who was standing beside Harrison. He cautioned against firing. Harrison ordered the artillery strike…The cannons boomed. The flashlights never reappeared. There was no way for Harrison to know what he had hit.[33]

Sometimes insurgents use the traces they leave behind to toy with their American adversaries. The *Washington Post* reports on an American unit searching for further evidence on a Taliban group that had successfully attacked American troops with an improvised explosive device. 'At the end of a long and largely fruitless day, the soldiers finally spotted something suspicious…A pair of black wires sticking out of the ground looked as if they might be part of a homemade bomb…A bomb-disposal expert carefully dug out the wires. Instead of a bomb, he unearthed a trio of playing cards, including an ace of spades, buried carefully in the dirt. "It almost feels like they're taunting us," Watson said, brushing off the cards.'[34]

On rare occasions where U.S. soldiers find themselves face-to-face with an insurgent, the effect is one of shock. The *Washington Post* says one seasoned U.S. soldier 'spotted a Taliban fighter[35] about 50 yards away carrying a rocket-propelled grenade launcher. It was the first time he had actually seen the face of one of the fighters trying to kill him. He fired his rifle at the insurgent and was certain he had hit him. But after the battle Broyles and his troops could find no body or blood trail.'[36] The Taliban combatant, encountered face-to-face in an electric moment, had converted back to a ghost. A *New York Times* account that describes two U.S. soldiers tracking Taliban through traces of blood on stone, takes this turn: 'two of Rice's squad mates appeared, eyes dilated. They couldn't believe they'd seen, up close, the ghosts they'd been fighting for the last five months. "I saw him in the eyes," Specialist Marc Solowski said. "He looked at me. I shot him."'[37]

In this starkly spare account the phrase 'I saw him in the eyes' comes as a jolting departure from the usual narrative accounts of fleeting encounters with the Taliban. It marks a rare human-to-human encounter between warriors before one of them dies.

Another trace used metonymically to regenerate the insurgent presence is, sometimes, their voices. However, their voices are represented in a very particular way. While American troops are constantly quoted by name in U.S. coverage of the Iraq and Afghan wars, thus gaining a voice and an identity, it has—until very recently at least—been rare to see insurgents quoted. However, sometimes insurgent radio chatter is picked up by U.S. soldiers, and this is quoted. By definition, such quotes are anonymous, adding to the sense that the Taliban especially are a sort of collective Islamist borg. Here is the *Washington Post*: 'on these mountain patrols, the Taliban insurgents typically reveal themselves as voices on Harrison's two-way radio. Sometimes the voices taunt Harrison in Pashto. Other times they threaten him. On a warm morning in early June the voices plotted how they were going to kill him. '"Do you see him moving?" one voice said. "I'm getting into position," another replied.'[38] In a *New York Times* account, 'on their hand-held radios, the old jihadis call the Americans "monkeys," "infidels," "bastards," and "the kids." It's psychological warfare; they know the Americans monitor their radio chatter.'[39] In other accounts, the insurgent voices are heard screaming 'Allah akhbar'—God is great. 'When they shouted "God is great," it was helpful to us, Colonel Baluch said. The voices gave away their location.'[40]

This is a classic orientalist image: insurgents defined by their religious fanaticism which, getting the better of them, pushes them into a life-threatening tactical *faux pas*. The religious nature of the Taliban is constantly foregrounded. Thus their titular leader, Mullah Omar, is referred to as a 'one-eyed cleric,'[41] and Kandahar is described as the Taliban's 'spiritual base.'[42] Death may not matter to such people because, in the words of Jeffrey Addicott, a former adviser to U.S. Special Forces, 'these are tribal people. They don't view life and death the way we expect them to.'[43] Richard Cohen, a syndicated columnist in the United States, agrees: 'As for the Taliban fighters, they not only don't cherish life, they expend it freely in suicide bombings. It's difficult to imagine an American suicide bomber.'[44] This sense of the insurgents as a religiously fanatical absolute other is perhaps best captured in this quote from a former human terrain team member in Afghanistan, Rafael Fermoselle, reacting to an attack that killed a fellow human terrain team social scientist, Paula Loyd:

Terrorists like the perpetrator of this attack had been attacking school age girls with acid attacks to disfigure their faces or blind them simply because they were walking to and from school. These insurgents are throwbacks to the Stone Age with very different ideas and convictions than we have. The same insurgents would probably place on the first lineup to be stoned to death the left-wingers who are critical of the [Human Terrain System] program. After all, their ideas and convictions are further away from theirs than those of more conservative right wingers. Want to talk to them about gay rights, women's rights, democracy, live and let live, respect for the rights of others, etc. with these insurgents? Go ahead![45]

Despite such sentiments, however, the media does quote U.S. soldiers as showing a grudging respect for the skill and courage of the insurgents. 'The Taliban is culturally primitive,' says the conservative syndicated columnist George Will, 'so any sign of tactical sophistication is unsettling.'[46] Although their skill is often represented as a sign of a sort of wily premodern cunning, it is skill nonetheless. 'As their use has multiplied several-fold in the past two years, bomb-disposal specialists and American officers say, the Taliban's bomb-making cells have sharpened their skills, moving away from smaller bombs in cooking pots to larger bombs encased in multigallon plastic water jugs, cooking-oil containers or ice coolers.'[47] Another article by the same journalist tells us that, 'to emplace the bombs where they are most likely to kill, the Taliban watch the Marines' habits carefully, including how small units react in the first instants of a firefight.'[48] The *Washington Post* quotes lieutenant Anthony Von Plisnky: 'These guys are smart. The Iraqi insurgent as a whole has really adapted well to our tactics and have learned a lot… They know how to bury things without us seeing them. They know how to trigger it without us knowing. Every time we react to a contact, they take that and learn from it. I hate to give credit to somebody who has no rules, but they're pretty good.'[49]

Violence

Most of all the insurgents are defined in U.S. media reports by their tactics—tactics characterized thus by Assistant Secretary of State Richard Boucher in the *Washington Post*: 'They keep hijacking buses, killing people, and chopping their heads off.'[50] To see what is at stake here, we need first to look at the way American fighting is portrayed. Usually in U.S. mainstream media articles, when American soldiers have killed civilians, the killing is carefully contextualized. The soldiers are first given names and stories— where they come from, what they hope to do after the war—and, if they kill civilians, it is in the confusion of battle, or when enraged by the killing of a beloved buddy, or when they miscalculate who is in a house from which U.S. troops are being fired upon or—to turn back the blame—when insurgents deliberately hide among civilians. Although one might argue that U.S. military commanders know that their counterinsurgency tactics will inevitably produce many civilian casualties, these casualties are invariably portrayed in the U.S. mainstream press as unintended accidents that belie the inherent goodness of American men and women in uniform; and while it is terrible to be blown apart or sliced up by shrapnel, the U.S. public is usually spared the grisly details of what American bombs do to the bodies of Afghan women and children.[51]

The insurgents, on the other hand, are essentially defined by their predilection for killing civilians, and for killing them in barbaric ways, such as by beheading, to terrorize civilian populations. Here is an example from the *Washington Post*: 'Fighters yanked a 60 year-old woman and her 7 year-old grandson off a bus in Dae Rawood. They interrogated the pair and, after finding a U.S. dollar bill in the boy's pocket, accused the two of spying and executed them in front of the other passengers.'[52] 'When Taliban fighters return to a village, they kill "collaborators" mercilessly, and publicly,' says the *Washington Post's* Charles Krauthammer.[53] And from the *New York Times:* 'Its [the Taliban's] methods were ruthless. Homeowners were coerced or paid to allow the militants to use their premises as bases. Those who resisted were killed, often by beheading.'[54] In a rare instance where a U.S. atrocity was reported—an incident where a G.I. raped a 14 year-old Iraqi girl, then murdered her and her family to cover up the crime—the reporter used an extraordinary rhetorical device to deflect it back on to the insurgents in a backhanded sort of way: 'The attack in 2006 in Mahmudiya, about 20 miles south of Baghdad, was so brutal that American commanders initially thought it was the work of insurgents.'[55] How could a journalist make it clearer that an American atrocity is an exception while insurgent atrocities are the norm? If the killing of innocents by Americans is an accident, an exception that can be forgiven if one knows the troops, for the insurgents it is the norm by which they will be defined. The insurgents, unlike American soldiers, are fixed in their essence by their tactics, and are not excused by who they really are. Who they really are is defined by their most innocent victims. Indeed, so depraved are they, that according to the *New York Times* Iraqi insurgents may even have been recruiting schizophrenics or women with Down Syndrome as suicide bombers.[56]

In being defined by their embrace of such tactics insurgents have, to borrow and adapt a phrase from Judith Butler, 'already suffered the violence of derealization.' Butler says, 'If violence is done against those who are unreal, then, from the perspective of violence, it fails to injure or negate those lives since those lives are already negated. But they have a strange way of remaining animated and so must be negated again (and again)....Violence renews itself in the face of the apparent inexhaustibility of its object.'[57]

I want to be clear here that I am not saying that insurgents in Iraq and Afghanistan do not behead people, execute suspects without due process and terrorize civilians. They surely do. Just as, in turn, American troops have been seen to bomb families from the air, torture people in Abu Ghraib, and shoot people at checkpoints. But in media accounts insurgents become defined by their most violent tactics. Where the abuse of violence by American troops is, if it is mentioned, put in a larger context, for the insurgents their violent tactics overwhelm the rest of their actions: the times they could kill someone but show mercy; the aid they give to widows and the poor; the development projects they undertake; and their institutions for resolving conflicts.

These tropes are hardly new in American war reporting. In his masterful account of media coverage of the Vietnam War, *The Uncensored War*, Dan Hallin describes U.S. television coverage of civilian casualties in Vietnam in terms that are eerily familiar. 'Television reports dealing with civilian casualties caused by American action usually were very specific. In keeping with the usual conventions of "objective" reporting, they described a single incident and were not concerned with higher policies or patterns. No television report I encountered ever suggested that the United States might have any sort of general policy of targeting civilians. Attacks on civilians by the enemy, on the other hand, were routinely assumed to result from a calculated *policy* of terror.'[58] The Vietcong were often portrayed as 'motivated by a love of cruelty for its own sake.'[59]

Hallin points out that, even after the U.S. press became more critical of the U.S. presence in Vietnam as the war ground on, these conventions for representing the enemy persisted unchanged. The Vietcong were always portrayed as 'shadowy figures'[60] defined by their use of violence, and U.S. media coverage placed 'them outside the political realm, making them appear more as criminals than as a political movement or rival government....Like most twentieth century war propaganda, television coverage of Vietnam dehumanized the enemy, drained him of all recognizable emotions and motives, and thus banished him not only from the political sphere, but from human society itself.'[61]

Even before the current institution of 'embedding,' then, mainstream U.S. media coverage of war was highly partisan. From Vietnam to Afghanistan and Iraq, the media has produced what we might call, after Haraway, a 'situated knowledge' of war, taking a point of view from just over the U.S. soldiers' rifle sights. It is from this very particular perspective that the insurgent is a spectral presence defined by his cruelty and unable to speak except in the staccato bursts intercepted by U.S. military radio operators.

Can the insurgent speak?

So finally we must ask, adapting a famous question asked by Gayatri Spivak, 'can the insurgent speak?'[62] Can insurgents speak to us not just to scream 'Allah akhbar!' and 'off with his head!' but in a discourse that would restore them to the political sphere and to human society? Do they, like their American counterparts, think of their wives as they die? Do they also anguish about the deaths of innocent women and children? When they look at other insurgents do they too feel a deep comradeship for which they would give their lives?

To make insurgents' voices heard, and to invite audiences to move into the insurgent subject-position, is deeply threatening to the ideological status quo. Thus Margaret Thatcher's government in the UK passed a law making it a crime for 'an identifiable individual to appear publicly as someone speaking for the IRA.'[63] IRA members' voices were not to be heard. In a similar vein, in 2008 RPI closed an art exhibit on campus because it invited audience members to experience the world from the subject-position of an Iraqi insurgent. The Iraqi American artist Wafaa Bilal created a fictitious character based on himself: 'a faculty member at the Art Institute of Chicago who loses his father and brother to the wars in Iraq. The character becomes an al-Qaeda recruit and hunts Bush. Bilal said he hopes to raise questions about the stereotypes of Iraqis, and about conceptions of what creates a suicide bomber. "I wanted to let people see how bad it feels to be labeled and hunted," he said.'[64]

Yet even as insurgent voices are repressed in one context, they are conjured in another. This is because the U.S. military needs a certain kind of insurgent—a faux insurgent—for training purposes. Thus the U.S. military has staged spaces where it incites faux insurgent speech from insurgents to see what might be learned from it. In Death Valley, for example, U.S. soldiers train in simulated Iraqi villages, matching their wits with mock insurgents—American soldiers coached in acting by Carl Weathers of *Rocky* movie fame. According to the *New York Times* these simulated villages feature 'insurgent uprisings, suicide bombings, and even staged beheadings in underground tunnels.' The mock insurgents, dressed in Arab gear, 'plant roadside bombs, booby-trap dead dogs…and drive suicide bombs into American checkpoints.' One of them, whose real name is Sergeant Wilson, and who roots for the Giants when he is not being an insurgent, goes by the pseudonym Mansour Hakim and runs the 'Kamel Dogs Café' in the simulated village. He tells the reporter, 'I'm a bad guy, and I'm looking for any weakness I can exploit.'[65]

As Derek Gregory has observed,[66] these faux insurgents may simulate the tactics and surface gestures of 'real' insurgents, but, unable to articulate the political grievances of actual insurgents, they are as capable of teaching U.S. soldiers about insurgency as a computer program would be of conducting psychotherapy. This attempt to ventriloquize insurgents, or to engage in counterinsurgency cross-dressing, does not get us much beyond the caricatured representations that collapse insurgents into their tactics of terror. These insurgents are empty signifiers, decorated with the name and dress of the other, but unable to speak authentically. They are guerilla simulacra—copies of copies of insurgents for which no originals exist.

To hear something closer to the authentic voices of insurgents one must go to the U.S. alternative media, to print journalism such as Nir Rosen's reporting for *Rolling Stone* on the Taliban and Patrick Graham's article for *Harper's* on his conversations with Sunni insurgents in Iraq, or to the PBS *Frontline* documentary, *The Insurgency*, or to Molly Bingham's and Steve Connor's filmed conversations with insurgents in the documentary film *Meeting Resistance*.[67] Whereas mainstream journalists prefer to talk to reformed insurgents who tell American readers what they want to hear about the moral bankruptcy or failing energy of the insurgency,[68] alternative journalists risk their lives to talk to active insurgents. Indeed, it is maybe the defining difference between mainstream and alternative media in the United States that mainstream media accounts are always from the point of view of U.S. troops with whom mainstream reporters are invariably embedded, always from what Judith Butler calls 'the narrative perspective of U.S. unilateralism,'[69] while alternative journalists such as Nir Rosen and Dahr Jamail[70] refuse embedding and seek their stories outside the sphere of U.S.

influence and protection. Here the natural reflex of U.S. mainstream journalists to gravitate toward official sources or, for a splash of color, toward their own troops may, ironically have been compounded by the effects of the insurgency itself. Philip Bennett, the *Washington Post's* foreign editor laments:

> It's now clear that we owe an enormous gap in our understanding of Iraq to the violence unleashed in early 2004, when kidnappings and beheadings, hundreds of suicide bombings and street fighting forced Western reporters to end the serendipitous daily contact with Iraqis that had produced the most telling stories. As The Post's foreign editor at the time, I started asking fewer questions about our coverage and constant questions about our reporters' safety. The media withdrew into armed convoys and hid behind blast walls, or abandoned the country altogether. (The Post and others stayed.) As Dexter Filkins of the *New York Times*, who emerged in those years as the premier combat journalist of his generation, wrote: 'Iraq disappeared for us then, and it never came back.'[71]

Still, courageous alternative reporters continued to seek their story among ordinary Afghans and Iraqis long after 2004, when Bennett saw this as too dangerous for his reporters. They might as well have been covering a different war, and indeed the people they spoke to did not even refer to the war in Mesopotamia as 'the Iraq War,' but as 'the invasion,' 'the events,' 'the Sectarian war,' and 'the collapse.'[72] In their alternative media accounts, one encounters complex, contradictory figures who defy our stereotypes. In the film *Meeting Resistance*, based on interviews with Iraqi insurgents, we meet Sunni and Shi'a insurgents, middle and working class insurgents, and, Donald Rumsfeld's characterization of these insurgents as 'deadenders' from Saddam Hussein's regime notwithstanding, we meet an insurgent who was tortured by the Baathist regime in the 1990s, but nonetheless takes up arms against the Americans.

Here is a description of insurgents from a PBS *Frontline* interviewer:

> The backbone of the insurgency are just professional military officers, otherwise ordinary guys who love their home and love their family and worry about their kids and want to make sure they get off to school OK and come back OK and they get a job and have a career and have children of their own.

> When [I'm brought blindfolded into their houses to meet with them], I'm in a living room, and we're sitting, and there's kids playing, and there's toys in the corner, and the wife's out the back making the food, and … the kids [are] joking and playing. These are ordinary men with ordinary family concerns, but to their minds there's a foreign occupier on their soil. And on a number of occasions these guys have said: 'Ask an American soldier to imagine he's in the Midwest, in the USA, and

a foreign occupying army is in his small hometown, and on his main street is a foreign tank and barbed wire and bunker positions with foreign troops who are searching the women of his home, and who at any moment can storm into his mother and father's house and turn it upside down. Ask him to understand that,' they'd say to me. That is the bulk of the insurgency in Iraq.[73]

Patrick Graham, reporting for *Harper's* Magazine, makes a similar observation. 'I had expected to be taken to some undisclosed location where paranoid men, their faces hidden behind scarves, would deliver a ten-minute rant against Zionism and the infidels before driving off in a Toyota pickup truck… I didn't anticipate the endless glasses of tea, or Mohammed, with a child sleeping on his lap, telling me that he didn't think Osama bin Laden was a good Muslim.'[74] This image of the insurgent with a sleeping child in his lap is extraordinarily dissonant in its humanization of the insurgent.

Alternative media accounts also help us make human sense of the factional groupings listed but not made real in mainstream media accounts. Mainstream media accounts sometimes give the reader the names of sectarian insurgent groups—names that are culled from jihadist websites or U.S. military briefers. For example, an Associated Press article tells readers that there is a syndicate of insurgent groups that includes the Jihad and Change Front, the Islamic Army in Iraq, Hamas Iraq, Ansar al-Sunnah, the Mujahedeen Army in Iraq and al-Qaeda in Iraq.[75] But this is hardly like telling readers that someone is a Republican, a Democrat, or a Libertarian, or that they belong to the United Autoworkers, the Teamsters or the Steelworkers union. The listing of the names conveys a sense of thoroughness on the part of the reporter, but it does not convey any meaningful information to American readers except that the insurgent population is riven by sectarian splintering. If anything, it amplifies the aura of strangeness around the insurgents, who are willing to die for groups that lie outside our social geography, segmented by differences that, for us, have no meaning. By contrast, in a background interview for the documentary film, *The Insurgency*,[76] Michael Ware explores the feelings and perceptions of a veteran Sunni insurgent deciding whether to ally himself with Zarqawi's al-Qaeda in Iraq—a more fundamentalist group of foreigners allied to Osama bin Laden. 'This is a man who himself had been in battle since the beginning of the occupation, this is a man who's killed goodness knows how many American soldiers…and he said, 'I was scared sitting with these men. From one moment to the next, you don't know what's going through their minds…It's as though they are from another planet…I realized midway through all of this that there [are] only two ways to leave their organization: you either die in battle or you die at their hands.' Ware's Sunni insurgent extricated himself and his men from that alliance. As we follow Ware's account, we learn that insurgents have their own moral economy of violence, and that they too are capable of fear.

Finally, in alternative media accounts insurgents speak to us about their motives. 'Did you see *Braveheart?*' an insurgent asks Patrick Graham. 'They throw out the British and the corrupt nobles. It is about hope. The people in the movie want freedom, and so do we. In the movie the problems start because the British invaded and take the beautiful women and hurt the people. Because of the hard times, they gather weapons and get rid of the spies and traitors. Isn't that right?'[77]

In the documentary film Meeting Resistance[78] one Iraqi insurgent has this to say about his feelings when the Americans occupied Baghdad:

The next morning I saw the American tanks and the American soldiers passing. I felt a fire in my heart. That was who we were waiting for, to show them the true nature of an Iraqi man. When I saw them, I didn't see them as an army that we would fight. I saw just one thing, that we had become an occupied country. When they occupied Iraq, they subjugated me, subjugated my sister, subjugated my mother, subjugated my honor, my homeland. Every time I saw them, I felt pain. They pissed me off, so I started working.

The insurgent's voice here articulates a distinctively Arab sense of honor with a patriotism which many Westerners can surely understand.

Another insurgent in the same film tells this story: 'The day before yesterday four young men were sitting there in the coffee house when two Humvees went past. The Americans went in, searched them, and pushed one of them against the wall. That pissed him off. So he went and bought a rocket launcher, and at 2 in the morning he fired it at them. He bought an RPG with his own money and attacked them with it.' Such stories not only allow insurgents to speak in broadly nationalist terms of their motives, they also disrupt conventional narratives in which American soldiers figure as innocents abroad who become victims of insurgent violence. In alternative media accounts insurgents share the victim position and may be moved to action by the experience of humiliation or unprovoked American violence.

There is, however, a recurrent danger of romanticizing the insurgents in these alternative media accounts, of simply reversing the dominant binary. Almost all of the films and articles discussed here took it for granted that the U.S. occupation would produce an insurgency and that the insurgents are motivated by a nationalism that should make complete sense to us. This is, however, just to scrape the surface of the situation. Not all occupations produce virulent insurgencies, and it remains an open question whether the insurgencies in Iraq and Afghanistan were an inevitable reaction to foreign occupation or were the product of disastrous but avoidable U.S. policies such as the immediate disbanding of the Iraqi military and the banning from public office of huge swaths of the Ba'ath Party in 2003.[79] Furthermore, not all Iraqis and Afghans have been equally sympathetic to insurgency. In Iraq Sunnis have been more supportive of the insurgency than Shi'ites and Kurds, though the Shi'ite community itself has been divided between Sadrists and others. Meanwhile in Afghanistan some ethnic groups, such as the Pashtun, have been more supportive of the Taliban than others, and the very term 'Taliban' belies myriad divisions over Islam, relations with Pakistan and so forth. Yet most alternative media accounts have shown a marked inability to think sociologically about the kinds of divisions within Iraqi and Afghan society that predispose some but not others to become insurgents, even as they legitimate these choices through the rhetoric of an all-encompassing nationalism.

But at least these alternative accounts do channel, however imperfectly, insurgent voices. The problem is that these alternative media spaces are rather like official protest zones at the national party conventions. Free speech takes place there, but safely out of sight of most of the American people. The insurgent will not really have spoken until he has been interviewed on *Sixty Minutes*.

Coda: the Taliban and the endgame

In the fall of 2009 U.S. media coverage of Afghanistan morphed in a fascinating way. Mainstream reporters began to quote Taliban spokesmen and shadow Taliban governors of provinces by name and also to report more on non-military ways in which the Taliban are often woven into the fabric of village life. A *New York Times* article mentioning that 'insurgent leaders... settle land and water disputes and dictate school curriculums' typified this new trend.[80] In October 2009 the *New York Times* even published a surprisingly neutral and factual portrait of Mullah Omar, the titular leader of the Taliban, in which they acknowledged his talents as an insurgent leader. A February 2011 article by Alissa Rubin showcased this new willingness to quote the Taliban and even accorded them some sense of concern about civilian casualties, while explaining, to some degree at least, the relationship between different insurgent factions:

The Taliban in the past have been careful not to single out civilians, though civilians are often killed in attacks. At least some Taliban factions seem worried about the latest tactics [which increase civilian casualties]. Zabiullah Mujahid, the Taliban spokesman for the north and east of the country, said an investigation was under way into the Jalalabad attack, which killed forty people, nearly half of them civilians.

'We are taking this issue seriously as we have appointed a delegate to assess the civilians [sic] casualties,' he said. 'We are not happy when there is even one civilian lost.'

American and Afghan officials now believe that Lashkar-e-Taiba, the group that planned the attacks in Mumbai, India, in 2008, has been working with the Haqqani network, which is based in North Waziristan. Lashkar-e-Taiba specializes in planning complex suicide attacks.

'The suicide bombings are we believe predominantly requested and funded by Haqqani but facilitated by LET and AQ,' said a senior American official, referring to Lashkar-e-Taiba and Al Qaeda.[81]

By January 3, 2012, as the Taliban moved to open a political office in Qatar with the quiet approbation of the U.S. government (which was seeking a neutral place to talk with Taliban leaders), the *New York Times* could even print a front page photograph of a lead Taliban negotiator, Tayeb Agha, in a group portrait with fellow Taliban. This picture, originally taken in 2001 by an Agence France-Presse photographer, breaks the conventional norms for representing the Taliban: the men all show their faces, some even smile, and only two have weapons.[82]

The start of this shift, in late 2009, was coincident in time with the protracted debate in Washington D.C. over the tens of thousands of extra troops General Stanley McChrystal was requesting from Barack Obama for counterinsurgency in Afghanistan. It also roughly coincided with rumors that the United States had begun quietly talking to some Taliban leaders, with reports of an increasingly public rift between Karzai and the Americans over the extent to which the highest Taliban leaders (as opposed to the rank and file) could be brought back into Afghanistan's political process, and even of a debate between the British government and the Obama Administration over the possibility of reaching out to Taliban leaders.[83]

When I asked an American reporter who covers Afghanistan about this new development of quoting Taliban spokesmen, he attributed the change to a new media savviness on the part of the Taliban.[84] I am in no position to evaluate the Taliban media strategy, but let me raise another possibility.

CAN THE INSURGENT SPEAK?

In his book *The Uncensored War*, media critic and historian Dan Hallin examines mainstream U.S. media coverage of the Vietnam War. Although it is often claimed in right-wing circles that the war was lost by the U.S. media, Hallin found that U.S. mainstream journalists were remarkably uncritical of the war in their coverage of it in the early years. He argues that, in print media coverage especially, reporting became more critical as splits developed over the war within U.S. elites in Washington, and that journalists essentially took their cues from the boundaries of permissible debate in Washington, which began to expand as the war bogged down. Among other things, as different factions in Washington struggled to exert control over the policymaking process in a context where elite consensus about the war was breaking down, insiders began to leak to the press, and this produced more critical coverage. Over time, a dialectical dynamic emerged where divisions among policymakers generated more critical media coverage which, in turn, provided more ammunition for elite disagreement. In Hallin's words,

the behavior of the media…is intimately related to the unity and clarity of the government itself, as well as to the degree of consensus in society at large. This is not to say that the role of the press is purely reactive. Surely it made a difference, for instance, that many journalists were shocked by the brutality of the war and by the gap between what they were told by officials and what they saw and heard in the field, and were free to report all this. But it is also clear that the administration's problems with the 'fourth branch of government' resulted in large part from political divisions at home, including those within the administration itself, which had dynamics of their own.[85]

One big difference between the Vietnam War and the wars in Iraq and Afghanistan is that mainstream U.S. reporters in Vietnam had remarkable latitude to go where they pleased and get behind the official story of that war, whereas in Iraq and Afghanistan they have been embedded inside the U.S. military apparatus which, without extensive resort to clumsy censorship, has shaped their perspective through a process of socialization and internalization. This may explain why U.S. mainstream reporting in Vietnam was better—more raw, more passionate, more inspired—and why reporters have been a little slow in Iraq and Afghanistan to rub their readers' noses in the gap between the official story and the messy reality. For that nose-rubbing readers who in 1969 could have read David Halberstam and Neil Sheehan in the *New York Times* this time around have had to seek out alternative media accounts.

Although the precise mechanisms whereby Taliban spokesmen suddenly end up being quoted in the *New York Times* are a mystery to me—whether reporters are responding to stimuli from editors or their unnamed sources in government or have arrived here by some process of their own—it seems clear that the shift in U.S. coverage of the Taliban is in some sense connected to the growing realization that the Islamists have at least fought the United States to a draw, and are maybe in the process of defeating it; far from being consigned to the dustbin of history as medieval relics, they will figure prominently in Afghanistan's future. The only question is to what degree they will continue, after NATO's departure from Afghanistan, to be portrayed in orientalist terms and to what degree the U.S. mainstream media can find new idioms in which to portray them. Based on U.S. media coverage of Vietnam's government in the years immediately after 1975, I am not hopeful.

6

COLONIAL WARS, POSTCOLONIAL SPECTERS

THE ANXIETY OF DOMINATION

Quỳnh N. Phạm and *Himadeep R. Muppidi**

Barely containable now

A suicide bomber, the *New York Times* tells us in its 'Breaking News,' hit a U.S. convoy in Afghanistan on Tuesday, May 18, 2010. The report, filed by Dexter Filkins, 29 minutes ago, notes:[1] 'A man driving a Toyota minivan crammed with explosives steered into an American convoy Tuesday morning here, killing 18 people, including five American troops....At least 47 people were wounded, nearly all of them civilians caught in rush-hour traffic.'

The video accompanying the text opens with the shot of an African American woman in an automobile factory talking about ideals. It takes a few seconds to realize that this message from a sponsor is also from Toyota. Very quickly, close-ups of three workers at an automobile plant occupy the screen, forcefully articulating the noteworthy values of Toyota:

'This company has been founded on standards,' says the first.

* Our thanks to Chris Chekuri and Mark Hoffman for critical comments on various versions of this paper.

'We have to work together in order that our customers will receive the best product we can give them,' says the second.

'Working towards the goal of getting it done and getting it done right; striving for perfection,' says the third.

Fifteen or so seconds is all it takes before these faces dissolve into the logo of Toyota and Reuters.

Then onto the 57-second video report showing us long shots of the Toyota van surrounded by soldiers, close-ups of a man with a bandaged head, a background shot of a battered Dar-ul-Alam (the former royal palace), the press conference of the Afghan interior minister, talk of a spring offensive by the Taliban, and then the reporter signing off with the logo of Reuters again.

Order. Disorder. Order.

In under a minute, the briefest of knowledge time, you have a window opening and closing on events in Afghanistan. You see Toyota suturing a smoothly functioning, value driven, productive space through a diversity of faces talking about standards and perfection. Then you see Toyota in a context of violence, destruction, guns, blood, and ruined buildings before the window closes again. Dexter Filkins' print report fills in the details you might not have seen: 'The blast sent a fireball billowing into the air, set cars aflame and blew bodies apart. Limbs and entrails flew hundreds of feet, littering yards and walls and streets. The survivors, many of them women and children, some of them missing limbs, lay in the road moaning and calling for help. In a passenger bus, an Afghan woman lay dead in her seat, cut in half; with her baby still squirming in her arms. Fifty yards away, a man's head lay on the hood of a truck.'

Your eyes scan the gory details till they come to rest, finally, in a differently colored text, about getting the 'full newspaper experience, and more, delivered to your Mac or PC. Times Reader 2.0: Try it FREE for 2 full weeks.'

Order here. Disorder there. Order here again.

The horror of disorder there is always framed before it is sent home. It is always sought to be contained.

But what if the order of the other is uncontainable, was never really contained? What if their orders exceed the framers' controlling grasp?

What then?

Barely containable before

Perfect image

Analyzing the 'virtual' realities of the U.S. war in Vietnam,[2] Bruce Franklin focuses on the fantasy of a perfect war image as a spotless landscape. What are the 'spots' to be purged? Franklin clues us in through the 'image interpreter['s]'[3] job in Stephen Wright's *Meditations in Green*. In this novel, the protagonist, Griffin, has the same job that Wright had in Vietnam: analyze photos that serve intelligence purposes for Operation Phoenix (1967–1972), a CIA-designed counter-insurgent assassination and torture program,[4] and Operation Ranch Hand (1962–1971), a 'defoliation' program that sprayed some 19 million gallons of herbicides, including an estimated 12 million of human-toxic Agent Orange, throughout southern Vietnam.[5] Scrutinizing films from aerial reconnaissance, the 'image interpreter' targets trees and humans. Any evidence of potential insurgency, i.e. any spot of life, must be eliminated: 'Trees, trees, trees, trees, rocks, rocks, cloud, trees, trees, road, road, stream, stream, ford, trees, road, road. He stopped cranking. With a black grease pencil he carefully circled two blurry shadows beside the white thread of a road. Next to the circles he placed question marks. Road, road, road, road, trees, trees, trees, trees…Wherever he put circles on the film there the air force would make holes in the ground.'[6]

Smudges were not just the rebellious natives on the ground, but as Franklin gathered from Wright's narration, also anyone in Griffin's unit who was disturbed by and might disturb these homicidal and ecocidal operations. Striving to be free of smudges, the perfect image aims at annihilating any sign of revolt. 'Holes in the ground' will put an end to them all. Intelligence analysts coordinate diligently with armed forces: They draw circles on the film, and make holes in the ground, with precision and productivity.

Draw circles. Make holes. Draw circles. Make holes. Circles. Holes.

'Working towards the goal of getting it done and getting it done right; striving for perfection,' says the third.

Holes and Smudges

Then we was [sic] in one valley, called the Que Son Valley, two miles wide, and ten, twelve miles long. We *cleaned out every living thing* in that valley—people and animals—and destroyed everything else. We just rounded them all up—four to five hundred people—and started moving them eleven klicks [kilometers] to some type of a camp. All their animals was [sic] killed. Then we made the valley a free-fire zone. After we cleaned it out, anything you saw was a legitimate target. *Two days later, half the people were right back in it.* They went back to nothing because we burned and destroyed everything.[7]

More than two decades after the U.S. troop withdrawals from Vietnam, George Watkins, an ex-infantry soldier, still marveled at what he had witnessed. His unit had done everything in their power to 'clean out *every living thing*': They removed everyone ('four to five hundred people') from the villages ('two miles wide, and ten, twelve miles long'), they killed all the animals, they burned, they free-fired, they destroyed everything. How many times did Watkins have to stress the deliberate totality of their cleansing that valley!

They had to be some good people to withstand all that. *They come right back to nothing and start over.* Go out and get some thatch or find some that wasn't burnt, tie it together with a couple branches over some poles, and sit up under it with their little beat-up aluminum pots. They's [sic] some of the most determined people I've ever run into.

To Watkins' astonishment, almost disbelief, these villagers came right back to the 'hole in the ground'—their ground—and started thatching and patching and tying and building again. They might have been circled out of their habitats for a day or two, but they returned and started from seemingly nothing in no time. They re-surged and in-surged right in the face of counter-insurgency. Not just the targeted 'insurgents' but also those very people whose hearts and minds need to be won. (Were they different?) No matter how many times Watkins' military made holes over their valleys, their villages, their families, their animals, they came back. And coming back, they smudged the immaculate screen all over again. They refused to be erased from the picture; they disordered the smooth production of perfection.

Circles. Holes. Smudges. Life.

But the story did not end there. Watkins soon found himself feeling the heat of the blasted hole and being cleaned out. He and two other men in his platoon were hit by a booby trap made out of the United States' own duds. One of them was saved by a radio from being pierced with a piece of shrapnel 'the size of your hand,' but the other lost his 'left eye, his left ear, and…some movement.' In the hospital, Watkins ran his hands down his body only to find his legs missing. The doctor told him that his eyes looked like scrambled eggs. 'Like you took an egg and you just scrambled it.'[8]

Does Watkins' body/vision carry a message yet to be read?

The weak in re-view

Confession

In his report 'Into Kandahar, Yesterday and Tomorrow,' John F. Burns[9] provides another perspective on order here and disorder there. His story begins with a helicopter shot of Kandahar showing a deeply browned landscape with low-walled houses, seemingly devoid of human beings. Burns reads the landscape as 'a grim warning.'

In the postcards of the mind, it is the starkest of all the images of Kandahar, dating back more than 20 years to the period immediately after Soviet troops withdrew from the city, and standing ever since as a grim warning of the folly of foreign military adventures in Afghanistan: hundreds of acres of rubble, whole quarters of the city reduced to fields of blasted concrete and steel, and further out, in the poorer districts, a shattered chocolate-box of a landscape formed by ragged mud walls that had once been home to tens of thousands of people seeking refuge from the war raging in the Afghan hinterland.

Burns' warning puzzles us. Why is a bombed out pile of concrete and steel and acres of rubble a warning and not a testament to the power of those who blasted it? How is the folly of the destroyer, rather than their power, apparent in the body of the devastated?

Outfought by the mujahedeen fighters of the 1980s, and desperate to hang on in the city that more than any other symbolizes Afghanistan's history of national resistance, *Soviet forces had resorted, like the Americans in Vietnam, to obliteration by bombing. That was as good as an admission that they had lost*, and when they finally pulled back across the Hindu Kush, they left behind little by way of a memorial to the 14,000 Soviet troops who lost their lives, or to the Kremlin's tens of billions of wasted rubles, beyond the scrap of blasted helicopters, tanks and armored vehicles that litter Afghanistan to this day.

The Soviet attempt to 'obliterate by bombing' comes after they had been 'outfought' by the mujahedeen. In coming after, this attempt to 'obliterate' (cleanse, destroy totally) signals desperation and is read as a sign of their defeat. This is a defeat so thorough that it cannot even be memorialized in terms of the (14,000) Soviet lives lost or the 'tens of billions' of Soviet rubles wasted. The destruction in the landscape, though caused by the Soviet Union, is bereft of any meaningful memorials for itself. All the signs speak only of the resistant power of the other and none of or for the Soviet Union.

What Burns reads into Kandahar is the dilemma of those who seek to dominate—their desire for domination running into the danger of a scrambling of the self, of its ability to see and read. ('Like you took an egg and you just scrambled it.') A self that defines itself as commander, and commander only, cannot but crumble when it proves unable to command. As graphed starkly above, Soviet efforts to crumple Kandahar speak to their poignant inability to order others in any meaningful fashion. It is the resistance to this crumpling that compels a closer look at the colonial desire to prevail over the other, a desire that stops just short of genocide, of a will to 'exterminate all the brutes.'[10]

In Burns' reading, the Soviet attempt to obliterate the Afghans ('like the [desire of the] Americans in Vietnam') arises only after their failure to dominate them and is more than anything else a sign of their desperation. Obliteration here hints of vengeance, not power, of frustration, not capability. It reveals an aggravation, and the impossibility of elevation, of the self over the other.

Our distinction between two colonial logics, one oriented toward extermination, and the other toward domination, is meant to focus our analysis on the different intersubjective relationships invoked by these processes. Let us first revisit what happened to the Hereros in German South West Africa when they rebelled against their colonizers in 1904. The response, Adam Hochschild tells us, was 'masked by no smokescreen of talk about philanthropy.' Lieutenant General Lothar von Trotha's *Vernichtungsbefehl* (an extermination order) pronounced, 'Within the German boundaries every Herero, whether found with or without a rifle, with or without cattle, shall be shot…' To ensure the transparency of this absolute order, an addendum was issued to emphasize that 'No male prisoners will be taken.' The Germans were ready to rid the occupied territory of all Hereros: they poisoned waterholes, drove people into desert to die of thirst, shot and bayoneted tens of thousands. That was, as Hochschild observes, 'a genocide, pure and simple, starkly announced in advance.'[11] The Germans were assured colonizers, and the Hereros exterminable objects. The colonized were effectively wiped out, with no possibility of coming back, at least not physically.

In more recent times, repeating what the Germans did might no longer be possible, since, as Jonathan Schell succinctly notes, postcolonial peoples not only have 'the will to resist' but also 'the means to do so.'[12] Domination, then, desperately needs to avoid provoking a direct will to resist from the other. Instead, it must search for ways to elicit an acceptance of its will, some acknowledgement from the very bodies it wishes to dominate. Thus, domination is both enabled and hampered by a paradoxical dependence, not on its own desire and will alone, but on that of the other.

Supporting the sending of more troops to Afghanistan, Senator John McCain of Arizona articulated this desire quite plainly, 'The way that you win wars is to *break the enemy's will*, not to announce dates that you are leaving.' The infliction of violence ('breaking' the other) is hostage to a yielding in the other, its willingness to concede and to accept the desire of the colonizer.

In the context of the Bush administration's discussions on Afghanistan, Richard Clarke points to the difficult-to-target nature of those bombed bare: 'Secy. Rumsfeld complained that there were no decent targets for bombing in Afghanistan and that we should consider bombing Iraq, which, he said, had better targets. At first I thought Rumsfeld was joking. But he was serious and the President did not reject out of hand the idea of attacking Iraq.'[13] You want to hit Afghanistan but no targets were 'decent' enough. What use is there in blasting that which has already been blasted to indecency? So you hit Iraq.

For those seeped in a colonial logic of domination, the differences among targets are not as relevant as their generally targetable nature. Thomas Friedman reiterates this point in his inimitable way:[14]

The 'real reason' for this war [in Iraq], which was never stated, was that after 9/11 America *needed to hit someone* in the Arab-Muslim world. Afghanistan wasn't enough because a terrorism bubble had built up *over there*... The only way to puncture that bubble was for American soldiers ...to go into the heart of the Arab-Muslim world...and make clear that we are ready to kill, and to die, to prevent our open society from being undermined by this terrorism bubble. Smashing Saudi Arabia or Syria would have been fine. But we hit Saddam for one simple reason: because we could, and because he deserved it and because he was right in the heart of that world. And don't believe the nonsense that this had no effect. Every neighboring government—and 98 percent of terrorism is about what governments let happen—got the message.

The order of open societies is threatened by the disorderly bubble of terrorism over there. Over where? Afghanistan, Syria, Saudi Arabia, Iraq... you know, over there...the 'Arab-Muslim world.' And the message to the 'Arab-Muslim world' was: 'we are ready to kill, and to die...' (the authors are not so sure about the willingness of the 'we' to die—unless, of course, it means sacrificing subaltern others of one's own) and we send that message out by hitting 'someone' in that world. Who should you hit? Anyone in that world would do. Saudi Arabia. Syria. Iraq. We can do Iraq. Let's hit Iraq. Iraq will do. It is over there.

This violence, contrary to its immediate appearance, is neither indiscriminate nor arbitrary. It is purposeful and deliberate in its willfulness to dominate the other, to send them a message about the self and its resoluteness. What it is less concerned about are the specificities of those it circles as targets. Targets are those that need to get the message; the differences amongst them do not matter, since hitting one, it is assumed, would somehow get the point across to others. They are all alike as a generalized Other.

More insidiously, the colonizer presents a façade of autonomy, of bravado—'because we could'—that conceals a fatal dependence, an anxiety: What if, however much you hit the other, the target just doesn't get the message? Hence Friedman's quick preemptive strike against that sort of 'nonsense': 'And don't believe the nonsense that this had no effect.' Colonial anxiety emerges here from the recognition that the target, somehow, might not get it, might not quite understand the meaning of your violence. You punch. You pummel. You blast. You bomb. And you desperately, desperately, want the other to understand, to at least acknowledge what you are doing to them as you intended it for them. To realize your purpose in beating them up, the goodness, the love for something better for all of us, behind that beating. The abuser aches for the abused's validation.

If someone says that your hitting had no effect, they must be lying. Nonsense! It had to have some effect. Surely, it must have hurt. And how can that hurt, that incredible pain that you inflicted on them not convey your desire to them? It had to. Colonial power, to the extent that it seeks domination over the other, is perennially haunted by the fear that the other does not 'understand it.' Its authority is plagued by a paranoid fear of smudges. However extreme its violence, colonial power awaits, apprehensively, an interpretive validation from the other. This is the anxiety of domination. Fear is the key. The colonizer's fear.

The order of the colonial self is captive to the disorders, the smudges, of the other. The willful bodies of the colonized constrain what colonizers can do to them. The violence may be 'awesome' as in Hiroshima and Nagasaki, or incessantly shocking as in Vietnam. The other will bleed, suffer, mourn, but they will also engage, endure, and re-narrate your violence. Might their understanding and re-narrating of your brutality, your torture startle you, shock and awe you in turn by its resilience, its unexpectedness, its humanness?[15] Are you, conceptually and ethically, in a position to hear/bear this?

Grim irrelevance

A specter haunts every colonial project, the specter of its hermeneutic inadequacy. It remains continually threatened that the violence it inflicts on the other in order to conquer, to punish, to communicate, will be rendered futile by the other's agentic reception. Because of its inter-subjective nature, even pain, sometimes read as strictly physical/material and somehow outside of hermeneutic translation, remains fundamentally open to interpretive and relational transfiguration. As Talal Asad astutely points out, pain can be 'eagerly embraced by those on whom it is inflicted and transformed into something other than what was intended.'[16] The colonized can reject and reinterpret not only the colonizer's messages and intentions but the entire economy of his purposeful violence. Insurgency is therefore first and foremost an interpretive rejection.

In 1975, Army Col. Harry Summers went to Hanoi as chief of the U.S. delegation's negotiation team for the four-party military talks that followed the collapse of the South Vietnamese government. While there, he spent some time chatting with his North Vietnamese counterpart, Col. Tu, an old soldier who had fought against the United States and lived to tell his tale. With a tinge of bitterness about the war's outcome, Summers told Tu, 'You know, you never defeated us on the battlefield.' Tu replied, in a phrase that perfectly captured the American misunderstanding of the Vietnam War, 'That may be so, but it is also irrelevant.'[17]

What lies in the American colonel's claim? Is Summers telling Col. Tu something that he suspects Col. Tu doesn't really know ('you never defeated us on the battlefield'; we really beat you, you know)? Or is he politely asking Col. Tu ('you know...'), implicitly beseeching him (Come on, you *know* that...), to agree on what he needs to affirm for himself? If the bitterness is about the outcome of the war (that the United States did not lose in the 'battlefield' but lost on another front) and Col. Summers is certain of that, why does he still want Col. Tu to acknowledge that? What hangs on the other's approval of that distinction?

Meanwhile, Col. Tu's response ('That may be so') denotes comfort with that ambiguous possibility. That prospect doesn't agitate him or induce resentfulness in him (which might have made him re-assert, in an anxious fashion similar to his counterpart's, something like 'you know, we won nevertheless.') Instead, simply and calmly, he replies: 'It may be so. But it's also irrelevant.'

Summers' 'American misunderstanding' reveals the anxiety of domination. A similar anxiety resurfaces when the deaths of U.S. soldiers in Iraq or

Afghanistan are claimed to be 'meaningless' if the U.S. withdraws now. Such a claim assumes that these deaths will be meaningful if/when the U.S. operations finally succeed. But what if success never comes and the corpses only pile up? The fragile meaningfulness of the colonial project (including combat deaths) is constantly deferred to the future, a future dependent on the other, producing a state of perpetual fear for the colonizer.

Ghostly battles

From the anxious perspective of the colonizer, Kandahar's rubble, its abused, visibly scarred body, appears as a warning, as a sign against trespassing. This is a body that has been battered before, has refused to yield, and then has been battered again, as revenge. But it survives. It lives. It just doesn't seem 'to know' its defeat. Is it possible that its scars scare us more than they scare it?

When you see an abused body like that, it brings back memories. Memories of the violence we inflicted on it. Memories of the bodies of others battered in a similar fashion. (After all, we cannot distinguish clearly amongst them.) Someone else we might have punched somewhere else before. Someone who put up with a lot of hurt but didn't break. How do such memories and bodies come back to haunt us? How do these specters appear in the contemporary language of international relations?

For Burns, these memories come 'rushing back,' as 'images of that dismal time,' in response to the Taliban's latest suicide bomb attack, 'rushing back' in a way that 'pressed the message home':

The *images* of that *dismal time* came *rushing back* last week when the Taliban, legatees of the mujahedeen, sent a suicide bomber in a vehicle loaded with nearly a ton of high explosives to attack a NATO convoy in western Kabul, killing at least 18 people, among them five NATO soldiers, four of them officers. In the grisly calculus of the current conflict, the attack was a Taliban triumph, and photographs from the scene *pressed the message home*. Behind the carnage, like *a forbidding sentinel*, stood the artillery-blasted ruins of the old royal palace at Darulaman, another *monument* to the Soviet disaster.

The 'photographs from the scene' (in accounts such as Filkins' or 57-second presentations sutured by Toyotas) set off powerful undercurrents for Burns. Their presentation of the visibly abused body of Afghanistan highlights the grisly scars of the past. These scars are not just any scars but are 'monumental' and stand as 'forbidding sentinels.' (Forbidding what? Fur-

114

ther abuse?) They are monumental in that they are an enduring sign of 'some abstract quality,' homage to a larger-than-life person/idea or 'heroic' deed.[18] Undeniably, Afghanistan is not just a recollection like any other; it is more a memory that 'refuses to take its place in history as done and finished with,' i.e., it is a trauma.[19] It represents not only the 'blasted' and the 'shattered' but also, as Burns admits, the heroic and the exemplary. But what is that abstract quality—'considered beyond question'[20]—to which Afghanistan's scars testify? For what is Burns paying tribute to Afghanistan and for whom is this monumental body a haunting trauma?

In Burns' explicit portrayal, the scars speak to Afghanistan's ability to bring catastrophe to the Soviets ('Behind the carnage, like a forbidding sentinel, stood the artillery-blasted ruins of the old royal palace at Darulaman, another monument to the Soviet disaster'). But how does a defeat of the Soviet Union, the Cold War adversary of the U.S., in a U.S. instigated and supported war, actually come back to haunt the victors, haunt Burns or his imagined American readers? It is strange that the Soviet Union and the United States are transformed from two enemies waging destructive battles the world over to intimates who suddenly co-suffer traumas. Even more strangely, a Soviet downfall in relation to the mujahedeen is now being brought to bear on a U.S. engagement with the Taliban, a different set of actors in a different historical setting. Why is the 'Soviet disaster' not seen as an intended and willfully achieved U.S. victory?

Burns bridges that gap by seeing the Taliban as the 'legatees of the mujahedeen,' a problematic conceptualization at best. Are the Taliban the legatees of the mujahedeen or is the U.S. the legatee of the Soviet Union? Under what conceptual assumption does that equation of the Taliban with the mujahedeen make sense?

[In 1989] the Soviet Union's collapse, hastened by the *imperial overreach* in Afghanistan, was barely three years away. Now, like others with experience of that time, I find recollections of the Soviet debacle sounding like a tocsin in the mind, warning of the miseries that await America *if the war's trajectory remains as it is*, toward expanding influence for the Taliban and their Al Qaeda cohorts, and mounting signs, for the corrupt Kabul government and its frustrated allies, that the war against the Islamic militants may ultimately be *unwinnable*.

The collapse of the Soviet Union haunts Burns. His 'recollections' of the 'Soviet debacle,' 'sounding like a tocsin in the mind,' forebode the 'miseries awaiting America.' It is intriguing that a Third World previously seen as a mere satellite and bearer of 'proxy' battles, suddenly comes alive as more than an object to be manipulated. Less so is how the Taliban and al-Qaeda might blur into the category of 'Islamic militants' since the orientalist discourse of domination does not, often enough, care to distinguish amongst such objects. Still, how does a former Cold War adversary, othered enough to warrant absolute violence to the point of mutual destruction, now become the self? Burns slips the U.S., un-scandalously, into the place of the Soviet Union and adopts its history and fate in Afghanistan as potentially the future of the U.S. But for the past of the Soviet Union to be the future of the U.S., certain other conceptualizations need to be in place.

One possibility is offered by the term 'imperial overreach.' Burns reads the defeat of the USSR in Afghanistan as the act of an overstretched empire rather than as a Cold War ideological struggle, and in doing so, puts the U.S.'s attempts to prevail in Afghanistan in the same category. Empire thus becomes the implicit subject position of the U.S. Are we all now, supporters (Ignatieff, Fergusson) and critics (Roy, Chomsky) alike, 'citizens' or 'subjects' of a U.S. empire?[21]

A second possibility is that our area-studies understanding of places like Afghanistan can provide only an imperial perspective. That is, whether it is political science, anthropology or classical discourses dating back to Alexander's wars, the expertise that we bring to bear on Afghanistan, in order to make it visible within the contemporary international system, offers us only the viewpoint of aspiring conquerors: how it appears to those who covet it and what has happened to unsuccessful conquistadors before. Most knowledge about Afghanistan is primarily an elaborate essay on the theme of 'Afghanistan is the graveyard of empires.'[22]

A third possibility lies in the parallel that Burns recognizes between Afghanistan and another body. Another body that made the Americans resort to obliteration by bombing, which, as Burns understood well, was 'as good as an admission that they had lost.' Another body that just did not 'get it,' not even after being blasted by an explosive power equivalent to hundreds of Hiroshimas.[23] Another monumental body that served as a grim warning against imperial 'folly.' In fact, it was the U.S. National Security Advisor to President Carter, Zbigniew Brzezinski, who had gleefully resurrected this body-cum-ghost in 'drawing the Russians into the Afghan trap' in 1979: 'We now have the opportunity of giving to the USSR its Vietnam War.'[24]

And indeed they did. The trap, as the U.S. National Security Advisor believed, 'brought about…finally the break-up of the Soviet empire.' Maybe it is not Afghanistan after all—the country, the people, the culture itself—that Burns is thinking of here. Maybe it is this very trap, notorious for its historical effectiveness—the trap that the U.S. once set up successfully for its archenemy, which was already a replay of an experience that had traumatized the U.S. itself—that preoccupied w(e)ary Americans like Burns. What comes back to haunt then is the ghost of an earlier war, not another empire's historical break-up but one's own hysterical 'break-down.' The tocsin rings the self's torment of having been here before.

> *...like the Americans in Vietnam...*
> We wanted the Soviets in Afghanistan to have our experience in Viet Nam
> They experienced our Viet Nam in Afghanistan
> They broke up
> But now we are in Afghanistan (and in Iraq)
> We don't want to be like the Soviets in Afghanistan
> We can't have another Viet Nam
> We can't have another break down
> *...like the Americans in Vietnam...*

'How Many Times Do I Have To Kill You?'[25]

Beginnings

In a haunted world, linear time is ruptured by ghost time, and ghost time murmurs in the ears of the haunted (whether they want to admit it or not): 'Everything begins before it begins.'[26]

Vietnam begins before Afghanistan begins before Iraq begins. Yes, Vietnam is *of* the present ('begins') and the U.S. has to keep battling it even though it is not *in* the present as a physical war for the United States anymore. Every time the United States attempts 'counterinsurgency' in a foreign land, every time it clamors to break the enemy's will, every time it campaigns for 'hearts and minds' even as it kills, Vietnam begins again: as a grim warning, as a curse. The ghosts watch the fated past repeat itself: after the surge comes the 'native-ization' of war (Vietnamization yesterday, Iraqization today),[27] then comes the complete withdrawal, then come McNamara-type regrets and Westmoreland-type we-could-have-won-if's.

But even if the United States had gone 'madder' than it was, even if it had inflicted yet more extreme violence on the entire people, would Vietnam have been subjugated? After all, Kissinger did repeatedly demand from his staff a 'savage, decisive blow' to break the enemy, a 'little fourth-rate power' that he couldn't believe did not have 'a breaking point.'[28] Nixon, the fourth U.S. president to try hopelessly to secure an illusory face-saving of some sort, despaired enough to resort to his Madman Theory: 'I want the North Vietnamese to believe I've reached the point where I might do *anything* to stop the war. We'll just slip the word to them that, "for God's sake, you know Nixon is obsessed about Communism. We can't restrain him when he's angry—and he has his hand on the nuclear button—and Ho Chi Minh himself will be in Paris in two days begging for peace."'[29] This feigned madness was premised on a distinction between good and bad threats. Both Nixon and Kissinger believed that a good threat would be a false threat that the enemy believed to be true while a bad one would be a genuine threat that was disbelieved by the enemy. Their mad minds never imagined an excess on the other side, a third (and fourth and fifth) possibility, an excess that allowed for a refusal to be blackmailed by either the threat of force or the force of threat: 'False or true, we Vietnamese don't mind. There must be a third category—for those who do not care whether the threat is true or not,' Nguyen Co Thach said to Kissinger in the Paris talks as he 'teased him about his views on the strategies of threat bargaining.'[30]

There is always a third category that exceeds the imagination of those in the dominant position, third worlds that they 'don't understand, even to this day.'[31] This ghostly category keeps coming back to haunt and traumatize them precisely for their inability to box it neatly in their break-it/fix-it technical schemas. For the powerful colonizers who expect to master all schemes of knowledge, to rule the direction and meaning of everything that happens, trauma occurs when they cannot comprehend their failure to control the other. They are scarred not from having received inconceivable injury from others, but from their unimaginable inability to effectively inflict violence on others. Trauma seeps in with the realization that nothing they could have done would have brought about their expected results. Nixon could have gotten madder; that too would have been irrelevant.

This is the moment of horror for the 'best and brightest:' Marlon Brando-Kurtz's brutal, weary hands wiping sweat from a clean-shaven head. Robert McNamara's stooped figure and thousand-yard stare, wearing 'the expression of a haunted man.'[32]

'Oh, the horror, the horror!'

Contrast that with the thoughtful, mutually elevating words from the ostensible enemy, passed along mournfully, playfully, humanely.

Nguyen Co Thach 'teas[ing Kissinger] about his views on the strategies of threat bargaining.'

Thich Nhat Hanh sowing the seeds of an alternative inter-being:

> You cultivate the flower in yourself,
> so that I will be beautiful.
> I transform the garbage in myself,
> so that you will not have to suffer.[33]

Even if the colonizer cannot see the contrast, they might sense the difference.

How could that be possible?
What do they even mean?
And why on earth are these fourth-rate people smiling?

How many times do I have to bomb you?

In August 1964, the U.S. Joint Chiefs of Staff (JCS) submitted to Secretary of Defense Robert McNamara a list of 94 most significant targets[34] to hit in Northern Vietnam as part of a bombing campaign codenamed Rolling Thunder. Built in 1899–1902 by the French to provide rail transport between Ha Noi and the important port of Hai Phong, the Long Bien Bridge by 1964 had become the highest to-break priority on the JCS-designated list; it was the bloodline that carried supplies and traffic into Ha Noi not only from Hai Phong but also from China and four of the five major rail lines. Scheduled to last eight weeks, Rolling Thunder dragged on for three years, failing to break either the bridge or Ha Noi's intransigence.

August 1967 marked the United States' first bombing raids on Long Bien Bridge.[35] Thirty-six F-105 Thunderchiefs delivered two 3,000-pound bombs each, felling three of the nineteen spans.[36] It was around the time of the Mid-Autumn Festival. Children were waiting for their star lanterns and *oản* cakes impatiently. Many mothers were coming home to prepare family feasts when the air raids blew them to sudden death, some lying next to lanterns and cakes. To collect the corpses straddled all over the bridge, people had to climb over the ruined parts and use ropes to lower the bodies to canoes and barges down in the river. 'It was the most desolate afternoon in the history of the bridge,' Nguyen Canh Chat, the chief supervisor of the reconstruction, recalled in grief.[37]

In grief and against mounting difficulties, the reconstruction team started work immediately though they had little experience in dealing with such a large bridge. To be safe from bombings, they had to disperse during day-time before resuming the repairs at night. The rainy season worsened the working conditions. Drenched, some worked despite fever (what little rain-covers existed were scraped together to protect solder joints) while others donated scarce food, even if only a bowl of watery porridge. A singer stayed up all night with the workers until she could sing no more. In less than ten days, the car track was rebuilt through to the fifteenth span and a few weeks later, the bridge's railway was completed.

Displeased, the United States launched another attack, in October, with twenty-one F-105s and put the bridge out of action again. Yet again, within a month Long Bien was back in operation. Desperate, in mid-December of the same year, the United States flew fifty F-105 sorties out and destroyed five consecutive spans in two heavy attacks. But after their bombing paused in March 1968, Long Bien was restored to vitality once more by May 1968. In 1972, they targeted it yet again, this time with updated weapons, i.e. first-generation 'smart bombs' (many of which 'smartly' missed the bridge in the initial attack, some by wide margins). That was the last time Long Bien was gravely damaged before it got immersed back into everyday life in March 1973 and continues to this day.

Throughout the war, each time the bridge was struck down, it was returned to life soon after, against Rolling Thunder, against all odds. Long Bien (or the Truong Son Trail or Kandahar…) underwent deadly abuse, repeatedly, but repeatedly, it withstood the pounding. It is this standing-up of the colonized, in suffering as well as in mourning, that traumatizes the colonizer. Even when the Long Bien Bridge was out of use, the United States never succeeded in halting the flow of supplies into the city. The Vietnamese improvised a network of pontoons, bamboo drafts, barges and other makeshift devices that temporarily made possible not only foot and car traffic but also the passing of whole trains across the Red River. Each night, the teams would assemble the devices, patiently and meticulously, to enable clandestine transportation. Each morning, they would disassemble and hide the network away from the bombing radar of U.S. planes. If reconnaissance planes neared the site at night, the lights would go out; as soon as they left, the lights would go back on for underground activities. Continually, off the (bomber's) radar, the bombed re-surge and in-surge, and the injured bodies spring back to life. Helplessly, fully on the (colo-nized's) radar, the colonizer cannot contain improvisations, cannot contain the making and shifting of resistant networks, cannot contain the singing and the porridge that breathe energy into the rebuilding, cannot contain the lights and lives that keep going back on. Cannot contain smudges.

> You are still alive… and singing?
> How many times do I have to bomb you?

The bombers wanted to give nightmares to the bombed, but it was they who suffered them; nightmares still possess them today and will possess them for as long as they continue to bomb others. If one could actually *hear* the subalterns of yesterday, 'They could not threaten us for we knew that they could not stay in Vietnam forever, but Vietnam must stay in Vietnam forever,'[38] it should not be too hard to hear the echoes that resound like an inescapable tocsin now.

Circles. Holes. Smudges. Life. Lives.

The picture cannot be perfect for long. The frame can contain the other only so much.

As Long As…

He's around my uncle's age, with half his hair grayed, lines etched on his brown arms and face, and most unmistakably, his eyes firm and his movements steady. With that firmness and steadiness, he was hammering nails into a small coffin. A very small coffin. It couldn't have held a baby more than four or five.

This one is small; there are a lot more for adults.

Many bombs, many coffins.

Eight to nine hundreds a week…

Many have died here, though it's nothing like in the countryside. Many more have died there.

But the countryside doesn't have this [He knocked on an empty coffin in the pile next to him].

This they don't have. Who would have the money to buy it…

Staring straight at the interviewer, uncle Mui Duc Giang, a coffin maker in Sai Gon, punctuated his sentences with pained glares, each heavy with grief and judgment.

'There are babies who have died right after they were born. Could you please tell us why?' the interviewer asked.

'Poison. Because of poison. Because of poison.' Uncle repeated, registering the crime a few times. 'Poison from these planes that keep spouting and spraying this stuff and so many people have died. It seems to destroy their intestines…Each day they drop hundreds of tons of bombs, can you imagine how many humans die?'

Uncle had lost seven children of his own. Choking with heartache, he could hardly find words to express the pain that he and many others had been enduring. But he wasn't in despair as he warned the United States:

No matter how many decades America fights it will never conquer Viet Nam—Never—I'm telling you so that you will go back and repeat it to president Nixon: Over here [he pointed his finger forward to address his audience forthrightly] as long as there is rice to eat we will keep fighting and if the rice runs out we will plow the fields and fight again!

His unwavering voice runs like an interminable breath of life, of dignity, of resistance. It pulsates not simply in a different time line ('We will outlast you') but in a different time world. A time world in which not everything ends with being flattened into a 'parking lot' or being bombed 'back to the Stone Age.' A time world in which not only pain but even death is transformed. Destroyed bodies do not 'give way to nothingness' but 'make way for the remainder.'[39] Speechlessness does not mute them. Death does not finish them. They only 'drop from existence to enter into that infinite time that is another piece of reality, the time of judgment.'[40] The colonized, even when dead, hang their judgment on those who thirst after colonial accomplishment but are never quite quenched; their judgment deters History from being made and turns history instead into the colonizer's 'hope of history.'[41]

Uncle Mui Duc Giang spoke in Vietnam 1974.[42]

Today we are still dwelling in Vietnam 1974, anxious in the time of judgment, shriveled by the hope of a phantasmal history.

Political exorcisms

In taking seriously the warning of Kandahar, Burns explicitly raises the issue of a gap between the West and the Afghans, between Christians and Muslims, between us and them. This gap was crystallized for Burns when a deputy leader of the Taliban discussed with him the different punishments for homosexuality.[43] That discussion generated a moment of certainty and understanding for him: the idea of an essentialized difference, in time (measured in 'centuries') between the world of the cosmopolitan Christian West (a world of 'Enlightenment' and 'freedoms') and the world of Islam

(with its 'ancient verities' of the 'Koran,' the 'rhythms' of 'Afghan traditions,' as well as the 'absence of Enlightenment').[44] What withstands American efforts to close this chasm by making the space of Islamic Afghanistan
more like the space of the West is the intransigence of the former (not
purging itself of 'barbarisms' so that it could be rebuilt better). The unwinnable option of prevailing over a resistant and radically different, pre-
Enlightenment other leads to a serious questioning of the trajectory of the
self (miseries…'await America *if* the war's trajectory remains as it is…').
Burns discloses a glimmer of self-doubt and self-questioning in the face of
the other's refusal to bend or break.

Nevertheless, with too much certitude about the 'impossible divide to
cross' between the West and the non-West, Burns imputes the futility of
U.S. and Soviet colonial enterprises to the intractable difference of the
Afghan other and therefore limits self-criticality only to self-consolidating
acts. We want, instead, to dwell on the tensions of colonial anxiety that do
not quickly reaffirm an orientalist certainty about the other, but rather,
produce moments of deep uncertainty and consequent re-examinations of
the self. Many a time, there is a promise here that the self can be open to
fundamental change. That promise, for example, is evident in the following account.

Stanley Karnow is the author of *Vietnam: A History*, generally regarded as the standard popular account of the Vietnam War. This past summer, Karnow 84, picked up
the phone to hear the voice of an old friend, Ambassador Richard Holbrooke…,
calling from Kabul…[Holbrooke passed the phone to General McChrystal.] His
question was simple but pregnant: 'Is there anything we learned from in Vietnam
that we can apply to Afghanistan?' Karnow's reply was just as simple: 'The main
thing I learned is that we never should have been there in the first place.'[45]

The question is simple—'Is there anything we learned from in Vietnam
that we can apply to Afghanistan?'—but pregnant with possibilities yet
unborn in our thinking. Karnow doesn't disappoint in delivering an imaginatively rich response: 'The main thing I learned is that we never should
have been there in the first place.'

For us, this is a politically productive moment that opens up the possibility of a radical self-critique and of an alternative politics. It re-imagines
history in order to enter the present differently. We should not have been in
Vietnam then and by implication in Afghanistan now. Or, we should not
have been in Vietnam then; draw your implications for what it means now
for being in Afghanistan.

In the article, this pregnant moment of self-critique is quickly aborted by the authors who note, patronizingly, that these were 'words of wisdom' but not very 'useful' to the general.

Words of wisdom, but not all that useful to General McChrystal. Like it or not, he is already in Afghanistan….McChrystal has been charged by President Obama with presenting a strategy for victory, generally defined as standing up the Afghan Army to beat back the Taliban and deny sanctuary to Al Qaeda. An avid reader of history, McChrystal has read Karnow's book but he has also read many others.

Maybe in an article titled, 'The surprising lessons of Vietnam: the perils of misconstruing the past,' this resolution in favor of the practical over the normative should not be surprising. The cover title is even more glaring in its slant: 'How we (could have) won in Vietnam.' The authors invoke Karnow's authority but quickly find themselves, along with General McChrystal, disavowing his advice. Karnow's suggestion raises specters that they are unable to deal with: not only the trauma of defeat but also the unjust nature of the founding violence. His words offer another way of engaging the other, one without a role for occupation. Yes, the United States is already in Afghanistan, but it never should have been there. Confronted with 'words of wisdom' that force an abuser to imagine an abuse-free relationship, the abuser refuses, in the name of 'usefulness.' Citing other texts and histories, he searches for an impossible 'victory' in an unjust relationship. Foreclosing the possibility of more ethical beginnings, he circles around past traumas for fresh 'lessons.'

We wish to foreclose the foreclosers and re-open the indispensible ethical questions. Let us take Karnow and uncle Mui Duc Giang and their warnings seriously and think wisely/humanely, and not simply usefully, about such situations. There is a beginning before the beginning that haunts contemporary international relations and must be remembered if we are to exorcise the specters of the abusers.

Disorder order disorder

Camouflage and distrust

Villagers are often stunned…to see women underneath the body armor. Inside compounds, the female Marines say they have been poked in intimate places by Afghan women who want to make sure they are really women…One morning in the village of Mamor, as Corporal Amaya and Corporal Gardner asked an Afghan woman if she would be willing to teach in a new school, other women and children—who said they had never seen non-Pashtun women—repeatedly asked two American women, a photographer and a reporter, to lift their shirts and pant legs so they could see what was underneath.[46]

Order

In the words of LTG Peter Chiarelli, former Commanding General, Multi-National Corps-Iraq:

'I asked my Brigade Commanders what was the number one thing they would have liked to have had more of, and they all said cultural knowledge.' Therefore, the Human Terrain System program seeks to integrate and apply socio-cultural knowledge of the indigenous civilian population to military operations in support of the commander's objectives. As one HTT member said, 'One anthropologist can be much more effective than a B-2 bomber—not winning a war, but creating a peace one Afghan at a time.'[47]

Disorder

Paula Lloyd was interviewing locals in the southern village of Maywand on Tuesday as part of her duties in a Human Terrain Team…She approached a man carrying a fuel jug and they began talking about the price of gas. Suddenly, the man doused Lloyd in a flammable liquid and set her on fire…

This is the latest in a series of attacks on Human Terrain personnel. In May, Michael Bhatia, an Oxford-trained political scientist working in eastern Afghanistan, was killed…Less than two months later, a bomb detonated inside the Sadr City District Council building in Iraq. Social scientist Nicole Suveges…and 11 others died instantly. Each incident has been scarring for the few hundred people in the tightly knit program. But the casualties are almost certain to continue.[48]

PART 2

WAR AS ORIENTALISM

7

ORIENTALISM IN THE MACHINE

Josef Teboho Ansorge *

I recently learned something quite interesting about video games. Many young people have developed incredible hand, eye, and brain coordination in playing these games. The air force believes these kids will be our outstanding pilots should they fly our jets.

Ronald Reagan, 1983[1]

For the weapons are nothing but the essence of the fighters themselves.

G.W.F. Hegel, 1807[2]

I

When the poet Rainer Maria Rilke was a student his physics teacher built a phonograph. To the young lyricist the unfamiliar sounds represented 'a new, still infinitely tender piece of reality.'[3] Today the visual displays and layered interfaces of battle spaces, video games and computer simulations

* Special thanks to Alex Anievas, Tarak Barkawi, Duncan Bell, John Mowitt, and Lisa Smirl for helpful comments. The usual disclaimers apply.

represent a similarly new, yet far from tender, fragment of the real. Used to project meaning onto foreign bodies and territories, this crowded medium is an essential link in a global kill chain. While these technical renditions and framings of the oriental other are innovative they recapitulate an old motif of orientalism. As Edward Said wrote, 'to divide, deploy, schematize, tabulate, index, and record everything in sight (and out of sight)' were 'features of Orientalist projection.'[4] In this desire to store, retain, and sort, orientalism 'embodies a systematic discipline of accumulation.'[5] Such accumulation entails expertise. At present, the nature of that expertise is one of technical and methodical data-management that subsumes knowledge about culture, history, and politics. Compared to earlier modalities, today the number—as code, data, and statistics—authorizes orientalist images projected on screens. Current orientalism is more concerned with arithmetizing and measuring the individual other than discovering any linguistic or civilizational essence. This technical expertise is about making the invisible—culture, danger, and political stability—visible, and thereby constitutes a particular type of military visuality.[6]

Vision is frequently invoked in *Orientalism*. The thinkers Said discusses have visions, are visionaries, revisionists and visualizers. 'Cromer envisions a seat of power in the West'; Dante has a vision of Mohammed; 'Averroes and Avicenna are fixed in a visionary cosmology'; Napoleon, de Lesseps, Balfour, and Cromer are 'men of vision'; 'the essential outlines of [Flaubert's] vision are clear'; Comte 'envisions' 'scientific regenerations of mankind'; Marx has a 'Romantic Orientalist vision'; Yeats too has 'visions of Byzantium'; then there is 'Smith's vision of the world'; 'Massignon's vision'; 'Giubb's later vision'; T.E Lawrence is a 'servant' of 'a certain conservative vision of the orient.'[7] Islam and the Orient are envisaged at the core of both *Orientalism* and orientalism. 'Orientalism was ultimately a political vision of reality' a 'manner of regularized (or Orientalized) writing, vision, and study.' The Orient is visualized and is 'something one illustrates.' Images of the Orient depend on a class of visualists and their practices. 'Neither "Europe" nor "Asia" was anything without the visionaries' techniques for turning vast geographical domains into treatable, and manageable, entities.' Methods of making the invisible visible, reign. 'Knowledge was essentially the *making visible of* material, and the aim of a tableau was the construction of a sort of Benthamite Panopticon.' Here the Panopticon is not so much understood as a mechanism for the self-disciplining of subjects, but rather as a regulative academic ideal, instrument for reform, and type of visuality in which an agent at the center sees but is not seen. 'The Orientalist surveys the Orient from above,' he must 'see every detail.' In the end though, this Panopticon itself is revealed as an untenable vision, a mirage, and a false presumption 'that the whole Orient can be seen panoptically.'[8]

I read Said's *Orientalism* as a story about the failure of the Panopticon, about the disenchantment with, and breakdown of, technical means of seeing the other. When considering the relationship of the Panopticon to orientalism it is worth retrieving an illustrative passage from Jeremy Bentham's twenty-first letter in his Panopticon writings. Bentham had no intention of sharing his panoptic insights with the Orient.

Neither do I mean to give any instructions to the Turks for applying the inspection principle to their seraglios: no, not though I were to go through Constantinople again twenty times, notwithstanding the great saving it would make in the article of eunuchs, of whom one trusty one in the inspection-lodge would be as good as half a hundred. The price of that kind of cattle could not fail of falling at least ten per cent., and the insurance upon marital honour at least as much, upon the bare hint given of such an establishment in any of the Constantinople papers. But the mobbing I got at Shoomlo, only for taking a peep at the town from a thing they call a minaret (like our monument) in pursuance of invitation, has cancelled any claims they might have had upon me for the dinner they gave me at the divan, had it been better than it was.[9]

Although Bentham is assured that the 'inspection principle' would bring economic benefits to 'the Turks'—'the price of that kind of cattle' (eunuchs) would fall 'at least ten per cent'—the 'mobbing' he received cancels any claims on hospitality or the reciprocal giving of gifts. This besieging occurs precisely when Bentham is seeking to undertake a quick visual inspection of the town, just a 'peep,' from a religiously significant tower. Despite an initial invitation to do so, such alien panoptic appropriation of the minaret, appears to have been met with great resistance. Many latent symbolic readings of this image of Bentham overwhelmed and disoriented by the Orient, exactly at the instant of attempted surveillance, are possible: the Orient itself rejects orientalists' endeavors for a sovereign vision; religious sites resist foreign annexation; technologies of surveillance have to be permitted to function by the population, etc. In this essay I pursue a slightly different line of argument: What happens when Bentham actually makes it up into the minaret? What transpires when the technical means of information accumulation and visual representation achieve such a capability that the Orient can, really, be seen continuously, perhaps even panoptically? Is this the 'highest stage of orientalism,' as some thinkers argue?[10] What does Bentham see?

I approach this question through three subsequent moves. Section II is an empirical engagement with technologies designed to see battle spaces and culture. I argue that modern military visuality should be treated as the latest stage in a statistical modality applied to the problem of the other: a structure of approaches characterized by quantifying and aggregating a plethora of disparate, indistinct, innocent, obscure, marginal, individually irrelevant and unnoticed signs and measurements into a standardized interpretation tending to prognosis and prediction. Section III considers what intellectual resources need to be developed when ocular surveillance is not up to the task of seeing the other or recognizing the foe. Vision does not deliver on its promises; Bentham does not find what he expects when he reaches the top of the minaret. To make sense of an unintelligible reality an underlying, invisible, ontology has to be postulated and then made visible on screens. This helps account for the great saliency of the term 'network,' a concept with curious historical precedents. Section IV considers whether and how orientalism manifests in video games for training and entertainment purposes. Although the visual projections of the Orient fall short of their stated tactical and strategic aims—despite the complex technical assemblages culture and danger are (still) not seen with great clarity—they nonetheless serve a variety of productive functions, akin to representations of the other in video games. Symbolic destructions and humiliations of the foe play an important role in constituting society and rearticulating an ideal of war, regardless of the medium they occur in. Here I draw on a tradition of writings on ritual and argue that what makes war games, simulations, and projections interesting is not their fidelity to, but rather their difference from, reality.

All attempts to see and project the Orient entail a physical and intellectual apparatus. In *Orientalism*, Said excavated the intellectual and academic components; in this essay I focus more on the physical and engineered instruments. Orientalism is 'an interpretive machine,'[11] but it also requires and demands machines of its own to see, sort, and inscribe illegible circumstances. When we look at the Orient we are also, always, looking with a machine. What is the newest version of that machine?

II

On February 23, 2008 a group of enlisted U.S. soldiers made a little bit of history in the Diyala province of Iraq when they became the first to use an

'Armed Warrior Alpha·Unmanned Aerial System' to 'neutralize targets.'[12] The significance of this event was that unlike predator drones, which are operated by trained pilots, the 'Armed Warrior Alpha Unmanned Aerial System' was controlled by ground troops—yet, it can also operate fully *autonomously*. This development was only the latest in a cluster of accelerating military tools for action at a distance. A historical account of these technical advances would include many moments of war in the 'Orient.' The first successful use of drones in battle was undertaken by Israel in the Bekka Valley in 1982. The first humans surrendering to a drone were Iraqi soldiers capitulating to a U.S. Pioneer Drone in 1991.

One consequence of advances in the field of unmanned aerial systems is a vast amount of data. The increase of drone flights is leaving the military with a huge, potentially debilitating, amount of visual information. Time is expanded and compressed as years of video footage are recorded of Afghanistan and Iraq in ever shrinking intervals. The projected developmental trajectory of these data streams is extremely steep. Reaper Drones will soon be able to record 10 angles simultaneously, are projected to record 35 shortly, and should be up to 65 after that.[13] This optical multiplication coincides with an overall increase in drones that has the potential to result in a startling total view of battle spaces; in 2008 the U.S. military already had twice as many drones as manned airplanes.[14] Northrup Grumman's marketing literature captures the spirit when it refers to its AN AAQ electro-optical distributed aperture system as 'seeing everything, everywhere, all the time.'[15]

A danger of such an increase is the Stasi syndrome: Drones may be looking 'everywhere, all the time' but actually see nothing, because there simply are not enough operators to watch and understand the images, to usefully archive and produce coherent narratives with them. New technical systems are regularly being developed to grapple with the staggering amount of information suddenly existing. In 2010, the basic operating platform for the military is Raytheon's Distributed Capability Ground System (DCGS). In Raytheon's words emphasizing dominance through speed, 'DCGS provides continuous on-demand intelligence brokering to achieve full-spectrum dominance so that U.S. and coalition warfighters can change the course of events in hours, minutes or even seconds.'[16] DCGS looks like a combination of screens of windows featuring live feeds and communication streams.

Technological assemblages and techniques used by the sports casting industry are also drawn on by the military. The means used to make a sports game legible to the disoriented viewer wondering 'are we winning?'—such as scores, overlays, tags keeping track of players, and commentators drawing on screens—are being studied and applied to live battle space images.[17] The system designed to tag and label objects in a battle space is called the Full-Motion Video Asset Management Engine, or FAME. It uses metadata tags, like pictures placed into Google earth. Once in service and online, drones permit one to produce, record and replay an ocular reality which previously did not exist; its level of detail would have been lost to the past and friction of war. One simple tactical practice is called 'backtracking': A fleet of drones maintain constant battlefield surveillance. When an improvised explosive device (IED) goes off, they simply rewind to see who placed it. The next, more strategic, step is to observe what kind of hitherto unrecognized patterns accompany the event to then begin to look for what phenomena might be tell-tale signs of similar future events. This method has a strong pedigree in the visual arts.

The 'Morelli method,' developed in the second half of the nineteenth century, sought to identify paintings by the masters through looking at typically ignored details. Indicative clues were supposed to be the particular style in which a hand or an ear was painted. According to an anonymous article written by Sigmund Freud, deducing the secret character of a piece of art from obscure clues has much in common with the psychoanalytic method. 'It seems to me that his method of enquiry is closely related to the technique of psychoanalysis' which also 'is accustomed to divine secret and concealed things from despised or unnoticed features, from the rubbish-heap ('refuse'), as it were, of our observations.'[18] This basic pattern of seeking to know a group through their mundane, hidden, but shared characteristics has resurfaced and failed with the development of every major technology to identify the individual: such as fingerprints, anthropometry, phrenology, bertillonage, and blood types.[19] What is novel about the current iteration is that by seeking to observe, measure, and categorize movement patterns and, as we will encounter further below, cultural and social reality itself, it displaces essence into a dynamic context.

While some of the subtleties of this visual register are akin to writing—they can be recorded, replayed, edited, spliced; tags are 'written' on to objects and events—they also differ in two very important regards. (a) Deployed in situations where immediacy is the primary design restraint and the medium is characterized by the combination of a large variety of data streams it can be difficult to trace the origin of information. Information on screens thereby manifests as a kind of revelatory knowledge; it does not exist as a text with a bibliography, which can be cross-referenced. (b) The dissemination of these systems means that we have more, and will continue to have more, visual traces of violence. It is easier to abstract and stomach bloodshed described in a text (just consider books VIII and X of the *Iliad*) or a column of numbers. Images are more visceral and moving images even more emotive. As many have argued, this is one of the reasons why drone pilots have such high levels of Post-Traumatic Stress Disorder (PTSD).[20]

Since drones don't immediately fly away after firing their missiles, these pilots see more of the damage they do than earlier generations. The foe is no longer simply a blip on the radar screen but a clearly discernible, often unwitting, individual that disappears in flashes of firepower and poses no immediate existential threat to the drone operator. Pilots are further faced with the knowledge that there is high definition visual evidence of the violence they commit, which can be replayed, copied, and leaked. This new visual battlefield record thereby represents novel challenges for the military's information warfare and public relations. This was demonstrated in 2010 when Wikileaks published classified footage of a gunship's video feed of two Reuters journalists being killed by U.S. soldiers.[21] The danger for the military is that it may lose control of the technical visual narrative of the war, of the moving images produced through its own machines, that have up until now stood for precision and competence.

The groundswell of information from various visual streams is also accompanied by a stark increase of human terrain data. As Said writes, the 'element preparing the way for modern Orientalist structures was the whole impulse to classify nature and man into types.'[22] Tagging and ethnic categorization are the expression of an age-old desire to classify and taxonomize that which is not clearly understood, in this case the social world of the other. A complex technological assemblage is used to keep track of the 'Muslim out of place'—one of the central themes of the global war on terror.[23] Such systems come out of a history of tools deployed by the state to identify individuals. These are typically field-tested and perfected on the external and internal other, where sovereign power experiences the most urgent, securitized, need to make human subjects legible. The technologies to identify individuals have gradually been moving away from visible physical markers—such as tattoos, conspicuous clothing, and badges—to more non-public identifiers, such as fingerprints, social security numbers, and IDs. The tag, only visible on the screen of the authorized operator, is the logical conclusion of the disappearance of material markers of identity. It is accompanied by the biometric iris and fingerprint scan, captured through a device such as the Hand-held Interagency Identity Detection Equipment (HIIDE) system, and stored on a secured database. Here, perhaps more than anywhere else, technical orientalism seeks to make the invisible visible for its operators.

The U.S. military's widely reported and discussed 'culture' turn in Counter-Insurgency (COIN)[24] is not just characterized by proto-anthropological methods, but is also high-tech—at this conjunction of COIN and the Revolution in Military Affairs (RMA) databases and programs to represent cultural data spring forth. An enabling implication of the widespread signifier of human-terrain is that culture can be measured and subsequently visually represented in colorful graphs, maps and diagrams with PowerPoint presentations. Applications have subsequently been custom-designed to facilitate the standardization, quantification and representation of cultural knowledge, which is always necessary to making it utile and legible. A suite of programs designed for the Human Terrain System (HTS), and based on DCGS discussed above, is called MAP-HT. That the software system for understanding culture is based on one designed to represent battlefields provides a good indication of the way culture is viewed in these systems. The HTS website describes MAP-HT in the following fashion:

It facilitates research, analysis, storage, archiving, sharing and other application of socio-cultural information relevant to the unit commander's operational decision-making processes....Map-HT Toolkit products include the following:

• Maps: for example, spatial distribution of tribes and related social entities.
• Link Charts: for example, power structures and social networks in informal economies.
• Time lines: for example, time sequence of key religious holidays.
• Visualization: for example, topographic views of Iraqi infrastructure.
• Reports: for example, role of ethnicity in Iraqi power sharing.[25]

MAP-HT is a synthetic multi-medial perspective that couples various people to a shared ocular reality, one that envisions ethnicity layered on top of infrastructure and topography. Images produced with this suite of programs are useless to the academic analyst if he treats them as some obvious representation or product of a surveyed reality. Instead these kinds of images need to be understood as profoundly enabled by statistics, as well as drawing on a particular history of visuality.

While there are accounts that the suite of programs is not being properly implemented in the field, the basic direction of this technology is apparent. Human Terrain Teams collect and analyze data in the field, it is then sent to a knowledge center based in the continental United States to be further processed and uploaded to databases and servers. To make the data legible it is projected on to maps, in effect it is built on top of widespread Geographic Information Systems (GIS), and tagged. The abstraction of the map is further layered with a simplified representation of culture in the form of inkblots.

The capability will provide a database augmented with specific sociocultural objects and an entity extraction capability for tagging narrative and freetext documents for ingestion into the local database.[26]

It has long been recognized that maps, and the practice of cartography in general, are distinctly political. Mark Monmonier has pointed out that not only do maps often lie, they actually have to misrepresent to create a meaningful image.[27] As Thongchai Winichakul reminds us, 'A map may not just function as a medium; it could well be the creator of the supposed reality.'[28] Moreover, one should recall Said's claim that 'neither "Europe" nor "Asia" was anything without the visionaries' techniques for turning vast geographical domains into treatable, and manageable, entities.'[29] What new cultural realities are being produced through the widespread manufacture of 'ethnic maps'? That maps of ethnic identity and culture are profoundly political, necessarily fictitious and can easily be abused should become apparent to the military in due course. The consciousness-raising moment to watch out for is when the issue arises of handing over vast amounts of biometric and other data to 'host' governments.

In basic outlook, these Human Terrain datasets hark back to an age of anthropological research where the guiding principle was completion and standardized recording. A recent critical report by an American Anthropological Association commission on the Human Terrain System raised 'questions about the integrity of data collected by HTTs, and where this data might end up.'[30] What else could be done with all of this data apart from providing the commander with cultural and political awareness? One answer to this question, discussed further below, is that the data should be used to simulate cultural environments for training purposes with higher fidelity.

Instead of understanding these new visual phenomena as results of surveillance, they should be read in the tradition of statistical thought and considered as a response to a failing Panopticon. Gathered terabytes of visual and cultural data are combined with other bits of information to form an aggregate baseline for the discovery of statistical patterns. Screens and computer programs offer opportunities for new immersive experiences, to empirically encounter information, to have thick experiences from thin data. It is important to bear in mind that all of this occurs for distinctly martial and predatory reasons. In the words of Carlo Ginzburg, 'lurking behind this model for explanation or prophecy one glimpses something as old as the human race: the hunter crouched in the mud, examining a quarry's tracks.'[31] In this reading technology is simply animated by primal instincts and practices of the hunt. What we observe with the creation of these machines, however, exceeds its animating principles and intended consequences. Writing at the beginning of the Great War, Emil Lederer managed to capture the dynamic of this relationship well:

Every military apparatus has as its aim the defeat of an enemy in war; there is, and can be, no military complex that does not have this aim. But as soon as this aim is fixed and held constant, the technology employed in the service of this end acquires an immanent necessity of its own.[32]

These various visualizing technologies culminate in a martial optic in which the experience of quasi-instantaneous legibility of a complex situation is produced through swiftly circulating standardized information that labels objects and events. If DCGS and MAP-HT are military apparatuses with the aim of seeing and finding the foe, and they are really as sophisticated as the marketing literature describes them, then why have the conflicts in Afghanistan and Iraq been such protracted illegible affairs? Why and how does the enemy persist if we see everything, all the time and everywhere? The short answer is that these systems don't deliver what they promise.

Finally up in the Minaret, Bentham sees the whole oriental town laid out before him; but now the shortcomings of the ocular mode become painfully apparent. Everybody looks the same. Seeing does not mean knowing or understanding. You can zoom in on one individual and not discover their essence; zoom out and not understand the town.

Who is that?

Are they dangerous?

How can one see the enemy in this environment? Can the enemy even be seen?

III

Conflicts in Afghanistan and Iraq, as well as the whole notion of a Global War on Terror, are characterized by a foe that cannot be seen, by a 'hidden' ontology. Metaphors and models are used to describe and make sense of this kind of political opponent. In 1622 Francis Bacon coined a theory of monstrosity that justified and called for the extermination of various different groups of society, as diverse as Canaanites, Anabaptists, and Amazons.[33] The metaphor he used to other and give form to this shapeless mass was that of a many-headed hydra, the mythological beast Hercules slew as his second duty. What is fascinating about this obscure historical fact is that the very same metaphor is commonly used in descriptions of Al-Qaeda and even Islam. The metaphor is both widespread, a Google search for 'Islam' and 'hydra' returns 218,000 hits,[34] and present in select U.S. government publications, most prominently in the 9/11 Commission Report, which speaks of the (false) image of al-Qaeda as 'an omnipotent, unslayable hydra of destruction.'[35]

Whatever its applicability, the use of this metaphor has the same implications in Bacon's time as it does in ours. The enemy is represented as a dehumanized, decentralized mass. Things are not as they look: forces appearing as separate individual components are recognized as belonging to one purpose and being, requiring utter destruction. The choice of words to describe a foe always has far-reaching consequences. An implication of this particular metaphor is that to insure that the heads of the hydra do not reproduce, it is necessary to turn to extraordinary means: Hercules decided to burn the neck. But most importantly, the basis for the conflict is produced as ontological: the hydra, like al-Qaeda, does not need to be battled because of political grievance but due to its very being. This move that conceptualizes the difference of the other to the self as the very cause of conflict produces difference as a problem and a threat; under these circumstances special intellectual (anthropology) and technical (primarily visual) resources are mobilized to understand the other's culture. Of course such mechanisms of othering are not particular to the War on Terror, but have many historical precedents.[36]

A term that plays a similar role to 'hydra' in modern military discourses is 'network,' where it is often used to refer to terrorist actors or insurgents. 'Network' has veritably exploded in to the intellectual life and discourse of the military. In a 1940 military handbook on illegible military circumstances approximating counter-insurgency campaigns, the Small Wars Manual (SWM), there is only one reference to network: 'connected with other towns in a large *network*,'[37] while in the new Stability Operations Field Manual (FM 3–07) of 2008 there are 15, and in the new Counterinsurgency Field Manual (FM 3–24) of 2007 there are 193 instances of 'network.' The following definition of network is provided in FM 3–24.

network is a series of direct and indirect ties from one actor to a collection of others. Insurgents use technological, economic, and social means to recruit partners into their networks. Networking is a tool available to territorially rooted insurgencies....[38]

Network is deployed as a very versatile concept in modern military discourses. It is described as a noun ('a series of direct and indirect ties from one actor to a collection of others'), as a verb ('networking is a tool'/to network), and as an adjective ('networked organization').[39] Instead of referring to a technical distribution network—as it does in SWM—it has been redefined to mean a form of social organization which is characterized by being relatively non-hierarchical, diffuse, and often secret in character. In contemporary military discourses, networks are typically described as organizational forms that the enemy successfully assumes and U.S. forces need to emulate.[40]

A positive feedback loop leading to the signifier of 'network' being more widespread is that operators in the U.S. military are finding that to receive the kind of logistical support they want it helps to refer to whatever opponent they are encountering as a network. Consider this email from an Intelligence Officer returning from a tour of duty in Afghanistan at the beginning of 2010.

The 'Network' thing is just an example of how using certain buzz words will better get your asset requests approved over the other guy. The shrewd intel or operations officer identifies those buzz words quickly and peppers his asset requests with them. 'Network' made Haqqani sounds like something extra special, and not just the Taliban in that particular area. Whereas I don't think Haqqani represents a Network as is traditionally thought of in intel work.[41]

Beyond these feedback dynamics, why does the notion of the 'network' take-off precisely during the illegible wars of Iraq, Afghanistan, and the Global War on Terror?

A paradigmatic moment in Gillo Pontecorvo's *The Battle of Algiers* (1966), which was watched with great interest at the Pentagon after the

9/11 attacks, may provide a clue.[42] In the middle of the movie Lieutenant-Colonel Mathieu is showing a video to a class of soldiers. The video shows soldiers searching people at checkpoints.

> MATHIEU
> Here is some film taken by the police.
> The cameras were hidden at the Casbah
> exits. They thought these films might be
> useful, and in fact they are useful in
> demonstrating the usefulness of certain
> methods. Or, at least, their inadequacy.

The soldiers are searching ordinary civilians to find FLN terrorists. The displayed action at the checkpoint does not go well: there is chaos and attacks still happen. Clearly, something is not working; the terrorists must have walked right by the checkpoint. When the video cuts out Mathieu draws the image of a network on the blackboard.

> MATHIEU
> We must start again from scratch. The only
> information that we have concerns the
> structure of the organization. And we
> shall begin from that…

The network is drawn when vision is not up to the task of seeing the foe. Contrasted to the video camera which surveys what is seen, the diagram of a network acts as an objectified and constructed image of a social reality that cannot be observed directly; it both complements visual reality, and undermines its positivist orientation. The network functions as representation and simulation of the social ontology of the foe.

The ontological shift from territory, to individuals, to network moves away from observed reality as well as politicized categories with established rights discourses. In this way, the emphasis on network can also be read as a depoliticizing practice, avoiding the more salient categories of race, individual, class or country. The use of particular terminology matters; it has the ability to connect contemporary ideas of the foe to historic scripts, to conjure up images from authorized memory as well as fantasy to understand the other. This is linked to the role games and training simulations play vis-à-vis orientalism. As I seek to show below, even though the eye does not deliver on the domination it promises, projecting oriental others on screens still performs important functions.

IV

There is a startling amount of design and aesthetic overlap between military training simulations, modern weaponry, and games created solely for entertainment. Controls to operate a robot in the field are inspired by a video game controller. 'We modeled the controller after the PlayStation because that's what these 18-, 19-year old Marines have been playing with pretty much all of their lives.'[43] Visionary technologies showcased in movies spur development of similar tools for the military. Inspired by the interactive display Tom Cruise used in Steven Spielberg's adaptation of Philip K. Dick's *Minority Report*, the U.S. military hired Raytheon to create a real version for the U.S. military. Raytheon promptly hired the same person who had proposed the technology to Spielberg in the first place.[44] Today Oblong Industries' G-Speak Gestural Technology System looks just like the technological artifact used in the movie. Gaming environments built for commercial gain are repurposed for training and simulation purposes.

AMERICAS ARMY project is based on UNREAL TOURNAMENT from Blizzard Entertainment, and DARPA's DARWARS AMBUSH product is derived from OPERATION FLASHPOINT by Bohemia Interactive Games.[45]

This close connection between 'real' and 'fake,' or virtual, visual machinery is a curious characteristic of simulation technologies.

The gaming entertainment industry is a significant economic and cultural force. Sales of the popular shooter Modern Warfare II (MWII) have exceeded $1bn, with some $500m worth of games being sold in the first five days. More money was spent on advertising for MWII than for Avatar.[46] Considering the time and energy it takes to play these games, video game consumers are more continuously exposed to the assumptions and stereotypes of games than they are of individual movies. Due to this special attention should be paid to how the other may be represented in them. A banal, blatant, and hackneyed kind of orientalism exists in video games. At first it would appear that oriental stereotypes still hold sway over the public imagination.

One aspect of the electronic, postmodern world is that there has been a reinforcement of the stereotypes by which the Orient is viewed....So far as the Orient is concerned, standardization and cultural stereotyping have intensified the hold of the nineteenth-century academic and imaginative demonology of 'the mysterious Orient.'[47]

The genre of first person shooters, in particular, features multiple armed opponents who exist as copies and caricatures of: North Koreans, Russians, Iraqis, Terrorists and Favela criminal gangs. Fictional narratives requiring the killing of many opponents are enriched through the hyper-realistic portrayal of certain aspects, such as the waves of a body of water or the military vehicles a game character can operate. This also applies to the game's politics; here too real reference points are embedded in imaginary worlds. For instance, the highly acclaimed Crysis (2007) is set in 2020 on an island in the Philippines. The first half of the gameplay is occupied with infiltrating an island and killing North Koreans. The North Korean characters all look alike and have a staple of simple lines: 'I see him!,' 'Die, Yankee Scum,' 'I kill you' and so on. But in the second half of the game, the enemy shifts. Now one plays the Special Forces soldier in a bionic suit pitted against aliens and has to defend humanity itself.

Another example of a trace of politics within a fictional setting can be discovered in Command and Conquer. The gameplay takes place at the strategic military-industrial level: players need to build weaponry and train soldiers to destroy enemy buildings and they require money to do so. The setting of the game is an entirely fictional world in which actors fight over some novel resource. The intro sequence, however, features the famous Bush era terrorism threat chart—what President Obama has referred to as the color coded politics of fear. There is no common thread connecting the way the enemy is represented in these games, what binds all of them however is an emphasis on technical know-how.

This affinity can also be discovered in the opening sequence of Modern Warfare II. While luminescent networks span the globe, interspersed by schematics of weapons and military vehicles, a single raspy voice delivers this monologue.

Shepherd's lament: The more things change, the more they stay the same.
Boundaries shift, new players step in, but power always finds a place to rest its head.
We fought and bled alongside the Russians. We shoulda known they'd hate us for it.
History is written by the victor. And here I am thinking we'd won.
But you bring down one enemy and they find someone even worse to replace him.

Locations change, the rationale, the objective.
Yesterday's enemies are today's recruits.
Train them to fight along you, and pray they don't eventually

> decide to hate you for it too.
> Same shit, different day.

World politics exists here as a confusing and disorienting backdrop. This is not the world of an unchanging, hostile Orient that can be known. A primitive kind of tragic realism can be sensed behind the account of sudden reversals of alliances, one in which the deep 'oriental' identity of the other is negligible. Shepherd continues:

> We are the most powerful military force in the history of man.
> Every fight is our fight.
>
> ...
>
> Learning to use the tools of modern warfare is the difference between the prospering of our people, and utter destruction.
>
> We can't give you freedom. But we can give you the know-how to acquire it.

What remains in Modern Warfare II is not an identity or ideology based conflict, but a worldview in which everybody can be a foe: insurgents, Russian Mafia, and traitors from your own ranks. The only reliable constant is the cryptic organizing concept of 'freedom' and an unabiding faith in military technology.[48] In this emphasis on know-how and utility we glimpse the possibility that there may be no extensive ideological investment in one or the other totalizing representation of the other.

The real characters of the game are actually the great variety of weapons one uses—from knives, to all forms of assault weapons and even military drones. The identity of the enemy you kill with this family of lethal objects is incidental. While the way you shoot a bullet is hyper-realistic in these games the identity of the person it is shot at is not. Read in this way the foe, as a complex entity that challenges the self, is absent from this game and from all commercially available shooters.

Like many other games the first part of MWII is a training component to let the player familiarize themselves with controls before the real game begins. The training component of Modern Warfare II has a twist though. In it the player is part of a training demonstration to foreign Arab-looking troops—named Fouad, Amin, Nasir, Fahd, Habib, and Bassam—who are being told that they are 'spraying from the hip too much.' This looks like Iraqi Security Sector Reform. The proper use of the 'tools of modern warfare' are treated here as a gift for the other.

Gaming was already taken on as a recruitment strategy by the U.S. Army before the 9/11 attacks. In 1999, after some of the worst recruitment numbers in 30 years, the U.S. Congress invested heavily into new recruitment tools and techniques. It was during this time that the foundation for America's Army was laid by Col. Casey Wardynski. America's Army is a widely popular freely available game that takes an Army recruit from training to different missions. Recently, in the midst of the global economic crisis, recruitment numbers have been met for the first time in more than 35 years.[49] This success can, in part, be attributed to the popularity of America's Army.

To play a game such as America's Army is to undergo more training experiences than to play any other shooter. The player's character has to spend a large amount of time running obstacle courses and qualifying on different weapons before they are 'ready' for combat. To play the game also means to be constrained at every turn by strict rules of engagement (RoE). Soldiers get sent to 'Leavenworth' for punishment when they violate the RoE, where they miss stages of the gameplay. As such America's Army is a fantasy of individual agency embedded in a team that delivers expert and legal violence. America's Army familiarizes the player with a U.S. military habitus, by getting a sense of the practices at fire ranges, the rules and types of weapons used. It permits a player to encounter a community of martially minded team-mates and to experience stages of success and qualification without having to leave their home.

The gaming reality produced in America's Army should not just be considered for its power to mimic human physical confrontations on earth; but rather for what it leaves out. America's Army does not provide an ideological narrative for violence in the confusing and disturbing world of actual conflict, but a repertoire of weaponry and a ritually ordered rehearsal for war. These games and simulations feel like the expression of a desire to control and rehearse, produce and perfect the delivery of force. While the kind of weapons you train on is hyper-realistic in America's Army, the fact that there isn't any 'collateral damage' isn't. What is also highly unrealistic, is the opponent. Whenever you see an enemy, he is to be shot: except if he is unconscious, which would be a violation of the RoE. The enemies exist in the game, but only as empty objects of violence. This cannot be said for new efforts to model cultural reality, in which the other arises as a highly complex set of behavioral functions.

Barry Silverman argues that human terrain data should be used to build serious games: training and simulation environments for cultural interaction. The gaming environment he has helped construct for the U.S. military is called 'non-kin village.' In it the player has to enter the houses of Afghan civilians and interact with them, the player needs to be polite and learn the local cultural terrain. These simulations create thick immersive experiences from thin data. Drawing on theories of bargaining and political grievance drivers, behavioural models are constructed in which the other is capable of highly complex interaction. Silverman claims that the modeling and simulation community would be remiss if it did not rise to the task of producing serious games from human terrain data. Today the computer programmer, or serious games constructor, is the heir to Said's scientists and men of vision; the gaming platform is the descendant of the laboratory.

To be able to sustain a vision that incorporates and holds together life and quasiliving creatures (IndoEuropean, European culture) as well as quasimonstrous, parallel inorganic phenomena (Semitic, Oriental culture) is precisely the achievement of the European scientist in his laboratory.[50]

Just like Said's 'laboratory' had much wider significance than the immediate output of its research, these type of training simulations fulfill many more important social functions than just the communication of information or technical know-how. Games and training simulations should also be read as modern forms of what James Frazer called homeopathic magic: 'the attempt which has been made by many peoples in many ages to injure or destroy an enemy by injuring or destroying an image of him.'[51] Examples of this kind of logic are 'North American Indians' who

believe that by drawing the figure of a person in sand, ashes, or clay, or by considering any object as his body, and then pricking it with a sharp stick or doing it any other injury, they inflict a corresponding injury on the person represented.[52]

As such, these training simulations do not only fulfill an exercising function, but are also important ritualistic humiliations and recurring symbolic destructions of a foe.

A key question for Silverman is 'if we use the data of human terrain systems to help model the "parts" and their microdecision processes, can we observe macro-behaviors emerging that are useful for analysts to know about?'[53] In other words, can the minutia of human terrain data describe societal processes and tendencies? This recapitulates a key question that has been haunting war games ever since their inception. Can these simulations somehow be used as a research methodology to provide different scenarios of what could happen in the real world? Are these gaming platforms actually laboratories? According to U.S. Admiral Hayward, the answer is a resounding no.

It is my conviction that wargaming as a training tool constitutes the overriding value of the wargaming technique, whether tactical or strategic. I would almost go so far as to say the only value. For I contend that using the wargame beyond the training dimension is fraught with flotsam that endangers the utility of the outcome unless managed with great care by the experts.[54]

What are the effects of simulation even when only used as a training tool? One concern is that the training simulation itself, and all of the orientalist or technophile assumptions that underlie it, come to frame and overdetermine real conflict, up to the point where the simulation structures the narrative and experience of what happens. This fear of the power of copies over the real is not only associated with computer simulations. Daniel Ellsberg recounts the following incident occurring at the time of the Cuban Missile Crisis:

[w]e were in…the Policy Planning Room. There were various cables coming in from minute to minute. One of them looked almost identical to one of the cables of the year before.…It looked very much like the message from the [Berlin] game. I tapped Walt Rostow on the shoulder and I said, 'Read this.' He read it. I said, 'This shows how realistic the Berlin game was.' He said, 'Or how unrealistic this is.'[55]

The basic schema of a homeopathic ritual can be discovered amongst people of many different times and places. Usually the central logic of these rituals is conceptualized as 'like producing like.' But does the representation of the other, either as a hollow container of violence or a complex set of behavioral functions, in games mean that soldiers will view non-Western peoples they encounter in the same fashion? The anthropologist Jonathan Z. Smith argues, in the case of sympathetic hunting magic, that the power of the ritual can also be understood in that it is actually 'unlike the hunt. It is, once more, a perfect hunt with all the variables controlled.'[56] Read from this position, these games and their various representations of the other are primarily symptoms of the desire to clearly see the enemy—of the desire for a world in which there is no collateral damage and force is delivered with technical precision and perfect legality.

V

In this essay I considered orientalism and military visuality through their technological basis; in the course of this exercise I identified the network as a model of the foe that is developed when surveillance is not up to the task. Orientalism in the machine (whether in the real battle space or on a com-

147

puter at home) appears now as the remainder of an equation seeking to square an ideal way of war with real conflict. It is the product of a particular genealogy as well the projection of deep-seated desires, not the 'empirical' results of surveying the other.

While technical means of seeing the Orient proliferate, the military itself can observe unintended consequences of technical systems in the field. It is in a privileged position to bear witness to the deficiencies of Bentham's view from the minaret—it was Mathieu's camera that displayed the French military's failure. It appears that strategic vision regularly requires liberation from the technical crutches it develops. For instance, an increasingly vocal anti-PowerPoint movement has been gaining speed amongst the defense intelligentsia. There also appears to be a growing discomfort and distrust of waging a Counter-Insurgency campaign through computers. Consider this comment from a security professional in Afghanistan.

I travel to all these bases throughout Afghanistan and I see the amount of wasted time that computers and TVs create. Things created on the computer are called 'products.' Most of the guys I have spoken with say that they rather be in the 'fight' than back creating products. If there were no computers, there would be less fancy PowerPoint slides about hearts and minds and more guys out working with the populace doing COIN....[57]

It has been argued that the more mechanized a military is, the less successful it is at fighting an insurgency.[58] It remains to be seen how a military whose information technology is automated and mechanized fares. For the military apparatus, as either DCGS, MAP-HTS, or war games, to function it has to be 'a closed world' in which the other is mediated and their representation is controlled.[59] The other can never surprise or exceed your knowledge when constrained to a game or a behavioralist function, or a cell in the Panopticon. You only see what you are looking for. This stands in clear contrast with the notion that 'There is no teacher but the enemy.'[60] And this is also why a reflective Bentham would have to be disappointed when he reaches the minaret; he thinks he will see the town, but instead he sees the foundations his vision is built upon.

The machine lays at the heart of our modern, technical, orientalism. With its dynamic development and future trajectory it will continue to play a more central role than academic traditions of representing the other. This leads to the unusual question: *will future artificial intelligence—* designed to identify the foe and produce battle space legibility—be racist? Will it inherit orientalist tropes? It appears that when the enemy is a network, one may not need a thick descriptive orientalism as a framing motif anymore, indeed this would only undermine the saliency and utility of the network concept. In this *Weltanschauung* the essence of the other is not anything in particular; it is simply a field of relations violently disrupted through military technology.

The weapon remains after this erasure of the other.

8

DIS/ORDERING THE ORIENT

SCOPIC REGIMES AND MODERN WAR

Derek Gregory

Orientalism and order

When Said described orientalism as a discourse he was calling attention to its performative power: to its capacity to produce the effect it names ('the Orient'). That capacity was—and remains—contingent. It depends on the constellations, conjunctures and circumstances in which orientalism is activated. Said focused on its imbrications with British, French and American modalities of power and their production of a particular 'Orient'—the 'Middle East'—whose designation was itself a profoundly colonial locution. There were other modalities and other 'Orients,' but in this case Said distinguished two cultural-political performances. First, 'the Orient' was summoned as an exotic and bizarre space, at the limit a pathological and even monstrous space: 'a living tableau of queerness.' Second, 'the Orient' was constructed as a space that had to be domesticated, disciplined and normalized through a forceful projection of the order it was presumed to lack: 'framed by the classroom, the criminal court, the prison, the illustrated manual.'[1]

The orientalist projection of order was more than conceptual or cognitive, for the process of ordering also conveyed the sense of command and conquest. Said identified the origins of a distinctively modern orientalism in Napoleon's military expedition to Egypt between 1798 and 1801.[2] And yet, even as he fastened on the catalytic importance of the French invasion, Said's focus was unwaveringly on the textual appropriation of 'ancient Egypt' by the engineers, scientists and artists who accompanied the French army. Their collective work was enshrined in the *Description de l'Égypte*, which Said described as a project 'to render [Egypt] completely open, to make it totally accessible to European scrutiny,' and to usher the Orient from 'the realms of silent obscurity' into 'the clarity of modern European science.'[3] The phrasing is instructive: visuality is a leitmotif of orientalism. Said noted that under its sign 'the Orient is watched,' that the Orient was always more than *tableau vivant* or theatrical spectacle, and that the orientalist technology of power-knowledge was, above all, about 'making visible,' about the construction 'of a sort of Benthamite panopticon' from whose watch-towers 'the Orientalist surveys the Orient from above, with the aim of getting hold of the whole sprawling panorama' in every 'dizzying detail.'[4]

Napoleon's military expedition was about more than annexing Egypt as what Said called 'a department of French learning,' however, and its execution inflicted more than cultural violence. Its capacity to do both these things was indeed visually mediated—though, strangely, there is not a single illustration in *Orientalism*—but so too was the conduct of the campaign itself. Historically, wars have always been shaped by (and have in turn shaped) visual fields, and there are close connections between (late) modern war and 'scopic regimes.' Metz proposed the latter term to distinguish the cinematic from the theatrical way of staging and seeing the world, but it has since been uncoupled from any specific forms, displays and technologies to denote a mode of visual apprehension that is culturally constructed and prescriptive, socially structured and shared.[5] Like its companion term visuality, which denotes culturally or techno-culturally mediated ways of seeing, the concept is intended as a critical supplement to the idea of vision as a purely biological capacity. Scopic regimes are historically variable, and different regimes can co-exist within a single cultural and social formation, but the closest attention has been paid to the ligatures between visuality and modernity. Apart from a handful of studies, however, of which Virilio's *War and Cinema* is probably the best known, little systematic attention has been given to the ways in which the conduct of modern wars is mediated by scopic regimes.

This blind spot has become ever more acute, because many of the wars fought directly by the United States and its allies during the Cold War took place in the 'Far East'—Korea, Vietnam, Laos and Cambodia—and since 9/11 they have taken place within the orbit of U.S. Central Command (CENTCOM) whose Area of Responsibility is a greater 'Middle East.' Yet there has been little examination of the ways in which these conflicts have been inflected by the visual codes of orientalism, by American fabrications of the 'Orients' in which they took place. For these reasons we need to establish how changing scopic regimes have mediated the triangulations of modernity, orientalism and war that frame our own, still profoundly colonial present. To fashion a preliminary answer to this question, I spool back to the French invasion of Egypt and then fast-forward to contemporary counterinsurgency operations in Afghanistan and Iraq.

Modernity, orientalism and war

Although Said says little about it, the French occupation of Cairo and the subsequent rampage through the Levant were hideously bloody affairs. In fact, Bell claims that the Napoleonic wars wrought such an 'extraordinary transformation in the scope and intensity of warfare' that they constituted 'the first total war' of the modern period.[6] This probably needs qualification, but the proximity of modern orientalism to modern warfare is reinforced in other ways too. Said notes more or less in passing that what most impressed the first Arab chronicler of the occupation, Abd al-Rahman al-Jabarti, 'was Napoleon's use of scholars to manage his contacts with the natives.'[7] This was expediency more than cultural sensibility; the *savants* grumbled that they were required to provide all sorts of practical information for the army on a more or less daily basis and to produce what was, in effect, military intelligence. Neither they nor the troops were prepared for their first contact with Cairo—it resembled 'a great intestine filled with houses stacked on top of one another,' complained one officer, 'without order, without regularity, without method'—and so it was necessary to transform its multiple opacities into a singular transparency. As I said at the start, this is a characteristically orientalist gesture—ordering what was assumed (incorrectly) to be disordered—and in this particular case Cairo was to be opened to the French military gaze: transformed into a spacialized object of knowledge that would make possible the surveillance, regulation and exaction of the city and its population.

This required a detailed mapping of the city and its environs. It was not difficult to establish a series of points from which to construct a *plan géometrique*—the first were fixed on the mounds of rubbish that ringed Cairo, from which an expanding series of triangles was folded out into the city using the minarets of the mosques as markers—but as the surveyors moved inside the city so their task became formidably difficult because the intricacy of the streets and the numerous dead-ends made it impossible to take the long sightings that would have expedited leveling.[8] When the map was finished it fell to one of the *savants* to provide its interpretative matrix. Jomard spent two months identifying the names of quarters and streets, numbering them and keying them to the map, and drafting a series of memoranda that were eventually incorporated into a plenary essay for the *Description* that was linked to illustrations prepared by other *savants*. The overall objective was to exhibit Cairo within a space of European reason, geometricized and systematized, for, as Jomard explained,

The internal plan of the city is nothing like European cities: not only are its streets and squares highly irregular but—with the exception of a few major streets—the city is almost entirely made up of very narrow streets and zig-zag branches that debouch into countless dead-ends. Each one of these districts is closed by a gate, which the inhabitants open as they please: with the result that the interior of Cairo is very difficult to know as a whole. This could not be done until the French were masters of the city.[9]

By these means Solé concludes that the *ingénieurs-géographes* succeeded in untangling the *'capitale-labyrinthe'* and 'forcing it to give up its secrets.'[10] During the first insurrection in October 1798 one of the targets of the crowd was the billet of 'the inspector for fortifications and trenches,' where 'many strange mechanical and optical devices' used by the surveyors were smashed or carried off. The French 'searched long for these instruments,' Jabarti recorded, 'and gave those who returned them huge rewards.'[11] Clearly occupiers and occupied alike understood that mapping was a weapon of war.

I have rehearsed the production of this map for two reasons. First, you might protest that there is nothing intrinsically orientalist about a modern, 'scientific' map, even one like this, and properly insist that cartography has never been an exclusively European or even colonial project. But this is to treat the map as an object—as what Latour calls an 'immutable mobile'—whereas a contrary, more powerful analysis views the map as an event and directs attention to the mappings through which it flickers into momentary presence and to the wider ensemble of practices within which they are activated.[12] Seen thus, situated within the web of military operations that produced and sustained Cairo as a city under French occupation, this is an unstable but profoundly orientalist inscription. Secondly, mapping Cairo, transporting it into the cognitive space of European reason, involved what an Arab writer once called *intizam al-manzar*, the organization of the view, which enabled the French to 'see' the paper city in a way that was impossible for them on the ground. By such means, a claim to certainty and truth was registered so that, as Mitchell puts it, 'everything seems ordered and organized, calculated and rendered unambiguous.' This was achieved through a novel machinery that installed a distinction between representation and reality—what Mitchell identifies as 'the world-as-exhibition'—whose distinctively modern 'exhibitionary order,' as he also shows, has an intimate association with colonialism and orientalism. This apparatus turns on the production of a detachment and distance between the viewing subject and the object of the gaze—on the power 'to separate oneself from the world and thus constitute it as a panorama'—and, by extension, on a radical difference between the city of the occupiers and the city of the occupants that is, I think, formally equivalent to the distinction between 'our space' and 'their space' rendered by Said's concept of an imaginative geography.[13] Both cartographic reason and the exhibitionary order depended on the establishment of what Mitchell calls 'viewing platforms' (like mounds of rubbish or minarets) from which, ideally, 'one could see and yet not be seen.'[14]

Both these ideas—mappings and exhibitionary orders—can illuminate the scopic regimes of American military adventurism in our own century. I do not mean to imply that nothing has changed in the intervening two hundred years. Orientalism is still abroad, and it is necessary to expose its reactivations of colonial imaginaries, dispositions and practices, but it is equally important to identify what is novel about the present constellation of neo-orientalism and late modern war. The counterinsurgency campaigns conducted by the United States and its allies in Afghanistan and Iraq provide vivid examples of this old-new paradigm.

Orientalism and counterinsurgency

There is a long tradition of military orientalism that counterposes different cultures of war, 'Occidental' and 'Oriental,' but there are other versions that seek to capitalize on a wider cultural knowledge of 'the Orient' that can also be traced to a colonial past but which continue to haunt military operations in 'the new counterinsurgency era.'[15] Counterinsurgency has a complex colonial genealogy but its most recent incarnation seeks to 'weaponize' culture itself.[16] Most discussions of this cultural turn fasten on the revised counterinsurgency doctrine issued jointly by the U.S. Army and Marine Corps in December 2006.[17] There are good reasons for this, not least the orchestrated fanfare of publicity that heralded its publication, but the new canon is not limited to a single text and counterinsurgency is not a purely textual construction: there are many differences, slippages and even reversals in the turbulent passages between doctrine, training and operations.

For these reasons (and others) counterinsurgency cannot be reduced to orientalism. But one of the most direct routes across the crowded terrain from orientalism to optics, from claims about Afghan and Iraqi culture to the scopic regimes that shape the conduct of American counterinsurgency, is through the figure of T.E. Lawrence: 'Lawrence of Arabia.' There are few modern experts in this 'graduate level of war' who do not acknowledge their debt to him. The title of an influential book on counterinsurgency, *Learning to Eat Soup with a Knife*, was taken from Lawrence's description of 'making war on rebellion' in *Seven Pillars of Wisdom*, and I doubt it is a coincidence that the U.S. Army's cultural war machine, the Human Terrain System, was based on 'seven pillars.' Its lead authors prescribed Lawrence as 'standard reading,' and a pre-deployment Primer reprinted his famous '27 Articles,' field notes which Lawrence saw as 'stalking horses for beginners in the Arab armies' that uncovered 'the secret of handling Arabs.' The seminal memorandum on counterinsurgency, written by General Petraeus's senior counterinsurgency adviser, went one better: '28 Articles.' Kilcullen's admiration for, even identification with Lawrence could not be plainer. No army will ever have 'more than a small number of individuals' with a gift for 'cultural leverage,' he wrote: mavericks 'in the mould of Lawrence.'[18]

This is more than intellectual homage.[19] For Lawrence is a powerful symbol of a close encounter with an other who remains obdurately Other. His talismanic invocation repeats the classical orientalist gesture of rendering 'the Orient' timeless: taking Lawrence as your guide to insurgency in modern Baghdad is like having Mark Twain show you round Las Vegas. Not surprisingly, both Iraq and Afghanistan are reduced to 'tribal society'—cartoons masquerading as anthropology[20]—and while the new doctrine acknowledges that 'American ideas of what is "normal" or "rational" are not universal' (perhaps the single most remarkable sentence in the manual) it leaves no doubt about whose ideas are 'right.'[21] In myriad ways the cultural turn continues the exorbitation of cultural difference that is at the heart of orientalism. It acknowledges that there are cultural practices and values to be understood—the Other is no longer an incomprehensible threat or an opaque signifier—but it locates these in a separate space that provides little accommodation for commonality, mutuality or transculturation. The emphasis on cultural difference—the attempt to hold the Other at a distance while claiming to cross the interpretative divide—produces a diagram in which violence has its origins in 'their' space, which the cultural turn endlessly partitions through its preoccupation with ethno-sectarian or tribal division, while the impulse to understand is confined to 'our' space, constructed as open, unitary and generous: the locus of a hermeneutic invitation that can never be reciprocated.[22]

When the new doctrine was published its focus was on ground operations; air operations were relegated to a supporting role outlined in the last appendix.[23] These may seem a world away from Lawrence, but long before he resigned his Army commission and re-enlisted in the Royal Air Force, he had been drawn to the wide open spaces of the sky as well as those of the desert. Deer suggests that in Lawrence's personal mythology 'air control in the Middle East offered a redemptive postscript to his role in the Arab Revolt of 1916–18.' He imagined the Arab Revolt 'as a kind of modernist vortex,' Deer argues, fluid and dynamic, 'without front or back,' and in *Seven Pillars* he recommended 'not disclosing ourselves till we attack.' To Lawrence, and to many others at the time, the intimation of a nomadic future war gave air power a special significance. 'What the Arabs did yesterday,' he wrote, 'the Air Forces may do tomorrow—yet more swiftly.' As Satia has shown, the practical implementation of this aspiration rested not only on a military orientalism that distinguished different ways of war but also on a cultural orientalism that represented bombing as signally appropriate to the people of these lands. This was, minimally, about intelligence, surveillance and reconnaissance. 'According to this perverse logic,' Satia explains, 'the RAF's successful persecution of a village testified to their intimacy with the people on the ground, without which they would not have been able to strike it accurately.' More than this, however, 'the claim to empathy ultimately underwrote the entire air control system with its authoritative reassurances that bombardment was a tactic that would be respected and expected in this unique land.' From this perspective, Satia continues, Arabs would see bombing as 'pulling the strings of fate from the sky.' They understood it 'not as punishment,' Lawrence informed his readers, 'but as misfortune from heaven striking the community.' And if women and children were killed in the process that was supposedly of little consequence to them: what mattered were the deaths of 'the really important men.'[24] As far as I know, Lawrence has not been invoked by any of the contemporary advocates of airpower in counterinsurgency, but many of these formulations, translated into an ostensibly scientific vocabulary, reappear in debates about the deployment of remotely piloted aircraft in Afghanistan. Their mission is not only to provide intelligence through their persistent presence over the war zone but to capitalize on that knowledge to conduct precision strikes; and many of those strikes, especially those conducted across the border in Pakistan by the CIA, were initially directed (im) precisely at killing 'high value targets': that is, 'the really important men.'

If Lawrence casts a long shadow, however, it is refracted through the prism of a decidedly contemporary counterinsurgency whose techno-cultural apparatus has transformed the battle space in two ways. First, conventional warfare has traditionally been fought in territorial terms that require the detection, capture or destruction of determinate objectives like buildings, gun batteries or missile silos that are for the most part fixed, whereas counterinsurgency is fought within a multi-dimensional battle space in which the contours of the enemy are indeterminate and fluid. This has necessitated the development of visual technologies that can overlay the object-ontology of conventional warfare with an event-ontology adequate to the speed at which these hybrid, late modern wars are conducted. Second, this in its turn has involved the operationalization of a scopic regime that is supposed to make the battle space transparent to the military gaze. Because counterinsurgency is now as much about the population as the insurgents—because it involves anatomizing the population, tracking the movements of insurgents through the population and their interactions with the population—it becomes necessary to expose the 'human terrain' to view in an intimate, continuous and time-critical manner. To probe the recesses of everyday life like this needs more than 'intelligence from three-letter agencies and satellite photographs,' as one colonel recognized, but it also involves more than Kilcullen's 'conflict ethnography' whose desire to expose the micro-details of the war zone mimics what Bickford calls 'the panoptic conceits of early anthropology.'[25] At the limit, as we will see, it requires a techno-cultural apparatus that can secure a militarized regime of comprehensive and constant hypervisibility, which Gordon defines as 'a kind of obscenity of accuracy that abolishes the distinctions between "permission and prohibition, presence and absence."'[26]

Securing Baghdad: counterinsurgency and the 'event-ful' city[27]

Visuality has played a central role in the implementation of the new counterinsurgency doctrine. On Mirzoeff's reading the field manual invokes a 'sovereign visuality' through which the commander is endowed with the capacity to see the battlespace as a totality, while unfamiliar territory (the 'human terrain') is transformed into 'a simulacrum of a video game' that subordinates can navigate with supreme confidence.[28] The first claim is broadly correct, though it is not peculiar to the Petraeus doctrine; its operationalization can be seen in the Command Post of the Future (CPOF), which was tested in Baghdad from 2004 and was specifically designed to allow commanders to see 'anywhere in the battlespace.' But the second claim needs qualification. The military uses video games in its pre-deployment training; but once in theatre troops move through a landscape where the rules of the game are constantly changing and they need to share their experiences with an immediacy that short-circuits the vertical protocols of the 'top-down view of the world' that characterizes what Mirzoeff calls 'command visualization.' In this regard the exemplary visual system is the Tactical Ground Reporting Network (TIGR).

CPOF is a networked visualization and collaboration system, a sort of super Geographical Information System, which was first used by the First Cavalry to track the real-time movement of troops and the incidence of events across the city (*Figure 8.1*). The effect was to produce Baghdad as what Croser calls the 'battlespace multiple' or the 'event-ful' city. In contrast to visualizations derived from static databases, CPOF operates on live data so its multiple screen images 'do not cohere but exist layered (side by side), and do not stay the same but alter moment to moment.' Within this system, Baghdad was 'never resolved into a single, definite picture,' therefore, and the battlespace was made to appear as 'constantly updated, fluid and always in the process of construction.'[29] While CPOF thus demanded 'the constant attention of users through its running display of the present'— what Croser calls its 'present-ing' of the battlespace—it could not specify 'which element of the present should be addressed at any given moment.' In order to prioritize the image stream, to navigate the digital city, users sought out events that disrupted the physical, almost physiological city,

Figure 8.1: Command Post of the Future (courtesy of U.S. Army).

scanning the screens for markers of 'abnormal functioning and distorted flows.'[30] This filtering allowed the military to assert visual and hence—at least in principle—operational control over the contingent, which is the fulcrum of late modern security practices. In Baghdad, those practices required a continuous audit that compiled Significant Activity Reports and correlated the incidence of those 'enemy actions' with a series of civil, commercial and environmental indicators of the population. Counterinsurgency involves the simultaneous pursuit of 'kinetic' (lethal) and 'non-kinetic' (reconstruction) operations, and these multiple, overlapping lines of operation reappeared on the multiple screens of the CPOF, so that there was a close correspondence between the technical and the conceptual. In Croser's view, therefore, 'CPOF was in some ways the perfect technology for [counterinsurgency] operations.'[31]

CPOF is a command-level system, however, and counterinsurgency also requires a closely textured local knowledge. The First Cavalry established a secure intranet to share reports among its patrols, and by 2007 CAVNET had been developed into the multimedia TIGR. This was a crowd-sourced virtual notebook, a militarized combination of Google Earth and a Wiki, into which troops uploaded their own digital images, videos and field observations to produce a different kind of collaborative database. Like CPOF, TIGR provided a map-based interface that allows users to pull back events, people and places along a patrol route or within a district (*Figure 8.2*). Unlike CPOF, however, the system was predicated on the rapid, horizontal transmission of information rather than the hierarchical chain of command and control. The transition from a sovereign model of information to a capillary model, where the threshold of visibility is lowered towards the close-in, meshed with the intrusive intimacy of the new counterinsurgency doctrine. It also reinforced the production of Baghdad as an event-ful city by inverting the pyramid in which satellite feeds and imagery from drones and other centralized resources were analyzed at command levels and filtered down to troops on the street, and substituting a much more fluid, 'just-in-time' system of monitoring, analysis and decision.

Bush's Baghdad was hardly the Corsican's Cairo, and the Iraqi capital was seen as a (degraded) modern city rather than an orientalist labyrinth. But the Americans had as much trouble reading its flickering signs as the French had had in Cairo, and the U.S. Army was just as determined to open the occupied city to its gaze. These two visual technologies, in concert with

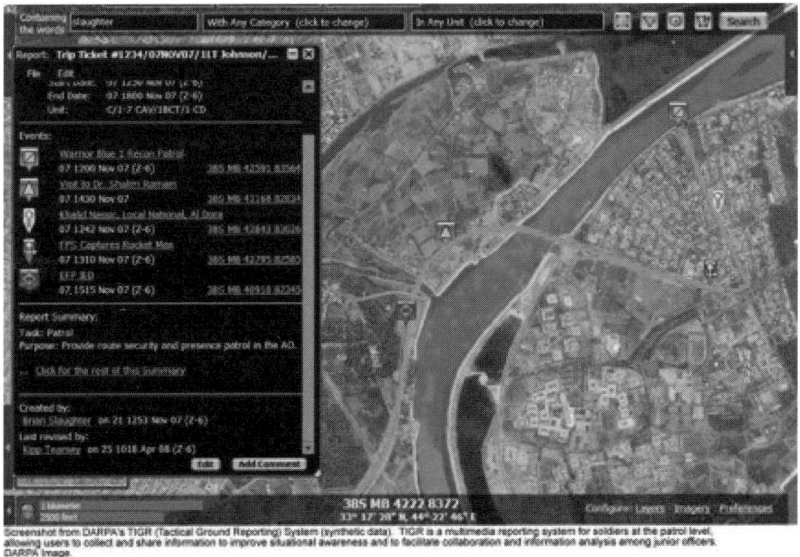

Figure 8.2: Tactical Ground Reporting Network screenshot (courtesy of DARPA).

others like the biometric scanning of the local population, provided a more intimate mapping than Napoleon's *ingénieurs-géographes* could ever have imagined: fluid rather than fixed, live rather than dead, interrogatory rather than inert. Yet when their mappings were re-presented to public audiences, their liquidity congealed into the conventional map. While the new systems produced Baghdad as 'messy, complex and ever-mutable,' capturing the quicksilver capacity of the insurgency, the public assertion of command—the public performance of that crucial operational competence—required the event-ful city to be staged as an ordered, coherent totality. This was achieved by exporting these mappings of the city to cartographies displayed at Press Briefings that worked to stabilize Baghdad visually, imaginatively and rhetorically.

As the violence in Baghdad intensified through 2006, it became increasingly dangerous for journalists to chase their own stories, and this gave the Press Briefings conducted by Multi-National Force in the Green Zone an extraordinary power. Briefers constantly asserted that only the U.S. military

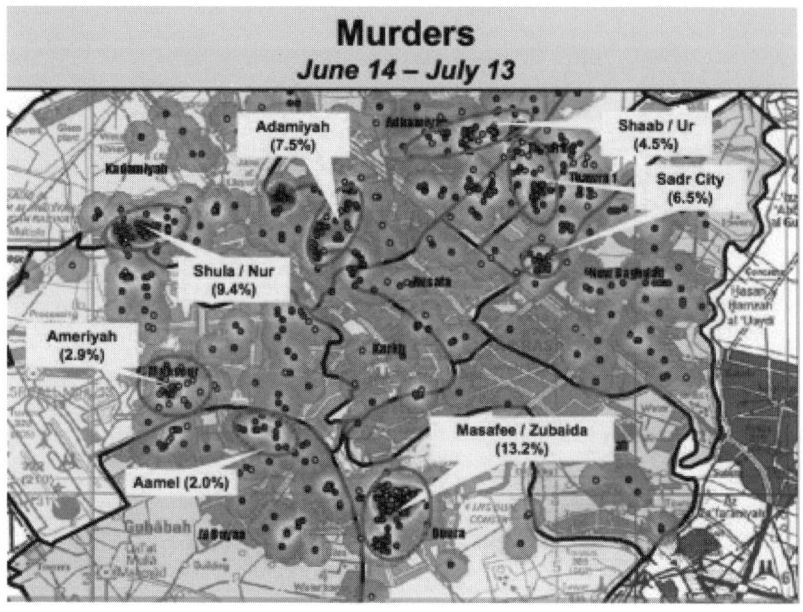

Figure 8.3: Murders in Baghdad, June 14–July 13, 2006 (courtesy of MNF-Iraq).

had the capacity for 'top sight'—the ability to integrate reporting chains 'at the top' and so see the city as a whole—and only the U.S. military could guarantee 'ground truth' through its armed patrols and aerial surveillance. This is the summation of 'sovereign visuality' whose counterpart is what Jacob calls the 'sovereign map.'[32] At these briefings Baghdad was staged cartographically through two sorts of plots: fleeting traces of terrorist and insurgent activity (*Figure 8.3*) and tracks of military operations against al-Qaeda in Iraq, insurgent cells and death squads (*Figure 8.4*).

The connection between top sight and ground truth was established by the metaphor of 'walking' reporters through the maps, a trope that became so commonplace that the distinction between the battle space and its representations was virtually erased. The conflation of map and city made it possible to walk through a virtual Baghdad at a time when it was desperately dangerous to walk through the physical city. But the reality-effect operated on another level too, because the parade of maps suggested that the event-ful city was known by virtue of being mapped. The storyboards

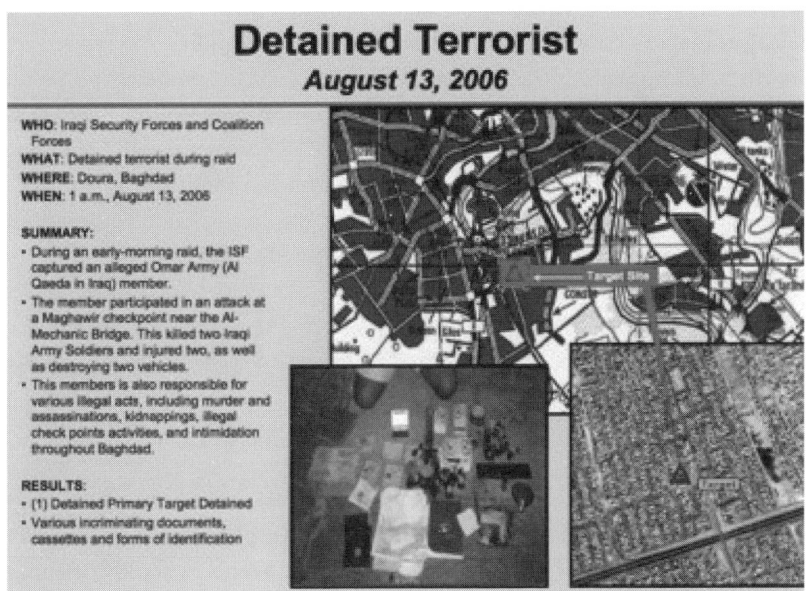

Figure 8.4: Detention of a terrorist, August 13, 2006 (courtesy of MNF Iraq).

were carefully composed and the spaces in which events occurred were calibrated, coded and located within a hierarchically nested grid put in place through maps and surveillance imagery (*Figure 8.4*). As Amoore notes, visualization strategies like these 'secure the presence' of an eternal, rational observer' with the power—the conjunction of Reason and resources—to bring order to the disordered.[33] The counter-view is put most succinctly by a subaltern in William Boyd's *Ice-Cream War* who finds himself in a war-zone for the first time: 'Gabriel thought maps should be banned. They gave the world an order and a reasonableness which it didn't possess.' But that was precisely the (counter)point: the maps were offered as a visible sign of operational competence, confirming the military's capacity to be on top of what was going down.

These mappings produced the city as a space pockmarked by and constituted through cascades of events that could be generalized into smooth surfaces that captured the intensification or diminution of the violence (*Figure 8.5*). If Baghdad was not reduced to the object-space of conventional combat, however, neither was it seen as the emergent field of practices that would have been consistent with a culturally informed analysis. Instead, within this event-ontology the framing narrative—the 'command message'—was one in which the actions of 'the enemy,' exhibited on one series of maps, were confounded by the actions of the military, exhibited on another. Interpretation was confined to a stark dualism, endlessly repeated, in which the intentions of 'the enemy' were contrasted with the aspirations of 'the people,' a strategy that repositioned the U.S. Army above the fray, watching over, making sense of but ultimately not responsible for the situation. It was as though the orientalist project was in suspended animation: the monstrous violence of the Other was captured—'framed'—by the map but it could not be contained by the military; the city-as-represented was ordered but the city-as-operationalized was spiraling out of control; and the 'abnormal functionings' displayed on CPOF screens were fast becoming the new normal on the streets.

From a view to a kill: drones and counterinsurgency in Afghanistan[34]

Less than a month after 9/11, one of Britain's most prominent military historians offered an explanation of those terrible events in starkly orientalist terms. 'Westerners fight face to face, in stand-up battle, and go on until one side or the other gives in,' Sir John Keegan declared, while 'Orientals,

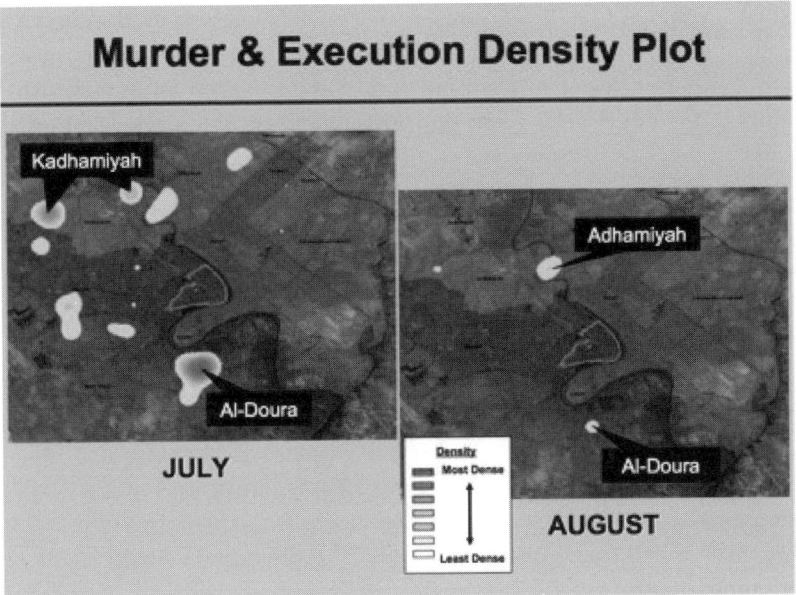

Figure 8.5: Murders and executions in Baghdad, July-August 2006 (courtesy of MNF-Iraq).

by contrast, shrink from pitched battle, which they often deride as a sort of game, preferring ambush, surprise, treachery and deceit as the best way to overcome an enemy.' On September 11, the 'Oriental' way of war 'returned in an absolutely traditional form. Arabs, appearing suddenly out of empty space like their desert raider ancestors, assaulted the heartlands of Western power in a terrifying surprise raid and did appalling damage.' He went on to claim that 'this war belongs within the much larger spectrum of a far older conflict between settled, creative, productive Westerners and preda-tory, destructive Orientals.'[35] With exquisite irony, on the same day that Keegan was composing his column the United States flew its first armed Predator mission over Kabul and Kandahar.

Keegan's intervention was not only absurdly racist; it conspicuously failed to recognize the predatory nature of the 'new imperialism.'[36] This was scarcely surprising for someone of Keegan's political views, but it was strange for him to ignore the military transformations of the last thirty years. Also writing in the shadow of the Twin Towers—and, let us not for-get, the Pentagon—Bauman offered a contrary, far more convincing reading when he argued that 'globalizing wars' conducted by advanced militaries were 'reminiscent of the warfare strategy of nomadic tribes' and depended on an 'ability to descend from nowhere without notice and vanish again without warning.'[37] This is the return of Lawrence with a vengeance, and Bauman saw this haunting as part of an aggressive re-enchantment of late modern war:

> Remote as they are from their targets, scurrying over those they hit too fast to witness the devastation they cause and the blood they spill, the pilots-turned-computer-operators hardly ever have a chance of looking their victims in the face and to survey the human misery they have sowed. Military professionals of our time see no corpses and no wounds.[38]

This was true of the high-level bombing campaign that preceded the invasion of Afghanistan, conducted by conventional aircraft and long-range missiles, which Feldman castigated as a 'new Orientalism.'[39] But it was—and remains—a far cry from the brutal intimacy of counterinsurgency on the ground. To many critics, however, the subsequent deployment of remotely piloted aircraft has made that optical detachment even more complete. Although these Unmanned Aerial Vehicles (UAVs) are launched from airbases in Afghanistan, most of their missions are controlled via Ku-band satellite link by operators in a Ground Control Station at Creech Air Force Base in Nevada.[40] When Robert Kaplan visited the base, he was told: 'Inside that trailer is Iraq, inside the other, Afghanistan.' The sense of time-space compression is exceeded only by its casual imperialism. 'Inside those trailers,' Kaplan explained, 'you leave North America, which falls under Northern Command, and enter the Middle East, the domain of Central Command. So much for the tyranny of geography.'[41] But critics insist that this replaces one tyranny of geography with another. The death of distance enables death from a distance, and these remotely piloted missions not only project power without vulnerability—as the Air Force frequently asserts—but also without compunction. Distance lends re-enchantment, you might say. Some see this as appallingly mundane—disparaging the pilots as cubicle warriors or commuter fighters—but others sense a no less terrifying Olympian power released through the UAV's Hellfire missiles. 'Sometimes I felt like a God hurling thunderbolts from afar,' one pilot admits, and Engelhardt spells out the metaphor's grim implications: 'Those about whom we make life-or-death decisions, as they scurry below or carry on as best they can, have—like any beings faced with the gods—no recourse or appeal.'[42]

As the Predators and Reapers flown by the USAF have become more closely integrated into counterinsurgency, however, that picture has become more complicated. The Air Force estimates that counterinsurgency requires three to four times as much intelligence, surveillance and reconnaissance (ISR) as major combat operations because it involves a fluid target set that requires the much longer dwell times that only UAVs can sustain. Ground operators can be changed at the end of a shift while the aircraft remains on station and the video stream is uninterrupted. In such circumstances ISR needs to be not only persistent but also pervasive: at the limit, 'gathering intelligence on fast, fleeting, hidden and unpredictable adversaries requires knowledge of everyone, everywhere, all the time.'[43] The multi-spectral targeting system in the Predator provides real-time full-motion video (FMV) at 30 frames per second, but its field of view is restricted and observers complain that zooming in is like looking through a soda straw. This has changed with the introduction of the Gorgon Stare, which provides lower resolution images (five cameras each shooting two sixteen-megapixel frames per second) but will stream sixty-five motion video feeds from a single Reaper by the end of 2012. The image streams will be quilted in-flight into a tiled mosaic and fed to networked users through a dedicated ground station in theatre that will control the sensors and coordinate operations with

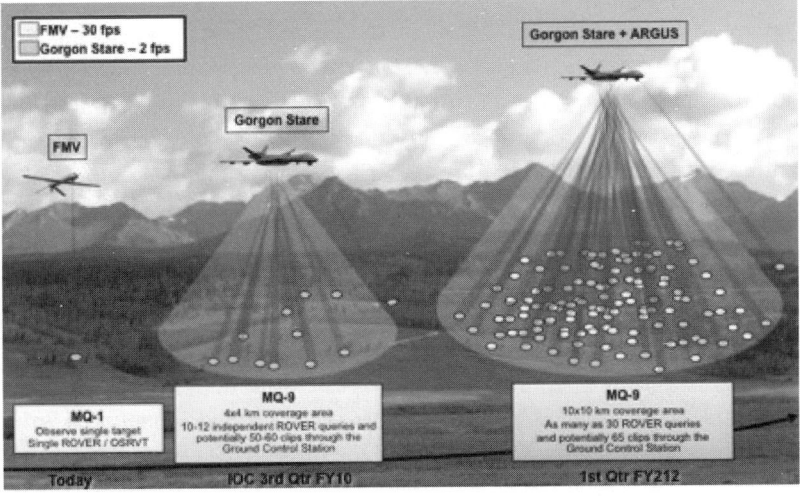

Figure 8.6: Wide-Area Airborne Surveillance (courtesy of USAF).

the flight crew in Nevada (who will still rely on the Reaper's sensor ball). The move to wide area surveillance will be reinforced with the introduction of the ARGUS-IS system, which will reintroduce high-resolution images; its multi-gigapixel sensor has a refresh rate of fifteen frames per second. These developments will allow individuals and movements to be tracked through multiple networks to establish a 'pattern of life' consistent with an emerging paradigm of 'activity-based intelligence' that is focal for counterinsurgency operations.[44]

The production of a macro-field of micro-vision solves one problem by creating another, however, and the USAF has become keenly aware of the danger of 'swimming in sensors and drowning in data.'[45] This is the same problem as the 'present-ing' of the battlespace on CPOF but multiplied and magnified thousands of times: in effect, Said's 'panopticism' and 'dizzying detail' transformed into techno-vertigo. A standard video camera collects over 100,000 image frames per hour, and the USAF has already archived 400,000 hours of video from its remote platforms; the rate of accession is rapidly accelerating as ISR coverage increases. To manage this image surge, the analytical field has been expanded. UAV operators in the United States are embedded in an extended network that includes not only Joint Terminal Attack Controllers on the ground in Afghanistan, but also senior commanders, mission controllers and military lawyers at CENTCOM's Combined Air and Space Operations Center at Al Udeid Air Base in Qatar, and data analysts and image technicians at its Distributed Common Ground System at Langley Air Force Base in the United States. Like CPOF this network performs two vital tasks. First, archived images are scanned to filter out 'uneventful footage' and distinguish 'normal' from 'abnormal activity.' Ideally this so-called forensic monitoring is based on some sort of cultural knowledge, but the image bank is so vast that experiments are under way with automated software systems for 'truthing' and annotating video imagery, and new TV technologies are being explored to tag and retrieve images. Second, live video streams are scanned to push time-critical information to UAV crews and troops who are responding to emergent events. These developments reinforce the rush to the intimate that characterizes counterinsurgency operations, but in this case the emphasis is as much on 'the rush' as 'the intimate.' The hierarchies of the network are flat and fluid, its spaces complex and compound, and the missions are executed through video feeds and online chat rooms that bring a series of personnel with different skills in different locations into the same zone. Time and space are telescoped so that, as one officer put it, 'We're mostly online with each other as we go.'[46]

The network is more than a late modern version of Mitchell's 'viewing platform,' the apotheosis of the desire to see and not be seen, because it is also a weapon system. The UAVs also fulfill the hunter-killer role conveyed by their hideous names.[47] The Predator carries two Hellfire missiles, and the Reaper can carry fourteen Hellfire missiles or two 500lb JDAM bombs and four Hellfire missiles. The information liquidity facilitated by the network has not made 'bombing at the speed of thought' a reality but it has dramatically compressed what the USAF calls the 'kill-chain' (*Figure 8.7*).[48] The networked kill-chain can be thought of as a dispersed and distributed apparatus, a congeries of actors, objects, practices, discourses and affects, that entrains the people who are made part of it and constitutes them as particular kinds of subjects.[49] During the Second World War and much of the Cold War the kill-chain was linear and sequential, directed mainly at fixed and pre-determined targets, and the time from identification to execution could extend over days or even weeks. Few of those involved could see the process in its entirety, which explains the commingling of what Harris calls 'the mundane and the monstrously violent.' The apparatus through which

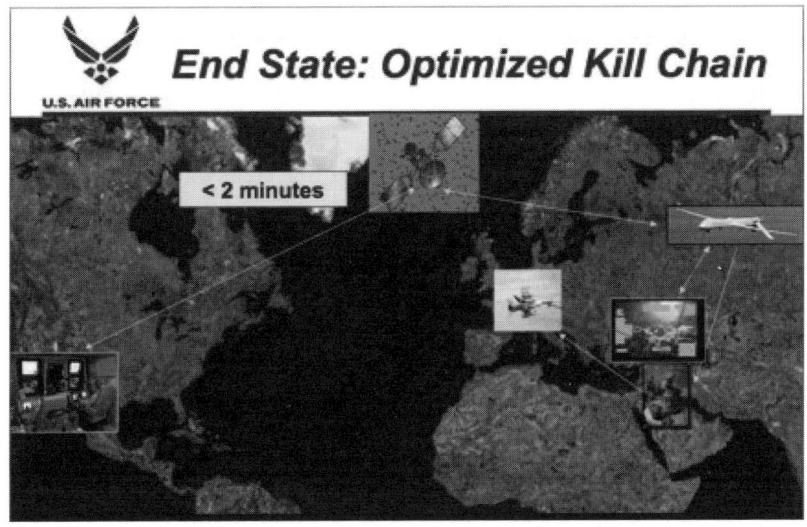

Figure 8.7: 'Optimized kill-chain' (courtesy of USAF).

the target was produced and passed through the links in the chain rendered the business of destruction unexceptional: 'extreme forms of violence and normal bureaucratic practices' were made 'co-extensive.'[50] The late modern kill-chain is increasingly directed at mobile and emergent targets, and the time-space compression that this entails has brought all those in the network much closer to the killing space. 'Traditional bomber pilots don't see their targets,' explains Singer, but in contrast to Bauman's characterization of 'pilots-turned-computer-operators,' he insists that those watching a UAV mission in near-real time 'see the target up close, [they] see what happens to it during the explosion and the aftermath. You're further away physically but you see more.'[51] In fact a constant refrain of those working from Nevada is that they are not 'further away' at all but only eighteen inches from the battlefield: the distance between eye and screen. This sensation is partly the product of the deliberate inculcation of a 'warrior culture' among UAV pilots, but it is also partly a product of interpellation, of being drawn into and captured by the visual field itself.

For this reason, characterizations of the remote missions as moments in a 'video war' that inculcates a 'Playstation mentality to killing' may be wide of the mark.[52] Critics often point to Grossman's study of 'learning to kill,' which identified distance as a powerful means of overcoming the resistance to killing. He pointed to first-person shooter video games as powerful agents of conditioning through which players become 'hardwired' for killing, and his anatomy of killing listed not only physical distance but also emotional distance, including social, cultural, moral and, crucially, 'mechanical' distance: the screen that separates the gamer from the game.[53] It seems a small step to infer that the long-distance killing of late modern war would radicalize those affective protections. Yet video games do not stage violence as passive spectacle; on the contrary, they are profoundly immersive, which is in part why the U.S. military uses them in its pre-deployment training.[54] The live video streams from the UAVs seem to produce the same reality-effect. 'You see a lot of detail,' one officer notes, so 'we feel it, maybe not to the same degree [as] if we were actually there, but it affects us.' 'When you let a missile go,' he explains, 'you know that's real life—there's no reset button.' At least one Predator pilot insists that the horror of watching two young boys on a bicycle ride into the frame seconds before his missile struck its designated target 'lost none of its impact' from being viewed on a screen: 'Death observed was still *death*.' Anecdotes cannot settle the matter, but reports of drone crews suffering from PTSD induced by constant exposure to high-resolution images of real-time killing and the after-action inventory of body parts should not be dismissed.[55]

There are also vital differences between video games and video feeds. Commercial video games staged in simulacra of Afghanistan show stylized landscapes prowled solely by 'insurgents' or 'terrorists' whose cartoonish appearance makes them instantly recognizable; the neo-orientalism of these renditions is a matter of dismal record.[56] But the video feeds from UAVs reveal a much more complicated, inhabited landscape in which distinctions between civilians and combatants become intensely problematic. The existence of so many extra eyes in that crowded sky—analysts, controllers, commanders and, significantly, military layers—is a (pre)caution that the presence of civilians is a constant possibility. The risk of 'collateral damage' has become a vital consideration throughout the kill-chain, driven by both the protocols of international law and also the prospect of international scrutiny. This marks another crucial difference between video games and video feeds because, as Grossman acknowledges, killing in combat is regulated by rules and legal sanctions, and defenders of the UAV missions routinely draw attention to the laws of armed conflict, the Uniform Code of Military Justice and the Rules of Engagement that govern them. Indeed, one informed commentator argues that the longer dwell times and enhanced video streams from the UAVs have considerably enlarged the role of military lawyers who provide expert counsel to commanders about the 'prosecution' of a target.[57] For deliberate targeting (where targets are typically developed over 36–40 hours) judge advocates review target folders, including imagery, collateral damage estimates and the weaponeering solutions proposed to mitigate those effects, and monitor the continued development of the target. For dynamic targeting the procedure is compressed (a matter of minutes) because the targets are time-sensitive, but a judge advocate must still validate the target. In both cases judge advocates are stationed on the combat operations floor of the Combined Air Operations Center to scrutinize image streams and live communications and inform the commander of the legal parameters of any attack. In consequence one senior judge advocate boasts that he and his colleagues 'explicitly guarantee extra benefits to civilians.'[58] This is too glib by far, and Beard makes it clear that these precautions (like the laws from which they derive) are not intended to prevent all civilians from being killed during military operations. The principle of discrimination between civilians and combatants is qualified by the principle of proportionality. This means that sometimes civilian deaths are accidental—the system is far from perfect—but in others they are incidental to what is deemed to be concrete and direct military advantage, in which case they have been anticipated in collateral damage estimates and endorsed by judge advocates.[59] The *Wall Street Journal* maintains that this heightened scrutiny makes 'for a more moral campaign': 'Never before in the history of air warfare have we been able to distinguish as well between combatants and civilians as we can with drones.'[60]

And yet when Beard writes repeatedly of the unprecedented level of 'transparency' made possible by the new visual technologies he is referring to the new visibility of military actions—to their exposure to public view—and to the possibility of sanctions if the laws of armed conflict are breached: not to the visibility of the battlespace.[61] This matters because contemporary counterinsurgency is often described as 'war amongst the people,' where it is constitutively difficult to distinguish between combatants and civilians. As the Pentagon's Defense Science Board noted: 'Enemy leaders look like everyone else; enemy combatants look like everyone else; enemy vehicles look like civilian vehicles; enemy installations look like civilian installations; enemy equipment and materials look like civilian equipment and materials...'[62] This central, existential problem would remain even if the battlespace could be made fully transparent. It may be mitigated by the persistent presence of UAVs and their enhanced ISR capability, and in some measure by the 'pattern of life' analysis this makes possible, but it cannot be erased.[63]

In fact, the 'intimacy' of time-space compression produced by the new visual technologies is highly selective. When a journalist compared the chat-rooms of the kill-chain to Facebook and marveled at 'how easily the distance could melt away,' he was describing the intimacy inculcated among those enrolled in the network. When officers at Creech told him that 'the amount of time spent surveying an area' from a UAV creates 'a greater sense of intimacy' than is possible from conventional aircraft, they were describing not their identification of a target but their identification with American ground troops. 'There's no detachment,' their commander explained. 'Those employing the system are very involved at a personal level in combat. You hear the AK-47 going off, the intensity of the voice on the radio calling for help. You're looking at him, 18 inches away from him, trying everything in your capability to get that person out of trouble.' Similarly, when a Predator pilot claimed that 'I *knew* people down there,' it was not local people he claimed to 'know': 'Each day through my cameras I snooped around and came to recognize the faces and figures of our soldiers and marines.' As these examples indicate, high-resolution imagery is not a uniquely technical capacity but part of a techno-cultural system that renders 'our' space familiar, even in 'their' space—which remains obdurately Other.[64]

Beard's point about the visibility of military actions is well taken, however, because there is another sense in which counterinsurgency is war amongst the people: the presence of the media means that the fight is conducted 'in every living room in the world as well as on the streets and fields of a conflict zone.'[65] In the face of the difficulty of distinguishing combatants, it is scarcely surprising that several tactics should have been used to mitigate the effects of civilian casualties on public opinion. The first is to dispute their civilian status and to call for a revision of international law to recognize what Dershowitz calls 'a continuum of civiliality' that would draw a 'line of complicity' between 'innocent' and 'non-innocent' civilians.[66] Despite the difficulties of distinguishing combatants from civilians, the civilian population can apparently be parsed. Referring explicitly to the use of UAVs to carry out targeted killings, Etzioni has proposed an identical distinction between 'innocent civilians' and 'abusive civilians' who 'refuse to separate themselves from the local population'; in doing so they forfeit their right to protection, he argued, and the responsibility for the deaths of the 'truly innocent' is theirs alone.[67] The U.S. military has not endorsed these maneuvers but its own casualty estimates, when they are released, reveal a remarkable ability to distinguish insurgents from civilians.

Second, while the new air war is not quite the 'war without witnesses' of the American invasion of Afghanistan in 2001, the space in which these continuing operations have been brought into public view is nevertheless strikingly limited. Media coverage in North America and Europe has focused on the spaces of the extended network, particularly Creech and the CAOC, while the space of the target has been radically underexposed. The Air Force issues terse daily airpower summaries in which Predators and Reapers provide 'armed overwatch for friendly forces' and 'release precision-guided munitions' that successfully attack 'enemy positions,' 'targets' and 'vehicles.' This is an artful reassertion of a conventional object-ontology in which ground truth vanishes in the ultimate 'God-trick,' whose vengeance depends on making its objects visible and its subjects invisible. This is compounded by the absence of the vigorous local press coverage of drone strikes across the border in Pakistan where, ironically, we consequently know much more about the impact of the CIA's 'secret war' (and correspondingly rather less about its kill-chain).

And, as I must finally show, there is one more move.

War, orientalism and biopolitics

In many ways the separations of the exhibitionary order—the world as exhibition now mutated into the world as target—have been compromised by visual technologies that both propel and make possible the intimacy of contemporary counterinsurgency. But even as those separations are dissolved they are reinstated; the screen morphs into the sovereign map, 'our space' is partitioned from 'their' space, and event-ontology reverts to object-ontology. These transformations are reinforced by a metaphoric that reactivates the performances of orientalism in concert with this new techno-cultural apparatus.

If orientalism produces 'the Orient' as a space of disorder, Euro-American diplomatic and geopolitical discourses have often produced the 'Middle East' as a corollary space of disease. From the middle of the nineteenth century the major powers treated the Ottoman Empire as a 'sick man,' hemorrhaging territories in an epidemic of disastrous wars, and in the early twentieth century Britain and France joined forces to impose their own 'cure.' Sir Mark Sykes, who negotiated the agreement with François-Georges Picot to partition the post-Ottoman Middle East between Britain and France—and evidently no stranger to the performative power of mapping—described their remedy as 'cutting out the cancer.'[68]

The metaphor has proved to be remarkably durable, and its rhetorical power has been enhanced through these new, advanced mappings that are so many performances of an intrinsically biopolitical field. Displays like *Figure 8.5*, for example, are the product of a smoothing algorithm that converts point data into a continuous surface. The technique was used to produce the maps of ethno-sectarian violence in Baghdad displayed by Petraeus in his reports to Congress in September 2007 and April 2008. These maps closely, even deliberately resemble medical scans of the body politic, so that violence is visualized as a series of tumors, and it is no accident that Petraeus described it as 'a cancer that continues to spread if left unchecked.'[69] The same techniques are used to visualize insurgent attacks in Afghanistan, and the same metaphor is deployed. Lt. General William Caldwell, who conducted many of the Press Briefings in Baghdad, now serves in Kabul, and he has provided an astonishing prescription for 'curing Afghanistan.' In his view, combat operations in Afghanistan should no longer be described 'in the language of war'; instead Afghanistan should be treated as 'an ailing patient—in many ways analogous to a weakened person under attack by an aggressive infection.' Caldwell describes the surge of combat troops and the increase in offensive operations as 'a late but powerful and much-needed dose of antibiotics' designed 'to allow the country's indigenous immune system to be restored.' He concedes that, 'similar to a powerful antibiotic, the use of large numbers of combat troops brings with it side effects that can cause discomfort and pain to the body politic of Afghanistan. The effects range from disruption of civilian day-to-day life to, regrettably, sometimes civilian casualties.' But Caldwell is adamant that 'senior NATO commanders seek to minimize civilian casualties and thus apply combat power with restraint and, to the extent possible, surgical precision.'[70] Kilcullen had anticipated this bio-medical diagnosis when he described the stages of counterinsurgency as infection, contagion, intervention and rejection. 'I use a medical analogy advisedly here,' he explained, to render insurgency in the language of 'immune systems.' The oncological metaphor raises the stakes much higher, of course, and licenses even more drastic measures: the Army Field Manual compares counterinsurgents to 'surgeons cutting out cancerous tissue while keeping other vital organs intact.'[71]

These are simple models and you might think that in these elementary forms nothing much turns on them. But they matter for two reasons. First, their techno-cultural translation into maps, screens and displays underscores the performative role of what Foucault once called the 'nomination of the visible.' The capacity to produce a target—to detect a 'tumor'—by rational-scientific means becomes inseparable from a series of truth-claims about the danger posed by the target-tumor. The lexicon has mutated—danger into risk, prevention into pre-emption, detection into destruction—and the tumor has metastasized: by November 2009 Obama was warning that 'the cancer is in Pakistan.' The aggressive propensity of biopolitics has been aggravated throughout these transformations—the second reason these tropes matter—because they make military violence appear to be intrinsically therapeutic. As the oncological metaphor depoliticizes and pathologizes insurgency, so it turns counterinsurgency's kinetic operations on the ground or in the air into chemotherapy—Caldwell's 'side-effects' that can cause 'discomfort and pain': killing insurgent cells and sometimes innocent bodies to save the body politic. Martial biopolitics and military orientalism march in lockstep through spaces of constructed visibility that are also always spaces of constructed *in*visibility.

9

NESTING ORIENTALISMS AT WAR

WORLD WAR II AND THE 'MEMORY WAR' IN EASTERN EUROPE

Maria Mälksoo *

This chapter argues that the contemporary 'war' over the remembrance of the legacy of the Second World War between Russia and its former satellites in Central and Eastern Europe is an example of nesting orientalisms at work where both 'fronts' regard each other as less European/civilized/developed than oneself. Milica Bakič-Hayden's notion of 'nesting Orientalisms,' extending on Edward Said's model of classical colonial orientalism, addresses the gradation of this type of marginalization, the construction of hierarchies of 'easternness' and 'otherness' in series running from west to east and south.[1] She demonstrates in relation to the Balkans, how the construction of an 'other' involves orientalization by those who have themselves been designated as such in orientalist discourse.[2]

The 'memory war' over the meaning and legacy of WWII in Eastern Europe is likewise both structured by as well as restructuring of orientalist

* Research for this article has been funded by the European Social Fund's Mobilitas fellowship (grant no. MJD60) and HERA (grant no. MSHRG10039).

standpoints. Besides the nesting orientalisms of the former Soviet satellites in Eastern Europe vis-à-vis Russia, there is also the orientalist experience of both Russia and its East European neighbors towards Western Europe. Just as the memory war over the role of the Soviet Union in the origins of WWII and the legacy of Soviet communism is fought on multiple fronts (national, regional, pan-European, and global), orientalism in this war comes in various different shapes, sizes, and disguises as well. As WWII has played a foundational role for the modern self-identities of Russia, Poland, the Baltic states, and Ukraine, the contested issue of its proper remembrance is of core importance for the ontological security (or the security of identity) of these states, for sustaining their consistent sense of their selves and securing the recognition of those selves by their significant other ('Europe'/'the West' being a common denominator here).[3] Moreover, these countries, which relate to the inheritance of the two totalitarian regimes of twentieth-century Europe in different ways, are struggling to translate their unique views of the Soviet communist legacy into the symbolic moral order and legal regime of the wider European community. As the contestants of this memory war are seeking to shape the emerging transnational memory of the Soviet communist legacy in Europe in their various ways, there is also an important Western 'front' in this East European mnemonical conflict.

Russia's and its former East European satellites' variegated readings of WWII each try to depict the other as more liminal, and thus as 'less European,' in the face of 'the West' in order to gain the latter's recognition of one's own comparatively 'more European' nature.[4] East European struggles for getting their narratives of WWII across as part of the 'core European' story of the war are illustrative of their politics of consolidating their recognition as 'fully European.' In the course of this effort, the other 'liminal European' cases get depicted as deviant from, if not directly violating, and thus generally non-suitable for the major Western narrative of WWII. Both Russia and its former satellites in Eastern Europe present themselves to the West as part of the Western tradition that is on the defensive, attacked by the 'alien,' or fundamentally different (albeit deceivingly claiming to be European) 'other' through their own frames of interpretation of WWII.[5] Overcoming one's own relatively orientalist experience of the war thus runs parallel to orientalizing others, exposing fundamental ontological insecurities. As a result, public remembrance of WWII and Soviet communism is securitized as a key temporal feature of respective state identities. Ontological security problems as enframed in the discourses of WWII get translated into concrete foreign policies and practices in turn, with acute political and social resonance.

These moves are marked by the ongoing attempts of Poland, Ukraine and the Baltic states to criminalize the Soviet communist legacy in Europe, on the one hand, and Russia's counter-attempts to condemn these efforts as 'falsifications of history,' on the other.[6] The mnemonical confrontation of the nested liminalities in Eastern Europe is displayed not only at the high-end political, but increasingly also at a popular level. As the massive riots following the decision of the Estonian government to relocate a Soviet-era monument in 2007 vividly demonstrated, the clash over 'proper' remembrance of the past can promptly take overwhelmingly physical proportions.[7]

The East European memory war has an inescapable relevance for the future of broader European remembrance of the war since both sides of this conflict direct their competitive discourses of conscience at an imaginary international audience. The fronts of this memory war include not only the multiple East European contexts and Russia, but also the broader European community as well as the imaginary 'Europe' in the respective discourses of the mnemopolitical contestants of this war. Aiming to translate their particular political and juridical mnemonic initiatives into the symbolic moral order and the legal regime of the broader European community (i.e., the EU, the Council of Europe, and the OSCE), the contestants of this memory war are all seeking to shape the emerging transnational memory of the Soviet communist legacy in Europe. At times, these debates are taken even to the global level and played out at the United Nations (UN).[8] Analyzing different East European undercurrents of the politics of universalizing, or cosmopolitanizing their particular remembrance of Soviet communism, allows for the probing of the future direction of (mnemo)political authority in Europe, or pinpointing the future practices of the 'common European mnemonic order' of WWII and twentieth-century totalitarianisms.

The politics of the 'common European remembrance' of the various experiences of totalitarianism reveals much about the current transformation of the modern European polity. The relative success or abandonment of the pan-European efforts to seek universal condemnation of the Soviet communist legacy inevitably reflect the power relations between the multiple mnemonic actors in European politics. The way in which the wider European community favors some histories over others lays bare the political balance between 'old' and 'new' Europeans, between traditional and emergent actors in European politics. Investigating the competing securitizations of the Soviet legacy in Russia and its former satellite states enables us to understand the central significance of normative solidarity in creating and maintaining security communities in international politics, and the controversial role orientalist tropes play in the process of consolidating collective identities.

The 'memory war' in Eastern Europe allows us to critically examine the applicability of the Saidian analytical apparatus of orientalism to the nations and states that were either left out from or relatively sidelined in the original Saidian account. Following Said's definition of orientalism as 'a Western style for dominating, restructuring, and having authority over the Orient' that (re)produces the alleged Western superiority and hegemony over the East,[9] the clarification of the meaning of orientalism in the discourses of these cultures and nations that have traditionally been the targets, not the sources of orientalist approaches and representations seems warranted. After all, as Larry Wolff argues, the overall 'invention of Eastern Europe' was 'an intellectual project of demi-orientalism' already at the age of Enlightenment.[10]

The question of interest for this chapter is therefore whether or not orientalism could be successfully conceptually stretched in order to capture essentially a(ny) counter-hegemonic move that is, by and large, the result of the 'travels' of Western (European) historically orientalist approach towards the nations and the region of Eastern Europe more generally. To what extent can we use this term metaphorically as a synonym for basically any mutually pejorative stereotypification and objectification, moving further from its original English and French colonial context, as devised by Said? Or should we rather characterize the Russian imaginary of its historic western borderlands, or its 'internal West,' such as the Baltic states, as a sub-type of occidentalism rather than orientalism proper?[11] In short, what does it mean to take orientalism to Russia, and having done so, what counts as 'typically orientalist' in that context?

Following Said's reliance on Gramsci's notion of hegemony in pointing out the historic Western desire to rule over the Orient, this chapter departs from the assumption that the notion of orientalism can be adjusted to the case in point since the struggle over memory in contemporary Eastern Europe is essentially a struggle for 'mnemonical hegemony' in Europe at large. Said defines orientalism as 'a certain *will* or *intention* to understand, in some cases to control, manipulate, even to incorporate, what is a manifestly different (or alternative and novel) world.'[12] The universalizing ambition within the concept of orientalism does not necessarily have anything to do with the Orient *per se*. The concept of orientalism, as John Mowitt points out in his attentive reading of Said in this volume, is, in effect, a form of knowledge/power—a discourse, or discipline; an interpretive (war) machine. War—be it fought physically or at the level of meaning—and the processes of 'othering' it entails could thus be more crucial to the concept of orientalism than the 'Orient' as such.[13] The characteristic representation of the other as backward and inferior applies equally to the usual suspects of the study of orientalism as well as to the cases in focus here. Just as the West has historically propped up its strength and identity by setting itself off against the Orient as sort of surrogate and subordinate version of itself, Russia's and its former Soviet dependents' mutual orientalizations serve to buttress their respective identities, to affirm their basic distinction in this conflict of interpretation over the meaning and legacy of WWII. While these nesting orientalizations are discursively constituted subject positions, they each aim at essentializing the other, thus generating real experiences and challenges for those designated as 'un-European' in the ongoing 'war of opinion.' Rhetorical constructions of 'easternness' and 'otherness' can, hence, go a long way in producing, legitimizing and sustaining the standard account of Russia and the former Soviet space as Europe's 'other.'

Russian 'brand' of orientalism towards the Baltic, Polish, and Ukrainian subaltern stories of WWII focuses on their alleged difference from the existing Western consensus of anti-fascism as the universally binding force in the war against Nazi Germany.[14] Bashing the putative Baltic 'fascists' enables Russia to plant its own experience of the war within the broader European consensus, if not boast it as the most exemplary instance of the fight in the anti-fascist league in WWII. Attempting to extend post-imperial control over the national re-ordering endeavors of the mnemonical spaces of its former satellites, Russia's post-Soviet foreign policy has displayed a traditional orientalist practice of seeking to dominate and rule over its former imperial subjects. The tropes of strength and weakness, prestige and humiliation that are so common in conflicts between the West and its orientalized others, are also an important part of the contemporary mnemonical conflict over WWII in Eastern Europe.

The conflict over the 'right remembrance' of WWII also serves as yet another illustration of the putative East European syndrome of permanent liminality which is, in turn, providing a rich ground for traditional Western (European) orientalist depictions about how different the Eastern European nations and peoples allegedly are (this time, in handling the business of coming to terms with the past).[15] The Western European discourse of the East European memory wars is therefore often a continuation of a much older colonial discourse. This Western vein of criticism could be described as the orientalist denunciation of East Europeans' allegedly nationalistic history-writing, or the nationalist 're-appropriation' of their respective pasts. Criticizing the Polish, Baltic, and Ukrainian emancipatory memory politics as another variation on the theme of Eastern (ethnic) nationalism that is supposedly essentially different from the Western civic brand,[16] the standard of 'proper democratic memory work' is linked to the Western European post-WWII experience while the Eastern European ways of post-Cold War *Vergangenheitsbewältigung* are orientalized as petty nationalistic, illiberal, and even aggressive. Yet again, Eastern European post-Cold War memory politics provides a convenient image for Western Europe to construct its own civility and superiority. Considering the striking similarity in the underlying logic and factual phases of the post-WWII and post-Cold War processes of 'coming to terms with the past' in the West and East of Europe respectively[17] hence affirms 'the internal consistency of Orientalism and its ideas about the Orient… despite or beyond any correspondence, or lack thereof, with the "real" Orient.'[18]

To unfold this argument the chapter first outlines some general characteristics of orientalism in Eastern Europe. Russian memory politics of WWII is sketched out next in order to suggest how it constitutes a counter-hegemonic attempt to redefine the normative contents of Europeanness, followed by critical cuts into East European orientalizations of Russia. The chapter concludes with reflections on the possible implications of the East European 'memory war' on the restructuring of nesting orientalisms in and out of Eastern Europe.

East European 'memory war' as decolonization

The contemporary 'memory war' in Eastern Europe illustrates the complexities of double-colonization. The Baltic states, Poland, and Ukraine have a post-colonial relationship to both Western Europe and Russia, although the latter is more recent and material while the former rather refers to the condition of mental (sense of) subjugation.[19] Russia, in its turn, has a complex identity of having historically colonized the respective East European countries while admitting, to a degree, its status as a mentally colonized subject by Europe(an culture). Meanwhile, the memory war over remembering the 'right' legacy of WWII highlights these countries' mutual importance for the constitution of their respective identities.

Russia displays fundamental ambivalence in its relation to 'Europe': its political elites are continuously fluctuating between seeking recognition as part of the European order and yet contesting it, denying it, protesting against it, constructing their own counter-hegemonic visions of 'Europe' and its contents instead. It is eerily reminiscent of the relationship between the colonized and the colonizer, as described by Homi K. Bhabha: hardly a clear and clean opposition, but rather an ambivalent and complex connection built on concurrent resistance and attraction between the two.[20] Kalpana Sahni maintains that 'the Russian elite became mentally colonized [by Europe] without having ever been a colonial subject. This was the weakness of Russian history and created the inherent contradictions of Russian orientalism, whereby the oriental attitude directed at them was accepted by the Russians and subsequently employed to downgrade the conquered people.'[21]

Russia's relative delay from all 'European' is well captured by Iver B. Neumann who has described Russia's specificity along the mnemonic, rather than spatial, dimension of European identity formation as the condition of being 'trapped in a time which (the rest of) Europe is forever leaving.'[22] Having been a target of orientalist depictions more often than not results in self-orientalization of some sort or the other. Adeeb Khalid has found this tendency to be particularly common to the Russian thought process (although not unique to it), distinguishing between the lachrymosian ('what hope could there be for orientals like us') and the heroic ('we are better than the West') attitude.[23]

As Bhabha argues, both the colonizer and the colonized are split subjects, although the effect and weight of their dividedness is different. Importantly, it is the internal division of the colonizer that enables the colonized to undermine its authority. Bhabha underlines the Janus-faced nature of the colonizer: on the one hand, it performs its role as a father-figure, or a caretaker; on the other, it comes across as the oppressor. On the one hand, the colonizer is a just ruler; on the other, a despot. The colonized is thus not a voiceless/silent sufferer, but (s)he entertains certain power over the colonizer as the latter is constantly seeking signs of the former's subjugation, being afraid of its possible resistance. Both Russia and its former satellites are colonial subjects in the Bhabhaian sense—albeit to a different degree and at different positions in this combined notion of a colonial subject bringing together the colonizer and the colonized. Historically, Russia has been the colonizer of the Baltic states, Poland, and Ukraine. Regarding the Russian-Baltic, or Russian-Ukrainian relations, Russia occasionally displays utter disbelief vis-à-vis its former colonized subjects refusing to behave as colonized and resisting openly the master narrative of their former colonizer. All six countries, moreover, display behavioral traits of the colonized vis-à-vis the common colonial master 'Europe'/'the West,' seeking at times to mimic what they regard as 'true Europe,' and at other times rebelling against it.

By stretching Bhabha's original argument, we can see how both sides of the 'mnemonic war' considered here accuse the other of 'unlawfully imitating' the European culture/values/predominant narrative of the war, and spoiling thus the 'truthful account' of it. In that vein, Russian politicians have occasionally accused the Baltic states of being a twisted parody of Europe, rather than a truthful reflection, less a rightful member of the European community of nations.

It can be argued accordingly that the contemporary memory war over the legacy of WWII and Soviet communism in Eastern Europe marks the most recent phase of cultural decolonization of the region. Mnemopolitically, both Russia and its former satellites are trying to catch up with Western Europe in their own ways, upon the realization that at the time of their crossing of the boundary of 'European community,' the normative consensus about the contents of the 'European remembrance' of WWII had already long been formulated, and the resistance of the old core towards shifting this consensus in either direction thus quite significant. Both the East European 'subalterns'[24] and Russia in essence represent a resistance culture towards the hegemonic Western representation of WWII, although, of course, with quite a different substance.

The re-nationalization of history and re-appropriation of national memories are presented accordingly as part of the mental decolonization process in the former Soviet satellite states. The underlying message emerging from the Polish, Baltic, and Ukrainian attempts to criminalize the legacy of Soviet communism in Europe is a call for a moral rebirth of Europe—quite in the vein of the earlier post-WWII project of 'renaming, dramatizing, reifying and ritualizing the Holocaust' that arguably contributed to the moral remaking of the (post)modern Western world.[25] Polish, Baltic, and Ukrainian 'memory warriors'' refutation of a common Western European allegation of nationalist tendencies behind these countries' post-Soviet processes of coming to terms with their past, points to the moral relativism of general lukewarmness towards the attempts to build a new condemning consensus on the Soviet legacy in Eastern Europe, as well as to the occasional double standards of the EU in relating to the multiple totalitarian experiences of its different member states.[26] The Western Europeans are criticized for tolerating, in a typically orientalist spirit, the Communists' crimes as 'normal aberrations' in the 'Russian borderland of Europe,'[27] as if something like this 'could only be expected to come from the East anyway.' Meanwhile, the establishment of '[Nazi] death factories in the heart of the shrines of Occidental culture' is depicted as having caused massive cognitive dissonance of an entirely different scale in the West for it happened inside the West itself.[28] Communism, by contrast, appeared in Russia—'almost "Asia" after all-where… civilization had never taken deep root.'[29]

Russian memory politics of WWII

Contemporary Russia's state-sanctioned memory politics of WWII and its ambivalent relationship to the Soviet communist legacy constitute a vivid example of counter-hegemonic attempts to redefine the normative contents of Europeanness. Trying to plant its victorious participation in the war into the broader Western narrative of WWII as the 'good war' of democracy fighting against tyranny, modern Russia's rulers generally distance themselves from bearing any historical responsibility for the crimes of the antecedent regime. The attempts of president Vladimir Putin to reconnect with the proud moments of Russia's communist past, seeking to reappraise segments of the Soviet legacy via state-orchestrated public remembrance of the period constitute a serious contestation of European values traditionally conceived, not the least as regards the notion of a democratic memory culture. Efficient leadership and the ability to play along in the European concert of powers have been underscored as key parameters of belonging to the European family of states instead.[30] Contra some liberal voices in Russia, who have regarded the Stalinist terror, or the overall Bolshevik Revolution rather than the Great Patriotic War as the constitutive rupture point for Russia in the twentieth century,[31] the current leadership has but sacralized and securitized the memory of victory in WWII. While trying to sift out something positive of the long century of suffering for the Russian people, the mainstream political discourse in Russia, with strong academic undercurrents supporting it, depicts the country's former satellites' allegedly petty nationalistic processes of coming to terms with the Soviet legacy as essentially deviant from the 'European way' of *Vergangenheitsbewältigung*.

On the surface, Russia seeks to present itself as part of the Western tradition that is on the defensive, attacked by the 'alien,' or fundamentally different (albeit also claiming to be European!) 'other' against the backdrop of WWII (i.e., historically Nazi Germany, and more recently Russia's former satellites in Eastern Europe with their anti-Soviet narratives of WWII).[32] Meanwhile, its official minimizing of the destructive totalitarian legacies of the Soviet period and glorification of the pricey military and political achievements of Stalin at the expense of large groups of people directly challenges the hegemonic Western interpretation of 'a good European' as essentially democratic, peaceful, and pluralistic, always putting human rights first. While some cracks have indeed begun to appear in the official use of the Soviet past,[33] maintaining a neat distinction between the mass crimes of Stalin's era and the great victory of the war achieved under the very same political leadership remains fundamentally problematic for the contemporary rulers of the country. Historians' debates over the role of the Soviet Union in the origins of WWII could potentially significantly disrupt the governmentally sterilized myth of the Great Patriotic War in Russia.[34]

Russia's state-sanctioned 'brand' of orientalism against the backdrop of its modern social memory of WWII is planted in the traditional idea of Russia's historical mission of 'saving Europe from itself.'[35] Anything endangering the heroic narrative gets immediately demonized—all the more so if the narrative competitor is regarded as small and politically insignificant. The Baltic states as small border states between Russia and the West thus emerge as especially conducive figures for respective orientalizing moves. Consequently, the categories of power and strength (against Russia's small neighbors' relative weakness), and the prestige of victory (against the humiliation of defeat or collaboration with the Nazi enemy) are invoked to prove the orientalist point vis-à-vis the Baltic states in the context of WWII. Displaying a general characteristic of the Western type of orientalism, modern Russia's leadership claims the country's involvement and politico-military movements in WWII were entirely defensive. Regarding themselves as nothing but victims of aggression in WWII arguably gave the Russian people not only 'a steadfast confidence in their own integrity and human superiority,' which was consequently 'routinized in an extra-moral, socially primitive, archaic, almost tribal distinction between "our people" and "not our people" as a basis for social solidarity,' but also provided the basis for deducing the right to violence from one's own righteousness.[36]

East European orientalizations of Russia

Polish, Ukrainian, and Baltic politicians seeking to secure a pan-European, if not universal, consensus on the criminal legacy of Soviet communism try, in their turn, to deconstruct the myth of Russia's Great Patriotic War as a solely defensive enterprise. They challenge the attempts to reinterpret the aggressive moves of the Soviet Union in the context of the unfolding of WWII as 'strategic necessities' that are consequently relativized in the context of the other European political developments of an arguably similar kind back in that time.[37]

Soviet totalitarianism is depicted as a variation on the theme of oriental despotism in the Baltic, Polish, and Ukrainian discourses seeking pan-European, or wider international condemnation of the Soviet legacy in Eastern Europe. Classical orientalist renderings (minus the racist distinction of white/dark) are clearly present in the various East European discourses on Russia, criticizing its ambiguous role in WWII and the problematic legacy of Soviet communism (e.g., the binaries of rational/irrational, civi-lized/barbarian; contrasting the individualistic political culture and that relying on the masses; distinguishing between freedom-loving and slave-like people). Orientalizing communism by presenting it as an Asian, barbaric force threatening European civilization has an additional bonus of allowing the political elites of these East European countries to externalize the com-munist experiences from their own national narratives.[38]

An archetypical orientalist theme in various East European discourses criticizing the 'imperialism of numbers' of the Russian war losses relates to the depiction of Soviet lives as infinitely expendable by the Stalinist regime. What for contemporary Russia counts as an example of the immensity of its national sacrifice in WWII ('the colossal price of Victory') is read in its formerly occupied or semi-colonized territories as an illustration of typically oriental carelessness about human lives, as the readiness of a totalitarian state to waste its own people in order to defend an idea of a state, as the barbarian fascination with turning individual lives into mass death.[39] A recent 'shock documentary' *The Soviet Story* (2008) by a young Latvian director Edvīns Šnore is particularly evocative in that regard. Stalin's care-lessness towards his own soldiers' 'infinitely expendable' lives is often pointed out as senseless human waste, typical of the Soviet state that, according to the witty observation of Aleksandr Solzhenitsyn, always put the needs of 'the People' before the concerns of the actual people.[40]

The boasts about the numbers of Soviet wartime deaths in contemporary Russia display, accordingly, an orientalist 'imperialism of martyrdom' by including also the victims of the occupied territories in the official count of the Soviet war dead as inherited by Russia, and are thus 'implicitly claiming territory by explicitly claiming victims,' as Timothy Snyder aptly puts the point.[41] Moreover, including all war dead under the same category of victims (i.e. embracing also those killed for trying to desert from the Red Army, or people dying during the war in the Soviet labor camps) has simultaneously made possible Russia's post-Soviet evasion from the thorny questions about its own inherited responsibility towards the different categories of the war dead.

This criticism sits comfortably with the inclination of modern Russia to handle its repressive Soviet legacy, both societally and by the current regime, as a series of essentially nameless, and thus also agentless tragedies.[42] Russian premier Putin's article published in the Polish newspaper *Gazeta Wyborcza* before attending the commemoration ceremony of the beginning of WWII in Gdańsk, Poland in 2009, as well as his more recent speech held in the ceremony commemorating the victims of the Katyń massacre of 1940 near Smolensk on April 7, 2010, provide rich evidence. Admitting, in the latter case, that the mass murder of Polish officers in Katyń in 1940 was a 'crime that cannot be justified in any way,' Putin nonetheless stopped short of identifying a clear carrier of responsibility for the 'tragedy,' not to mention issuing an apology that Poles so ardently expected from him on behalf of Russia. Instead, Putin pursued a common narrative of emphasizing Russians as being among the sufferers of Stalinist crimes, without actually naming any of the agents who caused these sufferings in the first place. In a similar vein, he labeled the beginning of WWII a 'tragedy' before the commemoration of the 70th anniversary of the Second World War in Gdańsk, neglecting to mention that the Soviet Union had invaded Poland just sixteen days after Nazi Germany attacked Poland from the west in 1939.[43]

It was therefore quite symptomatic for Putin to place Katyń in the relative context of the other wartime tragedies in his address at the ceremony to mark the 70th anniversary of the Katyń massacre held together with the Polish Prime Minister Donald Tusk. The alleged 'brotherhood in death' of those buried in Katyń's soil 'tied the fates' of 'Soviet citizens perished in the fire of Stalin's Great Purge of the 1930s, Polish army officers killed on secret orders, and Red Army soldiers killed by the Nazis during the Great War for Motherland.'[44]

By stretching the argument of the leveling ability of death in war to the extreme, Putin's message must have remained as perplexing to the relatives of the victims of Katyń ('the ceremony is held in connection with *common memory and shame*')[45] as it kept vague about the perpetrators of the 'tragedy' ('We bow our heads before those who boldly met their deaths here').[46] From a Polish viewpoint, however, the explicit confirmation of the Soviet Union's responsibility for the massacre would have been important, if only for raising awareness of the Russian public, a large majority of which still regarded Nazi Germany, not the Soviet Union, as responsible for the Katyń crime according to a poll conducted by the Levada Centre on April 6, 2010.[47]

Apparently then, Nikita Khrushchev's cunning idiom of 'unjustified repressions' for describing mass murders, arrests, and deportations of the high Stalinist era is a still-functioning formula for depicting modern Russia's rulers' relation to the darker chapters of the history of the Soviet Union.[48] Even though Putin's attendance at the commemoration ceremony of the victims of Katyń signified quite a rupture from his previous acts of rather sympathetic remembrance of the Soviet legacy, his acknowledgement of the event categorizes it as part of the many senseless acts of violence in wartime Soviet Union, without specifying agency, and therefore ultimately eluding responsibility. Putin's remarks at Katyń could be read at best as an expression of sorrow—the lowest or least meaningful type of utterance compared to an apology or request for forgiveness.[49] Similarly, his message for Poland before attending the WWII commemoration ceremony in Gdańsk on September 1, 2009 typifies the technique of expressing sorrow by saying 'We are sorry but....' In their effects, both statements are essentially self-defensive, serving to advance Russia's bilateral relations with Poland, true, but without indicating deeper repentance.

The victims of these 'senseless acts of violence' in the former satellite states of the Soviet Union, however, strongly refute the amassing of these crimes into nameless statistics. Instead, they affirm the importance of 'every name, every piece of information, every testimony'[50] and call specifically for speaking of 'people's deliberate actions instead of an impersonal force of nature'; finding out 'the fate of every single person who was imprisoned and deported' as well as identifying, 'without anger or prejudice... the ones who committed these crimes.'[51]

Refuting firmly the alleged *mission civilisatrice* of the Soviet Union in WWII, its engagement in the war is interpreted in Polish, Baltic, and Ukrainian 'memory warriors' accounts as an attempt of the communist expansion, as essentially another variation of the modernization idea which entails a belief that the transformation of backward peoples might require violence. Instead of the arguable extension of a protecting hand to the Western European peoples in order to save them from self-destruction, the Soviet Union's participation in the war is regarded as part of its wider world revolutionary endeavor to build a utopian society along with a New Man, in the course of which the remnants of the old and deficient order had to be wiped out, starting from Russia's own immediate vicinity. The putative 'civilizing mission' of the communist expansion to Eastern Europe is therefore at the heart of their critique of Russian orientalism.

Relatedly, Russian, Baltic, Polish, and Ukrainian competitive orientalizations fall back to the different interpretation of the Nuremberg principles. Russia understands them as rigidly referring to Nazism just as well as yet another source of its great and victorious European power status. East European 'criminalizers' of communism, however, interpret the black letter of the pertinent law much more broadly—as a legal source for their claims of equating the degree of criminality of Nazi and Soviet versions of totalitarianism, as the Nuremberg Principles 'do not mention any country by name.'[52]

A common trait in different Baltic, Ukrainian and Polish discourses is to orientalize Russia's problematic relationship towards its Soviet legacy as an example of its essential difference from Europe/the West; as a proof of its traditional, at times barbaric, and generally less civilized otherness. Russians' relation to the legacy of the country's communist experience is cited as an example of an infantile inability to come to terms with one's past as a mature nation and state, replaying thus the traditional orientalist thread of referring to the oriental Other as an immature cultural adolescent, permanently destined to the process of catching up with the West.[53] Russia's difficulties in issuing a proper political apology, and its leaders' long-time inability to express regret for their political forerunners' crimes towards Russia's neighboring peoples is implicated as a proof of Russia's putative difference from the European style of coming to terms with the past: '[e]ither there is remorse or there isn't. Just like you cannot demand that someone [apologize], because apologizing is a matter of conscience, upbringing and [civilization].'[54]

Russia's mnemopolitical 'special path' or *osobyi put* is thus seen as yet another proof of its fundamental difference from the European style of *Vergangenheitsbewältigung*.[55] An honest attempt to come to terms with one's past, to work through its problems not merely by acknowledging them, but also counteracting the tendency to deny, repress, or blindly repeat them,[56] is regarded as part of being a 'normal' European country. The political forces seeking to criminalize the public denial, condoning or trivializing of the communist crimes in Poland, Ukraine, and the Baltic states (as well as certain civil society organizations in Russia, such as Memorial) generally regard the way communities address the past and work through historical grievances as crucial to the prospects for the formation of communicative civil societies, able to learn and mediate diversity.[57] The state-sponsored historical narrative in post-Yeltsin Russia is largely read as aimed at preserving Russia's political identity as a great power over time instead of explicitly distancing the country from its prior repressive legacy.[58]

The issue of political apologies pertains directly to the ontological security problematique as having to admit to past crimes of the (predecessor) state would require the state to reconsider its sense of the self.[59] Accepting responsibility about past atrocities is consequently 'not a simple verbal act; on the contrary, it is nothing short of a reformulation of state identity from representing a group of people who are not capable of such an act, to representing a group of people who are both capable and apologetic about it.'[60] The temptation to emphasize the 'good' legacy at the price of disregarding the 'bad' is therefore always there.

Instead of reaffirming the liberalizing transitional identity of Russia, its current leadership's ambivalence towards the Soviet legacy is taken as yet another proof of its difference from the normative standard of the European way of working through one's past. The restitution of the 'good legacy' of Stalin under the leadership of Vladimir Putin is taken as evidence of Russia's 'inability for historical self-criticism and self-analysis.'[61] Putin's presidency is generally held responsible for relativizing the scale and meaning of the crimes committed in the name of the Soviet state during Stalin's time and thus hampering the process of coming to terms with the past in modern Russia.[62] Russia's reluctance to apologize explicitly for the crimes of its predecessor state is consequently quoted as a sign of its deviation from the European norm. The apparent lack of a sense of psychological guilt for the misdeeds and crimes of the Stalinist regime during and after WWII, or the inability to feel badly for acts that one has not in fact committed oneself is understood in Russia's former satellite states as an example of the Russian leaders' inability to take responsibility and thus their fundamental difference from the European code of conduct. Regarding the politics of official apologies as part of a liberal conception of state and society, the former victims of the Soviet oppression criticize the apparent unwillingness of today's Russia to apologize for its predecessors' crimes as a proof of the current regime's illiberal nature.[63] Critics relate Russia's long-time reluctance to acknowledge publicly the criminal legacy of the high-Stalinist regime, much less assume responsibility for the crimes committed in the name of communism, to the traditional Russian way of understanding responsibility in collective, rather than individual terms. This runs against the tide of modern democratic sensibilities that regard responsibility as an individual affair.[64]

This is also an important trope in Russian discourses of self-orientalization. Lev Gudkov, for instance, sees Russia as tied to the 'fetters of victory' of WWII, to the foot-cuffs that hamper its moral, intellectual and political working through of the negative and traumatic experience of Soviet times.[65] Instead of 'working through' its problematic legacy related to WWII—a notion loaded with generally positive connotations in the German *Aufarbeitung* style of addressing its difficult Nazi legacy—Russia is allegedly doomed to scarification of this 'traumatic tissue.'[66] Curiously, the sacralization of one's own remembrance of the war serves as a precondition for creating dichotomous negative images and representations of contending accounts not only in Russia but also on the other front of the current mnemonic conflict in Eastern Europe.

As an example of the current Russian regime's difficulties in coming to terms with the Soviet legacy in a democratic manner, the creation of the 'History Commission' by President Medvedev in May 2009 is often quoted. This special commission is designed 'to counteract attempts to falsify history that undermine the interests of Russia.'[67] Its establishment was preceded by a draft legislation 'On Countering the Rehabilitation of Nazism, Nazi Criminals, and Their Accomplices in the Newly Independent States of the Former Soviet Union' proposed to the Russian State Duma on the eve of Victory Day, May 9, 2009.[68]

The inclination of the contemporary Russian leadership towards picking and choosing elements of the Soviet times to their liking is criticized in former Soviet satellite states as the instrumentalization of history. The emphasis on the 'good' legacy of Stalin is pointed out as an essential, and therefore politically expedient, identity-building block for Putin's regime: oft-quoted examples by critics include Putin's re-instatement of the melody of the Soviet anthem as the national anthem of Russia; his decree of 2002, calling for the equation of the past employment in the Communist Party of the Soviet Union to Russian government service; the installation of monuments or memorials to former nominal Soviet security services figures; and the governmental/presidential approval of the new history textbooks according to which Stalin was first and foremost an 'effective manager' whose mass purges were 'adequate to the task of modernization.'[69]

The critical East European discourses build a direct connection between the internal power structure of the Putin regime and that of the Stalinist Soviet Union. The central significance of the security services in the public governance structures is just one of the oft-quoted common denominators of the Putinist and Stalinist regimes. The 'criminal morality' is yet another.[70]

Nevertheless, under President Medvedev the official attitude towards the Soviet legacy has become somewhat more nuanced compared to the Putin presidency. Medvedev has declared his conviction that 'the memory of national tragedies should be as important as the memory of victories.'[71] Somewhat bafflingly against the backdrop of the guiding logic of his recently established history commission, he claims to 'believe that no development of the country, none of its successes, or ambitions cannot be achieved at the cost of human suffering and loss; nothing can override the value of human life.'[72] He has thus reasoned his democratic agenda as follows:

Today is the first time in our history that we have a chance to prove to ourselves and the world that Russia can develop in a democratic way. That a transition to the next, higher stage of civilization is possible. And this will be accomplished through non-violent methods. Not by coercion, but by persuasion. Not through suppression, but rather the development of the creative potential of every individual. Not through intimidation, but through interest. Not through confrontation, but by harmonizing the interests of the individual, society and government.[73]

The Polish president's plane crash at Smolensk in April 2010, killing a good part of the Polish political and military leadership on their way to commemorate the 1940 NKVD massacres of Polish officers and intelligentsia, has been followed by a remarkable sequence of symbolic politics by Medvedev and Putin trying to outdo each other by acknowledging the controversial legacy of the Soviet era (although with many important reservations). In spite of the positively expectant attitude towards the recent change of the official Russian mnemopolitical tune, Polish and Baltic 'memory politicians' have been generally rather cautious at taking the recent criticism of the Stalinist legacy by Russian leadership at face value.[74] Suspicions loom large that Medvedev's newly conciliatory approach towards acknowledging the misdeeds of the Soviet wartime leadership might be just another means of competition with Putin over the future power-sharing and leadership of Russia.[75] Alternatively, it is regarded as just another cunning 'proxy tactic,' another democratic ritual without actual substance, aimed at improving the 'soft power' credentials of Russia in the eyes of the self-boasting 'civic power' Europe ('not through intimidation, but through interest'), taming thus the potential blockers, such as Poland, in developing further the EU-Russia strategic partnership, as well as hijacking the arguments of the domestic liberals.[76]

Regardless, Russia's current political elite clearly pays considerable attention to the country's ranking in the international community of states. Russia's gradual acknowledgement of the crimes of its predecessor state could therefore also be read as an attempt to deconstruct and ultimately disprove Russia's supposedly oriental nature (as defined by the West) by using the very mnemopolitical 'template' of the West (i.e., the acknowledgement and expression of some sort of regret for the past misdeeds as part of enhancing relations with one's neighbors). In a typically orientalist manner, Russia is deeply concerned about what the 'West' thinks about it.[77] It could be regarded as a 'frustrated great power'—essentially believing that it has not been given the position and status in international society/system of states and the rights (or privileges) it deserves.[78] Furthermore, Russian people display deep victim mentality according to which they would deserve an apology just as much as others.[79] Nonetheless, its recent mnemopolitical waltzes towards a more reconciliatory tone vis-à-vis Poland could also be taken as reflexive of Russia's willingness to respond more to the European normative expectations in order to improve its relative 'normative power' status in Europe.

In place of a conclusion: on the generative power of the East European memory war

A perfunctory look at the political and juridical translation of some East European initiatives pertaining to the criminal legacy of Soviet communism in and after WWII at the pan-European level lends support to the claim of the gradually shifting social frames of the wider European community's relation to the communist legacy in Eastern Europe. There has indeed been a flow of respective political declarations and resolutions by the European Parliament, the Parliamentary Assembly of the Council of Europe, and the

OSCE since 2005, condemning the criminal legacy of the Soviet Union in various ways.

More significantly perhaps, a recent judgment by the Grand Chamber of the European Court of Human Rights (ECHR) in the case of *Kononov v. Latvia* signifies a substantial change of tune in the legal side of the pan-European mnemopolitical discussions of WWII.[80] It marks a shift towards a more nuanced embracing of the subaltern East European narratives of WWII next to the hegemonic West European (that occasionally overlap with Russian) ones. With this judgment, the Grand Chamber reversed the previous judgment delivered by the ECHR on July 24, 2008, which had found Latvia to be in violation of Article 7 of the European Convention on Human Rights when convicting the former Soviet partisan Vasily Kononov for a war crime committed in Latvia during WWII. Instead, the Grand Chamber agreed with Latvian courts' previous rulings on finding Kononov guilty of war crimes for his acts against Latvian civilians who had allegedly collaborated with the Germans occupying the country in the village of Mazie Bati in 1944. The final ruling of the ECHR in this case established an important precedent in applying the standards of international law (i.e., the Nuremberg law) also to those who had been instrumental in establishing these standards—the winners of WWII.

In just two years, the discourse that had informed the original ECHR ruling in the Kononov case ('The Nazis and their collaborators were entirely in the wrong and those who fought against the Nazis were completely in the right')[81] has become significantly more nuanced about the controversial experiences of the war in these Eastern European countries that were consecutively subjugated to both Nazi and Soviet occupations. The lengthy 'abjectivity' of East European experiences from the pan-European memory of twentieth-century totalitarianisms has begun to gradually wane. The crystallization of the newly emerging European consensus on the meaning and legacy of WWII and Soviet communism into pan-European political declarations and court rulings is a vivid demonstration of the generative power of an ideological conflict, such as the 'memory war' analyzed in this chapter, to reshape its social and political contexts. The power of this mnemonical struggle to restructure the orientalist discourses of its various participants for the better—if not for good—remains yet to be seen.

10

VICTIMHOOD AS AGENCY

AFGHAN WOMEN'S MEMOIRS

Margaret A. Mills

Latent and overt orientalist stereotypes of Muslim women as passive and voiceless are part of the terrain to be negotiated by the Afghan women authors and the Western publishers of recent memoirs produced for English-speaking and other non-Afghan mass audiences.[1] The idea of female rescue, for example, from suttee or the 'harem' as a pretext for intervention by force, has a long history in orientalist-colonialist discourse, with a powerful romantic appeal, as in Western drama from Mozart to Valentino and beyond. But in the last decade, especially, Afghan women themselves as autobiographers have found access to audiences far beyond Afghanistan. A published personal memoir is, in itself, a substantial manifestation of personal agency and voice, representing or constructing images of self and others in social interaction and evaluating such actions in paratextual comments including dedications and disclaimers.

Intended for a primarily Western mass audience,[2] how do these self-presentations comport with the orientalist tropes of victimhood and rescue? Neither silenced nor hardly ever, in their own portrayals, passive, what kinds of subjecthood or agency do these women achieve or claim? What identities do they claim, vis-à-vis the East/West map of popular dichotomies? Must they ventriloquate the sovereign individual subjecthood of Western liberal ideology, in order to escape the orientalist stereotype of silenced victim? Each memoirist represents a distinct self and distinct history, to be sure, but is that self some version of the modernist, socially and ethically autonomous 'sovereign' self of the European genre of literary autobiography? Orientalism defined this form of selfhood as unattainable in 'oriental' societies. Or do representations of a given author confound or reject Western liberal individualism?

At least two forms of collective identity are at stake here, over against liberal individualism: one is the activist collective subjecthood of the testimony genre, another the networked collective subjecthood of the extended family as a basic economic, social, political and moral unit. Whether the latter collectivity is a retrograde survival from a pre-modern (and patriarchal) socioeconomic formation, and/or now emerging as an alternative form of (post)modernity in non-Western societies, is debatable. Yet a fourth form of female subjecthood, individual but not sovereign (because based on a primary commitment to Islam as submission to God's will) is argued by Saba Mahmoud, from research with Egyptian Muslim women engaged in religious self-realization.[3]

Part of the question of institutional, ideological and experiential formations comes down to forms of representation, in this case, literary genres. There is a prehistory to Afghan women's wartime memoirs, at least in some sectors of the Afghan female population, explored in Benedicte Grima's *The Performance of Emotion among Paxtun Women: 'The Misfortunes Which Have Befallen Me,'*[4] which analyzes the emic oral genre of Pashtun women's personal *gham-xádi* ('grief and joy') narratives, performed for each other in the context of traditional social visits of inquiry (*tapas* or *tahappos*). Grima ultimately argues that women's evaluations of their peers' narrative performances express an aesthetic of suffering, whereby individual Pashtun women earn empathy, respect and admiration from their peers both for their ability to endure hardships, and to evoke their own suffering in autobiographical oral narratives. Grima observes that these performances are essentially conservative, not spurs to remedial social action for structural injustice or social critique in any activist sense. The narrator's power or agency lies in her ability to evoke others' admiration for her endurance of things she cannot change. It was, at the time of Grima's research in the mid-1980s, primarily a rural women's tradition. Such a genre can be a protest genre without being reformist; social change may nonetheless come from other directions, economic and cultural (e.g. some urban women's access to education and paid professional work), obsolescing the genre. Young urban women she interviewed in Peshawar denied that they had such stories to tell.

In contrast to Grima's traditional Pashtun women self-narrators, all of the memoirists considered here except Ahmedi were highly educated urban dwellers raised in Kabul, some (Pazira, Zoya, Latifa) with highly educated, professionally employed mothers as well. All are children of progressive parents. In education and urban background they are not typical of the 85 percent of Afghan women who are of rural origin and mostly impoverished, or the 88 percent who were not functionally literate in the late twentieth century.[5]

Unlike the traditional narrations, these memoirs solicit empathy from audiences not sharing their social history or experience, using diverse discursive strategies and tropes. The memoirists present their and their families' aspirations to education, professions, and public-sphere activities in ways that evoke Western feminist goals and values. All the memoirs are calls for social change to one or another degree of explicitness, if only by the implications of involuntary displacement. Some Afghan male visiting university students, commenting on my discussion of the memoirs at Syracuse University in 2011, dismissed the writers as 'not real Afghans.' Such denial of Afghan identity to women or men with substantial experience abroad (especially in non-Muslim countries of refuge) is an important element in political debates, especially for those Afghans who stayed on, either in Afghanistan itself of in neighbouring Muslim countries (Pakistan or Iran), part of a distrustful critical assessment of the highly paid returned Afghans in the post-9/11 reconstruction effort.

How does the Euro-American literary genre of memoir, in particular, shape these Afghan women authors' public (indeed global) self-representation or self-fashioning as political acts?[6] Feminist literary critics argue that autobiography, as a European modernist genre, entails the construction of a radically individualist, liberal modern sovereign itself.[7] All these accounts are first-person narratives concerned with the writers' own developing knowledge, opinions, decisions and actions, and consequences thereof. The subjects' actions and plans are developed against one or more intolerably oppressive institutional presences. Thus their actions can be defined in feminist and subaltern studies terms as agency: the capacity for resistance or

subversive action to protect one's own interests against an oppressive dominant or hegemonic force.[8] This definition of agency has the virtue of not
instantiating any phantasms of autonomy: human subjectivities are *all* situated in hierarchies. Dominances are multiplex, in this case ranging from
Afghan indigenous hierarchical structures to 'foreign' ideological and physical interventions (as defined by Afghans) including foreign military occupation. Because of the multiplexity of dominance, and if following Mahmoud
we entertain the idea that not all agency need be resistant or adversarial, one
must try to hear where the dominated subject(s) say, implicitly or explicitly
to a given hegemon, 'This isn't about *you*, mate.' Despite orientalizing labe-
ling of oppressive structures or powers, there is plenty of represented
oppression to go around. But does the memoirist herself invite or partici-
pate in orientalizing interpretations thereof?

With these internationalized, mostly displaced Afghan women writing
for an orientalism-exposed Western mass audience, this disentanglement
yields multiple readings. One goal of the present analysis is to point out
places in texts that are more strikingly 'double-voiced,' likely saying one sort
of thing to a mass audience that derives most or all of its understanding of
the circumstances from ambient Western social opinion, and something else
to another audience with more access to Afghan viewpoints and experiences, an alternative context of interpretation. Double voicing may be quite
intentional or less obviously so, hard to tell which given the difficulty of
determining authorial intentionality in texts.

Double voicing as I define it recalls but does not duplicate aspects of
'coding' as defined by Radner and Lanser in *Feminist Messages*.[9] Radner and
Lanser define 'acts of coding' in gender politics as 'covert expressions of
disturbing or subversive ideas' that are not readily decodable by those (males
in their analysis) who would 'dominate, silence or marginalize' the producers, because they are expressed in female media or registers such as needle-
craft, lament or storytelling that are not regarded as significant by the
dominant.[10] The surface content of the expression may seem innocuous,
while it bears a different, coded message legible to the producers and their
co-subversives. Coding may be deniable (strategically or protectively) even
to the point of being below awareness for the perpetrator(s), yet perceived
by some of the complicit as critical, subversive or resistant.

Double voicing in these memoirs, while it partakes of qualities of ambiguous intentionality and possible gender solidarity as in Radner and Lanser's
subversive/resistant coding, is a more general phenomenon. The memoirs

do not appear to seek to convey covert messages, rather to witness openly to oppressive acts in various ways, to influence receptive members of a dominant other (Western readers). At the same time, they may offer circumstantial detail that authenticates the memoirs in the eyes of the more locally informed. Gender solidarity may not be gender-exclusive, as it is in Radner and Lanser's formulation, but in an orientalist version, both female and male readers (non-Afghan) empathize with the female authors as victims of (Afghan) gender oppression. Coding may nonetheless occur as messages are mediated by selected images or evaluations that have different associative triggers for different parts of a complex target audience.

Double voicing connects to Radner and Lanser's theorization of coding mostly in that readers who are party to structures of dominance or marginalization may read narrated events via orientalizing stereotypes of agency or victimhood, empathetically or voyeuristically, perpetuating structures of marginalization. In the same text, those more cognizant of pertinent Afghan viewpoints may evaluate narrated events and actors differently, seeing levels of complexity, ambiguity or even deniability at work in the authors' representations.

Agency is thus not at issue in these memoirs, but varieties and limits of autonomous agency are. Feminist differentiations of genres of subaltern self-representation (from subaltern memoir, defined as co-opting the individualist-modernist, hegemonic form, to life narrative, ethno-autobiography and testimony) are useful here. Whatever the critical assessments of genre, however, these self-accounts are susceptible to different kinds of readings. Whitlock has emphasized the memoirs' and memoirists' susceptibility to manipulation in support of imperialist projects, now prominently, the U.S.-led war in Afghanistan, but that trend does not exhaust these texts' interpretations.[11] Joya, Zoya, and Pazira among these memoirists vigorously and explicitly resist any such co-optation.

While detailed research on reader reception is lacking for these works, potential critical (sometimes uncritical) reception of these literary memoirs by representatives of the Western target audience is relevant. Some hints at writers' intentions for readers' engagement, such as use of an oral-conversational style of second-person address to the readers (especially Ahmedi) or use of American colloquialisms (Joya: 'clueless,' Ahmedi: 'My gosh!') assume or attempt forms of linguistic intimacy/familiarity to shepherd readers' affective reactions. Ahmedi's naïve voice and lack of literary polish may serve as indices of an authentic 'innocent' self: poor, young, uneducated, while Pazira and Gauhari in particular display crafted Euro-American writerly techniques: flashbacks, jump cuts, suspense, and especially recirculations of visual and circumstantial detail in metaphorized forms. Furthermore, the degrees and kinds of activism claimed by individual authors shape significant distinctions in the pragmatic intentions of the memoir as a witnessing act, employing certain kinds of reticence and coding (the authorial pseudonyms used by Latifa, the sisters Sulima and Hala, and Zoya being only the most obvious) while yet claiming a high level of truthfulness and disclosure; pseudonyms actually become an index of the accounts' critical authenticity. More directly, Sulima and Hala conclude their volume by recommending nongovernmental organizations whose work readers can support with donations; Zoya describes her experiences fundraising for the Revolutionary Association of the Women of Afghanistan (RAWA).

Variations in agentive positioning reflect the respective historical locations of the authors, ranging from an adult professional, wife and mother at the time of the 1978 Marxist coup (Gauhari), to those who recount coming-of-age narratives *in extremis*, coming to political consciousness, navigating childhood and young adulthood entirely in different fraught and unsafe post-1978 environments (Latifa, Nelufer Pazira, Farah Ahmedi, Hala, Zoya, Malalai Joya). These self-narratives, whether considered to be memoirs in some extended sense, ethno-autobiographies, or testimonies, reflect culturally constructed boundaries in reception between art and *cri de coeur*, the aesthetic, the political-instrumental and the personal-psychological.

The complexities of Afghan women memoirists' literary voicings, acts of narrative self-construction, representing their rescues by self and others, are complex in comparison with the very rudimentary orientalist-style rescue-the-victims proclamations from Laura Bush (2001) and George W. Bush (2002) to Hillary Clinton (2010). In each case, the memoirist's self-rescue is not a solo act of heroism but assisted at critical points by others whose roles are specifically described, in contrast to the malevolence or social dysfunctionality of others. Despite or because of this complex understanding of rescuer roles and indebtedness, some memoirists evaluated Western political calls for 'rescue' (e.g., Joya calls Laura Bush 'clueless,' though her statements were in Joya's view, nonetheless, more nuanced and less crude than her husband's).[12] As discussed below, self-representation, implied by the first-person voice used, is in all but three cases (Gauhari, Pazira, Sultan) complicated by co-authorship, 'as-told-to' attribution or translation, to which must be added various forms of editorial framing and manipulation enumerated by Whitlock, applying Genette's concepts of peritext, paratext and epitext.[13]

Textual analyses in this chapter are but short meditations on selected issues in the individual memoirs listed. Given the number and scope of the texts and space constraints, detailed textual analysis of thematic variations must be illustrative only, not to exclude other readings.

Voice and position, genre and power

Edward Said's theoretical legacy in discourses of war and conflict being the framing concept for the present anthology, we can share his agenda: 'I study Orientalism as a dynamic exchange between individual authors and the large political concerns shaped by the three great empires—British, French, American—in whose intellectual and imaginative territory the writing was produced.'[14] Said's core concern with the mechanisms of representation, with 'rhetoric, figures of speech, narrative structures and discursive formations' generally, and how political domination is propagated through and reciprocally propagates cultural formulations, bears on these writings, yet Afghan women memoirists address the orientalist project and Said's critique of it from at least two distinctly marginalized angles.[15] The first concerns Said's own position: specifically, the lack of any gendered dimension in his formulation of orientalist discourse, his 'never [having discussed] the position of colonized women, or consider[ed] that women on either side might speak for themselves.'[16] Paradoxically, Said's formulation perpetuates the silencing entailed in the stereotypes he critiques. The question of dominated groups having a voice, to 'steal the language,' to engage and co-opt the discourses of the dominant, and reciprocally their vulnerability to discursive co-optation in the process of claiming a voice, has been exhaustively discussed in feminist and subaltern studies circles with direct relevance to genre matters discussed below.

The second form of marginality concerns these memoirists' 'intellectual and imaginative territory' in Said's words. While all the memoirists speak to the orientializing West, they vary in the degree and manner in which they speak from it, either in physical or intellectual location. All were displaced from Afghanistan either temporarily or permanently. At two extremes are the protectively pseudonymous 'Latifa,' Malalai Joya and 'Zoya' on the one hand, and Masuda Sultan on the other. Zoya and Malalai Joya speak to the West, to the post-9/11 United States, from Afghanistan, in direct critique of an imperialist agenda. Both were displaced to Muslim countries only, Iran (Joya) and Pakistan (both), both returned to Afghanistan by choice as young, single, and clandestine female community organizers. Joya, furthermore, writes and speaks as an elected member of parliament who was ejected (amid threats of bodily harm) from that position due to her adamant demands for legal prosecution of 'warlords' also in parliament. Educated by, and working within, the still-covert RAWA,[17] Zoya is an avowed political secularist and gender rights activist. Neither woman intends to relocate to the West. No more did 'Latifa,' whose exile from Afghanistan was inadvertent. Her anonymity was destroyed and a fatwa issued against her and her family when she departed during the Taliban's control of Kabul, on what was meant to be a short incognito visit to France and Belgium to testify to Taliban abuse of women.

Others (Farooka Gauhari, Farah Ahmedi, 'Sulima' and 'Hala') speak as adult asylees permanently relocated to the United States, with explicit aspirations to cultural assimilation. Masuda Sultan was four years old when her family became refugees. Raised and educated in the United States, a U.S. citizen identifying herself as an Afghan-American, she returned to Afghanistan as a young, single woman while the Taliban were in power, to reconnect with relatives and Pashtun culture in Kandahar. After the Taliban's departure she returned as an organizer of the grassroots women's rights jirga (convention) which met in Kandahar prior to the national constitutional jirga, and latterly has worked, armed with a degree in public administration from Harvard's Kennedy School, as an economic development advisor to the Afghan Ministry of Finance and several organizations. While she speaks of Afghan economic marginalization and nascent capitalism with American entrepreneurial credentials, Sultan is not disconnected from Afghan viewpoints. Subsequent to the events in her book, nineteen of her relatives were killed when the United States erroneously bombed their village. Before and after that event she has written and spoken publicly to keep in Western view the loss of Afghan civilian lives due to NATO activities, a direct counter to facile assumptions that Western invasion is rescue.

Where individuals were exiled, whether in the West ('rescue' in orientalist terms) or in Afghanistan-adjacent locales, affected their ambit of activities and perhaps Western readers' identification with them. U.S. asylum policy specifically favors refugees fleeing areas of conflict dominated by our adversaries (the Afghan Marxists, the Taliban), less so those fleeing our 'ally' regimes, however violent. Reader identification with authors is invited (or not) if like Sultan, Ahmedi, Sulima and Hala, they offer considerable narrative detail about adjustments made between Afghan and American cultural values and practices, or if instead they do not appear to aspire to American-style cultural competence (Zoya, Joya).

Hardly discussed is the fact that returnees' place of exile has mattered very explicitly to Afghans who did not relocate. *Hijra*, flight to avoid religious persecution, is an Islamic principle that assumes protection will be secured in a Muslim society. In post-Taliban Afghan popular culture, prolonged residence in the non-Muslim West (unlike exile in Iran or Pakistan) potentially delegitimizes exiles' claims to Afghan identity, for at least three reasons. They are suspected of having forgotten Islam, having forgotten or abandoned Afghan cultural values and practices, in favor of Western values and practices which are 'not right for Afghanistan,' or as simply lacking historical experience of how Afghanistan has changed in the years of war and trauma since their departure. The Western-located memoirists do discuss in detail the identity and national-cultural loyalty issues that dogged them and their relatives in the process of deciding whether and when to seek refuge, and how to manage exile. But with the exception of Joya, and Sultan regarding her own return, memoirists do not discuss in detail issues attending the return of Afghans with Western technocratic credentials and claims. In this focus and this omission, the memoirists speak to the hegemonic West, more than to Afghans.

One telling scene in Pazira's case occurs not in her memoir but in *Return to Kandahar*, her documentary film made with Paul Jay in 2010 about her return to Afghanistan after the publication of her memoir, partly in search of her old friend Dyana. She conducts a group interview with women college students at Balkh University, in which most of the women describe their goals to pursue higher education for professional careers. Shortly thereafter, she is confronted, with cameras rolling, by male students who assert that 'foreigners' have no right to put 'our women into public view on film.' She protests vociferously in fluent Dari Persian that she, too, is Afghan, not 'foreign,' that the women students chose to be interviewed on film, and that she and all other Afghan women have the right to speak for themselves, no one has the right to deprive them of that choice.

This scene too is double-voiced, confirming for Western audiences the female-controlling and silencing agendas of Afghan men, and for those who have seen the pattern, additionally, the deep suspicions of Afghans (in my experience, not limited to men) concerning the non-Afghan identities, cultural tendencies and intentions of returnees. Afghan skepticism of both memoirs and film might rightfully include a rejection of voyeuristic orientalist interest in Afghan women and gender relations. Protective themes are not far to seek in the male students' objections to the filming of 'our women.'

Pazira's insistence on the women's right to self-expression in the filmed confrontation certainly resonates with Westerners' ideas of autonomous self and individual human rights as well as orientalist stereotypification of Afghan males. Yet this film and the memoirs if read by English-reading Afghans in Afghanistan, must be viewed in the light of commonly articulated reservations among the 'stayed-on' about cultural alienation in exile and the intentions and competencies of returnees. Such possible readerships and readings, confirmed in Afghan visiting students' comments to me that the memoirists were 'not real Afghans,' amount to unintentional double-voicing of the texts.

Genres, themes, tropes and topoi

The question of genre is pertinent to that of the varied forms of agency and selfhood claimed or achieved by the writers under discussion here. Western genre theory defines memoir, the term I am applying perhaps too generally to these self-writings, as focused on the writer's recall of events external to the self, while autobiography treats one entire individual life and personality as focus (as in Ahmedi's title, subtitle and highly affective personal narrative). Autoethnography may describe all these Afghan women's self-writings insofar as they assume and depict cultural differences between writer and reader. Beyond self-writing which is, in all its forms, an agentive act as such, a fourth, critical genre, that of testimony, applies insofar as these works bear witness to individual experience as an exemplar of the oppression of a larger group or class, intending to mobilize an audience for intervention or redress. Zoya's and Malalai Joya's accounts most clearly operate as testimony, both because they most assiduously draw parallels between their own individual experiences and a general Afghan experience, and because they narrate to mobilize not 'rescue' by outsiders, but rather their Western readers' critical consciousness to resist further hegemonic/imperialist claims of rescue by their own governments. By contrast, Sulima's detailed account of domestic abuse by Afghan relatives and her 'escape to freedom' in the West (per the book's subtitle) assigns no clear interventionist role to readers, and to that extent may leave readers in a voyeuristic position. Nevertheless, her call for action in the 'How You Can Help' list at the end of the book invites not Westerners riding to Afghan women's rescue against 'oriental' male abuse, but contributions to five Afghan women-run NGOs. Gauhari's account, in some years' retrospect, of the national tragedy of the 1978 Marxist coup and its aftermath for her family, reads not as an activist call but as elegy and lament for Afghanistan's prewar promise. Pazira's subtitle, *In Search of My Afghanistan*, aptly describes her memoir as at once a quest story and a claim to a continuing identity.

Despite these differences in overall trajectory, some specific themes, topics and tropes shared among the memoirs do mark them as a subgenre. Family members' relationships are a dominant theme, whether as living advocates of cultural/ideological (Sulima) or tactical (Pazira, Latifa) choices that challenge the authors, or as tragically lost members of a formerly strong protective group (Gauhari, Zoya, Ahmedi).

If the virtue of endurance of hardship without active resistance (*sabr*) as a female virtue finds a place in these memoirs, it is mostly in respectful portrayals of some memoirists' mothers (especially Pazira, 'Latifa,' 'Sulima,' and more ambivalently, Farah Ahmedi). Presentations of the mothers' positions on social action, contrasted with the memoirists,' suggest a generational shift in these Afghan women's varieties of expressed or performed agency. They may also lend themselves to double reading in that Western feminists may see more passivity, Afghans more stoical forbearance in the older women's attitudes and choices.

The first three authors' mothers are described as supportive in more or less explicit ways of their daughters' initiatives for education and self-choice, though seriously threatened by the risks posed by their social or political activism. In the cases where the memoirist sees a male family member as oppressor (especially Sulima), the mother counsels patience (*sabr*, again) and forbearance as a form of strength, privacy, and family honor. Only in portraits of their mothers can some confirmation of the orientalist stereotype of the passive, suffering oriental woman be read, but I do not find the memoirists encouraging such a reading. Sulima says she admires her mother's strength in forbearance, but cannot emulate it. Farah Ahmedi describing periods in Chicago when her mother stayed up all night cursing, weeping and mumbling to herself, sums up her mother's silencing as the loss in exile of a way of life that satisfied and protected her: 'She's quiet now because she has lost her whole family except me, her home, her way of life—everything…my mother had a set and sheltered way of life for so many years, and then she lost everything. That's why she's quiet.'[18] Nelufer Pazira, after a vivid and detailed portrayal of her father's intellectual, political and professional rise from poverty in a Kabul minority (Shi'a, ethnically Qizilbash) community, finally mentions in passing that her mother, working as a Dari literature teacher, publicly criticized President Daoud's decree for more stringent student college entrance examinations.[19] This is Pazira's entire discussion of her mother's professional career. Her portrait of her mother elaborates on her physical illnesses and emotional fragility under wartime conditions.[20] Pazira portrays her parents' marriage as a love match (innovative for Afghanistan at the time), her mother as a modernizing elite woman educated to the 'obedient modernity' of European-style elite secondary girls' schooling in Kabul in the 1950s.[21] But by the time Pazira is a very young adult, her father's idealistic determination not to abandon Afghanistan, leaves her to attend to emerging family crises. She portrays her mother as ready to flee for some time, yet dithering on the brink of flight about what to do with her valuable collection of jewelry. Yet Pazira also opines, 'I think my mother is the most courageous of us all' in the face of the need to flee.[22] Yet further, her mother is also the first to regret the flight decision audibly, during several days' very rough travel on foot across the Pakistani border. A portrayal of this complexity, if closely read, evades any easy stereotype of Afghan women facing the disorder and danger of thirty years of war, as either passive victims or agents.

Farah Ahmedi, as a very young, almost unschooled amputee mine victim, survives alone with her traditional, uneducated mother (the daughter of a Hazara village headman), after the last Taliban rocket attack on Kabul in 1996 that killed her 'modernizing' father and two sisters, and the subsequent disappearance (apparent death) of her two brothers, en route to refuge in Pakistan. Farah portrays her mother making the emergency decision that the boys must flee alone, leaving behind their less mobile sister and mother, in the face of the announced Taliban draft of young men and beginning of anti-Hazara reprisals one month after their occupation of Kabul.

This is about the last strategic decision she is shown making. Farah portrays her mother, family members and friends in Kabul as naïve and uninformed when arranging the boys' departure by public bus, lacking practical information about how to cross the border, or even of basic geography. A two-year NGO-sponsored rehabilitation in Germany has given Farah a taste of life in the non-war-torn West, but no practical survival skills. Her mother is asthmatic, and after their own flight, nearly killed by two years of hand-to-mouth life between refugee camp tents and exploitive employers in Quetta. They have only reached Pakistan with the crucial help of an intact Shi'a family, met by chance in flight at the bribe-blocked border. In Pakistan her mother retreats into insomnia and mental deterioration, her muttering and weeping punctuated by nearly-fatal asthma attacks and admonitions to Farah to bear with barely sublethal economic marginalization and avoid initiatives that seem risky to her. Farah describes her own descent into despair as a twelve-year-old amputee with a deteriorating prosthesis, sole support of her mother. Their eventual rescue, through Farah's own grimly determined applications to an American faith-based refugee resettlement NGO, lands them in Chicago, where on arrival Farah's mother's fear and resistance to the whole idea of the American transplantation erupts into a full-blown paroxysm of shared fear, as they flee the home of American temporary hosts with whom they have no common language.

Disability payments, intervention by a female NGO volunteer who becomes a friend, and Farah's success in American high school right their little ship to some extent over a couple of years. But Farah even by age 19, with graduation in sight, has become her still mentally fragile parent's permanent caretaker, a not-uncommon role reversal for refugees.

On the theme of rescue, Farah Ahmedi's narrative is the one that most stresses, in a regular refrain, the intervention of kindly bystanders and strangers who 'rescued me/us' or 'saved my life' at several crisis points, beginning with the day she stepped on the mine. She is further supported by a visionary dream experienced in the depths of her despair in Quetta, in which the Prophet Muhammad encouraged her. At some point all the memoirists depended, successfully or not, on non-family-member interveners, but Farah Ahmedi's descriptions of her rescues most stress her own moments of abject helplessness and the rescuers as reinforcing her faith both in humanity and in God. Despite the explicitly Islamic content of her Prophetic dream, her allusions to the power of faith and Divine help are otherwise carefully nonsectarian, asserting the commonality of Muslim and Christian concepts of faith. Yet her remarks echo Saba Mahmoud's portrayals of Muslim women whose agency includes an explicit submission to Divine will, not triumphal individualism. Yet she also describes extraordinary physical and psychological feats she herself performed, on behalf of her mother and herself from age ten onward.

Other vignettes of the memoirists' mothers contribute to dismantle any orientalist stereotype of passivity. Farooka Gauhari's mother, widowed at an

early age, raised six children alone from 1966 onward.[23] The most power-
fully univocal example of a mother's agency is Zoya's portrayal of her mother
as active in women's covert progressive organizing in RAWA from the
organization's inception in Kabul in the mid-1970s. Zoya's mother involves
her preadolescent daughter in aspects of the work. Zoya's father is also portrayed as an exemplary progressive male head of household, who supports
his wife's political work. First Zoya's father and then her mother were 'disappeared,' presumably killed, in 1992 during the Mujaheddin take-over of
Kabul. Zoya remained in the custody of another strong and resourceful
woman, her 'grandmother,' represented by Zoya as not her biological grandmother but a generation older than her parents. Despite her active contribu-
tion to two generations of activists, she is also the widowed survivor of an
unhappy arranged marriage, as she tells Zoya, something one could not
walk away from in her day due to physical and social dependency of women
on men. This elder later delivers the orphaned Zoya to a RAWA boarding
school in Pakistan. 'Grandmother' continues to play the role of a more
conservative female elder, moving from place to place to stay in proximity
to Zoya in her RAWA residences, but also fretting over loss of time with her,
and showing anger when she learns of the adult Zoya's perilous secret trips
back to Kabul in support of RAWA activities resisting the Taliban.

Farooka Gauhari, alone among this sample, writes as a middle-aged academic, herself a mother who had difficulty choosing between prewar opportunities for advanced study abroad and childrearing, ultimately choosing
the latter. She describes a peacetime of expanding professional and familial
opportunities in a progressive family. She deals indefatigably with the loss
of her highly supportive husband, who disappeared on the first day of the
Marxist coup in 1978. She narrates, from her diaries, her two-year quest for
definitive 'evidence' of his fate, and her painful decision to abandon the
quest when it becomes necessary to evacuate her two adolescent sons under
threat of the Marxist army draft. She details strategic actions to avoid being
co-opted politically, yet preserve her vital paid employment as a university
professor, and to avoid being arrested herself while inquiring high and low
in the Marxist government for definitive news of her husband. She has not
been politically invisible. As a highly educated progressive, she resisted
direct recruitment by Leftist parties before and after the coup and criticized
the infamous Hafizullah Amin even before the coup for failing to imple-
ment ideals of democratic, representative leadership. She fears and resists
some of her sons' risky behavior, but takes immense calculated risks herself.

Like other memoirists, she describes moments when she simply reached the end of her tether, dissolving into exhausted numbness, paralysis or tears of despair which (like other mothers portrayed) she tries to conceal from her children. Suppression emotional expressions for social reasons might be seen as the agentive flip side of traditional *gham-xádí* performance expectations, rather avoiding expressing vulnerability and despair, as a social intervention. Reciprocally, several of the memoirists recall being admonished as very young children not to cry in front of their mothers (e.g., when a family member is killed or imprisoned) so as to protect them from additional pain. Suppressing of expressions of grief and fear becomes a small child's form of agency, as well as a mother's. In Gauhari's case and others, emotional reticence and circumspection are not just female *sabr* but strategically necessary for physical survival.

The tension between endurance of the unaddressable (*sabr*) and indomitable action supplies the core dramatic motion in all these accounts. That this action almost always has the preservation of some tattered remains of a family, not achievement of personal agency as such, as its primary goal, is made clear by most memoirists' repeated motivation of their actions not in activist principles of resistance or liberation, but in family survival. In my reading of this recurrent theme, an Afghan valuation of family as the primary human emotional, moral, political and economic unit trumps any Western modernist ethos of personal liberation or self-realization in resistance.

Two polar variations on the theme of the primacy of family preservation are provided by Zoya and Sulima. The orphaned Zoya describes her socialization to adult activism as a member of RAWA, organizing boarding schools and residential work units providing family-like nurturance, promoting unswerving loyalty to the organization, its members and beneficiaries. RAWA's insistence on covertness can be seen as an instrumental extension of the urgent family value of privacy, in wartime not just a matter of honor but of physical survival. In one incident, Zoya remonstrates with a promising young RAWA-educated worker who has consented to a marriage arranged by her family, to a young man educated in a madrasa. In a precise mirror image of the moral outrage of conservative families faced with daughters' self-choice, Zoya questions her vehemently as to how she can choose to overturn all her RAWA education and its values of secularism and women's emancipation, betraying essential group loyalty by acquiescing to such a marriage. Zoya says she herself will seek no private (family) life, specifically no marriage, in her commitment to RAWA 'until Afghanistan is free.'

Sulima, alone among those reviewed here, focuses her critique and her activism primarily on male domestic abuse over two generations. She portrays her extended family as at times complicit in spousal abuse. Sulima presents her father as having first encouraged her high spirits and excellent performance in elementary school, using her example to browbeat her elder brother, then turning on her violently for her women's rights activism as a high school and college student in the 1970s. She dates his sudden change to a religious reawakening anomalous in the family. He accuses her of violating family honor with her political activism. Her adolescent and young adult politics were dedicated, under the banner of Marxism, to personal freedom and self-actualization in her account, very like Western secular feminism.

As a political refugee from Hafizullah Amin's regime, first in Europe and then in the United States, her main adversary is a psychologically and physically abusive husband. Her stated goal over several years is to save the marriage, partly in hopes of reviving what began as her strategic self-rescue from a threatened forced marriage and became an intense love relationship. She also portrays her reluctance to divorce as motivated by her Afghanistan-dwelling mother's concern for family honor. Her detailed description of cyclical physical attacks and reconciliations invites a very Western-style vision of the dynamics of domestic abuse. She herself does not ascribe her husband's abuse pattern, which developed only in Europe and America, to 'Afghan culture' as she has her father's aggression, nor does she psychologize or point out the similarity of her marital history to Western abuse patterns, but she certainly provides detail that invites a U.S.-style interpretation of the dynamics of the relationship. She blames her husband's elder brother for impugning her husband's masculinity and authority because she holds a more prestigious job, works with male non-relatives and earns more than he does in European exile. At the same time she gives details that support an Afghan reading of character flaws in her husband, even before the relationship became abusive (intense emotional dependency first on his mother and then on her, a weak work ethic, alcohol abuse once it is available). Such flaws would be read as such in Afghan cultural contexts as well. While Sulima works her way upward in each academic and business endeavor, in her narrative, he acts to sabotage them because he says for an Afghan man to live on his wife's income is shameful.

Whereas in the other memoirists' accounts, male failings are balanced by praise for other males' strengths, Sulima's narrative alone in this selection provides the reader so inclined with ample fodder for a blanket orientalist indictment of Afghan men's character and behavior in intimate relationships, of Afghan patriarchal customs and male privilege as the main basis for the power to abuse. She herself draws back from any such blanket indictment, however, leaving the breadth of implication to the reader. Like all the other memoirists, she regards progressive education, especially but not exclusively female, as key to Afghan women's rescue from oppression.

A trope of the unimaginable frames all the losses and failures of the memoirs, not any cultural predilection or inevitability attending Afghanistan's descent into chaos. The memoirists' chronotope of a gracious, secure, peaceful and cautiously progressive time/place called prewar Afghanistan, either in their own memories or their parents,' challenges the orientalist stereotype of Afghanistan and Muslim societies in general as violent by nature. The Afghan image of the family as the failed locus of security, identity and agency, dismantled by radical insecurity due to outside forces, introduces in turn high-risk rescue narratives in which non-family members (mostly Afghan) must be trusted to play crucial roles. Pazira's family relies on an extraordinary young, village-born female refugee-smuggler, orphaned in a Soviet raid, who as her jihad, her revenge for her parents' death, becomes a burka-clad guide for families escaping to Pakistan on foot. She represents her charges as her family, finessing checkpoints and safehouses along the way. Crippled Farah Ahmedi and her asthmatic mother, unable to pay the border guards' bribes, are smuggled across the Pakistani border by another escaping family. Friends and friends of friends shield Sulima and Hala from death threats at their own peril and arrange for their respective escapes. Extraordinary feats of rescue by strangers and the trust they entail are counters to the previously unimaginable trauma and betrayal of war, but these remarkable rescues are initiated for the most part by Afghans, not Western-mediated.

Historical consciousness as theme and trope

As appropriate to memoir in Western genre theory, each memoirist tells a story entangled in larger historical events. Though their competence and ambition as historians vary, all begin with an idyllic picture of a peaceful, secure, and to some extent progressive prewar Afghanistan, not a timeless utopia (far less a benighted oriental backwater) but a place situated in twentieth century change. Pazira and Gauhari are most knowledgeable and nuanced in their representations of a narrative context of global and national events and disasters. The two youngest witnesses, Farah Ahmedi and Latifa, born in the 1980s, manage the telling of history least perceptively. Latifa is conspicuously weak, mostly silent and sometimes inaccurate as an historian, yet she establishes historical authenticity by opening with a riveting 'I was there' historical vignette. On the first day of Taliban rule in Kabul, her businessman father, in a state of partial disbelief, took her and her flight attendant sister by car to see the bodies of ex-President Najibullah and his brother hanging mutilated in Aryana Square. Latifa, an aspiring adolescent journalist, had been 'publishing' a small magazine, hand-written and hand-circulated, for her friends, reporting on popular Western teen culture. This effort ended under Taliban restrictions. She describes her slide through boredom into depression and temporal disengagement, paralleling her mother's, only remedied when she started teaching others' children in a small clandestine home school.

Farah Ahmedi repeatedly builds her story around explicit disclaimers of historical knowledge. She says that her family in her early childhood lacked awareness of larger events unfolding around them. She describes her father as a progressive small businessman, trained as a tailor, who built a business importing and retailoring used Western garments into Western-style clothes popular with urban Afghans. The apolitical innocence of this first-generation, rural-to-urban-migrating, rising middle class minority family is consequential to her understanding of their fate, though she never implies that, had they engaged as informed activists, that fate would have been different. She portrays them as history's innocent victims. Her story is the most anti-ideological (or non-ideological) of the bunch. It also focuses most meticulously on personal psychological events, her own and her mother's. In this it most mirrors Euro-American modernist autobiography, with its introspective, psychologistic and developmental foci. In giving such entrée to the young adult author's psychic history, one might ask, does this account Americanize ('colonize') Farah, or rather establish for targeted American readers that Afghans also have (to them recognizable) psychological lives? Despite her stated desire to leave wartime Afghanistan forever as a young girl, certain elements of Afghan cultural experience remain strong. Farah reports some notably Afghan psychic experiences, for instance her dream vision of the Prophet that guides her and gives her hope in the most desperate conditions in Quetta. At the end of her memoir she proclaims a mobile identity: 'Today I feel I am both Afghan and American.

And today is not necessarily where it ends.'[24] By contrast, in other memoirs, the moment of departure from Afghan soil, even when fleeing for their lives, is a type scene of expressed ambivalence or sorrow. Further, the personal psychological history of other memoirists and their families is balanced and contexted by more detailed juxtapositions of historical and political data points.

Each memoirist's political position is implicit if not explicit: all the Harakat (Shi'a) party activists Nelufer Pazira identifies as such are progressives, while Hekmatyar's (primarily Pashtun Hezb-i Islami) people are brutal. Latifa speaks with unalloyed respect for 'General Masoud' (the Tajik Ahmad Shah Masoud) while Malalai Joya sees the Jamiat-e Islami, Masoud's party, as among the worst rapists and murderers. Hala and Sulima (sisters, Pashto speakers, sixteen years apart in age) are sketchy about historical time sequences such as the gathering strength of mujahed opposition, and they understate the overall level of Pashtun opposition to the Marxist regime. They leave totally unmentioned the loss of 2,000 or more killed in the first days of the Marxist coup in Kabul, so prominent in Gauhari's account. They extol the Marxists' progressive agenda, whom they nonetheless criticize as unrealistic about the pace of social change. Double-voicing again: the selective politico-historical perspectives of these writers are so understated as to remain invisible to a general American or European audience but palpable to readers Afghan or otherwise who have attempted to trace the political roots and history of the conflict. The deep, culturally and politically consequential rural-urban divide in Afghan experience and aspirations is also understated, though not totally ignored. One wonders if the selectivity or sketchiness of historical context in several of these accounts (Latifa, much of Sulima's and Hala's narratives, Farah Ahmedi) is a function of co-authorship and editorial choice as much as the primary authors,' assuming limited historical interest or acumen in a non-specialist Western readership primarily interested in highly personalized narratives.

Voicing and stylistics, not just data points, convey varieties of historical consciousness in these works. Farah Ahmedi's presentation style is a naïve, mostly linear circumstantial account. Her credited Afghan co-author, Tamim Ansary, an accomplished English-language memoirist himself, may have been instrumental in honing her nineteen-year-old voice, clear, uncomplicated, and largely devoid of metaphor, at times addressing the reader in second person as if to an American listener in a conversation. Her style contrasts with the more sophisticated and nuanced, metaphorically and imagistically rich voices of Pazira and Gauhari (working without co-authors). Pazira in particular uses a matrix of historical present tense for her core narrative, interspersed with past tense for flashbacks, to create a resonant, complex, temporal texture. Both Pazira and Gauhari build key remembered scenes into resonant interpretive metaphors. Sulima's narrative (as mediated by Batya Swift Yasgur), more starkly, uses present tense in italics only to report scenes of the highest emotion (the rapture of her wedding night; physical attacks by her father and later, by her abusive husband) and past tense for the rest. Some asides mediating between the cultures of the writer and the readers seem awkward, but as Yasgur explains in her own preface, she met the sisters as a refugee advocate supporting Haya's difficult asylum litigation, conducted from INS detention. Yasgur's motivation is general social justice for refugees in the American context, not Afghan cultural survival. The event content of the sisters' tales is compelling, but the expository style, the development of a plausible personal 'voice' in English, is possibly the least effective. Nonetheless, one highly effective dimension of this telling of two sisters' stories back to back is to illustrate (as they remark) how differences in birth order and exposure to different phases of Afghanistan's fraught recent political history, as well as the family history in that context, make for vastly different experiences and narratives even within one household. Sulima's narrative could be read as a handbook of failings of Afghan patriarchy in contemporary times; Haya's is not, leaving to the reader whether to imagine a timeless Afghan culture or radical historical disruption.

Burkas: the obligatory trope

Gillian Whitlock in *Soft Weapons* trenchantly critiques the othering power that the veil in general and the burka (called *chaderi* in Afghanistan) in particular exert over Western audiences, as exotic fetish objects: 'The image of the veiled woman…is a powerful trope of the passive "third world" subject, and it sustains the discursive self-representation of Western women as secular, liberated, and individual agents.'[25] 'The first time I put on a burka' is a type scene in all these memoirs. Only American-raised Masuda Sultan, first donning a burka to travel from Pakistan incognito to visit family in Kandahar during the Taliban period, describes the burka as inducing in her a sense of solidarity with her Afghanistan-dwelling women ancestors, as if becoming 'a native, organic Afghan, the person I would have been.'[26] The Afghanistan-raised memoirists describe the first burka experience as stifling, disorienting, physically encumbering, even deathly, but each goes on to describe their further experience with the burka as a tool of female mobility and strategic anonymity, especially in flight to refuge or in resistance activities. Zoya, Latifa and Malalai Joya all recount episodes of burka-theater advocated by Western well-wishers who either staged dramatic unveilings as Western-venue performance events (Zoya unveiled at the hands of Oprah Winfrey at a RAWA fundraiser organized by Eve Ensler in Madison Square Garden), paraded Afghan activist women to European speaking engagements and interviews in burkas (Latifa: 'So Shékéba and our little troop in chadris have made the rounds of important people,') or were resisted (Malalai Joya, who declined to wear then dramatically strip off a burka when receiving the International Human Rights Film Award in Germany in 2008).[27] Mahmoud, Abu Lughod, and numerous others writing on contemporary veiling practices concur on the complexities of the veil as social signifier and agentive resource. Rostami Poovy quotes Afghan women activists advising Westerners that the burka is not their problem, rather physical security, food, health and livelihoods.[28] The weaponized burkas figuring in January and June 2010 suicide bombings reported in Afghanistan are another dramatic example.[29] But whatever the complexities, pragmatic and symbolic, of burka-wearing in Afghanistan over the last century, from Queen Soraya's public doffing of the burka in the 1920s, Gillian Whitlock reminds us of the likelihood of recalcitrantly monothematic, even voyeuristic, Western readings of the burka featured on memoir book jackets, because the exoticized icon of Afghan women's victimization sells books.

Conclusion: slippages

Reading this sample of available themes and tropes, partly as an over-hopeful antidote to flattened dichotomous readings of Afghans as helpless victims or terrorists, I have endeavored to illustrate the possibilities of alternative readings and double voicings within memoir texts. In every case, agency is embedded in, and springs from, different forms of victimization, yet memoirists at various points transcend the merely reactive stance. Rescue narratives abound, but they portray the rescued as an agent together with a diverse cast of characters not including Laura or George W. Bush. Readers are also, however, offered an opportunity for some mixture of empathy (itself a dangerously seductive stance)[30] and voyeurism. Given that the memoirist (Afghan, female, usually young adult) is coming from a very different historical-political position than her target audience, what kinds of slippage (potential or actual) might be traced between the stated or implied instrumental intention of the text, and its effects in reception? Is a given memoir a call to admire the portrayed strengths of Afghan women (and men in specific cases), or to act politically? Is the invited response meant to be awe, intrigue, empathy, or action?

One major pattern of slippage in the co-optation/reception process, a triploid co-optative motion, is as follows:

(a) At least some of the appeal of these Afghan women's memoirs is orientalist or exoticist, a voyeuristic interest in 'behind the veil' imagery of silencing and rescue that is prominently invoked in or around some memoirs (book titles or subtitles, back cover text and cover photos of burka/chadari wearers) and in commentaries on them in the mass media.

(b) The memoirists engage and try to co-opt or subvert this voyeuristic energy through performed narrative intimacy, presenting through highly detailed descriptions of actions and feelings of private persons, in intimate or traumatic contexts, the 'real Afghan women' who are, almost to a woman, expressly concerned to convey personally the collective effects of extreme insecurity on their families and communities over thirty years of warfare. One generic example of this move is memoirists' 'The first time I put on a burka' narratives, which move the audience's angle of gaze from outside to inside the burka as worn, emphasizing how initially alienating the garment was to each of these female Afghan selves under dangerous conditions, but how the wearer subsequently realized and mastered its potential for tactical use.

(c) The memoirists' urgent desire for safe and peaceful self-determination may nonetheless be received by audience members with two other mental reinforcements of colonial-oid dominance:
   – Versions of the 'rescue the women' (from the men?) theme so well attested elsewhere in orientalist/general colonialist discourse (noted by Said, Spivak, Abu Lughod and others)
   – The argument that military intervention or other use of force toward men is necessary to provide this rescue.

As this thematic sampling illustrates, close reading of these memoirs alongside background history of contemporary Afghan insecurity and conflict, from local ethnohistory to global politics, discovers potential for double voicing about the nature of victimhood and its agency, between-the-lines subtexts on the historical emergence of forms of agency for Afghan women and men. This would not, however, prevent a flattened, recidivist reading of these accounts in which both the nature of the individual subject and her array of choices at home and abroad are construed in latently or overtly orientalist or Eurocentric feminist ways.

PART 3

ORIENTALISM AS WAR

11

FANON'S 'GUERRE DES ONDES'

RESISTING THE CALL OF ORIENTALISM

*John Mowitt**

'I was compelled therefore to conduct a sort of partisan war on behalf of my philosophical ideas.'

Georg Lukács[1]

I propose in the following that Edward Said's trilogy, *Orientalism*, *The Question of Palestine*, and *Covering Islam*, is less concerned with the intellectual tradition of 'really existing' orientalism, than with the intellectual and political task of producing the *concept* of orientalism. Because it is through the concept of orientalism that I aim to contribute to the topic, 'Orientalism and War,' it will be necessary at the outset to spend some time with Said's texts, and, in particular those moments in them where the concept of orientalism is, as it were, under construction. Moreover, because, as my title

* This chapter draws from 'Stations of Exception' in Mowitt, *Radio: Essays in Bad Reception*.

makes plain, I believe (indeed Said himself believed) that Frantz Fanon has something important to say about orientalism and war, especially that aspect of it that achieves distinctness in the context of anti-colonial struggle waged both on the battlefield, but also in the 'war of opinion,' I want to place special emphasis on the last text in Said's trilogy, *Covering Islam* where the concept of orientalism is produced through an explicit engagement with, as he repeats throughout the text, 'television, radio and newspapers.' My angle is this: perhaps the title, 'Orientalism and War' contains a typo. Perhaps what we, in fact, are concerned with is that orientalism *is* war, and if this is so, then perhaps what is understood by both orientalism and war requires renewed intellectual attention.

To make the case about Said's conceptual preoccupations, I will observe that the final chapter of the final installment in the 'orientalism' trilogy is titled, 'Knowledge and Power.' This is an unmistakable reference to the work of Michel Foucault, a figure who haunts the trilogy from beginning to end and whose invocation at its end invites us to recognize that Said sees his project as, properly speaking, 'genealogical.' Indeed, he appears to want deliberately to leave us with the impression that this is so. It is interesting, of course, that in Said's *Raritan* obituary for Foucault, he placed special emphasis on the importance for Foucault of his encounter with Iran—also at the core of *Covering Islam*—arguing that the precipitous rightward turn of the revolution importantly complicated Foucault's investments in the agency of knowledge/power. I stress this because it is precisely around the problem of agency that Said is most touchy about Foucault, preferring for that reason Antonio Gramsci's concept of hegemony to that of knowledge/power. In other words, it is precisely here that Said stakes a claim for his own agency as an analyst of orientalism and thus needs to take account of this in delimiting the concept of orientalism; about which, more in a moment.

What then do we learn about the concept of orientalism by and at the end of *Covering Islam*? Clearly, the insistent evocation of Foucault's work from the seventies functions to establish that orientalism is a form of knowledge/power, in effect, a discourse, or to invoke Foucault's own alternative, discipline. Said, concerned about the politics of knowledge, embraces this alternative. More particularly, and here one encounters a defining aspect of the concept of orientalism, he focuses on academic disciplines not merely because orientalism is at home among them, but because he understands academic disciplines as 'interpretive communities.' In other words, orientalism embodies knowledge/power in constituting an institutionalized means by which to produce, legitimate and disseminate a way of understanding a given object, in the case of orientalism, the Orient. Although Said rashly dismisses the history of science in his opening pass over the connection between knowledge and interpretation,[2] he does so in order to unleash the epistemological scandal of orientalism's constructed, and therefore interested, knowledge of its object. Thus, to grasp the concept of orientalism one must recognize its status as an interpretive machine. It is not that this status is unique to orientalism, rather that orientalism is inconceivable in the absence of such a machine. This is what it means to produce a concept.

But this is also only half the story. Throughout *Covering Islam* Said stresses, somewhat paradoxically, that orientalism is unconscious of its interpretive character. This expresses itself not only in orientalism's disavowal of the interested character of its knowledge, but also in its preemptive dismissal of 'every major advance in interpretive theory since Nietzsche, Marx and Freud.'[3] While this might appear to be simply a gesture of affiliation with Foucault's work—specifically his 1964 essay, 'Nietzsche, Freud, Marx'—here it has a more pedestrian structural function. Specifically, what such formulations do is tie together the various statements about interpretation that appear in the orientalism trilogy, statements that, in the end, produce what daylight there is between Said and orientalism. It is not just that, unlike orientalists, Said consciously *affirms* the interpretive character of his project, but that his construction of the concept of orientalism openly discloses its fraught character. Put succinctly, orientalism is an 'interpretive community' that cannot recognize this. In effect, it operates in denial of what makes it possible. Although easy to miss, this insight is tucked into Said's choice of the word 'covering' in his title. As he explains in his introductory chapter 'covering' is a pun, referring both to coverage—in the sense of media attention—and to cover up—in the sense of obfuscation; a rhetorical gesture that obliges one not only to pay careful attention to Said's own language, but also to the intimacy between media ('television, radio, and newspapers') and interpretation in his study.

A second defining aspect of the concept of orientalism derives immediately from Said's construal of it as an interpretive community. He writes:

In other words, what we are dealing with here are in the very widest sense communities of interpretation, many of them at odds with one another, prepared in many instances to go to war with one another, all of them creating and revealing themselves and their interpretations as very central features of their existence. No one lives in direct contact either with truth or with reality. Each of us lives in a world actually made by human beings, in which such things as 'the nation' or 'Christianity' or 'Islam' are the result of agreed-upon convention, of historical processes, and above all, of willed human labor expended to give those things an identity we can recognize.[4]

When summarizing this insight in 'Orientalism Reconsidered' from 1985 he sharpens what I take to be the salient point:

Far from being a defense either of the Arabs or of Islam—as my book was taken by many to be—my argument was that neither existed except as 'communities of interpretation,' and that, like the Orient itself, each designation represented interests, claims, projects, ambitions, and rhetorics that were not only in violent disagreement, but also in a situation of open warfare.[5]

What attracts attention here is the repeated reference to war in Said's analysis of interpretive communities. Indeed, in producing the concept of orientalism, Said not only renders it an interpretive machine, but—if I may be indulged a passing reference to *A Thousand Plateaus*—an interpretive war machine.[6] While it is true that in the passage from *Covering* he avers that interpretive communities like orientalism are prepared, 'in many instances' to go to war, in the subsequent sharpening of the point this hesitation disappears. Interpretive communities are 'not only in violent disagreement, but also in a situation of open warfare.' Thus, to summarize somewhat brutally, what the concept of orientalism entails is both interpretation and war.

That said, we ought not overlook the terms of Said's *apologia* in the passage from 'Orientalism Reconsidered,' for they highlight something otherwise easy to miss about the concept of orientalism. Refusing the mischaracterization of his partisanship on behalf of 'Arabs' and 'Islam,' Said includes both these and 'the Orient itself' under the capacious heading of 'interpretive communities,' stressing that warfare involves belligerent parties. Put differently, as I stressed earlier, while orientalism is an interpretive machine, it is not uniquely so. Here, 'Arabs,' 'Islam' and the 'Orient' all emerge not simply as interpretive communities, but as interpretive communities at war. There are two motivations for this emphasis. On the one hand, what this draws attention to is the difficulty one faces in trying to identify 'the other' per se as part of the concept of orientalism. Clearly, if interpretation is rooted in war, and if 'the Orient' is an interpretive community, then both it and 'the Occident' are party to the conflict that defines their relation. Certain tendentious—and largely identitarian—formulations within postcolonial studies notwithstanding, Said does not here situate the

Orient on the side of the other. Instead, in a surprisingly psychoanalytical gesture, he splits the other situating it within the violence that defines the belligerent encounter between warring interpretive communities, as if the other were a shared epiphenomenal projection that sustains the war itself. In this sense, 'othering' may well belong to the concept of orientalism, but the 'Orient' as other does not.

On the other hand, this very reading of the other urges us to think more carefully the relation between war and interpretation, and ask: in what sense do they imply or otherwise belong to one another? To answer, one is obliged to revisit the advances in interpretation that orientalism must disavow so as to sustain its interested character. In a nutshell, the work of Nietzsche, Marx and Freud. Earlier I proposed that Said's interest in this material was spurred by Foucault, and while this is almost certainly true it is also misleading, for what it fails to appreciate is the distinctive link perceived by Said between Foucault and Nietzsche. As he says in his obituary for Foucault: 'he is best understood, I think, as perhaps the greatest of Nietzsche's modern disciples.'[7] Indeed, while Said refers throughout the orientalism trilogy to Nietzsche, Marx and Freud, the figure whose work he cites at length is Nietzsche who also figures prominently in an essay written during the 'run up' to *Orientalism*, 'Conrad and Nietzsche,' from 1976. The obvious question—why Nietzsche?—is best answered by noting that a particular passage in Nietzsche's early work recurs in Said's texts from this period. It derives from, 'On Truth and Lie in an Extramoral Sense' and reads:

What, then, is truth? A mobile army (*Ein bewegliches Heer*) of metaphors, metonyms, and anthropomorphisms—in short, a sum of human relations, which have been enhanced, transposed, and embellished poetically and rhetorically, and which after long use seem firm, canonical and obligatory to a people: truths are illusions about which one has forgotten that this is what they are, metaphors which are worn out and without sensuous power, coins that have lost their pictures and now matter only as metal, no longer as coins.[8]

When re-cited in chapter three of *Orientalism* this passage is presented as the epistemology that underlies both Nietzsche's theory of language, and the theory of interpretation Said deploys to account for his 'political' definition of orientalism. Although here he characterizes orientalism as a 'school of interpretation,'[9] it is clear that he understands by this precisely what, only three years later, he calls a 'community of interpretation.' Also clear is the fact that the passage cited is understood to be suffused with the embellishments that appear around it in 'Conrad and Nietzsche,' embellishments that make explicit reference to the aphorism in *The Gay Science*, 'Our new infinite,' where Nietzsche writes: 'our world has become "infinite" for us all over again, inasmuch as we cannot reject the possibility that *it may include infinite interpretations*.'[10] In other words, it is because truth is rhetorical, figurative, that interpretation is infinite. Put differently, the world, our world, is interpretation all the way down. But then, to re-pose Freud's question to Einstein: *warum Krieg?*

It seems crucial here to note that in the passage repeatedly cited from Nietzsche, truth is characterized (*nota bene*, metaphorically) as a 'mobile army.' If this material contains the theory of language that supports Said's concept of interpretive community, then should we not conclude that war engages interpretation at the level of the very language deployed by any given interpretive community? More specifically, and this is a point that Said himself resists, truth is not only rhetorical, but it is precisely the alibi interpretive communities circulate to disavow their identities as interpretive communities, that is, as epistemo-political projects rooted in the infinity of interpretations. Truth, in other words, is the official story generated by interpretive communities hostile to or defensive about 'advances in interpretive theory.' It is, in a word, coverage.

But what does it mean to say that Said 'resists' the implications of his own insight? In fact, I had explained myself when earlier insisting that Said, 'rashly dismisses the history of science.' In other words, Said's account of interpretation and therefore interpretive communities, depends on a rigid, even ontological distinction between science and, in effect, the humanities and social sciences. The former is not historically conditioned, while the latter are. What is puzzling about this otherwise familiar hesitation, is that for Said, it is grounded in a theory of language in which no distinction between scientific statements (however formalized) and non-scientific statements is permissible. One can of course insist that the theory of language has come a long way since Nietzsche, but the point remains: Said does not say this. He simply produces a distinction between knowledge that is subject to interpretation and knowledge that is not, and then proceeds to ground this concept of interpretation in Nietzsche's theory of language and the rhetorical construal of truth it entails.

I think this awkward situation invites a somewhat different reading of 'the mobile army of metaphors, etc.' invoked by both Said and Nietzsche. If truth is, as it were, the effect of the activity, the campaign of this mobile army, then in a crucial sense interpretive communities are at war with themselves. Put differently, if truth is the alibi interpretive communities give themselves so as to disavow their interpretive character, then, in a certain sense, this truth depends—and depends fundamentally—on suppressing the trope movement (to crib from Avital Ronell) that sustains it, and by which, presumably, it is infinitely menaced. To claim that Said resists such conclusions is simply to point out that he does not believe the concept of orientalism to be false, or merely metaphorical. He believes that it is true, indeed he defended its truth vigorously throughout his career, and while he never simply declares his analysis to be true, he almost invariably follows his citations of Nietzsche with an anxious repudiation of their alleged nihilistic implications. He is, in short, keen to separate himself from those who read Nietzsche's theory of language as entailing a skeptical denial of the existence of the real world. Why? Not because he wants to cast his lot with scientists, but because he wants his analysis of orientalism to have, as we say, real world traction. This is, of course, entirely laudable but, and it is a big but, this betrays the concept of orientalism, precisely to the extent that it fails to recognize the war that must be waged within the concept to produce what truth can be claimed for it. Indeed, one might reasonably argue that the very distinction between interpretive and non-interpretive knowledge, is a metaphor caught up in a strategy of self-containment.

Here then is the most robust version of Said's concept of orientalism. It is not simply an interpretive war machine, it is also, and most deeply, an interpretive war machine at war with itself. With regard to the orientalism trilogy, this situation expresses itself in the ambivalence that haunts especially the first and third volumes, an ambivalence that might be brutally summarized in the question: does Said believe that the Orient truly exists outside orientalism? In the subtitle to *Covering*, Said puts the relevant matter thus: 'how the media and experts determine how we see the rest of the world.' On the Pantheon Books dust jacket of the text the title and subtitle are separated by a small graphic, a photograph of a photographer photographing two 'Islamic militants' who are quite shamelessly posing for the photograph. The abyssal image appears literally 'torn from the headlines.'

True, Said was not responsible for the cover design (it was done by Paul Gamarello), but he is clearly, perforce, implicated in the first person plural pronoun that appears in his subtitle. How 'we' (you and I) see the world through the eyes of the media, a world, as the cover graphic implies, posed for our view. Moreover, 'determine' is a strong and intellectually charged verb. In Said's hands it cannot but resonate in a Marxian context where it

Figure 11.1: *Covering Islam* cover (courtesy of Pantheon).

has long been used to understand the causal relation between the base and the superstructure, between, if you will, real events and their coverage. One might further adduce here the 'response to his critics' worked out in *Culture and Imperialism* where the concept of 'contrapuntal reading' expressly operates to include the 'speaking back' of the really existing subjects of imperialism, but I think the point is established. The war I am teasing out of the concept of orientalism is actively present in Said's relation to his materials, materials that include not only the media coverage of Islam (and in this text more often than not Iran), but Islam 'itself.'

So where then does Fanon fit? The *guerre des ondes* (war of the airwaves) of my title is a phrase that appears in an essay Fanon wrote during the Algerian war for independence, an essay, written by a partisan, on the use of radio as a weapon in the context of this anti-colonial confrontation. If I invoke it here it is because I propose that the distinctive resonance it produces between war waged against a quintessentially orientalist regime, and war waged within the concept of orientalism places vital theoretical and political pressure on Said's construal of this concept, particularly as it finds expression in *Covering Islam*.

Although my reading of Fanon's essay circles around the relation between the political stances of refusal and resistance it inscribes, it seems important to establish at the outset that even though the word 'orientalism' never appears in it, Fanon's essay is marked by what I have been calling its concept. The point can be made simply by noting that Fanon, in the framing of his radio study, writes: 'Radio-Alger [the local affiliate station of the French Broadcasting Network] sustains the occupant's culture, marks it off from non-culture, from the nature of the occupied. Radio-Alger, the voice of France in Algeria, constitutes the sole center of reference at the level of news. Radio-Alger, for the settler, is a daily invitation not to 'go native' (*se métisser*, more literally to 'cross breed') not to forget the rightfulness of his culture.'[11] Although recent historical research has complicated Fanon's presentation of Radio-Alger,[12] clearly here both the distinction between culture and non-culture as well as the anxious assertion of the priority, the rightfulness, of the former, are hallmarks of orientalist discourse. Moreover, as if directly anticipating Said's analysis in *Covering*, Fanon here stresses that French radio establishes the orientalist distinction between culture and non-culture in concert with its control of news about the city of Algiers and the country of Algeria. Put differently, Fanon grasps that radio belongs cortically to the project of sustaining the French presence in Algeria by interpreting that presence and its necessity for the occupier and the occupant alike. Although it may strike one as a bit of a stretch, it also seems that Fanon grasps radio as an interpretive war machine, that is, as a weapon already deployed for the purpose of what von Clausewitz called, in Book One of *On War*, 'intelligence,' not its gathering per se, but its control. If, as von Clausewitz specifies, intelligence concerns 'every sort of information about the enemy and his country,' then the constitutive belligerence of orientalism and the colonial apparatus of radio, strictly speaking, collaborate.[13]

I will take it that this settles, in general terms, the matter of whether Fanon indeed concerns himself with orientalism.

What then does Fanon have to say about the 'war of the airwaves'? As is generally known, 'This is the Voice of Algeria,' appears in 1959, in a collection of essays entitled, *L'an cinq de la révolution algérienne*. Both the essay and the collection are rallying cries. With the revolution hanging by a thread, Fanon is clearly seeking to snatch victory from the jaws of defeat, a situation largely obscured by Fanon's English translator who renders the title with the retrospectively confident *A Dying Colonialism*. As in the allegorical chapter that opens the volume, 'Algeria Unveiled,' the chapter on radio struggles to produce through the reliable and resonant metonymy of the voice, the national subject of Algeria, and it does so in the mood of anticipation. 'This' is the voice of an Algeria that is no longer French Algeria, where the deixis of the shifter 'this' clicks back and forth but also ahead to a condition that, in a quasi-performative gesture is being called into existence, but that strictly speaking does not yet exist. In addition, the shifter 'this' situates the radio broadcast both in the context of the struggle, but also in Fanon's words about that struggle. 'This' is spoken/written by Fanon and cannot but reference that. His is the voice of liberated Algeria. But 'this' (actually *ici*, or 'here' in French) also does something more challenging. In effect, it situates the revolutionary confrontation on the split stage of the text and the conflict. 'This/here,' the word in its idiomatic function, locates the voice of Algeria both on the radio, but also literally on the page, a page that unlike the radio broadcast, reanimates the voice of Algeria whenever and wherever it is read. This is rendered, I think, more effectively through 'here' than 'this,' although as shifters both are messages about codes. As such, this 'shifty' dynamic functions to elaborate a linguistic frame for the essay's reflections on resistance. In sketching the details of this reflection it will be my concern to underscore the way the essay brings resistance and reception into a relation that complicates the stability of both concepts, reminding us to think twice about them both and consider directly what they teach us about the war in and with orientalism.

As has been suggested, Fanon moves early in the essay to establish that because the radio was understood by Algerians as central to the projection of French colonial power it was, as he specifies, 'refused' by most sectors of the indigenous population.[14] In support of his contention that economic reason alone cannot adequately account for this refusal, he points out that Algerians aware of the content of Radio-Alger broadcasting refused to purchase receivers because of its sacrilegious character. Emphasizing the collective character of radio listening in the Maghreb, Fanon specifies that French radio addressed parents and children in ways thought to undermine the codes governing their relations largely as defined within a local variant of Islam. This matters because it allows him to advance one of his cortical themes, namely, that anti-colonial struggle necessitates some sort of negotiation with secular modernity. Hence, his opening stress on the refusal of radio receivers. Conceptually and politically, the essay thus begins by establishing radio reception as the object of what he will later refer to as the 'no,' the refusal of colonialism. This is a refusal grounded not in reception itself, but in a traditional defense against receiving what might well call tradition into question.

Significantly, the vocabulary of resistance is not deployed here, as if to set up a signal distinction between resistance and what he calls refusal, or at other times rejection, a decidedly more psychoanalytically inflected concept. In fact, Fanon later insists that the refusal to purchase radios was not an explicit act of resistance. Equally significant, however, is that when resistance does enter the essay, it does so as a characterization of the French reaction to the risk of 'Arabization.' After calling Radio-Alger an 'instrument of resistance,'[15] Fanon goes on to specify: 'Among the European farmers, radio is for the most part lived as the link to the civilized world, as an effective instrument of resistance to the corrosive influence of an indigenous society that is immobile, lacking in perspective, backward and without value.'[16] The prescient observation about the role of the radio in overcoming the urban/rural divide notwithstanding, what is emphasized here is the notion that the French resist the Algerians by receiving broadcasts characterized elsewhere in the essay as the French speaking to the French. Radio-Alger is the 'voice' of France in Algeria, an appeal to the voice that, in an essay titled 'This is the Voice of Algeria,' crackles with significance.

The text confronts us then with a founding conceptual and political distinction between refusal (on the part of the Algerians) and resistance (on the part of the French). Both pivot warily around reception. In the Algerian case we have a refusal to receive, while in the French case reception serves as the very medium of resistance. In addition, both refusal and resistance pivot around power and, perhaps surprisingly, in both cases a power perceived to be capable of calling into question traditional values. Predictably, the French see themselves threatened by the very absence of values, the Algerians simply by values other than their own. This monotony of power, its lack of differentiation in either substance or orientation, soon gives way however, as does the convenient logic whereby the distinction between refusal and resistance is indexed directly to the intentions giving 'voice' to one or the other. Put differently, Fanon presents us here with a standoff, a confrontation between two voices intent on circling around a homogeneity they are concerned to shelter from each other. Resistance, apart from indicating the stance of the colonizer, is also here structurally conservative. Precisely because it expresses a structural apartness, indeed the very apartness that distinguishes culture from non-culture, it must be re-evaluated.

This process is set in motion by the revolution itself. Specifically, as events begin to unfold throughout the country and Algerians increasingly realize that distorted coverage, biased information, is better than none, the refusal to consume receivers is reversed. According to Fanon, Algerians discover that the radio, precisely to the extent that its signals obey neither linguistic nor national boundaries, can bring international perspectives to bear on the conflict, a conflict whose representation would otherwise be utterly subject to the colonial control of the news. This movement away from a preemptive and largely religious refusal of reception, is decisively accelerated with the advent of 'La Voix de l'Algérié Libre,' the radio broadcast of the FLN (National Liberation Front). Primed by their discovery of the political and military importance of intelligence, Algerians, beginning in 1956, start to demand more radios—especially battery powered sets—than suppliers can supply. They are listened to eagerly both at home and in public. As a result, and Fanon is keen to emphasize this, the radio is deprived of its status as a modern, even 'evil' object. In becoming the channel through which Algerians attune with the revolution, the radio becomes 'a unique means *to resist* the ever increasing psychological and military pressures of the occupier.'[17] In short, the radio is taken up as the weapon the French have turned it into.

This is the decisive shift. Stated succinctly, refusal gives way to resistance, receivers are consumed, and reception valued as a site of political practice. Interesting here is that what Fanon presents us with, and not merely at the conceptual level, is a confrontation between two resistances, a confrontation that in challenging us to consider whether they are identical provokes us to recognize the critical importance of resisting resistance, of sensing that something within resistance menaces it. This is not a matter of abandoning resistance, but of challenging the assumption that resistance is resistance and as such opposes power at once directly and remotely (that is, from another, radically separate, ontological location). Radio as the transgressor, the delocalizer voids this location, urging partisans to gauge carefully the cost of what resistance repeats—in the case of the radio, the non-indigenous modernity of its technological conditions of possibility—in broadcasting truth to power. Fanon renders the matter with compelling clarity in his prescient deconstruction of the voice of Algeria.

This transpires in his discussion of '*la guerre des ondes*,' as his argument is beginning to turn toward the future, a future in which the persecutorial, super-egoic voice of the radio is transmuted into an inspiring, if all too familiar, voice of national consciousness. As the relevant passages have much to say about voice, resistance and reception they bear citing at length.

Here is situated a phenomenon sufficiently original to retain our attention. The extremely advanced French technical services, with experience acquired in the world wars, and familiar with the practice of 'airwave warfare,' were quick to pick up the wavelengths of the transmitters. The programs were then systematically jammed (*brouillés*), and the 'Voice of Fighting Algeria' became inaudible. A new form of struggle was born. Leaflets counseled Algerians to keep tuned in for durations of two to three hours. In the course of one broadcast, a second station, transmitting over another wavelength would relay the first jammed station. The listener thus incorporated into the battle of the airwaves, had to figure out the tactics of the enemy, and in a manner almost physical, muscular, outmaneuver the strategy of the adversary. Often, only the operator, his ear glued to the apparatus, would have the unanticipated chance to hear the Voice. The other Algerians present in the room received the echo of this voice through the device of a privileged interpreter, who, at the end of the broadcast, was literally besieged. Precise questions were then posed to this incarnated voice.[18]

And, half a page further on, Fanon continues his characterization of the voice, further delineating the rigors of its reception.

Poorly heard (*entendue*), blanketed by the incessant jamming, obliged to switch wavelengths two or three times in the course of a single broadcast, the Voice of Fighting Algeria could hardly ever be heard in a continuous fashion. It was a chopped, discontinuous voice. [...] Under these conditions to affirm having heard the Voice of Fighting Algeria was, in a certain sense, to alter the truth, but it was above all the occasion to proclaim underhandedly one's participation in the essence of the Revolution. It was to make a deliberate choice, even if not explicit in the first months, between the congenital lie of the enemy and the true lie (*proper mensonge*) of the colonized that suddenly acquired a dimension of truth. This voice, often absent, physically inaudible, that everyone felt welling up from within, founded on an interior perception of what was the Homeland (*la Patrie*) materialized in an undeniable fashion. Every Algerian, for his part, broadcast and transmitted (*émet et transmet*) the new language.[19]

In both passages, albeit differently, Fanon references and gives new meaning to what in Daniel Lerner's study of the psychological warfare waged against Nazi Germany is called, *Schwarzhören* (black listening), that is, acts of illegal radio reception carried out by ordinary citizens and members of the resistance alike. If the French are skilled in the ways of 'airwave warfare,' it is because they had been its targets barely a decade before. Thus, in the first passage we are presented with the noisy clash of resistances, one that seeks to tune into the anti-colonial struggle, the other seeking to interrupt this attunement. Both are struggling for power with power, in this case wattage, and the capacity to project one's message. However, Fanon insists that listening in this context was not simply motivated by curiosity, but by the inner need to fuse (*faire corps*) with the nation, thereby implicating the subjectivity of the colonized in the revolutionary struggle and drawing out the deep structure of the metonym of the voice. Indeed, as the passage concludes we are presented with the figure of an incarnated voice, the broadcast materialized in its receivers.

In the second passage this voice is properly described as chopped (*hachée*) and discontinuous. The noisy clash of resistances, in spacing out the voice, in separating the voice from itself, produces a reception context comprised of a collective charged with the urgent labor of suturing the tears in the voice. It is not simply that the operator is asked for details, the entire 'black' listening audience is called upon to piece together the shreds of the jammed broadcast. Aware, somehow, that this discussion has wandered onto the terrain of what Derrida, only eight years later, called 'phonocentrism,' Fanon draws the epistemological conclusion that the Voice of Fighting Algeria is not grounded in truth, but in the true or proper lie (*le propre mensonge*). Precisely because the radiophonic voice requires the active supplementation of reception, it cannot be grounded nor can it ground itself. It is delocalized and discontinuous. Perhaps this is why Fanon insists: 'every Algerian, for his part broadcast and transmitted (*émet et transmet*) this new language,' a formulation whose lexical details make it clear that the operator who earlier mediated the voice, has now given way to a heterogeneous, collective assemblage whose nearest conceptual analogue might be a disseminated network.

Perhaps because of Fanon's principled insistence that the revolution will be made by the subjects it makes (gone is the principle of a sheltered homogeneity), his discussion of radio underscores its antimetabolic status as both a site of resistance and a site within which resistance is called into question.

Not by power as such, but by resistance itself insofar as it lends itself to various articulations and incarnations, and insofar as it is always already conflicted by and over its duel with power. Under such circumstances the voice itself forks. Consider in this light that the motif, urgently foregrounded above, of the true lie—the proper as opposed to the congenital lie—is a deft, if unwitting, rewording of what Nietzsche called the mobile army of metaphors, etc. that constituted the truth. Put differently, consider that Fanon's deconstruction of the voice finds what footing it has in the theory of language to be found in 'On Truth and Lie,' a theory that Fanon picks up, as it were, over the radio. What this convergence urges is further consideration of what earlier I called Said's resistance, his blindness to his own insight.

Initially, this resistance was described largely in epistemological terms. That is, in arguing that Said was keen not to embrace the conclusion drawn by Foucault in 'Nietzsche, Freud, Marx,' that 'there are only interpretations,'[20] I proposed that he was committed to shielding his concept of orientalism as an interpretive war machine from its enabling theory of language. Politically, this gesture of epistemological prudence is indexed not simply to having truth on one's side, but to having a side at all, that is, a really existing Orient that might confront or otherwise resist orientalism. It seems important here to think through what if any relation there is between Said's resistance to his own concept and to the possibility of the Orient's resistance to the war that is orientalism. Put differently, what Fanon urges one to recognize is that despite the cortical status of war in Said's concept of orientalism, he in fact has no theory of war to support the particular emphasis he puts on it.

To pursue this I propose that we turn attention to Carl Schmitt's attentive reading of *On War* found in his important late essay, 'Theory of the Partisan,' from 1963. Written as an elaboration of *The Concept of Political*, this essay touches in intricate and provocative ways on both Nietzsche and Fanon, and does so through a theoretical elaboration of the crisis unleashed within the concept of 'bracketed war,' by partisan warfare, or what we might also call, following Mao Zedong, guerrilla warfare (*Youji zhan*).

As a reading of *On War*, Schmitt's essay develops the assertion that despite Clausewitz's fascination with war as waged by Napoleon, he failed to recognize the true importance of the French commander's innovations. Crucial was not the broad national character of military conscription in post-revolutionary France, or even the ferocity of Napoleonic campaigns, but rather the wisdom contained in Napoleon's order to General Lefèvre:

'in fighting the partisan anywhere, one must fight like a partisan.'[21] Thus for Schmitt what is remarkable about Clausewitz is that he theorized the logic of 'regular' or 'bracketed' war, precisely by factoring out of this concept the countervailing logic of partisan warfare. In effect, what he underscores is a version of the torturous procedure we have already encountered in Said's conceptual elaboration of the interpretive war machine of orientalism. Not surprisingly, this methodological dilemma does not fall directly within the cross hairs of Schmitt's attention. What does is the countervailing logic of partisan war, in effect, its war against war, or put differently, the resistance to resistance.

Although his orientation is typically philosophical he approaches the partisan historically. Several of his observations bear repeating here. First there is the matter of the origin of the partisan that Schmitt dates with the guerrilla war waged by the Spanish against the French in the early years of the nineteenth century. Here, what attracts Schmitt is the fact that for the first time 'irregular fighters' waged war against a regular army. Indeed, it is in this context that Napoleon's remarks about fighting the partisan as a partisan took shape.

A crucial subsequent development occurred with the 1813 Prussian Laws in which a monarch actually legalized partisan war against the French, insisting that every Prussian citizen has the duty to resist the invading army with every type of weapon. Axes, knives and pitchforks are listed. Although this law was later rescinded by a subsequent decree, it produced a decisive and far-reaching conceptual feature of the partisan, that is, the legalization in principle of irregularity. In Berlin around figures such as Fichte and Kleist this precise quality of the partisan received theoretical elaboration and thus appeared, for the first time, before what Schmitt, following Hegel, calls the world spirit. For reasons I shall later detail, it is significant that Schmitt locates the formal military encounter with the concept of the partisan in the Franco-Prussian War of 1870–1, a war that burdened the victorious Prussian state with the seemingly intractable legal problem of the 'irregular' fighter.

Once the partisan has entered philosophy, Schmitt's historical survey turns to focus on significant theoretical turning points: from Clausewitz to Lenin; from Lenin to Mao Zedong; and from Mao to Raoul Salan. What Schmitt traces here is the gradual and decisive transformation of the enemy. Stressing Lenin's attentiveness to *On War*, Schmitt shows how Lenin extrapolates the logic of Clausewitz's concept of 'war as a continuation of political activity by other means,' using it to develop a revolutionary strategy in the context, not of international enmity and conflict, but of civil war. Here the enemy emerges as a faction (the Mensheviks and the White Army) within the national polity. In marking the shift from Lenin to Mao, Schmitt stresses that the latter recognized more clearly than did the former what it means to grasp the revolutionary struggle for communism as an instance of partisan warfare. While both Lenin and Mao constitute the object of absolute enmity as a particular social class, a class with both national and international contours, Mao—because of his own deeply telluric formation—recognized the value of extending partisanship into the revolution itself. For Mao, peace becomes a moment within an enmity without bounds. Thus it too becomes a continuation of political activity by others means, prompting Schmitt to characterize Mao as the contemporary (in 1963) Clausewitz.[22]

Which brings us to Raoul Salan, a French officer who first encountered combat in WWII, who was then transferred to French Indochina (he supervised the internal investigation of the stunning French defeat at Dien Bien Phu) and in 1958 was transferred to Algeria where he was named the supreme commandant of the French forces. He was also, and it is this disturbing fact that brings him to Schmitt's attention, the founding member of the OAS, a clandestine group involved in carrying out terrorist activity against the FLN, Algerian non-combatants/citizens, but also French citizens in the urban centers of both Algeria and France. Needless to say, his presence in Algeria during the war for national independence places him in proximity to Fanon, but more important is how Schmitt sets up Salan's relation to the Clausewitz, Lenin, and Mao series. In effect, Salan exploits the appearance of the partisan before the world spirit, by drawing the logical conclusions of fighting the partisan like a partisan. He brings, as it were, the development of the concept of the enemy to its culmination. Schmitt puts it thus:

A declaration of war implies the identification of an enemy. That is obvious, and at the beginning of a civil war it is even more so. When Salan declared civil war he actually addressed two enemies: on the Algerian front, by announcing the continuation of regular and irregular war; against the French government, by launching an illegal and irregular civil war….Every war on two fronts always raises the question concerning who is considered the real enemy. Is it not a sign of inner conflict to have more than one real enemy. If the enemy defines us, if our identity is unambiguous, where does the doubling of the enemy come from?…Salan considered the Algerian partisan to be the foe. Suddenly, a worse and much more serious enemy appeared behind his back: his own government, his own superiors, his own brothers. In them he saw a new enemy. This is the core of Salan's case. Yesterday's brother turned out to be the more dangerous enemy. There must also be some confusion within the concept of the enemy, and it must be related to the theory of war.[23]

Two points seem warranted. First, it is clear that Schmitt sees the war for Algerian independence as a partisan war, a war that, as the Salan case demonstrates, confuses the theory of war by complicating the nature of the enemy. Second, in the passage cited the complication of the enemy takes the form of what is in effect a rhetorical question: 'if our identity is unambiguous, where does the doubling of the enemy come from?' Where indeed? In characteristic fashion Schmitt avoids pyschologizing Salan, preferring instead to see him as a subject caught up in a dynamic structure, in this case, a colonial war. While this risks a certain ultra-right recuperation of Salan, it also stresses something important, namely, that war has agency and when that agency is self-conflicted, ambiguous war, both theoretically and practically, is at war with itself.

It strikes me that Fanon grasps this state of affairs with precision. Although one might certainly point here to his anguished consideration, in 'Algeria Unveils,' of involving women ('irregulars') in the struggle as proof, my point is that the resistance to resistance teased out of 'Here is the Voice of Algeria' is an even more explicit confirmation. If we recall the early stand-off between refusal and resistance, where Algerians refused the radio through which the French resisted the effects of their occupation, followed by a resistance to this resistance, by a strategic acknowledgement that one cannot struggle on the enemy's terms, then we see the extent to which, for Fanon, *la guerre des ondes* was explicitly grasped as a partisan war, a war in which one was obliged to turn against the very assumptions supporting one's struggle with the enemy precisely because the enemy had made them. In effect, Fanon understood that the identity of the fighting Algerian *was* ambiguous and that one needed to probe continuously the friend/enemy distinction especially as it functioned within the very terms of the struggle. Put differently, what Fanon understood was the necessity of truly lying to one's brothers, not in the mode of betrayal or treason, but in the mode of fighting those who are fighting partisans as partisans…like a partisan.

At one level, this took a rather predictable form. Namely, throughout the war the FLN was keen to internationalize the conflict, to bring French atrocities before the international court of public opinion. The aim was to establish both that those tortured by Nazis could torture the likes of Djamila Boupacha or Pierre Vidal-Naquet, and to forge an alliance through 'television, radio and newspapers' with figures who might otherwise be construed as enemies: western powers in Europe and North America. But beneath or behind such a gesture—however indispensable—stands one that eludes even the conceptual subtlety of Said's understanding of 'coverage.'

To conclude, I will tease out this deeper gesture and thereby justify the proposition that what eludes Said here is indexed to what earlier I referred to as his resistance. One must start with the Franco-Prussian war. Why? If one recalls that in Schmitt's construal, it is here that the concept of the partisan revealed its disturbing legal paradoxes, paradoxes that preoccupied Prussia, then it becomes crucial to note that Nietzsche served in this conflict. Having executed his compulsory military service while still a student in Germany, he volunteered to serve in the Franco-Prussian war as a medical orderly, as his subsequent teaching post in Switzerland obliged him to abide by the strictures of Swiss neutrality. He could serve, but not fight. In his correspondence, one reads febrile reports about the pace and violence of the conflict. We also learn that his discharge prior to the cessation of hostilities was due to diphtheria. Literally, he lost the room to breathe.

Such facts might hold merely anecdotal value were it not for the extended discussion of this war and its outcome that appears in the first of the essays that comprise *The Unfashionable Observations*. This discussion constitutes the first part of 'David Strauss, Confessor and Writer,' and it launches the polemic against Strauss by impishly re-reading the German victory as a defeat. It is vital here to recognize the strictly partisan character of Nietzsche's gesture, his war against war, his re-construal of his brothers—the Germans—as his enemies. If, as Schmitt proposes, the concept of the partisan was, by the end of the nineteenth century, standing before the world spirit, then Nietzsche would appear to be taking tactical advantage of this development both to acknowledge the partisan character of modern war, and to continue this war by partisan political means. To, in effect, take advantage of the fact that the legal limbo into which fell captured French snipers (irregulars) extended the becoming-partisan of war indefinitely.

The first of the *Unfashionable Observations* was written in 1873. During the summer of 1872 Nietzsche wrote the lines, cited repeatedly by Said: 'What then is truth? A mobile army of metaphors, metonyms and anthropomorphisms…etc.' Indeed Nietzsche's notebooks from the period are filled with aphorisms and entries on truth, lie and language. Having already drawn attention to the bellicose figure of the *bewegliches Heer*, let me now propose that we hear precisely in the mobility of this army, (an otherwise peculiar emphasis), a distinctly partisan tone as if Nietzsche, in turning against Germany and truth, saw in his own gesture the implacable necessity of fighting like a partisan. After all, Schmitt himself characterized nineteenth century partisans as, 'a kind of very mobile *light troops.*'[24] Cleaving closer to my earlier reading of this passage, if truth is a mobile army at war with its own rhetorical character and in that sense at war with itself, it behaves essentially like Salan who believed that only by turning against France could French Algeria be saved. In short, the war between truth and rhetoric is a partisan one. What follows is that it is precisely this theory of war that Said smuggles into his concept of interpretive communities via Nietzsche's theory of language, and from there into his concept of orientalism. Thus, it is not simply that orientalism is war, it is war waged in the global context of the modern supersession of 'bracketed' or 'classical' war. In resisting the full implications of Nietzsche's theory of language—the becoming figural of truth and thus the interpretive (un)reality of the Orient—Said allows the figure of the partisan, and its impact on the concept of war to, as it were, slip through his mind. As a result, orientalism is constructed as an interpretive war machine, but one conceived as conducted in accord with the principles of 'bracketed' war, that is, a war between states, fought by regulars, within broadly legal parameters. Where truth, as it were, has a side to be on. One might have thought that his taking sides with Gramsci's concept of hegemony and its attendant distinction between 'war of position' and 'war of maneuver' might have provoked a more considered treatment of the theory of war, but it did not.[25] Even in his later reading of Fanon, for example in 'Traveling Theory Reconsidered' from 1994, Said, although attentive to what he calls the dialectic of colonial war, focuses almost obsessively on the general problem of violence as if the matter of sparing Fanon from the tedious charge of nihilism was job one.

If now we recall that Schmitt's 'Theory of the Partisan,' segues from its examination of 'turning points' to an enumeration of the aspects of 'modern partisan war,' then I can state concisely what is at stake in the distinction I have been agitating throughout between Said and Fanon on the politics of 'television, radio and newspapers.' Schmitt lists four aspects: the spatial, the social, the global, and the technological. Ultimately, he sees all aspects as subordinate to the technological one (he, anticipating Ronald Ray Gun, envisions astronauts warring in space), but in describing them it is plain that he recognizes the decisive role played by information technologies in opening up and thus politicizing new spaces, developments that shatter 'entire normative systems.'[26] He writes: 'Today, in the age of electric lights, long-range fuel supplies, telephones, radios and television, the expression "the home is inviolable" establishes limitations rather different than those of the time of King John and the Magna Carta of 1215, when the lord of the manor could raise the drawbridge.'[27] A discussion of the collapse of the distinction between land and sea follows, making it all but explicit that 'home' is a metonymy, that is, a part of a larger socio-political structure of identity that might now be antagonized by an enemy. Surely I am not alone in recognizing that this is precisely the set of concerns that dominate Fanon's early discussion of the reception of Radio-Alger in Algeria. It is not simply an apparatus by which the French speak to the French, but it is a means by which to destabilize, menace certain practices deemed normative in Islamic societies of the Maghreb. In addition, as an incursion in the war that *is* orientalism, Radio-Alger is a weapon wielded by an 'irregular.' Indeed, it is itself 'irregular.' It is always already a partisan maneuver, but one cloaked within plausible deniability, put differently, law. It is merely a legal, that is, licensed, public information service.

As Napoleon urged, one must fight the partisan like a partisan. In this context, it means turning radio against itself, resisting the way it asks to be resisted. One form this might take is what Fanon called refusal: when Radio-Alger calls, refuse to pick up. Another is the strategy embraced by Said, that is, a frontal assault on the bias that organizes the content circulated by media networks, and the fostering of a counter public sphere, say, in the present context, Al-Jazeera. Then, of course, there is the alternative of resisting resistance, of discovering in the belligerent deployment of radio the need to rework the apparatus, to turn one's weapon against its weapon-like character and denounce the fecklessness of the charge of bias when fueled by a rhetorical theory of truth. If, as the cover of *Covering Islam* graphically depicts, our seeing—and, I would add, our hearing—are in the hands of the media, then it is their role in the interpretive war machine that is orientalism that must be both challenged and changed. In the end, this is not about what they say, but what they do and how they do it. Either way, Gil Scott-Heron was right, the war that is orientalism and that must be waged within and against it 'will not be televised.' Not because it won't be covered, but because it is this very coverage.

12

THE PLEASURES OF IMPERIALISM AND THE PINK ELEPHANT

TORTURE, SEX, ORIENTALISM

Patricia Owens*

The issue of sex in the Arab world reminds me of the old story about the sorcerer's apprentice and the pink elephant. The master of alchemy, after explaining to his apprentice the complex steps to be followed in making gold, added: 'And, most importantly, through the entire process you must not think of the pink elephant.' Having been duly impressed by this warning, the apprentice tried desperately to heed it, but, of course, was unable to keep the forbidden subject out of his thoughts. At last he had to give up his attempts at making gold and sadly reproached his master: 'Why, O my master, why did you have to tell me not to think of the pink elephant? If you had not, I would never have thought of it.'

Raphael Patai[1]

* This chapter is a reprint of Owens, 'Torture, Sex and Military Orientalism,' *Third World Quarterly*, 31:7, 2010. Initial research for the paper was supported with a Small Research Grant from the Center for the Study of Sexual Minorities in the Military, University of California, Santa Barbara. I am grateful to Sara Ababneh for research assistance, Henry Shue, Bille Eltringham, and Lee Jones for comments. 'The Pleasures of Imperialism' in the title is taken from Chapter Two, Part V of Edward W. Said's *Culture and Imperialism*.

And he called…me 'faggot' because I was wearing the women's underwear, and my answer was 'no.' Then he told me 'why are you are wearing this underwear,' then I told them, 'because you make me wear it.'

Abu Ghraib Detainee #151108

It is hard to imagine the deliberate and reciprocal killing and maiming of other humans for political ends, that is, it is hard to imagine war, outside gendered relations of power. For most people there is an enormous resistance to killing other humans. If military strategy is the problem of translating what happens on the battlefield into the achievement of political intentions, then there is a prior problem of how to transform people into disciplined fighters in the combat zone. The oldest and most successful form of militarization is the creation of gendered war roles, the production of gendered subjects who are willing to fight or are otherwise constituted as civilians. Resistance to killing others is undone by the creation and continual maintenance of forms of masculinity in which to be honored is to be willing to fight—and fight well—under the most difficult conditions imaginable. Warriors are gendered masculine; enemies, subordinates, and those to be saved are gendered feminine. That is, they are emasculated. The first and primary masculine identity cannot exist without its binary and subordinated, secondary opposite. In other words, the dominance required to defeat an enemy in war borrows from—and is made possible by—subordination through gender hierarchy and the constitution of binary sexual difference, the construction of certain kinds of 'men' and 'women.' Historically, war has required misogyny and patriarchal systems and these systems have been served by war. Polities, economies, and societies are organized around both the preparation and fighting of war and gendered relations of power. This relationship crosses cultures and historical periods.[2]

The extent to which the motivation to fight is created through gendering combatants there is a necessary subordination and hatred of groups and activities that are coded 'feminine.' In the modern West, the disciplinary power exerted on the minds and bodies of soldiers during military socialization has traditionally not only reinforced misogyny, but also extreme cultural chauvinism and hatred of non-normative sexualities. This is not to say that all soldiers are misogynist, homophobic, and racist, or that all soldiers are gendered 'male.' Nor is it to suggest that there are no forms of gender disruption at the frontline, and not just as a form of military entertainment.[3] Rather that a common part of homosocial military training has been to prey on the most vulnerable and insecure elements of a young recruits sense of their own masculinity (an attribute possessed by both 'men' and 'women') and that this vulnerability is externalized onto racial, sexual and gendered 'others.'[4] Homosociality may be organized around fear and hatred of homosexuality, but it need not. The ancient Greeks eulogized the virtues of same-sex lovers in the army. Plato wrote that a small army composed of lovers would be more than a match for even larger armies.[5] Same-gender sex was prevalent and without moral censor in the Mamluk military system in medieval Egypt. Military-administrative elites passed on wealth to the state rather than to offspring so there was less incentive to form 'traditional' patriarchal families. Each new generation of Mamluk elites was recruited from young slaves from the Caucus and Central Asia.[6] There are many forms of sexuality and several are compatible with the masculinity deemed necessary to fight and to fight well.

Nonetheless, since the establishment of the binary opposition between homo- and hetero-sexuality in 1870s Europe, there has been a greater impetus to valorize forms of homophobic masculinity, alongside and indeed relying on misogynist socialization practices. The hegemonic masculinity of American combatants, for example, is made possible through a continual effort to define its sexuality relative to the sexuality of inferior others, setting it apart and protecting it.[7] Homophobic bonding includes targeting the masculinity of enemy combatants by raping and humiliating them and attacking their honored status as 'straight.' The depiction of enemy combatants as sexually deviant has been a common thread in the wars in Afghanistan (2001–) and Iraq (2003–).[8] In the days after the 9/11 attacks, posters appeared in Manhattan with an image of Osama bin Laden 'being anally penetrated by the Empire State Building' with the words, 'The Empire Strikes Back…So you like skyscrapers, huh, bitch?'[9] A USS Enterprise Navy officer scrawled 'high jack this fags' on a bomb attached to the wing of an attack plane bound for Afghanistan.[10] The first U.S. soldier convicted of murdering an Iraqi after the 2003 invasion used the 'gay panic' defense. After engaging in consensual sex with a seventeen-year-old, U.S. Private Federico Merida claimed he 'snapped' and repeatedly shot and killed a member of the Iraqi National Guard.[11] Others more optimistically claimed that the 'war on terror' could be to 'gay' Americans what the Great War was for women and World War II for African-Americans.[12] While at Abu Ghraib, Guantanamo Bay and elsewhere, acts of torture included rape and other violence appearing to imitate deviant sexual activity assumed to be especially humiliating for 'Muslims.'

This volume is about the effect and coherence of a particular binarism—Orient/Occident—on the conduct and justification of modern war, that is, how 'the West' dominates and restructures 'the East' through its constitution and use of organized violence, and how 'the West' defines itself through this process. Orientalism as a 'mode of discourse'[13] has been central to military, economic, and cultural dominance by justifying imperial domination. 'Military Orientalism,' notes Tarak Barkawi, 'identifies a linkage between Western military strategies in the non-European world and constructions of Western identity. The assumed superiority of the West is placed at risk in battles against supposedly inferior, irrational, weak, and uncivilized opponents. When these opponents fail to be defeated as expected, there are cultural as well as political and military consequences.'[14] There is no natural or primordial Orient expressed through some Eastern 'way of war' that must be discovered through anthropological examination or conquered by its opposite and nemesis, the West and its 'way of war.' The Orient at war is an historical construct, an image, a site of cultural production and power made possible by other discourses, those of sexuality, gender, and race. Indeed, it is difficult to imagine how orientalist discourse could function in the absence of two more fundamental binarisms without which modern and imperial war is inconceivable. These are the binaries of gender (masculine/feminine) and modern sexuality (hetero/homo).

Orientalist discourses have much in common with discourses about gender and sexuality. Like the Orient in the Western imagination, gender and sexuality are historical constructs; the reality of these distinctions is not uncovered through scientific inquiry or confession of one's true nature but is produced through discourse. The binary opposition of Orient/Occident is not a symmetrical relation and neither is that of male/female or homo/hetero. The feminized/homo/Orient is subordinated to the masculinized/hetero/Occident. The celebrated side of the binary only acquires its meaning through subordination and exclusion of the Other—the sexually deviant Orient. And yet, just as the actual experience of imperial 'small wars' disrupts orientalist categories, the homo-hetero binary ultimately contradicts and undermines itself. Efforts to construct stable sexual subjectivities must fail, belied by the ultimate instability of actual practice; there is no sexual being behind the doing. If, as Edward Said rightly argued, 'without examining Orientalism...one cannot possibly understand...[how] European culture was able to manage—and even produce—the Orient politically, sociologically, militarily, ideologically,'[15] then one cannot understand orientalism without examining how modern Western culture is fundamentally structured by the effort to establish a clear binary distinction between homo- and hetero-sexual populations. In Eve Sedgwick's words, 'an understanding of virtually any aspect of modern Western culture must be, not merely incomplete, but damaged in its central substance to the degree that it does not incorporate a critical analysis of modern homo/heterosexual definition.'[16] This binary distinction, which emerged—not coincidentally— alongside the rise of formal European empire, is central to all Western identity and social organization, including military socialization and associated forms of cultural and gender-based subordination.

This chapter asks how contemporary U.S.-led orientalist war is produced though discourses about sexuality as a marker of civilization. What happens when such war is explicitly sexualized in the context of the homo-hetero binary? How was sex put into wartime orientalist discourse? More specifically, what type of power did orientalist war bring to bear on the body and on sex in the effort to constitute objects of American torture? It is commonplace to note that interrogation techniques in recent U.S. wars were specifically designed to target cultures allegedly bound by honor and shame regarding sex. Presumed cultural and religious 'attitudes' toward sex among (always male) Muslim populations were incorporated into military, political and popular understandings of the enemy's thought, behavior and vulnerabilities. In other words, the assumed sexual conduct of Muslim men became an object of analysis and target of orientalist invention, regulation, and then intervention through torture. The commonly held instrumentalist account of American torture techniques is that detainees were 'softened up' through sexualized torture, forced to reveal private thoughts or admit to acts for which they would be dishonored and therefore more likely to 'talk.' Such an account reproduces the notion that there is, indeed, a special vulnerability in the realm of sex amongst Arab and Muslim men. It is argued here, in contrast, that just as the Orient at war is produced in the Western imaginary, the sexually repressed Muslim body was itself produced through American torture at Abu Ghraib appearing to prove through the forced re-enactment of deviant sexuality inane anthropological assumptions.

The chapter is divided into three parts. The first section revisits the debate about American torture practices, particularly focusing on claims that interrogators made use of anthropological texts and long-held assumptions about the sexual vulnerability of Muslim males (in contrast to their American counterparts). It argues that the relationship between sexualized torture and what American military strategist, General Anthony Zini, and others believed about 'the "proud Arab," hypersensitive to insult'[17] must be situated within an historical context of orientalist representations of Muslim sexual desires. The second section shows that despite the diversity of sexual practices and interpretations of religious texts, the dominant Western conceptualization of 'Muslim' sexuality and sexual identity as intolerant and repressed is the flipside of an older orientalist construction. The consolidation of modern European ideas about a binary distinction between hetero- and homo-sexuality coincided with colonialism and claims of rampant sodomy among adherents to Islam.[18] The third section returns to the sexualized torture. Both the enactment of the torture and much of the commentary was orientalist not only due to the discourse of the sexually repressed and perverse Muslim. The torturers were seeking to produce the subject of torture through gendered practices, to reveal the repressed and sexually perverse Muslim sexual subject that is said to have informed Pentagon torture techniques in the first place. The specific power relationship was constituted through the eliciting of a confession, which alongside scientific enquiry is *the* Occidental mode of acquiring knowledge about sex.

Torture and sexual orientalism

Military institutions have historically used sexual violence or the threat of sexual violence to motivate troops and humiliate enemy combatants. As already indicated, the sexualization of combatants is not a side issue to militarization and armed conquest. It is fundamental to it. The practice of combing torture and sexual humiliation in small wars is not new or unique to the United States. Belgian colonizers used such torture in the Congo, as did the French in Algeria.[19] The Indian Army practiced genital and anal torture against Sikh men in the Punjab.[20] Most recently, the military and security services of the United States have engaged in the torture of prisoners in multiple sites around the world, including secret locations and in collusion with subordinate allies such as Britain. According to Human Rights First, a nonpartisan organization, there have been almost six hundred criminal investigations into allegations of detainee abuse, including the murder of individuals in U.S. custody.[21] The most infamous case emerged from Abu Ghraib prison in occupied Iraq, which gained widespread media attention from April 2004 after the circulation of photographs of abuse by two units in the 800th Military Police Brigade. Earlier detailed reports of torture by several humanitarian organizations had not provoked much outrage; only the pictures of naked male detainees sparked the beginning of a critique of occupation within the establishment of the United States.

Despite efforts by feminists to dissociate rape from sex,[22] the primary focus of media and scholarly commentary was the purportedly 'sexual' character of the torture at Abu Ghraib: the rape of a male Iraqi teenager and several female prisoners, including the gang rape of a fourteen year-old girl; forcing one prisoner to rape a fifteen year-old fellow detainee and then write 'I am a Rapest' [sic] on his leg; the raping of one prisoner with 'a chemical light and perhaps a broom stick'; a male guard having 'sex with a female detainee' (for some reason not described as rape in the official army inquiry by retired General Antonio Taguba).[23] Most commentary focused on the images of Iraqi men being forced to masturbate, wear women's underwear, and lie on top of each other naked while being photographed, videotaped, and mocked. With the major exception of the canonical image of the man wired and hooded standing on a box, most of the photographs were of this kind.[24] Similar interrogation methods were used at Guantanamo Bay where detainees were forced to dance with each other, wear bras, called 'homosexual,' and told other detainees would find out they were 'gay.'[25] Other forms of 'gender coercion' included women guards straddling and/or touching detainees deliberately defying certain religious prohibitions on physical contact between women and men outside of the patriarchal family system.

The questions that framed much of the initial commentary about the torture were whether the tactic of humiliating Arab men by violating them by rape or simulated 'sex' acts was deliberately culturally-specific; whether they were especially shocking given the image of a rampantly homophobic male culture in the so-called 'Muslim world'; and whether the tactic of humiliating these men in this manner would have been effective in 'softening up' the detainees if Islam were not so 'homophobic' and had not produced a culture otherwise so 'sexually repressed.' There was virtually no discussion of the rape and other abuses of women, although much was made of the presence of women perpetrators of torture. The objects of sympathy and/or comment were defined as Arab/Muslim men or teenagers. The pictures were read almost exclusively through a purportedly homoerotic lens and the degree to which an assumed taboo regarding 'homosexuality,' and general sexual repression in 'Muslim culture,' were at work. Most significant in this regard was a widely discussed article by veteran reporter

Seymour Hersh claiming that the U.S. Department of Defense and Central Intelligence Agency used 'anthropological texts' to design specific torture techniques.[26] According to David Luban, 'obviously, someone in the government put this knowledge [*sic*] to use and ordered sexual humiliation as an interrogation tactic.'[27] The only specific text named in reports of torture and anthropology is *The Arab Mind* by the late orientalist Raphael Patai (1910–1996), reissued following the September 11 attacks. However, that the American Anthropological Association issued a resolution in 2006 that 'denounced the use of anthropological knowledge in torture,' suggests that the government was, indeed, supplementing strategy with anthropology, using cultural intelligence in violent subordination.[28]

One could read the torture instrumentally and focus on the United States' tactical goal of acquiring information; detainees may reveal intelligence after such 'softening up'; possessing photos of tortured bodies can be used as blackmail to turn prisoners into informants.[29] To be sure, violence targeting both the physical and mental vulnerabilities of the sexual body is never far from interrogators' mind and may even discount the significance of fine tuned techniques playing on the assumed vulnerabilities of a particular 'culture.' Nonetheless, it is clear that agencies of the United States sought to understand its presumed enemy in these terms, to devise torture techniques focusing on sexuality and the vulnerability of sexual identities (the enemies and, of course, its own). Of the various markers of cultural difference in the orientalist wars fought by the Bush and Obama administrations one of the most compelling for Western commentators has been the claim that Muslim cultures are especially sensitive when it comes to issues surrounding sex, what Michel Foucault referred to as the 'repressive hypothesis.'[30] This was the predominant theme in the discussion of sex in *The Arab Mind*. According to Patai, Arabs remain 'under the shadow of the ancient taboos';[31] 'the realm of sex is a more personal and more sensitive area of life than to the modern Westerner,'[32] or 'peoples who live in more northerly climes.'[33] Arab men are constantly thinking about sex because they are told not to; it has become a 'prime mental preoccupation…The very taboo of sex creates a kind of fixation on the subject.'[34] Like the imagined Victorian prudes of an earlier era, the way in which Arabs relate to sex is 'the product of severe repressions.'[35] Arabs remain behind the times, with an emotionally unhealthy preoccupation with sex. All social interactions and gender relations are dominated by the effort to prevent the possibility of sexual misbehavior, all of which results in what Patai called, 'the sexual repression-frustration-aggression syndrome of the Arab personality.'[36] But 'ultimately,' he predicted, 'the Arab mind will have no choice but to accept Western sex mores; and its innate ingenuity will find a way to modify and mold them until it will create…a special Arab subvariety of the new sexuality.'[37]

Such ideas about the sexually repressed Muslim male were reproduced in much media commentary, including those highly critical of the torture and in sub-cultures that might have viewed things otherwise. According to Faisal Alam, writer, activist, and director of a U.S.-based Muslim 'Gay' organization, 'Sexual humiliation is perhaps the worst form of torture for any Muslim…Islam places a high emphasis on modesty and sexual privacy. Iraq, much like the rest of the Arab world, places great importance on notions of masculinity. Forcing men to masturbate in front of each other and to mock same-sex acts or homosexual sex, is perverse and sadistic, in the eyes of many Muslims.'[38] According to Patrick Moore, writing for *The Advocate*,

Because 'gay' implies an identity and a culture, in addition to describing a sexual act, it is difficult for a gay man in the West to completely understand the level of disgrace endured by the Iraqi prisoners…This is not to say that sex between men does not occur in Islamic society—the shame lies in the gay identity rather than the act itself. As long as a man does not accept the supposedly female (passive) role in sex with another man, there is no shame in the behavior. Reports indicate that the prisoners were not only physically abused but also accused of actually being homosexuals, which is a far greater degradation to them.[39]

What does it mean to suggest that the apparently 'homoerotic' character of the torture was especially humiliating to Muslim men? What should we make of such discourses in the context of orientalist wars and the universalization of Western sexual identity that they represent? What are the origins of the notions that sexuality is repressed in Muslim majority societies and 'homosexuality' is a taboo?

Imperial and sexual binaries

Like orientalist identities, those surrounding sexuality are relational and performative. They do not exist objectively but are produced and reproduced through discourse. We cannot say that certain sexual identities cause certain sexual practices, as if 'being' homosexual causes a person to seek sex with persons of the same gender. Rather it is through sexual encounters with someone identified thus (the other binary of male/female) that the

identity of 'homosexuality' is produced. On the other hand, it is not possible to say that sexual relations with someone identified as the same gender causes homosexual identity. This identity is itself the product of
historically contingent and powerful constructions of 'homosexuality' as a
medical category in late nineteenth-century Europe. This identity is not
something someone innately possesses, but is based on the repeated performance of certain kinds of acts given certain kinds of meanings. Gendered and sexualized subjects conduct their lives based on these discourses
and interpret their sexual practices (acquire 'identities') based on specific
(binary) classifications (male/female, hetero/homo). In other words, there
is no such thing as being homosexual or heterosexual. There are only
diverse and complex sexual practices that come to be understood as cor-
relating with one side of the homo-hetero binary. To paraphrase Nietzsche,
there is no sexual being behind 'the doing, acting becoming…—the doing
itself is everything.'[40]

The modern construction of the homo-hetero sexual binary was codified
in late nineteenth-century Europe. Central to *The History of Sexuality*,
Michel Foucault's seminal study, is the claim that bourgeois society in this
period established quantitatively and qualitatively new discourses about sex.
The multiplication of scientific labels and medical theories—while privileg-
ing the male-female and homo-hetero binaries—ensured that sexual practices were analyzed and regulated as never before. The 'homosexual became
a personage,' Foucault observed, 'a past, a case history, and a childhood, in
addition to being a type of life…The sodomite had been a temporary aber-
ration; the homosexual was now a species.'[41] The term 'homosexual' dates
from an anonymous 1869 pamphlet opposing a Prussian anti-sodomy law,[42]
later and more commonly used in a medical context, alongside other terms
such as 'invert.'[43] More general discourses about sexuality, as well as specifically orientalist ones, rely on the trope of Victorian sexual repression.[44] In
fact, the Victorians rarely stopped talking about sex. (The apparent absence
of Western-style sexuality in the 'Muslim world,' of course, is taken to be
the product of religious and/or state repression of normal sexual practice
and identity—the 'repressive hypothesis'). Discourses named and regulated
rather than repressed sexual conduct. Their purpose, Foucault observed, was
to give sexuality 'an analytical, visible, and permanent reality…Not the
exclusion of these thousand aberrant sexualities, but the specification, the
regional solidification of each one of them.'[45]

The consolidation of modern European discourses about sexuality coincided not only with medicalization and classification but also with a wave

of imperialism. European narratives about 'homosexual' conduct in Europe were corroborated by 'evidence' from abroad. European thought was more formally structuring itself around a set of binaries in which rationality, order, and capitalist markets contrasted with (non-European) savagery, disorder and immaturity. Unsurprisingly, the sexual practices of the colonized and colonizer became a defining marker of civilizational difference.[46] The first and most obvious trope concerned the relationship between masculine/empire and feminine/colony. Just as the Orient was the site of military conquest, dynamic Western men could take sexual advantage of passive women and boys. This narrative persists in more recent orientalist/misogynist accounts of 'erotic encounters' between 'East' and 'West,' which also reproduce the 'repressive hypothesis.' As one orientalist has recently (and un-ironically) put it,

On one side was Christian monogamy in which sex was shrouded in religious meaning and prohibition, regarded as sinful when enjoyed outside of marriage, and even sinful within marriage when unconnected to procreation. On the other side was an Eastern culture wherein sex was strictly regulated, especially when it came to women, but where it was dissociated from both sin and love. The world, in other words, divided itself into two large zones. There was the Western erotic zone of guilt and repression and the Eastern zone of the harem, of multiple sexual partners, in which it was assumed, for good or ill, that it is entirely natural and healthy for a man to enjoy the favors of many women and that there needed to be a class of women to satisfy what were seen in the West as illegitimate and insalubrious desires, better repressed than indulged.[47]

The 'image of the imperial prude'[48] contrasted with that of the sexually decadent Other. Alongside misogynist discourses on the availability of women, emerged a series of colonial ethnographic accounts of homoerotic encounters, especially sodomy, as evidence for measuring and distinguishing civilizations.

Such accounts were not new to the Victorian period, as witnessed in descriptions of sodomy in ethnographic studies of earlier European conquest in the New World. 'They are all sodomites!' proclaimed Cortez in his first letter from the Americas in 1510.[49] During the Crusades, the 'sin of sodomy' was attributed to Europe's enemies. If captured the ultimate fear was of being subjected to Arab sexual demands, a fear that strengthened from 1249 as the Mamluks dominated Egypt.[50] As the political and military situation evolved so did discourse about sexuality. With the Ottoman Empire expanding into the Middle East, sodomy was more likely to be described as a Turkish vice without making 'redundant an ongoing association of sodomy with Islam in general.'[51] Joseph Pitts, author of *A True and Faithful Account of the Religion and Manners of the Mohametans*, noted in 1704, that 'it is common for men there to fall in love with boys as 'tis in England to be in love with women.'[52] Representations of sexuality became a boundary of civilization and central to discourses of cultural and religious difference. Muslims were represented as paedophiles, pederasts, and sodomites and, later, also somehow sexually repressed. Contemporary notions of repressed 'Muslim' sexuality are the reverse image of this older orientalist construction. They take their place in a long list of European failures to account for the ambiguities of sexual practice and identity, of ethnocentric theories of sexual behavior and sexual orientation.

Consider post-9/11 popular accounts of male Pashtun communities in Afghanistan in which cross-generational sexual activity between men is widespread. Western newspapers reported that one of the downsides of the end of Taliban rule, from the perspective of some locals, was the return of activities variously described as 'the Pashtun obsession with sodomy,' dandyism, paedophila, 'rape' and 'gay' or 'homosexual' activity. Before Taliban rule, reported *The Times*, the streets of Kandahar 'were filled with teenagers and their sugar daddies, flaunting their relationship. It is called the homosexual capital of south Asia…[L]ocals tell you that birds fly over the city using only one wing, the other covering their posterior—that the rape of young boys by warlords was one of the key factors in Mullah Omar mobilising the Taleban.'[53] With the American defeat of Mullah Omar the dandies were returning, with men walking 'about town in clumsy, high-heeled sandals.'[54] For the *New York Times*, such activity was the result of unnatural gender segregation (the other binary).[55] 'It might seem odd to a Westerner,' noted the *Los Angeles Times*, 'that such a sexually repressive society is marked by heightened homosexual activity.'[56] But if men can only see the faces of their mothers, sisters, and wives, they will have 'recreational sex' with each other. According to one local cleric, 'Ninety percent of men have the desire to commit this sin…But most are right with God and exercise control. Only 20 to 50% of those who want to do this actually do it.' We are invited to do the orientalist math: 'between 18% and 45% of men here engage in homosexual sex—significantly higher than the 3% to 7% of American men who…identify themselves as homosexual.'[57] Note the uncritical comparison between so-called 'homosexual' practice in Afghanistan and sexual identity politics in the United States, as if the only men in the United States having sex with other men call themselves 'gay.'

To investigate orientalist discourse is less to establish the accuracy of descriptions of the Orient, than, as Edward Said maintained, to interrogate 'the internal consistency of Orientalism.'[58] We can, nonetheless, remark on the obvious lack of adherence to the homo-hetero binary amongst many Arab and Muslim populations prior to, during, and after the binary's establishment in nineteenth-century Europe.[59] As Khaled El-Rouayheb observed, 'pre-nineteenth-century Arab-Islamic culture lacked the concept of homosexuality altogether, and operated instead with a set of concepts (like *ubnah* or *liwat*)…which were simply not seen as instances of one overarching phenomenon.'[60] The concept of 'homosexuality' falsely subsumes a number of distinctions central to the diversity of homosocial sexual relations across cultures and historical periods. These include 'passionate but chaste love and carnal lust' and 'permissible and prohibitive sexual acts,' both of which belie Western observers' obsession with sodomy.[61] If we are to address this one sexual act, the central distinction is not the hetero-homo sexual binary but the gendered (and militarist) binary of subordination, that is, the assumed existence of a passive (feminized) penetrated subject and an active (masculinized) penetrator. Given prevailing—and cross-cultural—patriarchal systems in which to be feminized is to be debased, made possible by the war system recall, clearly there is greater opportunity to dishonor the subject in the 'passive' role, hence the orientalist obsession with sodomy. Nonetheless, although even the best of the historical sources rely on accounts from learned male elites in the Ottoman Empire, there is historical and contemporary evidence of acceptance of same-sex sexual activity, including but not limited to sodomy, although this tolerance is circumscribed and ought not exclude other social responsibilities. Sex between men (and men and boys) may be officially prohibited but socially accepted as long as there is discretion and at least one of the participants also marry women and have children.

Contemporary orientalist versions of others' sexuality invariably ignore the effects of earlier such discourses on Arab and Muslim peoples' understandings of their own and others sexuality, that is, in the context of Western hegemony. Racialist and sexual discourse does not move in only one direction; the identity of the 'sexual' colonized became profoundly entangled with both the experience of colonization and colonial representations of seemingly deviant sexuality. For example, 'European colonialism and its influence in the Middle East,' suggests Bruce Dunne, 'may in large part bear responsibility for the…"official" non-existence [of "homosexuality"] in Arab countries.'[62] In our own context, at the height of the torture scandal at Abu Ghraib, street protestors in Cairo called for the removal of the 'homosexual American executioners.'[63] This reaffirmed the Egyptian state's view that homosexuality is an alien cultural import that must be stamped out. The state has pursued an aggressive crackdown on what it perceives as deviant sexual sub-cultures, including through entrapment, arrests, and torture with the collusion of medical doctors tasked with 'proving' men have had anal sex.[64] The protestors and government agencies may not—or indeed may well—have been aware that during the eighteenth-century many Europeans 'declared pederasty to be "the delight of the Egyptians"…distinguished from a more exclusive sodomy in Europe itself.'[65]

The reaction of mobs on the street and authoritarian states is easy to criticize, but it can be understood in the context of the universalization of the 'gay rights' discourse since the 1980s. Since this period, as Joseph Massad has put it, 'the rise of sexual identity politics in the West and international human rights activism would come to define…not only Arab nationalist responses, but also and especially Islamist ones, [with] implications…for the sexual desires and practices of…Arabs.'[66] Only very recently have some upper and middle class men in cities such as Cairo and Beirut adopted the discourse of gay identity and rights, along with many other things 'Western.' The vast majority of men who engage in same-sex relations in Muslim majority societies, as in the case of Pashtun men in Afghanistan, do not identify as gay or homosexual, nor do they feel the need to. They are not 'repressed' as a result. Yet, organizations such as the International Gay and Lesbian Association, as well as Amnesty International and Human Rights Watch, have been monitoring the treatment of 'gays' in Muslim societies assuming the existence of just such a 'cross-cultural, cross-gay identity.'[67] Such groups simply assume the existence of 'homosexual Muslim populations,' past and present, universalizing their struggle through an orientalist discourse, *producing what they seek to regulate*. In this respect, the 'Gay International'[68] movement and the American torturers would appear to possess something in common.

Knowledge, torture, confession

In a classic orientalist move, Michel Foucault described two 'great' traditions or 'procedures for producing the truth of sex,' the *scientia sexualis* of the Occident and the *ars erotica*, (with one exception) located in non-

Western societies: China, Japan, India, Rome, and 'Arabo-Moslem.'[69] Here, Foucault claimed,

pleasure is not considered in relation to an absolute law of the permitted and the forbidden, nor by any reference to a criteria of utility [as in the modern 'Occident'], but first and foremost in relation to itself; it is experienced as pleasure, evaluated in terms of its intensity, its specific quality, its duration, its reverberations in the body and the soul…[Here] there is formed a knowledge that must remain secret… because of the need to hold it in the greatest reserve, since, according to tradition, it would lose its effectiveness and its virtue by being divulged.[70]

In the East, Foucault asserted and without any textual or other evidence, sexual knowledge is held in reserve, only conveyed through the 'art of initiations and the masterful secret.'[71] This invention was a useful contrast to the Occident and its obsession with uncovering secrets, its construction of discourses to produce the truth of sex. Occidental power/knowledge negates oriental secrets and sexual reserve.

In the 'Christian West,' Foucault more persuasively claimed, there are fewer secrets or subtle initiations. While Europeans have established numerous discourses about sex they have simultaneously exploited sex 'as *the* secret.'[72] It is the task of experts, of medical science and psychiatry, to provide analytical and permanent reality to sexuality; the disciplined individual conducts him- or herself accordingly. Subjects are on one or other side of the gender/sex binaries—either male or female, homo or hetero, or occasionally some other (wholly derivative) in-between. If one is unable to act in accordance with proscribed practices, then this must also be known: one must confess to others and oneself. Christianity, after all, is a confessing religion and confessional practices are central to its sexual culture. In dramatic Christian rituals, individuals confess that they are sinners, what Jeremy Carrett describes as 'a kind of "coming out" as a Christian…The verbal act of confession was the verification of the "truth" of oneself.'[73] Occidental confession is rooted in the organization of both religious and civil authority, part of the moral apparatus of the Church, the effort 'to create a powerful, centralized organization against internal heresy and,' we should note, 'the external threat of Islam.'[74] No longer limited to the ritual of confessing sins to a priest offering absolution, modern confessional practices have multiplied and diffused throughout culture. The act has been transformed, incorporated into relationships, Foucault observed, between 'children and parents, students and educators, patients and psychiatrists, delinquents and experts,' and, we might add, prisoners and interrogators.[75]

The theme of confession is instructive for our discussion of orientalist torture, American torture that was deeply shaped by a 'will to knowledge regarding sex.'[76] Torture is the infliction of severe pain as punishment or in order to force an individual to do something and/or speak. In *The Body in Pain*, Elaine Scarry insisted that 'Torture consists of a primary physical act, the infliction of pain, and a primary verbal act, the interrogation. The first rarely occurs without the second…[:] the pain is traditionally accompanied by "the Question."'[77] The Question posed to the detainees at Abu Ghraib—with varying degrees of explicitness—concerned the precise nature of their sexual deviancy. 'Why are you wearing this?' one detainee was asked after being forced into rose cultured, flowery underwear.[78] The torture was not only to humiliate. It was to illicit confession as a form of knowledge/power. The prisoners/confessors were violently compelled to perform and or articulate their sexual abnormality.[79] 'When it is not spontaneous or dictated by some internal imperative,' as Foucault argued, 'the confession is wrung from a person by violence or threat; it is driven from its hiding place in the soul, or extracted from the body. Since the Middle Ages, torture has accompanied the confession like a shadow, and supported it when it could go no further: the dark twins.'[80] The infliction of pain was intended to produce very particular objects of torture—ones willing and able to confess their 'true' orientation in terms of a sexual code established in Europe. Moreover, the confession can revolve around more than rearticulating 'what was done—the sexual act—and how it was done; but of reconstructing, in and around the act, the thoughts that recapitulated it, the obsessions that accompanied it.'[81] This is the meaning of the forced masturbation and 'cross-dressing' with bras and flowery underwear, the rape, threats of rape and death, the leaving of men naked for days, forcing them to lie naked on each other, putting electrical wires on penises, sticking wires and phosphoric light in anuses, writing words on buttocks, drawing pictures of women on backs, constructing human pyramids, the name-calling and the photographs.

The United States enacted its military dominance and cultural superiority in constructing objects of torture in this way. It had the power to confirm, to prove, through confession and re-enactment their crude anthropological assumptions about the sexually repressed and deviant Arab mind/Muslim body, irrespective of the actual sexualities of those detained. The sexually repressed Arab/Muslim subject was more than an instrument of orientalist occupation; it was constituted through the torture.[82] The torturers sought to create a perverse form of what Patai in *The Arab Mind* had predicted would eventually evolve, 'a special Arab subvariety of the new sexuality.'[83] Not Muslim sexual modesty, then, but an Occidental culture of confessional practice, was revealed through sexualized torture, torture practiced to produce, regulate, and ridicule the secretive *ars erotica*. And yet it is crucial that we make the distinction between the intentions of those who perpetrated these acts of violence from the meaning of the violence itself. It was certainly the intention of the prison guards to perpetuate the idea that the worst form of torture for a Muslim man, indeed any man, is to be forced into feminizing acts of sodomy. The immediate goal was to dishonor by insinuating that the victims were sexually deviant, while reinforcing the hegemonic forms of masculinity central to the project of war in which to be the passive subject of sexual domination is to be feminized and humiliated. The forms of power enacted were through the performance of gender, as well as sexual, roles, the maintenance of the masculine-feminine dichotomy and the homo-hetero binary. The violence was not shameful due to some essential prohibition against same-gender sexual activity in Muslim societies. What happened at Abu Ghraib and elsewhere was torture because it was violence that targeted for humiliation and ridicule the most intimate of acts not because the victims were male or Muslim. It was shameful because all torture reveals an intimate form of vulnerability that humiliates, whatever the form. The essence of the torture was violence, not sex of any kind.

Conclusion

It is commonplace to observe that recent U.S.-led wars have been deeply 'gendered,' not least by political leaders in Europe and North America who have repeatedly and opportunistically evoked the domination by bearded men of shrouded women as part of a justification for military action. In the violent and political struggles over the terms of social governance in Afghanistan and Iraq, how 'men' 'treat' 'women' structures competing claims of who is civilized and who is not. To the extent that such narratives reduce the relationship between war, sex and gender to competing systems of patriarchy the significance of gender and sexuality for military cultures are elided, superficially understood in the form of a clash of civilization and forms of misogyny. This particular orientalist discourse about 'women,' the ontological, epistemological and hierarchical distinction between 'East' and 'West' in how 'women' are 'treated' has been widely criticized, as has Said's own paternalistic neglect of the woman question in his path-breaking study, *Orientalism*. This chapter has shown some of the ways in which the language of sexual identity disrupts and transforms orientalist and military languages. A hierarchy of civilization—necessary to fight imperial wars—has been made possible, in part, through ahistorical and orientalist wartime constructions of 'Muslim' sexuality while supporting confessional torture techniques aiming to produce what it assumed—Muslim sexual deviancy. Orientalist war brought violence to bear on the body and on sex in the effort to constitute objects of American torture. While sex was put into wartime orientalist discourses, the seeming humanity of the United States, rather than the brutality of its government, was produced through such rhetoric about 'homophobia' in the Muslim world. Highlighting the assumed sexual repression of Muslim prisoners served to distract attention away from the torture itself and toward the United States' apparently more liberal values, its supposedly fewer inhibitions and insecurities regarding sex—exactly what was (and is always) on display.

13

AFTERWORD

Patrick Porter

Now is as good a time as any to consider the relationships between war and visions of the East, a frontier of the study of orientalism where attention is long overdue. This Afterword synthesizes contributions from the volume to make an argument about how war both destroys and reintroduces orientalist myth. It then considers future directions of research and inquiry that flow out of the insights here. And it suggests where we need to work harder to strengthen this fledgling research agenda.

It is vertiginous to read the contributions in this volume at the very time that our presumed knowledge of regions such as North Africa and the Persian Gulf has been again shocked and ruptured by armed uprisings. 'Orientalism' encompasses a set of traditions not only about Western intellectual curiosity, but about the linkages between expertise, authority and power. But war is in the realm of chance and shock, and is a fatal reciprocal dance between adversaries with their own dynamic will. The oriental subject gazed upon repeatedly returns fire and confounds our polished predictions. The near-implosion of Iraq surprised triumphalists who presumed that a Western invasion would release market democracy in the Greater Middle East at the timetable and convenience of the liberator. Equally, revolts in Egypt and Tunisia also shatter the opposite established beliefs. The humanist and universal slogans of the protesters defy the fantasy that Arabs live in an alien, unconnected world and are doomed to be enslaved subjects of tyrants or mystics, or can only be emancipated by a benign Occident.

The pursuit of cultural knowledge about adversaries also touches a showdown that could have very high stakes indeed. As Iran, Israel and the United States move steadily towards a triangular crisis over Iran's nuclear program, it is worth recalling that nothing is culturally written in stone in Tehran either. Cultures in conflict operate more as a repertoire than a fixed script, even for regimes that are often portrayed as stubbornly theocratic. The Supreme Leader Ali Khamenei in 2005 issued a *fatwa* against the production and use of nuclear weapons. Yet should the regime be moved to develop a latent nuclear capability, or even an actual one, they have another doctrine to deploy to legitimize change. During the Iran-Iraq War of the 1980s, Ayatollah Ruhollah Khomeini pronounced a doctrine of 'maslahat-e nizam' or 'expediency of the system,' 'by which the needs of the Islamic Republic as a political institution might trump even Islamic law.'[1] Precisely because security communities don't always follow the dictates of cultural traditions—because they reinvent those traditions as they go—strategic history like life is full of surprises.

Yet as this chapter argues, there is a paradox in the relationship between war and Orientalism. Just as war shocks established perceived truths about the non-Western, the exotic and the alien, it generates chaos that tempts us to reintroduce cultural knowledge as a way of restoring order.

Indeed, the effort to resist potent cultural mythologies often seems like a losing struggle. Powerful and contradictory myths endure: the belief that there is an overarching oriental meta-culture, that orientals are servile and culturally prone to respect Western power, along with the belief that they are irrational when they resist it. The concept of the irrational alien people warring against an implicitly logical and rational West has been the fallback explanation for 'Eastern' behaviour, whether for Ambassador Joseph Grew in 1943 on Japan's bid for regional power in Asia, President Dwight Eisenhower on China in 1955, or American viceroy L. Paul Bremer III's judgements on Ayatollah Sistani and Iraq society from 2003: 'developments in Iraq were not always logical…Certainly Ayatollah Sistani operated on a different rational plane than we Westerners.'[2]

Softer, more seductive forms of orientalism also persist. In a leaked report by the British Army on operations in Iraq, a senior Officer commented '… we failed to understand how important appearances are to the Arabs.' The challenge is to improve understanding of Islamic culture, the Arab 'mind,' their views of allegiances and way of doing business in Iraq, and to address the shortage of linguists able to speak (and read) Arabic with Iraqi dialects.'[3] Striving to grasp this elusive thing 'culture' amidst the communal bloodletting and anarchy in occupied Iraq, it was easy to fall into reductionist concepts of Iraqi politics as superficial street theatre with material power struggles left out. It was also tempting to reduce the wildly difficult task of winning local consent to a technocratic matter of pushing the right symbolic and ethnographic buttons.

Viewing themselves as bringers of order into chaos, powerful states can unleash anarchy and then reach for metacultural ideas of the 'Oriental personality' to explain it. You do not have to be Edward Said to notice the different standards that are applied to the strategic behaviour of the non-West. As John Dower observes, had the Bush II Administration planners for the post-invasion disaster in Iraq been Japanese, 'a legion of white pundits would have materialised to explain that they simply did not think logically, as Westerners do.'[4]

It seems that war inevitably drives security communities back towards cultural myths to render the chaos intelligible, and there is not much scholars can do about it. As I tried to argue while the architects of the military surge in Afghanistan-Pakistan spoke confidently of 'flipping' tribes, 'We may never banish the mythologized oriental from our consciousness. Like fear of death and darkness, it is too powerful to be fully exorcised and will remain a silhouette on our mental horizon. But we can be more conscious of its presence, more alert to its myths, and allow evidence and observation to subvert our preconceptions rather than the other way around.'[5] If the aim of critical scholarship is to eliminate myths and primordial fears from the collective mind, then the academy has failed monumentally. The exotic warrior and primeval barbarian figure too strongly, serve too many purposes, are too evocative artistically, and as I argue later, peoples at war may gain from having a reputation for irrational savagery. But if we scale down our aim, to engage in a never-ending dialogue and argument with our own prejudices, then this volume is a promising step in that direction.

War as a fatal dance

War in its violent entanglements and brutal irony is the ultimate disrupter of the certainties of cultural knowledge. At the same time, armed conflict is the site and occasion which heightens desire for authoritative knowledge about the chaos that it produces. Thus there is a never-ending search for a controlling master knowledge about other cultures, or for visions of the East through which to debate the fate of the West. Grandiose judgements about civilizations seem to be frequently reintroduced to comprehend the surprises and chaos of war. War subverts received knowledge, and it recreates it.

So in the Israel-Lebanon war of 2006, the Israel Defence Forces (IDF) entered the battlespace convinced that it knew the story in advance, that weaker foes with their asymmetric methods would hit and run, shrinking back in the face of the armoured advance and overwhelming firepower. But as it turned out, the Hezbollah guerrillas mixed regular and irregular methods. They had prepared classical 'hedgehog' defences, designed to resist Israel's firepower head-on. The irony was summed up by an Israeli soldier. His Lebanese adversaries 'had never heard that an Arab soldier is supposed to run away after a short engagement with the Israelis.'[6] Israel's shock was compounded by the fact that its own combatants had been conditioned by the experience of the West Bank to imagine a dispersed guerrilla enemy fleeing their hammer blows. The IDF had reformed itself to de-emphasise classical combat and excel in fighting irregular insurgents and policing occupied territories. But by comparing Hezbollah's style against typologies of military behaviour, Stephen Biddle has shown that it developed pseudo-conventional, state-like methods as a counter-response, wounding more Israelis per fighter than any previous Arab effort, confounding the archetype of the shadowy guerrilla. It was a hybrid force that fought to hold territory rather than embracing purely population-centric methods.[7]

Yet orientalism lives on and is remade, with the theme of Israel as an island of civilization in an ocean of barbarism showing no sign of abating. Just as war fatally jumbles and entangles cultures, its wounds inspire fresh attempts to depict security communities as separate and antagonistic blocs. And as the exterminationist charter of Hamas or the Holocaust denial of Iranian President Ahmadinejad show, Israel's adversaries are also prone to the war rhetoric of cultural separation and violent 'otherness.'

The chapters in this book also point to the never-ending dynamic of war destroying and creating orientalist visions. Arjun Chowdhury's work on the shock of the Indian Mutiny of 1857 demonstrates the resilience of orientalism, as a way of thinking that can adapt itself to unexpected new political realities, as the shock of revolt quickly yields to a new technique and knowledge of colonial rule, through the mediating authority of 'traditional leaders.' As after Pearl Harbor, complacent beliefs in the yielding weakness of the oriental, are shattered by a shock offensive, but the surprise attack can then become perceived evidence of the treacherous ways of the East. Neither consent nor resistance can overthrow the urge to turn back to orientalist knowledge as the key to understanding the world. Orientalism's resilience can also be seen in Bruce Cumings' work on the reinvention of Chinese communists in American public debate, or in Quỳnh N. Phạm and Himadeep R. Muppidi's portrayal of evolving fears that the Afghan enemy will not accept defeat, a stark contrast from the self-confident prophecies of inevitable victory in the early days of the war in Afghanistan. Indeed, we can extend Hugh Gusterson's insight about media portrayals of fighter-insurgent, a figure that is emptied and denied a voice, so that we can project any fear or agenda onto it. If this is a matter of 'controlling' images of the enemy, it may also be true of representations of the terrorist, mad mullah or scheming warlord, who can be endlessly reinterpreted to fit an orientalist ideology about Eastern weakness, insanity or fanaticism. As will be suggested, we need to know more about the enemy's capacity to return fire.

Thus far, the discussion here has been logo-centric, just as Edward Said's interpretation focused mainly on high literary or documentary sources. But as the contributors Derek Gregory and Josef Ansorge here demonstrate, orientalism works through many prisms and visual media which create a different kind of aesthetic. There are the recent visual representations of foreign cultures through the technologies of video games, satellite surveillance and unmanned aerial vehicles. These in turn were anticipated in the urban mapping conducted during Napoleon's occupation of Egypt. The new technology vastly increases the scale of information and surveillance, but with its appearance of comprehensive and orderly oversight, and its promise of intimacy, could also reinforce the delusion that cultures can be systematically known and 'captured' in the eye of the beholder. Just as utopians over-reached themselves during the Revolution in Military Affairs by claiming that new surveillance tools could 'lift the fog of war,' so too could the tools of hi-tech observation dangerously create the illusion that such wars are easy, that a natural order of panoptic supervision will prevail, and present a bloody and chaotic business as an exhibition or even trivialize it as an amusement.

Orientalism, imperial hierarchy and Western pessimism

In unpacking the nature of orientalism, I owe a response to one contributor, Patricia Owens, who argues that my own attempt to push the frontier a few inches, *Military Orientalism* gets the concept of orientalism very wrong. Owens claims that placing the concept in the context of 'anxiety about the longevity of Western superiority and as a critique of progressive movements in the West' does not count as evidence of the absence of a fundamental hierarchy of West over East.[8] She also objects that my use of the concept of orientalism contributes to helping states 'do culture better.' She argues that to strip the concept of orientalism from this 'imperial, hierarchical context' is to rob the concept of 'critical meaning.'[9]

Owens effectively argues here that only those who agree with her and Edward Said are 'critical,' unlike those of us attempting to help militaries understand the complexities of culture. Why this is so, she does not explain, so that point need not detain us. More broadly, as a matter of logic, if orientalism can and does work to articulate fears of Western decline or inferiority, then that is evidence that orientalism does not always work simply to downgrade the East rhetorically to reinforce an imperial hierarchy.[10] This is a basic disagreement, between my work and those with a narrower view of Western orientalism as the playing out of supremacist ideology and self-aggrandizement.

Empirical accounts of military-strategic history point to a strand of Western self-doubt, beyond the mere recapitulation of imperial hierarchies. Asli Cirakman, for example, shows that military observers in early modern Europe were dissatisfied with their own undisciplined and volatile mercenary armies, and looked with envy at Turkey's alternative system.[11] They contrasted their unruly mercenaries with the good order, courage and self-control of Ottoman forces. If such scholarship is mistaken, and it all really is just a history of Western self-aggrandizement, why did a whole generation of American strategic culture theorists worry that an authoritarian and steadfast Soviet Union would prevail in a future conflict against an unsteady American democracy?[12] Why does a whole genre of literature and film, from *Dances with Wolves* to *The Last Samurai* view the 'Easterner' ambiguously as more primitive but purer and more virtuous, as a foil against corrupting Western materialism? Why do American nationalists like Ralph Peters warn that fanatical suicide bombers are tougher and more agile than the hi-tech, deluded Pentagon?[13] Why does Robert Kaplan, not exactly a bastion of post-colonial criticism, argue that Marines should be more like Apaches?

Orientalisms of this kind operate not to stifle but to accentuate doubts, to surface the possibility that the East might be both inferior yet tougher. In the military-strategic context especially, even those affirming a West-East pecking order can still fear that a combination of Western weakness and Eastern strength will overturn the natural hierarchy. This ambiguity runs through literature, such as Rudyard Kipling's simultaneous belief in the primitiveness and resilience of the Afghan or African warrior who could not be ultimately subdued by a self-defeating British Empire. Consider the paradoxes within the most pronounced Edwardian voice of imperialism and racial hierarchy:

where Kipling excelled—and where he most deserves praise and respect—was in enjoining the British to avoid the very hubris that he had helped inspire in them. His 'Recessional' is only the best-known and most hauntingly written of many such second thoughts…There is also 'The Lesson,' a poem designed to rub in the experiences of defeat in Africa, and (though it is abysmal as poetry) 'Fuzzy Wuzzy,' a tribute to the fighting qualities of the Sudanese. 'Arithmetic on the Frontier' is a memorable, sardonic warning against imperial overstretch in Afghanistan.[14]

Ambivalence also runs through the history of Western policy. Some of the most pronounced voices of orientalism reflect not confident superiority but a sense of Western fragility and, in terms of policy, opposition against rather than support for imperial military adventures. In recent times, figures with pronounced orientalist views such as Colin Powell or Lawrence Eagleburger have opposed armed interventions in the Gulf, the Horn of Africa or the Balkans precisely on the basis that the West with its limited power and knowledge cannot impose itself over primordial others and their 'ancient ethnic hatreds.' Lawrence Eagleburger, a U.S. advisor on Yugoslavia, insisted in September 1992 that the Bosnian war was 'not rational. There is no rationality at all about ethnic conflict. It is gut, it is hatred; it's not for any common set of values or purposes.'[15] This fatalism helped obstruct or delay international military intervention. General Colin Powell, his influence and prestige heightened by the 1991 Gulf War, staked his opposition to intervention on the idea that war sprang from 'deep ethnic and religious roots that go back a thousand years.'[16] If orientalism often implies hierarchy, this does not necessarily mean it is always 'imperial.'

Neither are grand cultural visions directed necessarily against those perceived Easterners. Western nations historically have not been unitary actors merely turning the guns of their power against perceived Eastern targets, but against their own internal Others, whether Roman Catholics, Irish nationalists or the working class, or in what they saw as fratricidal international struggles for the soul of the West. When Kipling wrote of 'lesser breeds without the law,' he was referring not to Africans, Asians or Arabs but to the German *Kaiserreich*. Self-styled Western traditions can be more interesting and ambivalent than Said's followers allow, and contain multitudes.

Then there is the question of the role of academics themselves. Owens finds suspect my view that academics should help militaries. This is a difficult question that divides the academy and turns anthropologists against one another. In case anyone is asking, on balance I think academic engagement is wiser than isolation. The fact remains that military forces find themselves in wildly difficult wars in Afghanistan-Pakistan and Iraq, and are more conscious than most that they can unwittingly be forces of chaos and disorder abroad. They want to reform themselves and think harder about the people and societies they are fighting amongst. They have become interested in how to depress the levels of violence, at least in theory, and think twice about the social impact of their presence. Aspects of this are objectionable, such as the revival of colonial anthropology, 'drive by' ethnography and the dressing up of ancient bigotry in the language of cultural awareness, as *Military Orientalism* argues. But the only thing more dangerous—to itself and others—than a culturally curious military force is one that doesn't care at all, and kills indiscriminately. This is the basis for having a critical dialogue with the military, and the state, and whoever wields power, even if that compromises our political virtue.

Future directions

An emerging disagreement lies at the core of this volume, foreshadowed in Owens' critique of *Military Orientalism*. Most contributors to this volume agree with the thrust of Edward Said's argument, that 'It is therefore correct that every European, in what he could say about the Orient, was consequently a racist, an imperialist, and almost totally ethnocentric.'[17] They share his view that the driving force of orientalism is western supremacism, and view with deep suspicion the movement to assist military and state power with anthropological insight. Against this, there is a minority view, argued by the likes of Robert Irwin, Asli Cirakman and myself, which finds the above approach ahistorical and reductionist.[18] While there is no question that racism, imperialism and ethnocentrism are important parts of the story, or that the weaponizing of anthropology can be highly mischievous, we argue that orientalism is a richer, more conflicted tradition, and not just the intellectual arm of Western imperialism.

Some caveats are necessary, before this debate becomes too caricatured. It should be stressed that self-aggrandizement and self-doubt can both be found in orientalist traditions. As in Kipling's poetry, they can constitute one another. Many of the chapters in this volume bring such tensions to the surface. No doubt Western fears, say, of the primordial Balkans, indicate certain assumptions of hierarchy—but the use of 'Balkan ghosts' images by anti-interventionists was hardly imperialistic. This flies in the face of the argument that orientalism and imperialism are forever yolked. Also, to argue that Western intellectual curiosity is driven by multiple urges and not just the urge to reinforce imperial hierarchy, is not necessarily to argue naively that it is politically disinterested. The argument of *Military Orientalism* is that some of the most potent orientalist visions sprang from furious political battles about identity and military power within the West as well as expansion beyond it. And in terms of hard politics today, to argue that militaries and anthropologists can legitimately teach one another is not necessarily to endorse the Human Terrain programme specifically or to cheer on the conduct of the War on Terror. Here is a chance for the academy to practice what it so often preaches: a commitment to pluralism and diversity.

Out of this volume, we can identify three other potential directions of future research.

The first is the question of agency and power. In the post-colonial tradition, it is customary to approach orientalism as a rhetoric that marginalizes, silences and disempowers its target peoples whether they be the shadowy and muted Afghan insurgents or Chinese communists during the Korean War. Orientalism, as Susan Jeffords reminds us, is partly about the authority to assign rhetorically loaded labels to others (whether 'terrorist' or 'liberator') with weighty policy implications. If orientalism is often intended to work as a tool of imperial domination, we are understandably tempted to assume that this is how it takes effect. But as with the study of medieval witch-hunting, we might also consider that the very archetypal images linked to exotic non-Western 'Others' may not just be there because Westerners foist those ideas upon them, and those images may not simply work to the disadvantage of the perceived oriental. The Taliban might want worldwide observers to perceive them as medieval and savage, as a horde of unstoppable fanatics wedded to a cult of death, even while they strive to persuade Afghans that they have technical modernity and can out-do NATO and ISAF in the provision of government services. As one young Afghan fighter bragged on the eve of war in autumn 2001: 'The Americans love Pepsi Cola, but we love death.'[19] This raises a question that flows out of Gusterson's chapter: the fact that these images are so pervasive in our media coverage might be partly due to the adversary's own deliberate self-portrayal, overcoming the silencing power of orientalist rhetoric and speaking directly to us. This potential of the 'terror image' to work in favour of the perceived barbarian was probably not lost on Sheikh Nasrallah when after the IDF left Lebanon, he boasted that he possessed the 'heads, the hands, the feet and even a nearly intact cadaver' of Israeli soldiers during a speech in Beirut.[20] We have little trouble recognising our own attempts at 'strategic communication.' In our own time, the United States and its allies have sought to impress enemies that their power is awesome and irresistible. As Clausewitz argued, war is at root a psychological undertaking, waged to change an adversary's mind or compel them to do one's will. The very concepts of orientalist rhetoric—the barbaric, the fanatical, the dreadful—might become weapons of the weak, skilfully co-opted and turned back against audiences in the United States and its allies. From a different direction, Margaret A. Mills has demonstrated how the observed subject can reclaim a voice. Have we been too quick to assume the overwhelming power of the West in imposing itself, its story and its icons upon its adversaries?

A second line of inquiry should be about change and continuity within orientalist traditions as well as their sources, and our need to work harder at understanding the traditions historically. At its most ambitious, orientalism as a grand schema for understanding representations of the non-Western can be a relatively timeless concept, finding continuities through time from the Greco-Persian Wars to the War on Terror of recent time. This can lead to the one-dimensional portrayal of orientalism as little more than the rhetorical handmaiden to imperialism, reducing a rich history to a boring tale of monotonous Western supremacism. East-West relations, the very history of the dichotomous concept of East and West, have not been constants historically. With shifting politics, how much have representations shifted also?

Even the medieval Crusades, often invoked as a climactic, prototypical period of orientalism, are a problematic case. Crusades to reclaim real estate and holy sites for the Latin Christian West were launched also against heretics within the faith and closer to home, not to mention the sack of Constantinople (an Orthodox, Christian East) in an opportunist diversion; they featured convenient strategic alliances between Crusaders and Fatimid Sultans, as between Ottomans and Venetians later; and in terms of cultural representation, the warrior aristocracies might abhor the Muslim masses while identifying with and trying to rebrand elite opponents like Saladin as knightly, virtual Christians. Clearly, it is possible to take these caveats too far. The Crusades were obviously not a moment of intercultural or interfaith harmony. But a glib 'East-West' narrative does little justice to the historical record. The forces that shape and shove orientalism are all there: shifting politics and power balances, internal and intra-faith conflicts, and a phenomenon strong in military history, that war in its reciprocities and homogenizing effects can prompt recognition as well as 'Othering.' 'War...is not simply a clash of Others, made possible by an ignorant horror of difference. The warrior looks out at the enemy and sees men who are, in crucial respects, recognizably like himself.'[21] This is obviously not always the case. But the mental worlds of warring cultures are often full of multiple divides and Others: there can be a horizontal cultural divide between societies at war, but there can also be a vertical class divide between commanders and those who fill the ranks. Other periods testify to this. The militaries of European dynastic states in the mid-eighteenth century, for example, shared much of each other's professional cultures, and reserved their worst atrocities not for each other, but for civilian populations unfortunate enough to get in their way.[22]

Finally, a challenge for scholars in this field is to turn our own high-powered analytical perception upon ourselves. If we are quick to point to the power of cultural myth, and to discover that in time of war our compatriots fall prey to chauvinist world views, academic critics of orientalism must also contend with their own fallibilities. In our enthusiasm to puncture the prejudices of Western observers whether soldiers, spies or Hollywood, we are prone to forget our own mythologies. Our reductionist caricatures of the United States in particular are also open to critique. In the wake of the Greco-Persian wars of the fifth century BC, an archetype emerged everlastingly of the ancient Persian Empire as an enslaving force, little more than a self-celebrating imperial power ruled by a grasping emperor and an opulent elite, driven only by unspeakable motives. How much have the intellectual heirs of Edward Said recycled this image to orientalize America, robbing it of its contradictions and its multiplicities? That kind of approach impoverishes our understanding of Washington's policymaking. And it damages our understanding of complex orientalist figures like Paul Wolfowitz, for example, whose long record of sophisticated engagement with scholarship on Islamic history and whose criticisms of Israeli occupation can be forgotten, as he is reduced misleadingly into an envoy of American cultural bigotry. Crude stereotyping is not just something that others are guilty of. A deeper understanding of Occidentalism should also be part of the widening frontier of research in this field. By rightly interrogating the politics of cross-cultural representation, we have set a standard by which we too will be judged.

NOTES

1. INTRODUCTION: ORIENTALISM AND WAR

1. Played by Robert Duvall in Coppola (dir), *Apocalypse Now*, 1979.
2. See Coward, *The Newspaper India*; Hamlin, '"Wo sind wir?,"' pp. 424–52; Kalmar and Penslar (eds), *Orientalism and the Jews*.
3. See for example Said, *Orientalism*; Said, *The Question of Palestine*; Said, *Covering Islam*. The lasting influence of these arguments can be seen in Jones, *The Image of China in Western Social and Political Thought*; Klein, *Cold War Orientalism*; Lockman, *Contending Visions of the Middle East*; Lowe, *Critical Terrains*; Lye, *America's Asia*; McAlister, *Epic Encounters*. Critiques include Ahmad, *In Theory*; Halliday, *Islam and the Myth of Confrontation*; MacKenzie, *Orientalism*.
4. Some exceptions include Attridge, *Nationalism, Imperialism and Identity in Late Victorian Culture*; Belich, *The Victorian Interpretation of Racial Conflict*; Cameron, *American Samurai*; Chakravarty, *The Indian Mutiny in the British Imagination*; Cooper, *The Anglo-Maratha Campaigns and the Contest for India*; Porter, *Military Orientalism*; Renda, *Taking Haiti*; Said, *Culture and Imperialism*.
5. Said, *Orientalism*, p. 1.
6. Ibid., p. 6.
7. See, Brunner, 'Occidentalism Meets the Female Suicide Bomber,' pp. 957–71.
8. See Foucault, 'Truth, Power, Self: An Interview with Michel Foucault,' pp. 145–62.
9. See, Krepinevich Jr., 'How to Win in Iraq,' 2005, pp. 87–104; Jones, *Counterinsurgency in Afghanistan*.
10. Mann, *States, War and Capitalism*, p. 147.
11. See, Delbrück, *History of the Art of War*; Howard, *Captain Professor*; Clausewitz, *On War*.
12. Herbig, 'Chance and Uncertainty in *On War*.'
13. Morrillo, *What is Military History?*

275

14. Clausewitz, *On War*, pp. 592–93.
15. Shaw, *Dialectics of War*.
16. See, Tilly, *Coercion, Capital, and European States, AD 990–1990*; Elshtain, *Women and War*; McNeill, *The Pursuit of Power*.
17. Fussell, *The Great War and Modern Memory*, p. ix.
18. Lévinas, *Totality and Infinity*, p. 21
19. Clausewitz, *On War*, p. 87.
20. Ibid., p. 89.
21. Strachan, *Clausewitz's On War*, pp. 176*ff.*
22. For a fuller discussion, see Barkawi and Brighton, 'Powers of War.'
23. Said, *Orientalism*, p. 7.

2. SHOCKED BY WAR: THE NON-POLITICS OF ORIENTALISM

1. 'Editorial,' Sept. 16, 1857, p. 6.
2. Said, *Orientalism*, p. 71, emphasis mine; 6.
3. Mitchell, *Colonising Egypt*, p. 165.
4. Said, *Orientalism*, p. 123, emphasis in original.
5. Ibid., p. 2, 73.
6. Ibid., pp. 31–49.
7. Ibid., p. 21, 94.
8. Ibid., pp. 71–2.
9. Ibid., p. 6; Stanski, 'So These Folks are Aggressive,' p. 89.
10. Kaye, *History, Vol. 1*, pp. 343–4.
11. Young, *Colonial Desire*, pp. 99–117.
12. Said, *Orientalism*, p. 72.
13. Ibid., p. 95.
14. Lacan, *Ecrits*, p. 64, emphasis mine; Hegel, *Phenomenology*, p. 111.
15. Hegel, *Phenomenology*, p. 113; Kojève, *Introduction to the Reading of Hegel*, pp. 4–40.
16. Quoted in Mitchell, *Colonising Egypt*, p. 95.
17. Bhabha, *Location*.
18. Zizek, 'Desire: Drive = Truth: Knowledge.'
19. Because the Self-Other relationship cannot be a Friend-Enemy relationship, Said cannot theorize war in a colonial context; Mowitt, 'Fanon's "guerre des ondes."'
20. Fabian, *Time*.
21. Miles, 'On the Late Mutinies in India,' *Times*, Jul. 6, 1857, p. 11, emphasis mine; Kaye, *History, Vol. 1*, pp. 256–60, 348–9; Malleson, *Indian Mutiny*, pp. 9–15.
22. Malleson, *Indian Mutiny*, p. 13.
23. Barthes, *Eiffel Tower*, p. 103.

24. Put otherwise, in the European context, people were shocked by the outcome/duration of war; Blainey, *Causes of War*, pp. 35–43. In the colonial context, they were shocked that there was war at all.

25. Cited in Bayly, *Empire and Information*, pp. 315–6.

26. Kaye, *History, Vol. 1*, p. 487.

27. Ibid., p. 491.

28. Duff, *Indian Rebellion*, p. 99, emphasis in original. John Norton similarly noted that English civilians 'are so wedded to the perfections of the Indian government that they cannot conceive it distasteful to the people'; quoted in Nayar, *1857 Reader*, p. 183.

29. Duff, *Indian Rebellion*, p. 113.

30. Ibid., pp. 105–6.

31. Guha, 'Prose of Counterinsurgency,' pp. 336–7.

32. 'Editorial,' Jun. 10, 1857, p. 9.

33. 'Editorial,' Sept. 16, 1857, p. 6.

34. 'Editorial,' Oct. 26, 1857, p. 6.

35. 'American Views of the Crisis in India,' *Times*, Aug. 19, 1857, p. 10. Other foreign commentators viewed the Mutiny in realpolitik terms, forecasting the downfall of Britain in India, and the geopolitical weakening of Britain. Equally, British justifications for reconquest warned of Britain becoming a second-rate power; e.g. Kaye, *History, Vol. 1*, p. 342–3.

36. Lt. Col. J. H. MacDonald, 'The Bengal Army,' *Times*, Aug. 20, 1857, p. 10.

37. 'An East Indian Director on the Indian Mutiny,' *Times*, Oct. 20, 1857, p. 7.

38. Quoted in Chakravarty, *Indian Mutiny*, p. 23, emphasis in original.

39. Counter-intuitively, letters in the *Times* can be considered private information, namely the personal observations of individuals, often dissenting from official policy.

40. 'The Earl of Shaftesbury on the Mutiny in India,' *Times*, Nov. 2, 1857, p. 6.

41. Ball, *History*, p. 40.

42. Quoted in Chakravarty, *Indian Mutiny*, p. 25.

43. 'Lord Brougham on Popular Education and the Mutiny in India,' *Times*, Nov. 5, 1857, p. 5.

44. Malleson, *Indian Mutiny*, pp. v–vii, p. 33, 45, 51; Roberts, *Letters*, p. 13; Metcalf, *Aftermath*, p. 290.

45. Kaye, *History, Vol. 1*, p. 456.

46. 'The Earl of Harrowby on the Indian Mutiny,' *Times*, Oct. 30, 1857, p. 10.

47. Malleson, *Indian Mutiny*, p. 146, emphasis mine.

48. Roberts, *Letters*, p. 51, emphasis mine.

49. X.X. 'The Indian Mutinies,' *Times*, Aug. 8, 1857, p. 12; 'The Bengal Army,' *Times*, Aug. 20, 1857, p. 10.

50. 'The Indian Mutinies,' *Times*, Aug. 3, 1857, p. 5.

51. Ibid.
52. Quoted in Nayar, *1857 Reader*, p. 40.
53. Roberts, *Letters*, p. 6.
54. Ball, *History*, p. 60, p. 97; Duff, *Indian Rebellion*, pp. 19–20, 43–4, p. 59.
55. Ball, *History*, p. 97, pp. 105–6.
56. P., 'The Indian Mutinies,' *Times*, Aug. 5, 1857, p. 9.
57. The historiography of the Mutiny located the proximate cause of the revolt in the sepoys' belief that their cartridges were being greased with pig or cow fat, violating Muslim and Hindu tenets respectively.
58. Malleson, *Indian Mutiny*, p. 38; Ball, *History*, p. 116; Kaye, *History, Vol. 1*, pp. 348–352.
59. 'Editorial,' Sept. 12, 1857, p. 6; Ball, *History*, pp. 34–7; Dirks, *Castes*, 130–131.
60. Metcalf, *Aftermath*, p. 298.
61. Judex, 'The Indian Mutiny,' *Times*, Jan. 29, 1858, p. 12; Duff, *Indian Rebellion*, pp. 93–4.
62. J.C. Wilson, 'The Indian Mutiny,' *Times*, Mar. 24, 1858, p. 5.
63. Lt. Col. J.H. MacDonald, 'The Mahommedans in India,' *Times*, Sept. 11, 1857, p. 5; Duff, *Indian Rebellion*, pp. 46–47, 121–2.
64. Malleson, *Indian Mutiny*, p. 53, pp. 50–53.
65. E.g. Roberts, *Letters*, pp. 4–5, p. 17.
66. In a letter that *did* advocate the withdrawal of British rule, the author wrote, 'let the entire body of Sepoys be placed *hors la loi*…they have rebelled against English institutions…let them cease to protect them…in a week every Sepoy would be a pauper, his house in flames, himself fleeing from men who will hunt him like a wolf'; Anglo-Bengalee, 'The Indian Mutinies,' *Times*, Aug. 8, 1857, p. 12. The withdrawal of empire here is a punishment for the Indians, reiterating the value of British rule.
67. Quoted in Nayar, *1857 Reader*, p. 281.
68. Guha, *Elementary Aspects*; Bhadra, 'Four Rebels.'
69. Lt. Col. J.H. MacDonald, 'The Bengal Army,' *Times*, Aug. 20, 1857, p. 10.
70. Quoted in Metcalf, *Aftermath*, p. 292.
71. Kaye, *History, Vol. 2*, p. 401; Nayar, *1857 Reader*, p. 142, 162, 166.
72. Lt. Col. J.H. MacDonald, 'The Indian Mutinies,' *Times*, Aug. 8, 1857, p. 12.
73. 'Capture of Delhi and Relief of Lucknow,' *Times*, Nov. 16, 1857, p. 7.
74. One advocated India become a settler colony; 'How to Establish Our Empire in India,' *Times*, Oct. 27, 1857, p. 12.
75. 'Editorials,' Jul. 24, 1857.
76. E.g. Centurion, 'The Siege of Delhi,' *Times*, Aug. 5, 1857, p. 9.
77. Ne Cede Malis, 'The Indian Rebellion,' *Times*, Aug. 3, 1857, p. 5.
78. E.g. Ne Cede Malis, 'The Indian Rebellion,' *Times*, Aug. 3, 1857, p. 5; 'Lord Brougham on Popular Education and the Mutiny in India,' *Times*, Nov. 5, 1857, p. 5.

79. This argument had been previously made by Edmund Burke; Dirks, *Scandal*.
80. 'Editorials,' Feb. 13, 1858, p. 9; 'Editorials,' Feb. 15, 1858, p. 6.
81. 'India Reform,' *The Times*, Dec. 18, 1857, p. 7.
82. Viscount Palmerston, 'Speech to the House of Commons,' Feb. 12, 1858, *Hansard*, Vol. 148: cc 1282, emphasis mine.
83. Quoted in Guha, *Dominance without Hegemony*, p. 77.
84. Kaye, *History, Vol. 1*, p. xii.
85. Chakravarty, *Indian Mutiny*, p. 71.
86. Ibid., p. 13.
87. Metcalf, *Aftermath*, p. xviii.
88. Kaye, *History, Vol. 1*, p. 153.
89. Ibid., p. 260.
90. Ibid., pp. 180–6; Norton quoted in Nayar, *1857 Reader*, pp. 183–7.
91. Dirks, *Castes*, pp. 127–130.
92. Kaye, *History, Vol. 1*, pp. 194–5.
93. Quoted in Metcalf, *Aftermath*, p. 136.
94. Godley, 'Copies,' p. 2.
95. U.S. Army/Marine Corps, *Field Manual 3–24*, p. 3–63, 3–64.
96. Ibid., p. 1–73.
97. Kilcullen, *Accidental Guerilla*, p. 199, emphasis in original, 203.
98. Ibid., p. 169.
99. See Said, *Orientalism*, p. 106.
100. On (mis)understanding Orientals in the context of war, see Porter, *Military Orientalism*.
101. Bayly, *Empire of Information*, pp. 4–5.
102. This trope remains alive: as a US intelligence officer in Iraq explained, 'in this country, everyone is lying to everyone else…you know that…they are all doing each other in'; Filkins, *Forever War*, p. 288.

3. AMERICAN ORIENTALISM AT WAR IN KOREA AND THE UNITED STATES: A HEGEMONY OF RACISM, REPRESSION, AND AMNESIA

1. This essay draws in part on themes developed in recent books of mine: *Parallax Visions*; *Dominion From Sea to Sea*, and *The Korean War*, 2010.
2. Whitman quoted in LaFeber, *The Clash*, p. 24; Perry, *Narrative*.
3. Stoddard, *Rising Tide*, pp. vi-vii, p. xiv, xxxi, 50, 196.
4. Lye, *America's Asia*, p. 16, 25, 30, pp. 40–1. Meredith Jung-en Woo first brought 'The Unparalleled Invasion' to my attention. On Professor Adams, see George L. Henderson's brilliant dissection in *Fictions of Capital*, pp. 91–6.
5. Ngai, *Impossible Subjects*, p. 3, 8, 40, original emphasis; Heizer and Almquist, *Other Californians*, pp. 189–90; Henderson, *Fictions of Capital*, pp. 91–6; Beard, *Open Door at Home*, pp. 93–5; Palumbo-Liu, *Asian/American*, p. 39.

6. Palumbo-Liu, *Asian/American*, p. 40; Clements quoted in McWilliams, *Factories in the Field*, p. 139.

7. Steiner, *Japanese Mask*. The commanding interpretation of this dark period in U.S.-Japan relations is Dower, *War Without Mercy*.

8. Quoted in Bernstein, 'Understanding the Atomic Bomb,' p. 268.

9. Judge Radhabinod Pal of India quoted this in his famous dissent from the Tokyo War Crimes Trial; cited in Holmes, *War and Morality*, p. 188.

10. Several veterans have told me that they thought fragging was more common in Korea than in Vietnam. I have no way of judging this matter.

11. Thompson, *Cry Korea*, p. 39, 44, 84, 114.

12. Princeton University, John Foster Dulles Papers, John Allison oral history, April 20, 1969; Ibid., William Sebald oral history, July 1965. Sebald quotes from his diary 'words to that effect' from MacArthur; see also Casey, *Selling the Korean War*, p. 28, 68.

13. *New York Times*, Jul. 14, 1950.

14. *New York Times*, Jul. 19, 1950.

15. *New York Times*, Aug. 21, 1950. See Christopher Simpson's searing account of the bloody Nazi suppression of guerrillas in the Ukraine, which he considered 'without equal in history.' Simpson, *Blowback*, pp. 13–26.

16. Letter to *New York Times*, Jul. 16, 1950. Taylor noted that these precepts have not always been followed by Western armies.

17. Hanley *et al.*, *Nogun-ri*, pp. 236–7.

18. Associated Press, 'G.I.'s Tell of a U.S. Massacre in Korean War,' p. 1.

19. Struck, 'U.S., South Korea Gingerly Probe the Past,' p. A24.

20. Osborne, 'Report from the Orient,' pp. 74–84.

21. Karig, 'Korea—Tougher Than Okinawa,' pp. 24–6.

22. Quoted in Falk, 'The Vietnam Syndrome,' p. 22.

23. David Oshinski quotes the 'sockful' line in *A Conspiracy So Immense*, p. 111; for 'Communists and queers' and 'egg-sucking liberals,' see *New York Times*, Apr. 21, 1950.

24. Capehart is quoted in Hodgson, *America in Our Time*, p. 34. Emphasis added.

25. Or what one did not look like: Thomas F. Murphy, Federal prosecutor in the Alger Hiss case, said 'The Communist does not look like the popular conception of a Communist. He does not have uncropped hair, he does not wear horn-rimmed glasses nor carry the Daily Worker. He doesn't have baggy trousers.' See *New York Times*, Mar. 13, 1950.

26. I recently read a forthcoming autobiography by John Paton Davies Jr., and he has skillful portraits of, and pungent comments about, most of McCarthy's targets—Owen Lattimore, John Service, John Carter Vincent, Jack Belden, Agnes Smedley, Anna Louis Strong, McCarthy's ally Freda Utley, and others; he met all of them in China in the 1930s and 1940s, as diplomats, journalists, and

leftists who all sought to understand the nature of the communists in their Yanan base.

27. The investigations of Grajdanzev and others are in MacArthur Archives, Charles Willoughby Papers, box 18, 'Leftist Infiltration into SCAP,' Jan. 15, 1947 and thereafter; Willoughby supplied his 1947 studies to Benjamin Mandel of the McCarran Subcommittee after Mandel solicited them, and also stated that he had given them to McCarthy (box 23, Mandel to Willoughby, Feb. 19, 1954). See also Willoughby to W.E. Woods of HUAC, May 1, 1950, Willoughby Papers, box 10

28. *New York Times*, Mar. 14, Mar. 22, Mar. 27, and Mar. 31, 1950.

29. *New York Times*, Apr. 4, 1950.

30. *New York Times*, May 16, 1950.

31. 'Transcript of Round Table Discussion on American Policy toward China,' State Department, Oct. 6–8, 1949, declassified in Carrolton Press, CRC 1977, item 316B. On Lattimore's support for the U.S. role in the Korean War, see *New York Times*, Aug. 1, 1950.

32. *New York Times* editorials, Apr. 5, 1950 and Apr. 19, 1950. Other responsible officials who held this 'shocking view' were for example, most of the high Army Department officials in 1948–1949, who were ready to write off the ROK even if it meant a communist takeover; Gen. Lawton Collins told the 1951 Senate MacArthur Hearings in testimony deleted at the time, that Korea 'has no particular military significance,' and if the Soviets were fully to occupy the peninsula, Japan would be in little greater jeopardy than it already was from Vladivostok and the Shantung Peninsula.

33. McAuliffe, *Crisis on the Left*, p. 147.

34. Hodgson, *America in Our Time*, p. 89, 97.

35. Wittfogel, *Oriental Despotism*.

36. Poppe's defection is discussed in more detail in Christopher Simpson, *Blowback*.

37. Anderson, *Lineages of the Absolutist State*, pp. 462–549.

38. See for example Chong-sik Lee, 'Stalinism in the East,' pp. 114–39.

39. Friedrich, *The Fire*, pp. 14–17, 50, 52, 61–2, 71, 76.

40. Quoted in Ibid., p. 82, 485.

41. Princeton University, J.F. Dulles Papers, Curtis LeMay oral history, April 28, 1966. South Korean cities were only bombed when North Koreans or Chinese occupied them, and the destruction was much less than in the North.

42. Townsend, 'They Don't Like Hell Bombs'; 'Napalm Jelly Bombs Prove a Blazing Success in Korea'; Bullene, 'Wonder Weapon.'

43. Crane, *American Airpower*, pp. 32–3, 66–8, 122–5, 133; Knox, *Korean War*, p. 552.

44. Lovett, Matthew Connelly Papers, 'Notes on Cabinet Meetings,' Sept. 12, 1952.

45. Knell, *To Destroy a City*, p. 25, 334.

46. Crane, *American Airpower*, p. 133.
47. Friedrich, *The Fire*, pp. 85–7, 110, 151.
48. Lautensach, *Korea*, p. 202.
49. Crane, *American Airpower*, pp. 160–4.
50. Dean, *General Dean's Story*, p. 274.
51. Dormer *et al.*, 'Korea: The Unknown War.'
52. See Springer, *North Korea Caught in Time.*
53. Friedrich, *The Fire*, p. 75, 89; Knell, *To Destroy a City*, p. 266; Crane, *American Airpower*, p. 126; Foot, *Substitute for Victory*, p. 208; Crane, *American Airpower*, pp. 168–71.
54. Karig *et al.*, *Battle Report*, pp. 111–12.
55. Crane, *American Airpower*, pp. 168–71.
56. Knell, *To Destroy a City*, p. 329.
57. Kim Jong Il tried to get American attention 'by appearing to be barmy—a gambit aided by the fact that he almost certainly is.' Coll, 'No Nukes,' p. 31.
58. Sneider, 'Let them Eat Rockets,' p. 6.
59. Jameson, *Political Unconscious*, pp. 295–6, 298.
60. Quoted in Von Laue, *Why Lenin?*, p. 182. See also p. 155.

4. TERROR, THE IMPERIAL PRESIDENCY, AND AMERICAN HEROISM

1. Lieberman, 'Lieberman Statement.'
2. Quoted in Grim, 'Faisal Shahzad Arrest.'
3. In *The American Spectator*, Ben Lerner asserts that 'To be sure, jihadist terrorists generally could care less whether they are citizens of any specific country—after all, their unifying goal is global Islamic rule under a Caliphate implementing shariah law, an arrangement rendering the nation-state system irrelevant.' Lerner, 'Citizenship as Sword.'
4. Quoted in Condon, 'McCain: Faisal Shahzad Should Not Have Been Mirandized,' May 4, 2010.
5. For the purposes of this discussion, I will use the capitalized Terrorist to refer to the constructed category that forms part of the U.S. narrative of terror.
6. For a discussion of whether enemy combatants are 'lawful' or 'unlawful,' see Cohen, 'No Unlawful Enemy Combatants at Guantanamo.'
7. Owens, 'The Pleasures of Imperialism and the Pink Elephant,' p. 244.
8. For an example, see the case of Khaled el-Masri, who was detained in custody by the CIA even after concerns about his innocence were raised.
9. For a discussion of Masri's case, see Mayer, *The Dark Side*, pp. 282–7.
10. Mowitt, 'Fanon's "guerre des ondes," p. 219.
11. Kateb, 'A Life of Fear,' p. 892.
12. McClintock, 'Paranoid Empire,' p. 55.
13. Singh, 'The Afterlife of Fascism,' p. 88.

14. Kateb, 'A Life of Fear,' p. 898.
15. Ibid., p. 900.
16. Said, *Orientalism*, p. 57.
17. Ibid., pp. 59–60.
18. Ahmed, 'The Politics of Fear in the Making of Worlds,' p. 378.
19. Ibid., p. 389
20. Ibid., p. 387.
21. Elliott *et al.*, 'For Times Sq. Suspect, Long Roots of Discontent,' p. A1.
22. 'The Ballot Box.'
23. Vaughn, 'Faisal Shahzad.'
24. Singh, 'The Afterlife of Fascism,' p. 88.
25. Ahmed, 'The Politics of Fear in the Making of Worlds,' p. 393.
26. Rudalevige, *The New Imperial Presidency*.
27. Genovese, *Memo to a New President*, p. 163,188.
28. Daynes and Sussman, 'The Imperial Presidency Revisited,' p. 12.
29. Wayne, 'Presidential Decision Making,' p. 136.
30. Yoo, *Crisis and Command*, p. 403.
31. Ibid., p. 404.
32. 'There Were Orders to Follow,' p. 22.
33. Goldsmith, *The Terror Presidency*, p. 213.
34. Der Derian, 'Imaging Terror,' p. 32.
35. Ignatieff, *The Lesser Evil*, p. 150.
36. Briggs and Briggs II, 'Bush and the Psychology of Incompetent Decisions.'
37. Singh, 'The Afterlife of Fascism' p. 73, quotation from Mamadani, 'Good Muslim, Bad Muslim.'
38. Quoted in Hannah, 'Torture and the Ticking Bomb, p. 635.
39. Ibid.
40. Zizek, 'What Rumsfeld Doesn't Know that He Knows About Abu Ghraib.'
41. Canada, Australia, New Zealand, as well as countries in Africa, Asia, Europe and the Middle East.
42. Jones, 'The End of *24* and Hopefully of the Idea that Torture Works.'
43. Quoted in Dougherty, 'You Can't Make this Stuff Up,' p. 19.
44. Beverley, 'The Question of Torture, the Spanish Decadence, and Our Own,' p. 196.
45. Ibid., p. 191.
46. Jonah Goldberg, 'When Push Comes to Torture.'
47. Flynn, *Protect and Defend*, p. 329.
48. Flynn, *Extreme Measures*, p. 340.
49. Ibid., p. 341.
50. Ibid.
51. Ibid. p. 429.

52. Flynn, *American Assassin*, p. 2.

5. CAN THE INSURGENT SPEAK?

1. David Halberstam, 'From a Helicopter,' p. 77.
2. Without attempting a comprehensive mapping of this literature, some texts include: Chomsky, *Interventions*; Chomsky, *Power and Terror*; Der Derian, *Virtuous War*; Englehardt, *The End of Victory Culture*; Evans, *Celluloid Mushroom Clouds*; Faludi, *The Terror Dream*; Gibson, *Warrior Dreams*; Gusterson, 'Paranoid, Potbellied Stalinist Gets Nuclear Weapons'; Hammond, *Media, War, and Postmodernity*; Henriksen, *Dr. Strangelove's America*; Herman and Chomsky, *Manufacturing Consent*; MacArthur, *Second Front*; Masco, 'Target Audience'; Mermin, *Debating War and Peace*; Mitchell, *So Wrong for So Long*; Pedelty, *War Stories*; Robb, *Operation Hollywood*; McChesney, *The Problem of the Media*; Schechter, *Media Wars*; Sharp, *Condensing the Cold War*; Thussu and Freedman, *War and the Media*; Turse, *The Complex*; Weber, *Imagining America at War*; Zelizer and Allen, *Journalism After September 11*.
3. Notable exceptions include Shaheen, *Guilty*, and *Reel Bad Arabs*; and Said, *Covering Islam*.
4. On the general importance of war and enmity in the dialectical construction and securing of identity, see Connolly, *Identity/Difference*; Weldes *et al.*, *Cultures of Insecurity*.
5. Gusterson, 'Presenting the Creation'; Robin, *The Making of the Cold War Enemy*.
6. See Klare, *Rogue States and Nuclear Outlaws*, for a discussion of the emergence of the term 'rogue state' and of a more generalized concern about the Middle East as a source of threat shortly after the end of the cold war.
7. Although I have not studied British media coverage of the wars in Iraq and Afghanistan systematically, I have read enough of it to conclude that many of the arguments made here would not apply to British mainstream newspapers, especially but not uniquely the *Guardian* and the *Independent*. British mainstream newspapers on the left tend to be more open to critical ideas than American mainstream newspapers, partly because the British dailies are organized along an ideological spectrum while the American mainstream newspapers serve regional markets where they try to speak to and represent the center of gravity.
8. Porter, *Military Orientalism*. On the importance of metrics of technical advancement and backwardness to ideologies of colonial or neocolonial superiority, see Adas, *Machines as the Measure of Men*.
9. This article is a sequel to earlier research I undertook (Gusterson, 'Nuclear weapons and the Other') on orientalist themes in Western media coverage of nuclear proliferation. Third World countries seeking nuclear weapons, especially those in South Asia and the Middle East, have often been portrayed as too irrational or technically backward to be trusted with the ultimate weapon. These countries are

often metaphorized as women and children who should be under the tutelage of the West, so that their nuclear arsenals are fundamentally incongruous.

10. For an Associated Press archive of coverage of Bilal Hussein and of AP statements on his behalf, see http://www.ap.org/bilalhussein. Accessed Dec. 16, 2010. See also Layton, 'Behind Bars.'

11. Curley, 'In Iraq, a Journalist in Limbo.'

12. In this Hussein's pictures follow a certain visual convention in the representation of insurgents. See, for example, John Alpert's documentary film, *Chiapas: The Fight for Land and Liberty*, where subcommandante Marcos is also featured in a mask in his interview footage.

13. Butler, *Precarious Life*, p. xviii.

14. Rubin, 'Battle Company is Out There.'

15. King and Loiko, 'U.S. Now in Afghanistan as long as Soviets Were.'

16. Ricks, *Fiasco*, p. 355.

17. Chivers, 'In the Taliban, Marines Find Evolving Foes,' p. A1.

18. Stockman, 'Anthropologist's War Death Reverberates.'

19. Rubin, 'Battle Company is Out There.'

20. Notwithstanding the often noted difficulty of telling insurgents apart from innocent civilians among whom they hide, mainstream media accounts do tend to present insurgent affiliation as absolute and binary: either you are an insurgent or you are not and, as with pregnancy, it is not possible to be partly insurgent. In fact, however, some alternative media accounts suggest that some people may move in and out of the insurgency, depending what else is happening in their lives, and there are even descriptions of men moving back and forth between working for American occupying forces and fighting with the insurgents. See, in particular, Graham, 'Beyond Fallujah,' pp. 37–48.

21. Gray, 'Battle for Iraq's Third City.'

22. Gall, 'Ragtag Taliban Show Tenacity'; 'US Says Taliban Use Pakistani Lair to Widen Attacks' was the headline of a *New York Times* story on Aug. 24, 2009.

23. Londono and Partlow, 'Afghan Prison an Insurgent Breeding Ground.'

24. Perlez, 'Militant den is Penetrated by Pakistan,' p. A4.

25. Nordland, 'Taliban Hit Back with a Campaign of Intimidation,' p. A1.

26. Jaffe and Partlow, "Scaling Back Ambitions."

27. Brulliard and Khan, 'Pakistanis Tie Slayings to Surge in U.S. Strikes' p. A1.

28. Rondeaux, 'For Pakistan's Tribesmen, a Difficult, Deadly Choice,' p. A14

29. Ignatius, 'Questions for Gen. Petraeus,' p. A13.

30. Chivers, 'Afghan Attack Gives Marines a Taste of War,' p. A1.

31. Perlez and Shah, 'Pakistan is Mired in Brutal Battle to Oust Taliban,' p. A1.

32. Chivers, 'G.I.s in Remote Afghan Post Have Weary Job, Drawing Fire.'

33. Jaffe, 'A Personal Touch in the Taliban Fight,' p. A1.

34. Will, 'A Tet in Afghanistan?,' p. A25. Will is borrowing this account from a story by Yochi J. Dreazen in the Dec. 4 issue of *National Journal*.

35. It is one of the conventions of American reportage that U.S. combatants are referred to as soldiers, while Taliban combatants are invariably called 'fighters.'

36. Jaffe, 'Fighting to Get out of the Way,' p. A1.

37. Rubin, 'Battle Company is Out There.'

38. Jaffe, 'A Personal Touch'

39. Rubin, 'Battle Company is Out There.'

40. Perlez and Shah, 'Pakistanis Mired in Brutal Battle.'

41. Gall, 'Ragtag Taliban.'

42. Shanker and Rubin, 'Quest to Neutralize Taliban.'

43. Porter, 'CIA Drone Operators Oppose Strikes.'

44. Cohen, 'Does Obama Have the Backbone?,' p. A23. For a critique of Cohen's claim that it would be hard to imagine an American suicide bomber, see Gusterson, 'An American Suicide Bomber?.'

45. Human terrain teams are assemblages of military and intelligence personnel, contractors and social scientists who advise the U.S. military on indigenous culture while surveying the needs and preferences of local populations. As a human terrain team social scientist, it is, ironically, Fermoselle's job to teach cultural sensitivity to U.S. military personnel. He posted this remark at http://zeroanthropology.net/2009/05/07/whitewashing-a-us-war-crime-in-afghanistan-the-trial-of-don-ayala-human-terrain-mercenary. Accessed Jan. 4, 2012. A concise overview of the human terrain team program is given by Gonzalez, *American Counterinsurgency.*

46. Will, 'A Tet in Afghanistan?,' *Washington Post*, p. A25.

47. Chivers, 'Foot on Bomb,' p. A1.

48. Chivers, 'In the Taliban,' p. A1.

49. Partlow, 'Troops in Diyala,' *Washington Post*, p. A1.

50. DeYoung, 'Obama to Explore New Approach,' p. A1.

51. For an example, see Rubin, 'Battle Company is Out There.'

52. Moore, 'NATO confronts surprisingly fierce Taliban,' p. A1.

53. Krauthammer, 'Afghanistan: The 7/11 Problem,' p. A19.

54. Perlez and Shah, 'Pakistanis Mired in Brutal Battle,' p. A1.

55. Santora and Al-Salhy, 'Iraq Tribes are Upset by Sentence Given to G.I.,' p. A5.

56. Oppel, 'Files for Suicide Bombers,' p. A6.

57. Butler, *Precarious Life*, p. 33.

58. Daniel Hallin, *The Uncensored War*, p. 156.

59. Ibid., p. 158.

60. Ibid., p. 55.

61. Ibid., p. 158.

62. Spivak, 'Can the Subaltern Speak?.'

63. Cooke, 'Paramilitaries and the Press in Northern Ireland,' p. 84. The BBC got around this prohibition by having anonymous actors read the exact words of IRA spokespersons in interviews.

64. Shulman, 'Terror-Themed Game Suspended,' *Washington Post*, p. A3. Bilal also staged an exhibit, 'Domestic Tension,' where viewers could log on to the internet to interact with him via webcam, then choose whether to shoot him with a paintball gun. See http://wafaabilal.com/html/domesticTension.html.

65. Filkins and Burns, 'Mock Iraqi Villages,' p. A1.

66. Gregory, 'The Rush to the Intimate.'

67. In his ethnography of war reporters in El Salvador, the anthropologist Mark Pedelty makes a distinction between 'A team' and 'B team' reporters. The A team reporters have staff positions for major dailies and are often sent to 'parachute' in on temporary assignment to cover foreign war stories. The B team reporters are stringers who may do support work for A team correspondents for a particular newspaper, or they may be freelancers who sell their work to various outlets. In the context of war reporting from Iraq and Afghanistan, it is mainly these B team journalists who allow the insurgents to speak. See Pedelty, *War Stories*.

68. For an example, see Cocks, 'Iraqi Sunni guards join Shi'ite government payroll.' General Petraeus's strategy of buying the Sunnis out of the insurgency produced a number of model reformed insurgents suddenly available for U.S. media interviews.

69. Butler, *Precarious Life*, p. 7.

70. Jamail, *Beyond the Green Zone*.

71. Bennett, 'In the War's Cast of Characters,' p. B1.

72. This point is taken from Bennett, who derived it from the *Washington Post* reporter Anthony Shadid, an Arab-American mainstream reporter who has operated extensively outside embedded contexts and has been wounded by Israeli soldiers and kidnapped by Libyan security forces. See Shadid, *Night Draws Near*.

73. See http://www.pbs.org/wgbh/pages/frontline/insurgency/interviews/ware.html.

74. Graham, 'Beyond Fallujah.'

75. 'Insurgents Vow to Resist Security Pact,' Associated Press, Nov. 11, 2008. Similarly, an article in the *New York Times* tells readers that Taliban fighters from the Quetta Shura Taliban, Haqqani network, and Hekmatyar clan, traditionally rivals, have been cooperating to attack U.S. troops, but without explaining any of the differences between the factions named in the article. Tellingly, the sources of evidence for this new cooperation in the article are all NATO military and intelligence officials, many unnamed. One of these sources cites identification found on the dead bodies of Taliban as evidence. No insurgents— indeed no Afghans of any kind—are quoted or cited as sources on this supposed development. Shanker, 'Rival Factions Unite,' p. A1.

76. Roberts, *The Insurgency*.

77. Graham, 'Beyond Fallujah.'

78. Connors and Bingham, *Meeting Resistance*.

79. See Ricks, *Fiasco*.
80. Rivera, 'Inroads by the Taliban,' p. A8. However, the article's description of how the Taliban dictate the school curriculum follows narrative conventions about the Taliban's invisibility: 'At a school of about 1,300 boys and 30 teachers in the nearby village of Chawni, the Taliban recently posted a letter on the wall detailing the curriculum that was to be taught.'
81. Rubin, 'Taliban Bet on Fear Over Brawn as a Tactic,' p. A6.
82. The *New York Times* article, together with the photograph, can be seen at http://www.nytimes.com/2012/01/04/world/asia/taliban-to-open-qatar-office-in-step-toward-peace-talks.html?scp=2&sq=taliban&st=cse. The photograph itself (the reproduction of which in this article Getty Images refused to allow without extravagant payment) can be seen online at http://ramkshrestha.files.wordpress.com/2012/01/jp-afghanistan–1-articlelarge.jpg.
83. DeYoung and Partlow, 'Karzai's Overture Sets off Discord, Confusion,' p. A1.
84. For an account that shows the Taliban had had an aggressive media strategy for some years, see Porter, *Military Orientalism*, p. 167.
85. Hallin, *The Uncensored War*, p. 213.

6. COLONIAL WARS, POSTCOLONIAL SPECTERS: THE ANXIETY OF DOMINATION

1. Filkins, 'Taliban Car Bomb,' p. A1.
2. Franklin, *Vietnam and Other American Fantasies*.
3. Wright, *Meditations*, p. 43.
4. See Zepezauer, *CIA's Greatest Hits*. Also see Lendman, 'Afghanistan's Operation Phoenix': 'In 1975, Counterspy magazine said it was "the most indiscriminate and massive program of political murder since the Nazi death camps of world war two." It even targeted certain US military personnel considered security risks and members of the South Vietnamese government.'
5. The toxic chemicals were also sprayed on parts of Laos. Dioxin-concentrated Agent Orange continues to inflict deformities and incurable diseases, through human genes and the poisoned environment, on Vietnamese babies being born today. See 'United States-Viet Nam Scientific Conference,' 2002.
6. Wright, *Meditations*, p. 43.
7. Appy, *Patriots*, p. 23. In this essay, all italics in quotes are our emphasis unless otherwise stated.
8. Ibid., p. 24.
9. Burns, 'Into Kandahar.'
10. Lindqvist and Tate, *Exterminate*.
11. Quoted references are from Hochschild, *King Leopold's Ghost*, p. 281–82.
12. Schell, *Unconquerable World*.

13. Clarke, *Against All Enemies*, ch. 1.

14. Friedman, 'Because We Could.'

15. In 1965, Maxwell Taylor, U.S ambassador to South Vietnam and former Chairman of the Joint Chiefs of Staff, was stunned by the resilience of the 'insurgency' that his forces encountered: 'The ability of the Vietcong continuously to rebuild their units and make good their losses is one of the mysteries of this guerilla war. We still find no plausible explanation for the continued strength of the Vietcong…[They] have the recuperative power of the phoenix [and] an amazing ability to maintain morale.' Quoted in Record, *Beating Goliath*, p. 5.

16. See Asad, *Formations of the Secular*, ch. 2.

17. Carter, 'Irrelevant Exuberance.'

18. 'Monument.'

19. Edkins, *Trauma*, p. 59.

20. See fn. 19.

21. Roy, 'Seize the Time.'

22. Jones, *Graveyard of Empires*.

23. From 1965 through 1973, the US Air Force dropped '*at minimum* over eight million tons of munitions,' an explosive power equivalent to 640 Hiroshima-size bombs, onto Vietnam, Laos, and Cambodia. See Gibson, *The Perfect War*; Tanaka & Young, *Bombing Civilians*.

24. Quoted in Johnson, *Nemesis*.

25. Mbembe, *Postcolony*, p. 205.

26. See Derrida's hauntology in Derrida, *Specters of Marx*.

27. Nordland, 'Ready or Not.'

28. Kissinger quoted in Hersh, *Price of Power*, p. 126.

29. Quoted in Tanaka and Young, *Bombing Civilians*, p.165, original emphasis.

30. The story is footnoted in Hersh, *Price of Power*, p. 134.

31. As Former Secretary of State Dean Rusk confessed, 'Hanoi's persistence was incredible, I don't understand it, even to this day.' See Rusk, *As I Saw It*, p. 472.

32. Weiner, 'McNamara.'

33. Excerpt from the poem 'Interrelationship' in Thich Nhat Hanh, *Call Me*.

34. Van Staaveren, *Gradual Failure*, p. 46.

35. In what follows, we have drawn on both US records and Vietnamese accounts of the bombing and restoration of the Long Biên bridge.

36. See Price, 'Bridge Busting.'

37. Nguyên, 'Kỳ tích.'

38. Nguyen Co Thach, Former Foreign Minister of Viet Nam, quoted in Hersh, *Price of Power*, p. 134.

39. Mbembe, *On the Postcolony*, p. 205.

40. Ibid.

41. Ibid., p. 206.

42. The scene and dialogue are taken from Peter Davis' documentary 'Hearts and Minds' (1974). We have edited some of the translations.

43. 'The issue, he [one of Mullah Omar's deputies] said, was what to do with the incidence of homosexuality among Taliban fighters…. Should the offenders be buried alive, or taken atop the old city wall and cast down? The question carried me back across the centuries to a time when similar barbarisms were an everyday occurrence in the Christian West.' See Burns, 'Into Kandahar.'

44. 'At that moment, I understood what remains so hard for many in the West to grasp, as our troops fight to secure freedoms for Afghans that we have long enjoyed at home: that for many in Afghanistan…,*our world and theirs are, indeed, centuries apart,….*' Ibid.

45. Thomas and Barry, 'Surprising Lessons,' p. 36.

46. Bumiller, 'In Camouflage or Afghan Veil.'

47. U.S. Army, 'Welcome to the HTS Home Page.'

48. Shachtman, 'Army Social Scientist.'

7. ORIENTALISM IN THE MACHINE

1. Speaking to students at the Epcott Center on Aug. 8, 1983.

2. 'Denn die Waffen sind nichts anderes als das Wesen der Kämpfer selbst.' Hegel, *Phänomenologie Des Geistes*, p. 308.

3. Kittler, *Aufschreibesysteme 1800/1900*, p. 239.

4. Said, *Orientalism*, p. 86.

5. Ibid., p. 123.

6. While vision refers to the physical act of seeing, visuality refers to the social fact of seeing. The difference is 'between the mechanism of human sight and its historical techniques.' Foster, *Vision and Visuality*, p. ix.

7. Said, *Orientalism*, p. 44, 68, 70, 95, 113, 14, 54, 230, 37, 70, 76, 40.

8. Ibid., p. 43, 202, 40, 113, 27, 239, 40. Cf. Gregory in this volume.

9. Bentham, *The Complete Works of Jeremy Bentham*, pp. 65–6.

10. Davis, *Planet of Slums*, p. 205. See also Gregory, '"The Rush to the Intimate" Counterinsurgency and the Cultural Turn,' *Radical Philosophy*, p. 150; Graham, 'The Urban "Battlespace."'

11. Mowitt, 'Fanon's "guerre des ondes,"' p. ???.

12. 'Unmanned Aerial System First to Fire Missiles in Combat.'

13. Drew, 'Drone Flights Leave Military Awash in Data.'

14. Singer, *Wired for War*, p. 37.

15. Northrup Grumman, 'An Aaq–37 Eo Das for the F–35,' Available at http://www.es.northropgrumman.com/solutions/f35targeting/assets/eodasvideo.html.

16. http://www.raytheon.com/capabilities/products/dcgs/.

17. Choi, 'Military to Adopt NFL's Instant Replay Technology.'

18. Freud, 'Der Moses Des Michelangelo,' p. 24. See also Ginzburg, 'Morelli, Freud and Sherlock Holmes,' p. 10.

19. For failed attempts and dashed hopes at connecting finger prints with race and class see Galton, *Finger Prints*, pp. 17–19; 192–97. For the colonial history of fingerprints see Sengoopta, *Imprint of the Raj: How Fingerprinting Was Born in Colonial India*.

20. Saletan, 'Ghosts in the Machine: Do Remote-Control War Pilots Get Combat Stress,' *Slate*, Aug. 11, 2008; For more on drones see Singer, *Wired for War*, pp. 36–37, 47, 58, 59, 64, 119, 45, 306. See also Gregory in this volume.

21. WikiLeaks, 'Collateral Murder,' http://www.collateralmurder.com/.

22. Said, *Orientalism*, p. 119.

23. Li, 'A Universal Enemy?,' p. 358.

24. U.S. Army and U.S. Marine Corps, *Field Manual 3–24*; Porter, *Military Orientalism*.

25. U.S. Army, 'HTS Components.'

26. Jay, 'Mapping the Human Terrain.'

27. Monmonier, *How to Lie with Maps*.

28. Winichakul, *Siam Mapped*, p. 56.

29. Said, *Orientalism*, p. 113.

30. AAA Commission on the Engagement of Anthropology, 'Final Report on the Army's Human Terrain System Proof of Concept Program,' p. 15.

31. Ginzburg, 'Morelli, Freud and Sherlock Holmes,' p. 14.

32. Lederer, 'On the Sociology of World War,' p. 247.

33. Linebaugh and Rediker, *The Many-Headed Hydra*, p. 39.

34. A Google search for 'Al-Qaeda' and 'Hydra' produces 35,800 hits.

35. National Commission on Terrorist Attacks upon the United States, *The 9/11 Commission Report: Final Report of the National Commission on Terrorist Attacks Upon the United States*, p. 364.

36. For an overview of U.S. constructions of otherness in the past see Campbell, *Writing Security*.

37. United States Marine Corps, *Small Wars Manual*, p. 2–46, f (2). Emphasis added.

38. U.S. Army and U.S. Marine Corps., *Field Manual 3–24*, §1–94.

39. Ibid.

40. 'This enemy is better networked than we are.' Gen John Abizaid, Jun. 20, 2007, Tranformation Warfare 2007. 'In bitter, bloody fights in both Afghanistan and Iraq, it became clear to me and to many others that to defeat a networked enemy we had to become a network ourselves....It takes a network to defeat a network.' McCrystal, 'It Takes a Network,' *Foreign Policy*, 185, Mar.-Apr. 2011, p. 66.

41. Confidential email exchange. U.S. Army Intelligence Officer. May 24, 2010

42. Thank you to John Mowitt for bringing this to my attention. For more on the Battle of Algiers see Mowitt, 'The Battle of Algiers.'

43. Official in charge of a ground robot program quoted in Singer, *Wired for War*, p. 68.

44. Ibid., p. 69.

45. Smith, 'The Long History of Gaming in Military Training,' p. 6.

46. http://www.trustedreviews.com/video-games/news/2010/01/15/Modern-War-fare-2-As-Successful-As-Avatar/p1.

47. Said, *Orientalism*, p. 26.

48. This stands in a tradition of defining western and non-western peoples through the technological artefacts they produce. For more on this see Adas, *Machines as the Measure of Men*.

49. Tyson, 'A Historic Success in Military Recruiting.'

50. Said, *Orientalism*, p. 145.

51. Frazer, *The Golden Bough*, p. 15.

52. Ibid.

53. Silverman, 'Human Terrain Data—What Should We Do with It?,' p. 1.

54. Admiral Thomas B. Hayward, USN (Ret.) Foreword in Peter p. Perla, *The Art of Wargaming*, p. xiii.

55. Quoted in Ghamari-Tabrizi, *The Worlds of Herman Kahn*, pp. 158–9.

56. Smith, 'The Bare Facts of Ritual,' p. 127.

57. COIN academy participant on battlefield immersion in Afghanistan. Confidential email exchange. May 8, 2010.

58. Lyall and Wilson, 'Rage against the Machines.'

59. Edwards, *The Closed World*.

60. Card, *Ender's Game*, p. 262.

8. DIS/ORDERING THE ORIENT: SCOPIC REGIMES AND MODERN WAR

1. Said, *Orientalism*, pp. 41, 103.

2. Ibid., p. 87. More recently Cole, *Napoleon's Egypt*, p. 247 has endorsed a parallel claim. In invading Egypt, he argues, 'Bonaparte was inventing what we now call "the modern Middle East,"' and 'the similarities of the Corsican general's rhetoric and tactics to those of later North Atlantic incursions into the region tell us much about the persistent pathologies of Enlightenment republics.' So they do, but the 'Middle East' has its origins in European and eventually American discourses of diplomacy, geopolitics and security, whereas 'the Orient' has a more diffuse cultural inflection. The conjunction of the two in the French occupation of Egypt is of crucial importance, and the same can be said of the American-led invasion of Iraq in 2003.

3. Said, *Orientalism*, pp. 85–6.

4. Ibid., pp. 103, 127, 158, 239.

5. Metz, *Imaginary Signifier*, p. 61; Jay, 'Scopic Regimes.

6. Bell, *First Total War.*

7. Said, *Orientalism*, p. 82; al-Jabarti, *Journal.*

8. Jacotin, 'Mémoire,' pp. 546–7.

9. Jomard, 'Description de la Ville,' pp. 115–6.

10. Solé, *Les Savants de Bonaparte*, p. 163.

11. al-Jabarti, *History of Egypt*, p. 49.

12. Kitchin and Dodge, 'Rethinking Maps.'

13. Mitchell, *Colonising Egypt*, pp. 12–13, 24, 29; Idem, 'World-as-exhibition'; Idem, *Orientalism and the Exhibitionary Order*; Said, *Orientalism*, p. 55.

14. Mitchell, *Colonising Egypt*, p. 24.

15. Porter, *Military Orientalism*; Ucko, *New Counterinsurgency Era.*

16. Gregory, 'Rush to the Intimate.'

17. U.S. Army and U.S. Marine Corps, *Field Manual 3–24.*

18. Nagl, *Learning to Eat Soup*; Kipp *et al.*, 'Human Terrain System'; Lawrence, '27 Articles'; Kilcullen, 'Twenty-Eight Articles'; idem, Countering Global Insurgency, p. 614; idem, *Counterinsurgency*, pp. 29–50.

19. Lawrence was of course an insurgent, but it is his experience of working with Arabs and conducting guerilla war that explains his significance for American counterinsurgency: see Young, 'Lost in the Desert.'

20. Cf. Eisenstadt, 'Tribal Engagement;' González, 'Going "Tribal"'; Meinshausen and Wheeler, 'Tribes and Afghanistan.'

21. U.S. Army and U.S. Marine Corps, *Field Manual 3–24*, §1–80.

22. Gregory, 'Rush to the Intimate,' p. 18.

23. U.S. Army and U.S. Marine Corps, *Field Manual 3–24*, § E.5-E.11.

24. Deer, *Culture in Camouflage*, pp. 64–73; Satia, *Spies in Arabia*, pp. 242, 249–51, 256–8.

25. Kilcullen, *Accidental Guerrilla*, pp. 304–6; Bickford, 'Anthropology and HUMINT,' p. 147.

26. Gordon, *Ghostly Matters*, pp. 15–16.

27. This section is derived from Gregory, 'Seeing Red.'

28. Mirzoeff, 'War is Culture,' p. 1741.

29. Croser, 'Networking Security.'

30. Croser, *New Spatiality of Security*, pp. 103, 105.

31. Idem, 'Organising Complexity,' p. 38.

32. Jacob, *Sovereign Map.*

33. Amoore, 'Vigilant Visualities,' p. 226

34. This section is confined to the missions flown by the USAF in Afghanistan, and is derived from Gregory, 'From a View to a Kill'; for a wider discussion, including CIA-controlled missions in Pakistan and beyond, see Gregory, 'Lines of Descent.'

35. Keegan, 'War of Civilizations.'

36. Harvey, *New Imperialism*; cf. Said, *Orientalism*, p. 322: 'Orientalism has been successfully accommodated to the new imperialism.'
37. Bauman, 'Wars of the Globalization Era,' p. 15.
38. Ibid., p. 27; see also Coker, *Future of War*; Der Derian, *Virtuous War*.
39. Feldman, 'Ground Zero Point One.' Here the painstaking work of Marc Herold in recovering the record of those killed by US air strikes in Afghanistan is indispensable.
40. The 7,000 mile distance imposes a delay in control inputs that makes it impossible for them to perform take-offs and landings, which are the responsibility of forward-deployed Launch and Recovery crews that use a line-of-sight data link.
41. Kaplan, 'Hunting the Taliban.'
42. Martin, *Predator*, p. 3; Engelhardt, 'War of the Worlds.'
43. Biltgen and Tomes, 'Rebalancing ISR.'
44. Ibid.
45. The phrase was coined by Lt. Gen. David Deptula, the Air Force's deputy chief of staff for ISR, and has become a leitmotif in discussions of ISR.
46. Tirpak, 'Beyond Reachback'; Drew, 'Social Networking,' p. B1. One (2009) estimate suggested that 168 personnel were required to support a single UAV during one Combat Air Patrol; this excluded staff at Al Udeid.
47. They are also described as MALE (Mid-Altitude Long-Endurance) drones, and since the US military is evidently fixated by its acronyms it would not be difficult to read this as a techno-cultural version of the voyeurism of the orientalist gaze in which 'the Orient' reclines unsuspecting beneath their persistent, penetrating stare. Thus, for example, Martin, *Predator*, p. 81 describes his role as 'a voyeur in the sky' and notes that 'the poor bastards never once considered looking up, way up, from which height Predator crews observed their every move.' Hypervisibility then becomes a climactic voyeurism. Such a reading also draws attention to the 'techno-masculinization' that advances the abstract disembodiment of late modern war: Masters, 'Bodies of technology.'
48. Cullather, 'Bombing'; cf. Herbert, 'Compressing the Kill Chain'; Cheater, 'Accelerating the Kill Chain.'
49. The term derives from Foucault, but Deleuze's gloss is particularly apposite: *dispositifs* or apparatuses comprise 'curves of visibility and curves of enunciation,' in other words, 'they are machines which make one see and speak': What is a *Dispositif?* p. 160.
50. Uecker, 'Full-motion Video;' Grant, 'All-seeing Air Force; Harris, Omniscient eye,' p. 102, 114. Harris was describing the targeting cycle during the first Gulf War.
51. Singer, 'War Porn.'
52. Alston, 'Report of the Special Rapporteur,' p. 25; Cole *et al.*, *Convenient Killing*.

53. Grossman, *Killing*, pp. 79, 102, 188–9, 312, 323. Cf. O'Connell, 'Unlawful Killing,' pp. 9–10, who claims that the central factors in Grossman's study also 'characterize drone operations' which in her eyes look 'very much like a video game.'

54. The military also uses them for recruitment, which is much more problematic; the Air Force, for example, stages the hunter-killer missions as entertainment: see 'Fly the MQ–9 Reaper' at http://www.airforce.com/games-and-extras.

55. Zucchino, 'Drone Pilots'; Martin, *Predator*, p. 212; Lindlaw, 'UAV Operators'; McCloskey, 'Two Worlds.' Others may be more blasé; the vice chairman of the Joint Chiefs of Staff described jaded analysts watching archived hours of what he callously called 'Death TV' in order to detect targets. Lake, 'Drone Footage.'

56. Höglund, 'Electronic Empire.'

57. Beard, 'Law and War,' p. 422. Beard was Associate Deputy General Counsel (International Affairs) at the Pentagon, 1990–2004.

58. I have condensed this idealized account from *Targeting*; *Air Force Operations and the Law*, ch. 16. See also Shanker, 'Civilian Risks,' p. A1; Mulrine, 'Warheads on Foreheads'; Kurle, 'Lawyers.'

59. Beard, 'Law and War,' p. 43; cf. Owens, 'Accidents.'

60. 'Drone Wars,' p. A12; see also Phillips, 'Civilians in Cross-hairs,' p. A1.

61. Beard, 'Law and War,' p. 410 and passim.

62. *Transition to and from Hostilities*, p. 154.

63. One example: a Predator operated by the CIA killed Baitullah Mehsud, the leader of the Pakistan Taliban (TTP), on Aug. 5, 2009; but it took 16 strikes over the preceding 14 months before he was assassinated, in the course of which 200–320 other people were killed: Mayer, 'Predator War.'

64. Drew, 'Social Networking,' p. B1; McCloskey, 'Two Worlds'; Martin, *Predator*, p. 121.

65. Smith, *Utility of Force*, p. 17.

66. Gregory, 'In Another Time-Zone.'

67. Etzioni, 'Unmanned Aircraft Systems'; see also idem, 'Drone Attacks.' Etzioni claims that criticisms are 'written by people who yearn for a nice clean war, one in which only bad people will be killed using "surgical" strikes that inflict no collateral damage.' This is an extraordinary inversion, since it is proponents of UAVs that consistently connect them to a surgical-strike capacity.

68. Sykes, 'Future'; Renton, 'Changing Languages,' pp. 652–6.

69. Gregory, 'Biopolitics of Baghdad.'

70. Caldwell and Hagerott, 'Curing Afghanistan.'

71. Kilcullen, *Accidental Guerilla*, p. 35; U.S. Army and U.S. Marine Corps, *Field Manual 3–24*, §1–26.

9. NESTING ORIENTALISMS AT WAR: WORLD WAR II AND THE 'MEMORY WAR' IN EASTERN EUROPE

1. See Bakić-Hayden, 'Nesting Orientalisms.' Cf. Todorova, *Imagining the Balkans*; Wolff, *Inventing Eastern Europe*.

2. 'Teutons orientalize Italians. Italians orientalize Slovenians. Slovenians orientalize Croats. Croats orientalize Serbs. Serbs orientalize Bosniaks, Bosniaks orientalize Turks, and Turks keep it up regarding "their" Orient.' See Neumann, 'Series Editor Preface,' pp. xi-xii. Similar process was at play in the self-differentiation attempts of the candidate countries in the earlier phases of the European Union (EU) and NATO enlargement when being considered as part of 'Central Europe' was preferred to 'Eastern Europe,' due to the former's allegedly stronger degree of 'Europeanness.'

3. Ontological security theory emphasises the importance of identity for the sense of security: states are accordingly not only seeking physical survival, but survival and surpassing as certain sort of social beings, i.e. the security of their 'selves.' See Steele, *Ontological Security in International Relations*; Mitzen, 'Anchoring Europe's Civilizing Identity' and 'Ontological Security in World Politics.'

4. For the subtleties of 'true' and 'false' Europe in Russian discourse, see Neumann, *Russia and the Idea of Europe*; and Morozov, 'The Baltic States in Russian Foreign Policy Discourse.'

5. Cf. Medvedev, 'Interview to Der Spiegel.'

6. The intensity of mnemonical politics has varied along the shifts in domestic power-sharing of the respective states. The rule of the national conservatives from *Prawo i Sprawiedliwość* in Poland (2005–07), and the presidency of Viktor Yushchenko in Ukraine (2005–10) are distinct from both their predecessors and successors in that regard.

7. Mälksoo, 'Liminality and Contested Europeanness.'

8. Russia has sponsored resolutions in the UN opposing the resurgence of Nazism since 2003; Ukraine, in its turn, attempted to seek (ultimately unsuccessfully) international condemnation of the artificially created Great Famine of 1932–3 (*Holodomor*) as an act of genocide of the Ukrainian people.

9. Said, *Orientalism*, p. 3.

10. Wolff, *Inventing Eastern Europe*, p. 7.

11. Cf. Buruma and Margalit, *Occidentalism*.

12. Said, *Orientalism*, p. 12.

13. Mowitt, 'Fanon's "guerre des ondes,"' in this volume.

14. Already in 1930s, depicting oneself as anti-fascist had lent 'a Western veneer' to Soviet communists, as argued by Furet, *The Passing of an Illusion*, p. 326.

15. E.g., Chauvier, 'Fallait-il collaborer avec le IIIe Reich?'

16. Cf. Jutila, 'Taming Eastern Nationalism.'
17. As regards the initial subordination of the memory of Holocaust to the remembrance of one's own 'national tragedies' first, for example.
18. Said, *Orientalism*, p. 5.
19. Cf. Mälksoo, 'The Memory Politics of Becoming European.'
20. Bhabha, *The Location of Culture*.
21. Sahni, *Crucifying the Orient*, p. 15.
22. Neumann, 'Europe's post-Cold War memory of Russia,' p. 135.
23. Khalid, 'Russian History and the Debate over Orientalism.'
24. Cf. Mälksoo, 'The Memory Politics of Becoming European.'
25. Cf. Alexander, 'On the Social Construction of Moral Universals.'
26. E.g., Masso, 'Habras ja haavatav tóde.'
27. Cf. Malia, 'Foreword: The Uses of Atrocity,' pp. ix-xx.
28. Hvostov, 'Lääne haritlaskonna kommunismimeelsuse psühholoogia.'
29. Malia, 'Foreword,' p. xii.
30. See Filippov, *Noveishaia Istoriya Rossii*.
31. E.g., Khapaeva, 'Historical Memory in Post-Soviet Gothic Society.'
32. E.g., Medvedev, 'Speech at Ceremony Awarding Decorations to Veterans of the Great Patriotic War'; Putin, 'Address on the 60th Anniversary of the Beginning of the Great Patriotic War.'
33. Cf. Putin, 'Remarks at the Butovo Shooting Range.'
34. Cf. Uldricks, 'War, Politics and Memory.'
35. The Communist effort itself was arguably an example of an incessant Russian aspiration to play a special role on the basis of its alleged moral superiority over the West. See Kotkin, *Magnetic Mountain*, p. 12. Cf. Gudkov, 'The fetters of victory'; Medvedev, 'Remarks at the News Conference.'
36. Gudkov, 'The fetters of victory.'
37. E.g., Putin, 'Pages of History.' Cf. EU Council and European Commission, Hearing on 'Crimes committed by the totalitarian regimes'; Tannberg, 'Eesti saatust kujundanud välistegurid,' p. 15.
38. Cf. Zhurzhenko, 'The Geopolitics of Memory.'
39. Cf. Carleton, 'Victory in Death.'
40. Solzhenitsyn, *Cancer Ward*.
41. Snyder, 'Holocaust: The Ignored Reality.'
42. Etkind, 'Post-Soviet Hauntology'; Khazanov, 'Whom to Mourn and Whom to Forget?.'
43. Putin, 'Pages of History.'
44. Putin, 'Remarks at the commemoration ceremony of the victims of Katyń.'
45. The trope of 'common grief and mutual pardon' (cf. Putin, 'Pages of History') stems from the logic of comparing, as Putin implicitly did both at Gdańsk and Katyń commemoration ceremonies, the Katyń massacre(s) to Polish POW camps in the 1920 Soviet-Polish War. Emphasis added.

46. Putin, Remarks at Smolensk.
47. Cf. Śmigielski, 'Commentary on the Ceremony to Mark the 70th Anniversary of the Katyń Massacre.'
48. Cf. Etkind, 'Post-Soviet Hauntology,' p. 184.
49. Cf. Coïcaud, 'Apology: A Small Yet Important Part of Justice'; Löwenheim, 'A haunted past'
50. Tusk, 'Remarks of the Prime Minister of Poland at the Commemoration Ceremony of the Victims of the Katyń Massacre.'
51. Ilves, 'The President of the Republic at the 60th anniversary commemoration conference of the March deportation.' Cf. Kaczyński, *Undelivered speech at Katyń.*
52. Luik, 'Our Duty.'
53. Meanwhile, Russia's political elites tend to depict the Baltic states as morally, rather than culturally, backward in their relation to the legacy of WWII.
54. Ilves, 'The President of the Republic of Estonia on the Anniversary of the Tartu Peace Treaty.' Drawing an implicit connection between 'the West' and 'civilization' (i.e., 'civilization-in-the-singular') is a symptomatically Orientalizing move. Cf. Jackson, *Civilizing the Enemy.*
55. Of course, there is hardly a definite European style of a sort in reality; yet the argument is frequently, if implicitly, made by East European representatives criticising the Russian way of addressing its recent past.
56. Cf. LaCapra, *History and Memory after Auschwitz,* p. 54.
57. Cf. Ray, 'Mourning, Melancholia and Violence.'
58. Cf. Teitel, *Transitional Justice,* p. 117.
59. Cf. Zarakol, 'Ontological (In)Security and State Denial of Historical Crimes,' p. 7.
60. Ibid.
61. Masso, 'Habras ja haavatav tõde,' p. 229.
62. E.g., Śmigielski, 'Commentary on the Ceremony.'
63. See Andrieu, 'Sorry for the Genocide.'
64. Cf. Olick, 'The Guilt of Nations?,' p. 109.
65. Gudkov, 'The Fetters of Victory.'
66. Ibid. See also Ferretti, 'Memory Disorder.'
67. Medvedev, 'On Great Patriotic War, Historical Truth and Our Memory.'
68. The law includes punishment by fine and three to five years in prison, introducing criminal liability for the 'denial of the victory of the USSR in the Great Patriotic War.' Furthermore, the wording of the bill suggests extraterritoriality: the 'rehabilitation of Nazism' is to be punishable under the Russian Administrative and Criminal Code regardless of whether or not it is allegedly committed in Russian territory.
69. E.g., Herkel, 'Vene võitlus ajaloo pärast'; cf. Hiio, 'Ametlik ajalugu kehtestuks vaid mõnede mõtete ärakeelamisega.'

70. Cf. Hvostov, 'Urkade moraal, allalastute tõde.'

71. Medvedev, 'Address of the President of the Russia Federation on the Day of the Political Prisoner.'

72. Ibid.

73. Medvedev, 'Go, Russia!.'

74. Except for one of the most prominent 'criminalizers' of the communist legacy in Estonia and the harshest critics of Russia's democratic deficiencies, the former Estonian prime minister and Minister of Defence Mart Laar who recently gave a prize of European Memory and Reconciliation to Russian President Dmitry Medvedev. The other receivers of the award included the European Parliament and the Swedish Foreign Minister Carl Bildt.

75. As vividly expressed, for instance, by the director of the Baltic Centre of Research on Russia, Vladimir Juškin, 'Uus "Lavrovi doktriin" ei muuda Venemaa poliitika olemust.'

76. Cf. Frolov, 'Shared Agenda of Gorbachev and Medvedev.'

77. Zarakol, 'Ontological (In)Security and State Denial.'

78. Cf. Suzuki, 'Seeking "Legitimate" Great Power Status in Post-Cold War International Society.'

79. Cf. Carleton, 'Victory in Death.'

80. European Court of Human Rights, *Grand Chamber Judgement on the Case of Kononov v. Latvia*.

81. Judge Myjer, *Concurring Opinion in the Kononov v. Latvia Judgement*.

10. VICTIMHOOD AS AGENCY: AFGHAN WOMEN'S MEMOIRS

1. An extensive reception-focused reading of this predicament (framed as critical interpretation, not based on reader reception studies) can be found in Whitlock, *Soft Weapons*. See Tucker, 'Pensée 2,' pp. 19–21 and references for assessment of continuing Orientalist gender stereotyping in Middle Eastern studies disciplines, especially History and Political Science.

2. The eight memoirs (of nine individuals) under consideration are Ahmedi, *The Story of My Life*; Gauhari *An Afghan Woman's Odyssey*, 1996/2004; Joya, *A Woman among Warlords*; Latifa, *My Forbidden Face*; Pazira, *A Bed of Red Flowers*; 'Sulima' and 'Hala,' *Behind the Burqa*; Sultan, *My War at Home*; 'Zoya,' *Zoya's Story*.

3. Mahmoud, 'Feminist Theory, Agency, and the Liberatory Subject,' pp. 111–52; Mahmoud, 'Feminist Theory, Embodiment, and the Docile Agent,' pp. 202–36.

4. Grima, *The Performance of Emotion among Paxtun Women*, 1992.

5. CIA *Factbook: Afghanistan*.

6. I here define the political in the broadest possible way, as having to do with distributions of power in all interpersonal relationships.

7. Watson and Smith, 'Introduction,' pp. xiii-xxxi; Beverley, 'The Margin at the Center: On *Testimonio* (Testimonial Narrative),' pp. 91–114.

8. For alternative definitions of agency, see Mahmoud, 'Feminist Theory, Agency, and the Liberatory Subject,' pp. 202–36; Mahmoud, 'Feminist Theory, Embodiment, and the Docile Agent,' pp. 111–52.

9. Radner and Lanser, 'Strategies of Coding in Women's Cultures,' pp. 1–30.

10. Radner, *Feminist Messages*, p. vii.

11. Ibid.

12. Joya, p. 178. She goes on to say that Laura Bush's remarks were 'meaningless, mere dust in the eyes of the world, considering the brutal policy they have helped to justify.'

13. Whitlock pp. 14, 56–7, 61.

14. Said, *Orientalism*, p. 14.

15. See Shohat, 'On the Margins of Middle Eastern Studies,' p. 22.

16. Kennedy, *Edward Said*, p. 41.

17. See Brodsky, *With All Our Strength*.

18. Ahmedi, pp. 245–6.

19. Pazira, *A Bed of Red Flowers*, p. 65.

20. Ibid. p. 23, 180.

21. Ibid., p. 139.

22. Ibid., p. 200, 204.

23. Gauhari, *An Afghan Woman's Odyssey*, p. 5.

24. Ahmedi p. 249.

25. Whitlock, *Soft Weapons*, p. 49.

26. Sultan, *My War at Home*, p. 91.

27. Zoya, *Zoya's Story* p. 211; Latifa, *My Forbidden Face*, p. 196; Joya, *A Woman among Warlords*, p. 172.

28. Mahmoud, 'Feminist Theory, Agency, and the Liberatory Subject'; Abu-Lughod, 'Do Muslim Women Really Need Saving?,' pp. 783–90; Rosatni-Povey, Elaheh, 'Women in Afghanistan: Passive Victims of the Borqa [*sic*] or Active Social Participants?,' *Development in Practice* 13:2–3, pp. 266–77.

29. See Brunner, 'Occidentalism Meets the Female Suicide Bomber,' pp. 957–71.

30. Shuman, *Other People's Stories*.

11. FANON'S 'GUERRE DES ONDES': RESISTING THE CALL OF ORIENTALISM

1. Quoted in Eorsi, 'The Right to the Last World,' p. 12.

2. Edward W. Said, *Covering Islam*, New York: Pantheon, 1981, p. 154.

3. Ibid., p. 140.

4. Ibid., pp. 41–2.

5. Said, *Reflections on Exile and Other Essays*, p. 201.

6. As Walter Kauffman was perhaps too quick to point out, Nietzsche's 'hammer' (as in 'philosophize with a hammer') was also a 'tuning fork.' Similarly, readers of

Deleuze and Guattari will insist that a 'war machine' is not simply a troop carrier or explosive device. While accurate, it seems crucial to hold onto both readings especially if one of the things at stake here is the very concept of war itself.

7. Said, *Reflections on Exile and Other Essays*, p. 187.
8. Ibid., p. 72.
9. Said, *Orientalism*, p. 203.
10. Said, *Reflections on Exile and Other Essays*, p. 74.
11. Fanon, *A Dying Colonialism*, p. 71.
12. Cf. Rebecca Scales, 'Subversive Sound,' pp. 384–417.
13. Clausewitz, *On War*, p. 117.
14. Fanon, *A Dying Colonialism*, p. 70.
15. Ibid., p. 72.
16. Ibid.
17. Ibid., p. 84, my emphasis.
18. Ibid., p. 85.
19. Ibid., pp. 86–7.
20. Foucault, *Aesthetics, Method, and Epistemology*, p. 278.
21. Schmitt, 'Theory of the Partisan,' p. 18.
22. It should be stressed that Schmitt largely overlooks the fact that Mao's discussion is entirely focused on the anti-imperial confrontation with Japan, and that
Mao therefore downplays the theoretical discontinuity between 'regular' and
partisan warfare. Thanks to Tina Mai Chen for insisting upon this.
23. Schmitt, 'Theory of the Partisan,' pp. 71–2.
24. Ibid., p. 16.
25. It is interesting to note in passing that in Mao's *On Guerilla Warfare* he makes
persistent reference to what he calls 'war of position' and 'war of movement'
without anywhere acknowledging whether Gramsci's remarkably similar distinction matters to him.
26. Schmitt, 'Theory of the Partisan,' p. 59.
27. Ibid.

12. THE PLEASURES OF IMPERIALISM AND THE PINK ELEPHANT: TORTURE, SEX, ORIENTALISM

1. Patai, *The Arab Mind*, p. 126
2. Goldstein, *War and Gender*.
3. Boxwell, 'The Follies of War.'
4. On the rejection of martial masculinity among British conscientious objectors
see Lee Jones, 'The Others.'
5. Burg (ed), *Gay Warriors*.
6. Murray, 'Male Homosexuality.' Unfortunately, the title of this text is anachro-
nistic. The term 'homosexual' dates only to the 1870s and, as others have shown,

pre-nineteenth century Arab-Islamic culture possessed no such concept or binary distinction. See El-Rouayheb, *Before Homosexuality in the Arab-Islamic World*.

7. But see Zeeland, *The Masculine Marine*. In 1993, Congress passed the policy of 'Don't Ask, Don't Tell' that prevented military commanders from actively rooting out service-members with unorthodox sexualities, but mandated the discharge of those who openly claimed a gay, lesbian, or bisexual identity. The Obama Administration has vowed to repeal the law.

8. For a similar analysis of the 1990–1 Gulf War see Norton, 'Gender, Sexuality and the Iraq of Our Imagination.'

9. Puar, *Terrorist Assemblages*, p. 38.

10. Dotinga, 'Navy Photo Shows Antigay Slur on Bomb.'

11. Price, 'Guardsman killed Iraqi after Sex.'

12. Sullivan, 'Our War Too: Gay Heroes and Gay Necessities.'

13. Said, *Orientalism*, p. 1.

14. Barkawi, *Globalization and War*, p. 109. For an effort to account for military orientalism in terms of 'cultural realism' (culture as instrumentalized) in contrast to Said's and Barkawi's emphasis on imperial hierarchy see Porter, *Military Orientalism*, p. 14, pp. 25–6. That orientalist discourse can be strategically used in the context of anxiety about the longevity of Western superiority and as a critique of progressive movements in the West is *not* evidence of the absence of an assumed fundamental hierarchy of West over East. To strip the concept of orientalism from this imperial, hierarchical context, to co-opt the terminology to help imperial states 'do culture better,' is to rob the concept of critical meaning.

15. Said, *Orientalism*, p. 3.

16. Sedgewick, *Epistemology of the Closet*, p. 1.

17. Porter, *Military Orientalism*, p. 57.

18. Goldberg, *Sodometries*; Bleys, *Geography of Perversion*.

19. Maran, *Torture*

20. Axel, *The Nation's Tortured Body*.

21. Human Rights First, 'Torture: Quick Facts.'

22. See Brownmiller, *Against Our Will*.

23. The transcript of the March 2004 'Taguba Report.'

24. Sworn statements by Abu Ghraib detainees can be found in Danner, *Torture and Truth*.

25. Limpkin and Baldor, 'New Instances Of Using "Gay" As Means Of Torture.'

26. Hersh, 'The Grey Zone'; also see Hersh, *Chain of Command*.

27. David Luban, 'Torture and the Professions.'

28. The press release of the American Anthropological Association is available at http://www.aaanet.org/pdf/iraqtorture.pdf. Last accessed Jun. 1, 2010; also McCoy, *A Question of Torture*. Barkawi has rightly suggested that the Pentagon

may simply have supplemented long-standing orientalist prejudices with any 'scholarship' that might support them rather than using such texts to devise new torture techniques. Correspondence with author.

29. Hersh, 'The Grey Zone.'
30. Foucault, *The History of Sexuality*, pp. 15–49.
31. Patai, *The Arab Mind*, p. 150.
32. Ibid., p. 136.
33. Ibid., p. 149.
34. Ibid., p. 126.
35. Ibid., p. 136.
36. Ibid., p. 137.
37. Ibid., p. 151. The general assumption about the difference between oriental and occidental sexual mores is that the 1960s represented an important break. After the sexual revolution and 'gay rights' movement, the West became more liberal; there were greater sexual freedoms among 'the Arabs' prior to this time.
38. 'Al-Fatiha Condemns Sexual Humiliation.'
39. Moore, 'Weapons of Mass Homophobia.'
40. Nietzsche, *On the Genealogy of Morals*, p. 29; for a seminal discussion of the implications see Butler, *Gender Trouble*.
41. Foucault, *History of Sexuality*, p. 43.
42. The pamphlet was written by Austrian-born novelist Karl-Maria Kertbeny. See Feray and Manfred 'Homosexual Studies and Politics in the 19th Century.'
43. Sedgwick, *Epistemology of the Closet*, p. 2. Foucault, *History of Sexuality*.
44. The Victorian prude of bourgeois society is foundational for Marxist and social-ist feminist critiques of the role of the family under capitalism in which sexu-alities (and 'women') are repressed in the interests of reproducing labor and the desirability of private property.
45. Foucault, *History of Sexuality*, p. 44.
46. See Trexler, *Sex and Conquest*; McClintock, *Imperial Leather*; Aldrich, *Colonial-ism and Homosexuality*.
47. Bernstein, *The East, The West, and Sex*, pp. 29–30.
48. Foucault, *History of Sexuality*, p. 3.
49. Freccero, 'They are All Sodomites!'
50. Murray, 'Male Homosexuality.'
51. Bleys, *Geography of Perversion*, p. 21.
52. Quoted in Ibid., p. 22.
53. Reid, 'Kandahar comes out of the closet.' For an account of Orientalist assump-tions about Afghan warlords see Stanski, 'So These Folks are Aggressive.'
54. Reynolds, 'Kandahar's Lightly Veiled Homosexual Habits.'
55. Smith, 'Shh, It's an Open Secret: Warlords and Pedophilia,' p. A4.
56. Reynolds, 'Kandahar's Lightly Veiled Homosexual Habits.' The designated pun-

ishment for sodomy under Taliban rule was to be crushed to death under a brick wall driven down by a military tank.

57. Reynolds, 'Kandahar's Lightly Veiled Homosexual Habits.'

58. Said, *Orientalism*, p. 5.

59. Some scholars point to the fact that the Quran treats same gender sexual activity far less harshly than does Judaic or Christian texts and that male sexual pleasure is not confined to procreation. See Schild, 'Islam.'

60. El-Rouayheb, *Before Homosexuality*, p. 6

61. Ibid., p. 153. There were a 'multiplicity of ideals that coexisted in the Arab-Islamic world in the early Ottoman period. A survey of the literature of the period—historical, belletristic, religious—indicates a complex and variegated reality; a reality that cannot adequately be captured by notion of "tolerance" contra "intolerance," or "ideal" contra "practice."' Ibid., p. 155.

62. Dunne, 'Homosexuality in the Middle East: an Agenda for Historical Research.'

63. Letellier, 'Egyptians protest "gay" abuse in Iraq.'

64. Human Rights Watch, 'In a Time of Torture.'

65. Bleys, *Geography of Perversion*, p. 79.

66. Massad, *Desiring Arabs*, p. 48.

67. Massad, 'Re-Orienting Desire,' p. 373.

68. The term is taken from the title of Massad's article, 'Re-Orienting Desire: The Gay International and the Arab World.'

69. Foucault, *History of Sexuality*, p. 57.

70. Ibid., p. 57.

71. Foucault, *History of Sexuality*, pp. 58, 61. For a critique see Stoler, *Race and the Education of Desire*.

72. Foucault, *History of Sexuality*, p. 35.

73. Carrett, 'Beyond Theology and Sexuality,' p. 223.

74. Hepworth and Turner, *Confession*, p. 79; Foucault, *History of Sexuality*, pp. 58–59.

75. Foucault, *History of Sexuality*, p. 63.

76. Ibid., p. 65.

77. Scarry, *The Body in Pain*, p. 28.

78. Statement by Kasim Mehaddi Hilas, Detainee no. 151108, reprinted in Danner, *Torture and Truth*, p. 242.

79. According to Oliver S. Buckton, 'the desire for certain kinds of secrecy…is relative to a specific historical context in which homosexuality is associated with a range of perverse, antisocial, and subversive practices and characteristics. To "confess" to homosexuality, therefore, is inevitably to go beyond the statement of sexual preference for other men. It is, inescapably, to receive the label of the "homosexual" or "invert" as ideologically and prejudicially defined by official Victorian discourse.' Buckton, *Secret Selves*, p. 4.

80. Foucault, *History of Sexuality*, p. 59.

81. Ibid, p. 63.

82. For good discussions, but which do not emphasize the role of confessional practice, see Kaufman-Osborn, 'Gender Trouble at Abu Ghraib?'; Puar, *Terrorist Assemblages*, ch. 2; Butler, *Frames of War*, pp. 125–31.

83. Patai, *The Arab Mind*, p. 151.

13. AFTERWORD

1. Disney, 'Pushing Iran Towards a Nuclear Bomb.'

2. Cited in Dower, *Cultures of War*, p. 19.

3. 'Stability Operations in Iraq (Op-Telic 2–5),' p. 30.

4. Dower, *Cultures of War*, pp. 19–20.

5. Porter, 'Culture Wars in Afghanistan,' p. 3.

6. Cited in Matthews, *We Were Caught Unprepared*, p. 43.

7. Biddle and Friedman, *The 2006 Lebanon Campaign and the Future of Warfare*.

8. Owens, 'The Pleasures of Imperialism and the Pink Elephant,' p. 296.

9. Ibid.

10. For a more extended historical critique of Said's thesis, showing that it is possible to oppose imperialism while recognising the complexities and multiple functions of Orientalism see Irwin, *For Lust of Knowing*, pp. 277–310.

11. Cirakman, *From the 'Terror of the World' to the 'Sick Man of Europe,'* p. 79.

12. Ermath, 'Contrasts in American and Soviet Strategic Thought,' pp. 138–55; Gray, 'National Style in Strategy,' pp. 21–47; Revel, *How Democracies Perish*; Lord, 'American Strategic Culture,' pp. 269–94.

13. Peters, 'The Counter-Revolution in Military Affairs.'

14. Christopher Hitchens, 'A Man of Permanent Contradictions,' pp. 29–43, 36.

15. Cited in Power, *A Problem from Hell*, p. 282.

16. Powell, 'Why Generals get Nervous,' p. A35.

17. Said, *Orientalism*, p. 204.

18. Irwin, *For Lust of Knowing*; Cirakman *From the 'Terror of the World' to the 'Sick Man of Europe.'*

19. Blair, 'The Americans love Pepsi Cola, but we love death.'

20. Black, 'Grave Failings All Round'; 'Hezbollah has Israel Body Parts.'

21. Ehrenreich, *Blood Rites*, p. 141.

22. On this point, see further Strachan, 'A General Typology of Transcultural Wars—the Modern Age,' pp. 85–103.

BIBLIOGRAPHY

AAA Commission on the Engagement of Anthropology with the US Security and Intelligence Communities (CEAUSSIC). 'Final Report on the Army's Human Terrain System Proof of Concept Program,' 73, 2009.

Abu-Lughod, Lila. 'Do Muslim Women Really Need Saving?,' *American Anthropologist*, 104:3, 2002, pp. 783–90.

Adas, Michael. *Machines as the Measure of Men: Science, Technology, and Ideologies of Western Dominance*, Ithaca: Cornell University Press, 1989.

Ahmad, Aijaz. *In Theory: Classes, Nations, Literatures*, London: Verso Press, 2000.

Ahmed, S. 'The Politics of Fear in the Making of Worlds,' *International Journal of Qualitative Studies in Education*, 16:3, May-Jun. 2003, pp. 377–98.

Ahmedi, Farah. *The Story of My Life: An Afghan Girl on the Other Side of the Sky*, with Tamim Ansary, New York: Simon Spotlight Entertainment, 2005.

Air Force Operations and the Law, 2nd ed, Judge Advocate General's School, Maxwell Air Force Base, 2009.

Aldrich, Robert. *Colonialism and Homosexuality*, London: Routledge, 2003.

Alexander, Jeffrey C. 'On the Social Construction of Moral Universals: The "Holocaust" From War Crime to Trauma Drama,' *European Journal of Social Theory*, 5:1, 2002, pp. 5–85.

'Al-Fatiha Condemns Sexual Humiliation of Iraqi Detainees, Calls for National LGBT Groups to Denounce Homophobic Human Rights Abuses.' Available at http://www.lavendergreens.us/lavender_greens_009.htm.

al-Jabarti, Abd al-Rahman. *History of Egypt*, Vol. III, Thomas Philipp and Moshe Perlmann (ed), Stuttgart: Franz Steiner, 1994.

—— *Journal d'un notable du Caire durant l'expédition française 1798–1801*, Joseph Cucocq (tran), Paris: Albin Michel, 1979.

—— *Napoleon in Egypt: Al-Jabarti's Chronicle of the French Occupation, 1798*, Princeton: Markus Wiener, 1993.

BIBLIOGRAPHY

Alpert, John. 'Chiapas: The Fight for Land and Liberty,' DCTV, 1994.

Alston, Philip. 'Report of the Special Rapporteur on Extrajudicial, Summary or Arbitrary Executions; Addendum: Study on Targeted Killings,' United Nations General Assembly, Human Rights Council, May 28, 2010.

'American Views of the Crisis in India,' *Times*, Aug. 19, 1857, p. 10.

Amoore, Louise. 'Vigilant Visualities: The Watchful Politics of the "War on Terror,"' *Security Dialogue* 38:2, 2007, pp. 215–32.

Anderson, Perry. *Lineages of the Absolutist State*, London: Verso, 1974.

Andrieu, Kora. '"Sorry for the Genocide": How Public Apologies Can Help Promote National Reconciliation,' *Millennium*, 38:1, 2009, pp. 3–23.

Anglo-Bengalee. 'The Indian Mutinies,' *Times*, Aug. 8, 1857, p. 12.

Appy, Christian G. *Patriots: The Vietnam War Remembered from All Sides*, New York: Penguin, 2004.

Asad, Talal. *Formations of the Secular: Christianity, Islam, Modernity*, Stanford: Stanford University Press, 2003.

Associated Press, 'G.I.'s Tell of a U.S. Massacre in Korean War,' *New York Times*, Sept. 30, 1999, p. 1.

Attridge, Steve. *Nationalism, Imperialism and Identity in Late Victorian Culture: Civil and Military Worlds*, Houndmills: Palgrave, 2003.

Axel, Brian Keith. *The Nation's Tortured Body: Violence Representation, and the Formation of a Sikh Diaspora*, Durham: Duke University Press, 2001.

Bakiç-Hayden, Milica. 'Nesting Orientalisms: The Case of the Former Yugoslavia,' *The Slavic Review*, 54:4, 1995, pp. 917–31.

Ball, Charles. *The History of the Indian Mutiny, Vol. 1*. New Delhi: Master Publishers, 1981 [1858].

'The Ballot Box: The Terrorist Next Door,' Oct. 8, 2010, Available at http://www.thepakistanupdate.com/2010/10/the-ballot-box-disaster/.

Barkawi, Tarak. *Globalization and War*, Oxford: Rowman and Littlefield, 2006.

Barkawi, Tarak and Shane Brighton. 'Powers of War: Fighting, Knowledge, and Critique,' *International Political Sociology*, 5:2, 2011, pp. 126–43.

Barthes, Roland. *The Eiffel Tower and Other Mythologies*, Richard Howard (trans), New York: Hill and Wang, 1979.

Bauman, Zygmunt. 'Wars of the Globalization Era,' *European Journal of Social Theory*, 4:1, 2001, pp. 11–28.

Bayly, Christopher. *Empire and Information: Intelligence Gathering and Social Communication in India, 1780–1870*, Cambridge: Cambridge University Press, 1996.

Beard, Charles A. 'Law and War in the Virtual Era,' *American Journal of International Law*, 103:3, 2009, pp. 409–45.

——— *The Open Door at Home: A Trial Philosophy of National Interest*, with G.H.E. Smith. New York: MacMillan, 1935.

Belich, James. *The Victorian Interpretation of Racial Conflict: The Maori, the British and the New Zealand Wars*, Montreal and Kingston: McGill-Queen's University Press, 1986.

Bell, David. *The First Total War: Napoleon's Europe and the Birth of Warfare as We Know It*, Boston: Houghton Mifflin, 2007.

'The Bengal Army,' *Times*, Aug. 20, 1857, p. 10.

Bennett, Philip. 'In the War's Cast of Characters, Where are the Iraqis?,' *Washington Post*, Mar. 15, 2009, p. B1.

Bentham, Jeremy. *The Complete Works of Jeremy Bentham*, vol 4, John Bowring (ed), Edinburgh: W. Tait, 1843.

Bernstein, Barton J. 'Understanding the Atomic Bomb and the Japanese Surrender: Missed Opportunities, Little-Known Near Disasters, and Modern Memory,' *Diplomatic History* 19:2, Spring 1995, pp. 227–73.

Bernstein, Richard. *The East, The West, and Sex: a History of Erotic Encounters*, New York: Alfred A. Knopf, 2009.

Beverley, John. 'The Margin at the Center: On *Testimonio* (Testimonial Narrative)' in Sidonie Smith and Julia Watson (eds), *De/Colonizing the Subject: The Politics of Gender in Women's Autobiography*, Minneapolis: University of Minnesota Press, 1992, pp. 91–114.

———— 'The Question of Torture, the Spanish Decadence, and Our Own,' *Boundary*, 34:3, 2007, pp. 189–205.

Bhabha, Homi K. *The Location of Culture*, London: Routledge, 1994.

Bhadra, Gautam. 'Four Rebels of Eighteen Fifty-Seven' in Ranajit Guha and G.C. Spivak (eds), *Selected Subaltern Studies*, New Delhi: Oxford University Press, 1988.

Bickford, Andrew 'Anthropology and HUMINT,' in Network of Concerned Anthropologists, *The Counter-Counterinsurgency Manual*, Chicago: Prickly Paradigm Press, 2009, pp. 135–51.

Biddle, Stephen and Jeffrey A. Friedman. *The 2006 Lebanon Campaign and the Future of Warfare: Implications for Army and Defence Policy*, Carlisle: Strategic Studies Institute, 2008.

Biltgen, Pat and Robert Tomes. 'Rebalancing ISR,' *Geospatial Intelligence Forum*, 8:6, Sept. 2010, pp. 14–16.

Black, Ian. 'Grave Failings All Round: The Winograd report's criticism of Israel's government and military may give Hizbullah reason to smile, but Lebanon remains as volatile as ever, writes Ian Black,' *Guardian*, Jan. 30, 2008.

Blainey, Geoffrey. *The Causes of War*. New York: Free Press, 1988.

Blair, David. 'The Americans love Pepsi Cola, but we love death,' *Daily Telegraph*, Sept. 24, 2001.

Bleys, Rudi C. *Geography of Perversion: Male-to-Male Sexual Behaviour Outside the West and the Ethnographic Imagination*, New York: New York University Press, 1995.

Boxwell, David A. 'The Follies of War: Cross-Dressing and Popular Theatre on the British Front Lines, 1914–18,' *Modernism/modernity*, 9:1, 2002, pp. 1–20.

Briggs, John p. and J.P. Briggs II, 'Bush and the Psychology of Incompetent Decisions,' *Trutthout*, Jan. 18, 2007. Available at http://www.truth-out.org/article/briggs-and-briggs-bush-and-psychology-incompentent-decisions.

Brodsky, Anne E. *With All Our Strength: The Revolutionary Association of the Women of Afghanistan*, New York, Routledge, 2003.

Brownmiller, Susan. *Against Our Will: Men, Women and Rape*, New York: Ballantine Books, 1993.

Brulliard, Karin and Haq Nawaz Khan. 'Pakistanis Tie Slayings to Surge in U.S. Strikes,' *Washington Post*, Dec. 24, 2010, p. A1.

Brunner, Claudia. 'Occidentalism Meets the Female Suicide Bomber: A Critical Reflection on Recent Terrorism Debates; A Review Essay,' *Signs*, 32:4, 2007, pp. 957–71.

Buckton, Oliver S., *Secret Selves: Confession and Same-Sex Desire in Victorian Autobiography*, Chapel Hill: University of North Carolina Press, 1998.

Bullene, E.F. 'Wonder Weapon: Napalm,' *Army Combat Forces Journal*, Nov. 1952.

Bumiller, Elizabeth. 'In Camouflage or Afghan Veil, a Fragile Bond,' *New York Times*, May 29, 2010, p. 1.

Burg, B. R. (ed). *Gay Warriors: A Documentary History From the Ancient World to the Present*, New York: New York University Press, 2002.

Burns, John F. 'Into Kandahar, Yesterday and Tomorrow,' *New York Times*, May 22, 2010, p. 1.

Buruma, Ian and Avishai Margalit. *Occidentalism: The West in the Eyes of Its Enemies*, New York: The Penguin Press, 2004.

Butler, Judith. *Frames of War: When is Life Grievable?*, London: Verso, 2009.

——— *Gender Trouble: Feminism and the Subversion of Identity*, London: Routledge, 1990.

——— *Precarious Life: The Powers of Mourning and Violence*, New York: Verso, 2004.

Caldwell, William and Mark Hagerott. 'Curing Afghanistan,' *Foreign Policy*, Apr. 7, 2010.

Cameron, Craig. *American Samurai: Myth, Imagination and the Conduct of Battle in the First Marine Division, 1941–1951*, Cambridge: Cambridge University Press, 1994.

Campbell, David. *Writing Security: United States Foreign Policy and the Politics of Identity*, Minneapolis: University of Minnesota Press, 1992.

'Capture of Delhi and Relief of Lucknow,' *Times*, Nov. 16, 1857, p. 7.

Card, Orson Scott, *Ender's Game*, New York: Tom Doherty Associates LLC, 1977.

Carleton, Gregory. 'Victory in Death: Annihilation Narratives in Russia Today,' *History & Memory*, 22:1, 2010, pp. 135–68.

BIBLIOGRAPHY

Carrett, Jeremy. 'Beyond Theology and Sexuality: Foucault, Self and the Que(e) rying of Monotheistic Truth' in James William Bernauer and Carrett (eds), *Foucault and Theology: the Politics of Religious Experience*, Surrey: Ashgate, 2004.

Carter, Phillip. 'Irrelevant Exuberance' *Slate*, Aug. 1, 2007. Available at http://www. slate.com/articles/news_and_politics/war_stories/2007/08/irrelevant_exuberance.html.

Casey, Stephen. *Selling the Korean War: Propaganda, Politics, and Public Opinion in the United States, 1950–1953*, New York: Oxford University Press, 2008.

Centurion. 'The Siege of Delhi,' *Times*, Aug. 5, 1857, p. 9.

Chakravarty, Gautam. *The Indian Mutiny and the British Imagination*. New York: Cambridge University Press, 2004.

Chauvier, Jean-Marie. 'Fallait-il collaborer avec le IIIe Reich? Comment les nationalistes ukrainiens réécrivent l'histoire,' *Le Monde diplomatique*, Aug., 2007, pp. 4–5.

Cheater, Julian. 'Accelerating the Kill Chain via Future Unmanned Aircraft,' Center for Strategy and Technology, Air War College, Apr. 2007.

Chivers, C.J. 'Afghan Attack Gives Marines a Taste of War,' *New York Times*, Feb. 14, 2010, p. A1.

———— 'Foot on Bomb, Marine Defies a Taliban Trap,' *New York Times* Jan. 24, 2010, p. A1.

———— 'G.I.s in Remote Afghan Post Have Weary Job, Drawing Fire,' *New York Times*, Nov. 10, 2008, p. A1.

———— 'In the Taliban, U.S. Marines Find Evolving Foes,' *New York Times*, Feb. 2, 2010, p. A1.

Choi, Charles Q. 'Military to Adopt NFL's Instant Replay Technology,' *LiveScience. Com*, Jun. 1, 2010.

Chomsky, Noam. *Interventions*, San Francisco: City Lights, 2007.

———— *Power and Terror: Conflict, Hegemony, and the Rule of Force*, Boulder: Paradigm, 2011.

'CIA Factbook—Afghanistan'. Available at https://www.cia.gov/library/publications/the-world-factbook/geos/af.html.

Cirakman, Asli. *From the 'Terror of the World' to the 'Sick Man of Europe': European Images of Ottoman Empire and Society from the Sixteenth Century to the Nineteenth*, New York: Peter Lang, 2002.

Clarke, Richard A. *Against All Enemies: Inside America's War on Terror*, New York: Free Press, 2004.

Clausewitz, Carl von. *On War*, Michael Howard and Peter Paret (ed and trans), Princeton: Princeton University Press, 1976.

Cocks, Tim. 'Iraqi Sunni guards join Shi'ite government payroll,' *Reuters*, Nov. 11, 2008.

Cohen, Majorie. 'No Unlawful Enemy Combatants at Guantanamo,' Jun. 6, 2007.

BIBLIOGRAPHY

Available at http://jurist.law.pitt.edu/forumy/2007/06/no-unlawful-enemy-combatants-at.php.

Cohen, Richard. 'Does Obama Have the Backbone?,' *Washington Post*, Oct. 6, 2009, p. A23.

Coïcaud, Jean-Marie. 'Apology: A Small Yet Important Part of Justice,' *Japanese Journal of Political Science*, 10:1, 2009, pp. 93–124.

Coker, Christopher. *The Future of War: The Re-enchantment of War in the Twenty-First Century*, Oxford: Blackwell, 2004.

Cole, Juan. *Napoleon's Egypt: Invading the Middle East*, New York: Palgrave Macmillan, 2007.

Cole, Chris, Mary Dobbing, and Amy Hailwood. *Convenient Killing: Armed Drones and the 'Playstation' Mentality*, Oxford: Fellowship of Reconciliation, 2010.

Coll, Steve. 'No Nukes,' *New Yorker*, Apr. 20, 2009, pp. 31–2.

Condon, Stephanie. 'McCain: Faisal Shahzad Should Not Have Been Mirandized,' May 4, 2010. Available at http://www.cbsnews.com/8301–503544_162–2000 4087–503544.html.

Connolly, William. *Identity/Difference: Democratic Negotiations of Political Paradox*, Minneapolis: University of Minnesota Press, 2002.

Connors, Steve and Molly Bingham (dirs). *Meeting Resistance*, Washington D.C.: Nine Lives Documentary Productions, 2007.

Cooke, Tim. 'Paramilitaries and the Press in Northern Ireland' in Pippa Norris, Montague Kern, and Marion Just (eds), *Framing Terrorism: The News Media, the Government, and the Public*, New York: Routledge, 2003.

Cooper, Randolf G.S., *The Anglo-Maratha Campaigns and the Contest for India: The Struggle for Control of the South Asian Military Economy*, Cambridge: Cambridge University Press, 2007.

Coppola, Francis Ford (dir). *Apocalypse Now*, San Francisco: Zoeptrope Studios, 1979.

Coward, John M. *The Newspaper India: Native American Identity in the Press, 1820–90*, Urbana: University of Illinois Press, 1999.

Crane, Conrad C. *American Airpower Strategy in Korea, 1950–1953*, Lawrence: University Press of Kansas, 2000.

Croser, Caroline. 'Networking Security in the Space of the City: Event-ful Battlespaces and the Contingency of the Encounter.' *Theory and Event*, 10:2, 2007.

———— 'Organising complexity: Modes of Behaviour in a Networked Battlespace,' Australian Army, Land Warfare Studies Centre, Working Paper, 133, 2007.

———— *The New Spatiality of Security: Operational Uncertainty and the US military in Iraq*, London: Routledge, 2010.

Cullather, Nick. 'Bombing at the Speed of Thought: Intelligence in the Coming Age of Cyberwar,' *Intelligence and National Security*, 18:4, 2003.

Cumings, *Parallax Visions: Making Sense of American-East Asian Relations*, Durham: Duke University Press, 2002.

———— *Dominion from Sea to Sea: Pacific Ascendancy and American Power*, Yale University Press, 2009.

———— *The Korean War: A History*, New York: Modern Library, 2010.

Curley, Tom. 'In Iraq, a Journalist in Limbo,' *Washington Post*, Sept. 23, 2006, p. A19.

Danner, Mark. *Torture and Truth: America, Abu Ghraib, and the War on Terror*, New York: New York Review of Books, 2004.

Davis, Mike. *Planet of Slums*, London: Verso, 2007.

Davis, Peter (dir). *Hearts and Minds*, New York: BBS Productions, 1974.

Daynes, Byron W. and Glen Sussman. 'The Imperial Presidency Revisited: Lessons from the Administration of George W. Bush,' paper presented at 2008 Annual Meeting of the American Political Science Association.

Dean, William F. *General Dean's Story*, New York: Viking Press, 1954.

Deer, Patrick. *Culture in Camouflage: War, Empire and Modern British Literature*, Oxford: Oxford University Press, 2008.

Delbrück, Hans. *History of the Art of War*, 4 vols., Lincoln: University of Nebraska Press, 1990.

Deleuze, Gilles. 'What is a *Dispositif?*' *Michel Foucault Philosopher: Essays*, Timothy Armstrong (trans), New York: Routledge, 1992.

Der Derian, James. 'Imaging Terror: Logos, Pathos and Ethos,' *Third World Quarterly*, 26:1, 2005, pp. 23–37.

———— *Virtuous War: Mapping the Military-Industrial-Media-Entertainment Network*, 2nd ed, New York: Routledge, 2009.

Derrida, Jacques. *Specters of Marx: The State of the Debt, the Work of Mourning, and the New International*, New York, Routledge, 1994.

DeYoung, Karen. 'Obama to Explore New Approach to Afghanistan War,' *Washington Post*, Nov. 11, 2008, p. A1.

DeYoung, Karen and Joshua Partlow. 'Karzai's Overture Sets off Discord, Confusion,' *Washington Post*, Mar. 3, 2010, p. A1.

Dirks, Nicholas. *Castes of Mind: Colonialism and the Making of Modern India*. Princeton: Princeton University Press, 2001.

———— *The Scandal of Empire: India and the Creation of Imperial Britain*, Cambridge: Harvard University Press, 2008.

Disney, Patrick. 'Pushing Iran Towards a Nuclear Bomb,' Al Jazeera, Jan. 13, 2012. Available at http://www.other-news.info/2012/01/pushing-iran-towards-a-nuclear-bomb/.

Dormer, Mike, Max Whitby, and Phillip Whitehead (dirs). *Korea: The Unknown War*, London: Thames Television, 1986.

Dotinga, Randy. 'Navy Photo Shows Antigay Slur on Bomb,' *Gay.com/PlanetOut. com Network*, Oct. 12, 2001.

Dougherty, Michael Brendan. 'You Can't Make this Stuff Up,' *American Conservative*, 7:23, Dec. 1, 2008, pp. 18–19.

Dower, John W. *Cultures of War: Pearl Harbor, Hiroshima, 9–11, Iraq*, New York: W.W. Norton, 2010.

———— *War Without Mercy: Race and Power in the Pacific War*, New York: Pantheon Books, 1986.

Drew, Christopher. 'Drone Flights Leaves Military Awash in Data,' *New York Times*, Jan. 10, 2010, p. A1.

———— 'Military Taps into Social Networking Skills,' *New York Times*, Jun. 7, 2010, p. B1.

'The Drone Wars,' *Wall Street Journal*, Jan. 9, 2010, p. A12.

Dunne, B.W. 'Homosexuality in the Middle East: An Agenda for Historical Research,' *Arab Studies Quarterly*, 12:3–4, 1990, pp. 1–18.

Duff, Alexander. *The Indian Rebellion: Its Causes and Results*, London: James Nisbet, 1858.

'The Earl of Harrowby on the Indian Mutiny,' *Times*, Oct. 30, 1857, p. 10.

'The Earl of Shaftesbury on the Mutiny in India,' *Times*, Nov. 2, 1857, p. 6.

'An East Indian Director on the Indian Mutiny,' *Times*, Oct. 20, 1857, p. 7.

'Editorial,' *Times*, Jun. 10, 1857, p. 9.

———— *Times*, Jul. 24, 1857, p. 9.

———— *Times*, Sept. 12, 1857, p. 6.

———— *Times*, Sept. 16, 1857, p. 6.

———— *Times*, Oct. 26, 1857, p. 6.

———— *Times*, Feb. 13, 1858, p. 9.

———— *Times*, Feb. 15, 1858, p. 6.

Edkins, Jenny. *Trauma and the Memory of Politics*, Cambridge: Cambridge University Press, 2003.

Edwards, Paul N. *The Closed World: Computer and the Politics of Discourse in Cold War America*, Cambridge: MIT Press, 1996.

Ehrenreich, Barbara. *Blood Rites: Origins and History of the Passion of War*, London: Henry Holt, 1997.

Eisenstadt, Michael. 'Tribal Engagement: Lessons Learned,' *Military Review*, Sept.-Oct. 2007, pp. 16–31.

El-Rouayheb, Khaled. *Before Homosexuality in the Arab-Islamic World, 1500–1800*, Chicago: University of Chicago Press, 2005.

Elliott, Andrea, Sabrina Tavernise, and Anne Bernard. 'For Times Sq. Suspect, Long Roots of Discontent,' *New York Times*, May 15, 2010, p. A1.

Elshtain, Jean Bethke. *Women and War*, New York: Basic Books, 1987.

Englehardt, Tom. *The End of Victory Culture: Cold War America and the Disillusioning of a Generation*, New York: Basic Books, 1995.

———— 'War of the Worlds,' *TomDispatch*, Oct. 8, 2009.

Eörsi, István. 'The Right to the Last World' in, Georg Lukács, *Record of a Life: An Autobiographical Sketch*, István Eörsi (ed), Rodney Livingstone (trans), London: Verso, 1983), pp. 9–25.

BIBLIOGRAPHY

Ermath, Fritz W. 'Contrasts in American and Soviet Strategic Thought' *International Security*, 3:2, 1978, pp. 138–55.

Etkind, Alexander. 'Post-Soviet Hauntology: Cultural Memory of the Soviet Terror,' *Constellations: An International Journal of Critical and Democratic Theory*, 16:1, 2009, pp. 182–200.

Etzioni, Amitai. 'Drone Attacks: The "Secret" Matrix,' *The World Today*, 66:7, 2010, pp. 11–14.

———— 'Unmanned Aircraft Systems: The Moral and Legal Case,' *Joint Forces Quarterly*, 57:2, 2010, pp. 66–71.

EU Council and European Commission. Hearing on 'Crimes Committed by the Totalitarian Regimes,' Apr. 8, 2008.

European Court of Human Rights. *Grand Chamber Judgement on the Case of Kononov v. Latvia*, Strasbourg, May 17, 2010.

Evans, Joyce A. *Celluloid Mushroom Clouds: Hollywood and the Atomic Bomb*, Boulder: Westview, 1998.

Fabian, Johannes. *Time and the Other: How Anthropology Makes its Object*, Matti Bunzl (trans), New York: Columbia University Press, 1982.

Falk, Richard. 'The Vietnam Syndrome,' *Nation*, Jul. 9, 2001, pp. 18–23.

Faludi, Susan. *The Terror Dream: Fear and Fantasy in Post–9/11 America*, New York: Metropolitan, 2007.

Fanon, Frantz. *A Dying Colonialism*, Haakon Chevalier (trans), New York: Grove Press, 1967.

Feldman, Allen. 'Ground Zero Point One: On the Cinematics of History,' *Social Analysis*, 46:1, 2002, pp. 110–9.

Feray, Jean-Claude and Herzer Manfred. 'Homosexual Studies and Politics in the 19th Century: Karl Maria Kertbeny,' *Journal of Homosexuality*, 19:1, 1990, pp. 23–47.

Ferretti, Maria. 'Memory Disorder: Russia and Stalinism,' *Russian Politics and Law*, 41:6, 2003, pp. 38–82.

Filippov, Aleksandr. *Noveishaia Istoriya Rossii: 1945–2006. Kniga dlya Uchiteley* [A New History of Russia: 1945–2006. A Manual for Teachers], Moscow: Prosveschenie, 2007.

Filkins, Dexter. *The Forever War*. New York: Random House, 2009.

———— 'Operators of Drones are Faulted in Afghan Deaths,' *New York Times*, May 29, 2010, p. A6.

———— 'Taliban Car Bomb Strikes U.S. Convoy in Kabul,' *New York Times*, May 18, 2010, p. A1.

Filkins, Dexter and John F. Burns. 'Mock Iraqi Villages in Desert Prepare Troops for Battle,' *New York Times*, May 1, 2006, p. A1.

Flynn, Vince. *American Assassin*, New York: Atria Books, 2010.

———— *Extreme Measures*, New York: Atria Books, 2008.

———— *Protect and Defend*, New York: Atria Books, 2007.

Foot, Rosemary. *A Substitute for Victory: The Politics of Peacemaking at the Korean Armistice Talks*, Ithaca: Cornell University Press, 1990.

Foster, Hal. 'Preface' in Hal Foster (ed), *Vision and Visuality*, Seattle: Bay Press, 1988, pp. ix-xiv.

Foucault, Michel. *Aesthetics, Method, and Epistemology* in James Faubion (ed), Robert Hurley and others (trans), New York: New Press, 1998.

———— *The History of Sexuality: an Introduction*, Vol.1, London: Vintage, 1990 [1978].

———— 'Truth, Power, Self: An Interview with Michel Foucault' in L.H. Martin. Gutman, H. and P.H. Hutton (eds) *Technologies of the Self*, Amherst: University of Massachusetts Press, 1988, pp. 145–62.

Franklin, H. Bruce. *Vietnam and Other American Fantasies*, Amherst, University of Massachusetts Press, 2000.

Frazer, James George. *The Golden Bough: A Study in Magic and Religion*. Abridged ed, Penguin Twentieth-Century Classics. Harmondsworth, England ; New York: Penguin Books, 1996.

Freccero, Carla. 'They are All Sodomites!,' *Signs: Journal of Women in Culture and Society*, 28:1, 2002, pp. 453–5.

Freud, Sigmund. 'Der Moses Des Michelangelo,' *Imago. Zeitschrift für Anwendung der Psychoanalyse auf die Geisteswissenschaften*, III, 1914, pp. 15–36.

Friedman, Thomas L. 'Because We Could,' *New York Times*, Jun. 4, 2003, p. 31.

Friedrich, Jörg. *The Fire: The Bombing of Germany, 1940–1945*, Allison Brown (trans), New York: Columbia University Press, 2002.

Frolov, Vladimir. 'Shared Agenda of Gorbachev and Medvedev,' *The Moscow Times*, May 17, 2010.

Furet, François. *The Passing of an Illusion: The Idea of Communism in the Twentieth Century*, D. Furet (trans), Chicago: The University of Chicago Press, 1999.

Fussell, Paul. *The Great War and Modern Memory*, New York; Oxford: Oxford University Press, 1975.

Gall, Carlotta. 'Ragtag Taliban Show Tenacity in Afghanistan,' *New York Times*, Aug. 4, 2008, p. 1.

Galton, Francis. *Finger Prints*. London: MacMillan and Co., 1892.

Gauhari, Farooka. *An Afghan Woman's Odyssey*, Lincoln: University of Nebraska, 1996.

Genovese, Michael. *Memo to a New President: The Art and Science of Presidential Leadership*, New York: Oxford University Press, 2008.

Ghamari-Tabrizi, Sharon. *The Worlds of Herman Kahn*, Cambridge: Harvard University Press, 2005.

Gibson, James William. *The Perfect War: Technowar in Vietnam*, Boston: Atlantic Monthly Press, 1986.

BIBLIOGRAPHY

——— *Warrior Dreams: Violence and Manhood in Post-Vietnam America*, New York: Hill and Wang, 1994.

Ginzburg, Carlo. 'Morelli, Freud and Sherlock Holmes: Clues and Scientific Method,' *Historical Workshop Journal* 9:1, 1980, pp. 5–36.

Godley, Arthur. 'Copies of the Proclamation of the King, Emperor of India, to the Princes and Peoples of India, of the 2nd day of November 1908, and the Proclamation of the Late Queen Victoria of the 1st day of November 1858, to the Princes, Chiefs, and People of India.' London: HMSO. 1908.

Goldberg, Jonah. 'When Push Comes to Torture,' *National Review Online*, Sept. 27, 2006. Available at http://www.nationalreview.com/articles/218829/when-push-comes-torture/jonah-goldberg.

Goldberg, Jonathan. *Sodometries: Renaissance Texts, Modern Sexualities*, Stanford: Stanford University Press, 1992.

Goldsmith, Jack. *The Terror Presidency*, New York: W.W. Norton, 2007.

Goldstein, Joshua. *War and Gender: How Gender Shapes the War System and Vice Versa*, Cambridge: Cambridge University Press, 2001.

González, Roberto. *American Counterinsurgency: Human Science and the Human Terrain*, Chicago: Prickly Paradigm Press, 2009.

——— 'Going "Tribal": Pacification in the 21st century,' *Anthropology Today*, 25:2, 2009, pp. 15–19.

Gordon, Avery. *Ghostly Matters: Haunting and the Sociological Imagination*, Minneapolis: University of Minnesota Press, 2008.

Graham, Patrick. 'Beyond Fallujah: A Year with the Iraqi Resistance,' *Harpers*, Jun. 2004, pp. 37–48.

Graham, Stephen. 'The Urban Battlespace,' *Theory Culture Society*, 26:7–8, 2009, pp. 278–88.

Grant, Rebecca. 'The All-seeing Air Force,' *Air Force Magazine*, 91:9, Sept. 2008.

Gray, Colin S. 'National Style in Strategy: The American Example' *International Security*, 6:2, 1981, pp. 21–47.

Gray, Dennis. 'Battle for Iraq's Third City hangs in the Balance,' AP, Nov. 11, 2008.

Gregory, Derek. 'The Biopolitics of Baghdad: Counterinsurgency and the Counter-city,' *Human Geography*, 1:1, 2008, pp. 6–27.

——— 'From a View to a Kill: Drones and Late Modern War,' *Theory, Culture and Society*, 28:7, pp. 188–215.

——— '"In Another Time-Zone the Bombs Fall Safely…" ': Targets, Civilians and Late Modern War,' *Arab World Geographer*, 9:2, 2006, pp. 88–111.

——— 'Lines of Descent,' available at http://www.opendemocracy.net/derek-gregory/lines-of-descent, Nov. 8, 2011.

——— 'Seeing Red: Baghdad and the Event-ful City,' *Political Geography* 29:5, 2010, pp. 268–79.

——— 'The Rush to the Intimate: Counterinsurgency and the Cultural Turn in Late Modern War,' *Radical Philosophy*, 150, Jul./Aug., 2008, pp. 8–23.

BIBLIOGRAPHY

Grim, Ryan. 'Faisal Shahzad Arrest: Lieberman Proposes Taking Away Citizenship of Suspected Terrorists,' *Huffington Post*, May 4, 2010. Available at http://www.huffingtonpost.com/2010/05/04/faisal-shahzad-arrest-lie_n_562834.html.

Grima, Benedicte. *The Performance of Emotion Among Paxtun Women: 'The Misfortunes which have Befallen Me,'* Austin: University of Texas, 1992.

Grossman, Dave. *On Killing: The Psychological Costs of Learning to Kill in War and Society*, Boston: Little, Brown and Co., 1995.

Grumman, Northrup. 'An Aaq–37 Eo Das for the F–35.' Available at http://www.es.northropgrumman.com/solutions/f35targeting/assets/eodasvideo.html.

Gudkov, Lev. 'The Fetters of Victory,' *Eurozine*, Mar. 5, 2005.

Guha, Ranajit. *Dominance without Hegemony: History and Power in Colonial India*, Cambridge: Harvard University Press, 1997.

———— *Elementary Aspects of Peasant Insurgency in Colonial India*, New Delhi: Oxford University Press, 1983.

———— 'The Prose of Counterinsurgency' in Nicholas Dirks, Geoff Eley, and Sherry Ortner (eds), *Culture/Power/History: A Reader in Contemporary Social Theory*, Princeton: Princeton University Press, 1994.

Gusterson, Hugh. 'An American Suicide Bomber?,' *Bulletin of Atomic Scientists Online*, Jan. 20, 2010. Available at http://www.thebulletin.org/web-edition/columnists/hugh-gusterson/american-suicide-bomber.

———— 'Nuclear Weapons and the Other in the Western Imagination,' *Cultural Anthropology*, 14:1, 1999, pp. 111–43.

———— 'Paranoid, Potbellied Stalinist Gets Nuclear Weapons: How the U.S. Print Media Cover North Korea,' *Nonproliferation Review*, 15:1, 2008, pp. 21–42.

———— 'Presenting the Creation: Dean Acheson and the Rhetorical Legitimation of NATO,' *Alternatives*, 24:1, 1999, pp. 39–57

Hacking, Ian. *The Taming of Chance*, Cambridge: Cambridge University Press, 1990.

Halberstam, David. 'From a Helicopter,' *Media Studies Journal*, Summer 2001.

Halliday, Fred. *Islam and the Myth of Confrontation: Religion and Politics in the Middle East*, New York: I.B. Tauris, 1995.

Hallin, Daniel. *Uncensored War: The Media and Vietnam*, New York: Oxford University Press, 1986.

Hammond, Philip. *Media, War, and Postmodernity*, New York: Routledge, 2007.

Hamlin, David D. '"Wo sind wir?" Orientalism, Gender and War in the German Encounter with Romania,' *German History*, 28:4, 2011, pp. 424–52.

Hanh, Thich Nhat. *Call Me By My True Names: The Collected Poems of Thich Nhat Hanh*, Berkeley: Parallax Press, 1993.

Hanley, Charles J., Sang-Hun Choe, and Martha Mendoza. *The Bridge at No Gun Ri: A Hidden Nightmare from the Korean War*, New York: Henry Holt and Company, 2001.

BIBLIOGRAPHY

Hannah, Matthew. 'Torture and the Ticking Bomb: The War on Terrorism as a Geographical Imagination of Power/Knowledge,' *Annals of the Association of American Geographers*, 96:3, 2006, p. 635.

Harris, Chad. 'The Omniscient Eye: Satellite Imagery, "Battlespace Awareness" and the Structures of the Imperial Gaze,' *Surveillance and Society*, 4:1/2, 2006.

Harvey, David. *The New Imperialism*, Oxford: Oxford University Press, 2003.

Hegel, Georg W.F. *Phänomenologie Des Geistes*, Paderborn: Voltmedia, 1973.

Hegel, G.W.F. *The Phenomenology of Spirit*, A.V. Miller (trans), Oxford: Oxford University Press. 1977.

Heizer, Robert F., and Alan J. Almquist. *The Other Californians: Prejudice and Discrimination under Spain, Mexico, and the United States to 1920*, Berkeley: University of California Press, 1971.

Henderson, George L. *California and the Fictions of Capital*, Philadelphia: Temple University Press, 1998.

Henriksen, Margot. *Dr. Strangelove's America: Society and Culture in the Atomic Age*, Berkeley: University of California Press, 1997.

Hepworth, Mike, and Bryan S. Turner. *Confession: Studies in Deviance and Religion*, London: Routledge, 1982.

Herbert, Adam. 'Compressing the Kill Chain,' *Air Force Magazine*, 86:3, Mar. 2003.

Herbig, Katherine. 'Chance and Uncertainty in *On War*' in Michael Handel (ed), *Clausewitz and Modern Strategy*, London: Frank Cass, 1989.

Herkel, Andres. 'Vene võitlus ajaloo pärast' [Russia's Fight for History], *Isamaa ja Res Publica Liidu häälekandja Eesti Eest*, Jan. 15, 2009.

Herman, Edward and Noam Chomsky. *Manufacturing Consent: The Political Economy of the Mass Media*, New York: Pantheon, 2002.

Hersh, Seymour M. *Chain of Command: The Road from 9/11 to Abu Ghraib*, New York: Allen Lane, 2004.

———— 'The Grey Zone,' *The New Yorker*, May 10, 2004.

———— *Price of Power: Kissinger in the Nixon White House*, New York: Simon & Schuster, 1984.

'Hezbollah has Israel Body Parts' *BBC News*, Jan. 19, 2008. Available at news.bbc. co.uk/2/hi/7197679.stm.

Hiio, Toomas. 'Ametlik ajalugu kehtestuks vaid mõnede mõtete ärakeelamisega' [Official history could be implemented only by prohibiting certain thoughts], *Sirp*, Jan. 15, 2010.

Hitchens, Christopher. 'A Man of Permanent Contradictions' in *Love, Poverty and War: Journeys and Essays*, New York: Nation Books, 2004.

Hochschild, Adam. *King Leopold's Ghost: A Story of Greed, Terror, and Heroism in Colonial Africa*, Boston: Houghton Mifflin, 1998.

Hodgson, Godfrey. *America in Our Time: From World War II to Nixon—What Happened and Why*, New York: Doubleday & Co., 1976.

BIBLIOGRAPHY

Höglund, Johan. 'Electronic Empire: Orientalism Revisited in the Military Shooter,' *Game Studies*, 8:1, 2008.

Holmes, Robert L. *On War and Morality*, Princeton: Princeton University Press, 1989.

Howard, Michael. *Captain Professor*, London: Continuum, 2006.

'How to Establish Our Empire in India,' *Times*, Oct. 27, 1857, p. 12.

Human Rights First. 'Torture: Quick Facts.' Available at http://www.humanrightsfirst.org/us_law/etn/misc/factsheet.aspx.

Hvostov, Andrei. 'Lääne haritlaskonna kommunismimeelsuse psühholoogia' [The Psychology of the Western Intellectuals' Communism-Mindedness], *Sirp*, Jan. 15, 1999.

Hvostov, Andrei. 'Urkade moraal, allalastute tõde' [The morale of the *urkas*, the truth of the underdogs], *Eesti Ekspress*, Jun. 28, 2005.

Ignatieff, Michael. *The Lesser Evil: Political Ethics in an Age of Terror*, Princeton: Princeton University Press, 2004.

Ignatius, David. 'Questions for Gen. Petraeus,' *Washington Post*, Dec. 29, 2010, p. A13.

Ilves, Toomas Hendrik. 'The President of the Republic of Estonia on the Anniversary of the Tartu Peace Treaty,' Tallinn, Feb. 2, 2007.

———— The President of the Republic at the 60th anniversary commemoration conference of the March deportation, Tallinn: The Museum of Occupations, Mar. 25, 2009.

'The Indian Mutinies,' *Times*, Aug. 3, 1857, p. 5.

'India Reform,' *Times*, Dec. 18, 1857, p. 7.

Irwin, Robert. *For Lust of Knowing: The Orientalists and their Enemies*, New York: Penguin, 2006.

Jackson, Patrick Thaddeus. *Civilizing the Enemy: German Reconstruction and the Invention of the West*, Ann Arbor: The University of Michigan Press, 2006.

Jacob, Christian. *The Sovereign Map: Theoretical Approaches in Cartography Throughout History* (Tom Conley trans), Chicago: University of Chicago Press, 2006.

Jacotin, Pierre. 'Mémoire sur la construction de la carte de l'Égypte,' in *Description de l'Égypte*, 17, Paris: Panckoucke, 1824, pp. 546–7.

Jameson, Fredric. *The Political Unconscious*, Ithaca: Cornell University Press, 1981.

Jaffe, Greg. 'A Personal Touch in the Taliban Fight,' *Washington Post*, Jun. 22, 2009, p. A1.

———— 'Fighting to Get out of the Way,' *Washington Post*, Dec. 27, 2010, p. A1.

Jaffe, Greg and Joshua Partlow. 'Scaling Back Ambitions,' *Washington Post*, Oct. 7, 2011.

Jamail, Dahr. *Beyond the Green Zone: Dispatches From an Unembedded Journalist in Occupied Iraq*, Chicago: Haymarket Books, 2007.

Jay, Erin Flynn. 'Mapping the Human Terrain,' *Geospatial Intelligence Forum*, 7:2, Apr. 2009, 10–12.

BIBLIOGRAPHY

Jay, Martin. 'Scopic Regimes of Modernity' in Hal Foster (ed), *Vision and Visuality*, Seattle: Bay Press, 1988, pp. 3–23.

Johnson, Chalmers. *Nemesis: The Last Days of the American Republic*, New York: Metropolitan Books, 2007.

Jomard, Edme. 'Description de la Ville et de la Citadelle du Kaire,' *Description*, 18, pp. 115–6.

Jones, David Martin. *The Image of China in Western Social and Political Thought*, Houndmills: Palgrave, 2001.

Jones, Lee. '"The Others": Gender and Conscientious Objection in the First World War,' *Nordic Review of Masculinity Studies*, 3:2, 2008, pp. 99–113.

Jones, Michael A. 'The End of 24 and Hopefully of the Idea that Torture Works,' May 24, 2010; Available at http:// humanrights.change.org/blog/view/the_end _of_24_and_hopefully_the_idea_that_torture_works.

Jones, Seth G. *Counterinsurgency in Afghanistan*, Vol. 4, Santa Monica: RAND Corporation, 2008.

——— *In the Graveyard of Empires: America's War in Afghanistan*, New York: W. W. Norton & Co., 2009.

Joya, Malalai. *A Woman among Warlords: The Extraordinary Story of an Afghan Who Dared to Raise Her Voice*, with Derrick O'Keefe, New York: Scribner, 2009.

Judex, 'The Indian Mutiny,' *Times*, Jan. 29, 1858, p. 12.

Juškin, Vladimir. 'Uus "Lavrovi doktriin" ei muuda Venemaa poliitika olemust' [The new 'Lavrov doctrine' does not change the essence of Russian politics], Interview to Argo Ideon, *Postimees*, May 19, 2010.

Jutila, Matti. 'Taming Eastern Nationalism: Tracing the Ideational Background of Double Standards of Post-Cold War Minority Protection,' *European Journal of International Relations*, 15:4, 2009, pp. 627–51.

Kaczyński, Lech. *Undelivered speech at Katyń*, Apr. 10, 2010.

Kalmar, Ivan Davidson and Derek J. Penslar (eds). *Orientalism and the Jews*, Lebanon: Brandeis University Press, 2005.

Kaplan, Robert. 'Hunting the Taliban in Las Vegas,' *Atlantic Monthly*, Sept. 2006.

Karig, Walter, Malcolm W. Cagle, and Frank A. Manson. *Battle Report: the War in Korea*, New York: Rinehart, 1952.

Karig, Walter. 'Korea—Tougher Then Okinawa,' *Collier's*, Sept. 23, 1950, pp. 24–6.

Kateb, George. 'A Life of Fear,' *Social Research*, 71:4, Winter, 2004, pp. 887–926.

Kaufman-Osborn, Timothy. 'Gender Trouble at Abu Ghraib?' *Politics & Gender*, 1:4, 2005, pp. 597–619.

Kaye, J.W. *A History of the Sepoy War in India, 1857–1858*, Vol. 1. London: W.H. Allen. 1872.

——— *A History of the Sepoy War in India, 1857–1858*, Vol. 2. London: W.H. Allen. 1878.

Khalid, Adeeb. 'Russian History and the Debate over Orientalism' in M. David-

Fox, p. Holquist, and A. Martin (eds), *Orientalism and Empire in Russia*, Bloomington: Slavica, 2006, pp. 23–31.

Khapaeva, Dina. 'Historical Memory in Post-Soviet Gothic Society,' *Social Research*, 76:1, 2009, pp. 359–94.

Khazanov, Anatoly M. 'Whom to Mourn and Whom to Forget? (Re)constructing Collective Memory in Contemporary Russia,' *Totalitarian Movements and Political Religions*, 9:2–3, 2008, pp. 293–310.

Keegan, John. 'In this War of Civilizations the West will Prevail,' *Daily Telegraph*, Oct. 8, 2001.

Kennedy, Valerie. *Edward Said: A Critical Introduction*, Cambridge: Polity Books, 2000.

Kilcullen, David. *The Accidental Guerrilla: Fighting Small Wars in the Midst of a Big One*, New York: Oxford University Press, 2009.

——— 'Countering Global Insurgency,' *Journal of Strategic Studies*, 28:4, 2005, pp. 597–617.

——— *Counterinsurgency*, New York: Oxford University Press, 2010.

——— 'Twenty-Eight Articles: Fundamentals of Company-level Counterinsurgency,' *Military Review*, May-Jun. 2006, pp. 103–8.

King, Laura and Sergei L. Loiko. 'U.S. Now in Afghanistan as Long as Soviets Were,' *Los Angeles Times*, Nov. 27, 2010.

Kipp, Jacob, Lester Grau, Karl Prinslow, and Don Smith. 'The Human Terrain System: A CORDS for the 21st Century,' *Military Review*, Sept.-Oct. 2006, pp. 8–15.

Kitchin, Rob and Martin Dodge. 'Rethinking Maps,' *Progress in Human Geography*, 31:3, 2007, pp. 331–44.

Kittler, Friedrich A. *Aufschreibesysteme 1800/1900*, München: Fink, 1985.

Klare, Michael. *Rogue States and Nuclear Outlaws: America's Search for a New Foreign Policy*, New York: Hill and Wang, 1996.

Klein, Christina. *Cold War Orientalism: Asia in the Middlebrow Imagination, 1945–1961*, Berkeley: University of California Press, 2003.

Knell, Herman. *To Destroy a City: Strategic Bombing and its Human Consequences in World War II*, Cambridge: Da Capo, Press, 2003.

Knox, Donald. *The Korean War: Pusan to Chosin: An Oral History*, New York: Harcourt Brace Jovanovich, 1985.

Kojève, Alexandre. *Introduction to the Reading of Hegel: Lectures on the Phenomenology of Spirit*, James Nichols (trans), Ithaca: Cornell University Press. 1982.

Kotkin, Stephen. *Magnetic Mountain: Stalinism as a Civilization*, Berkeley: University of California Press, 1995.

Krauthammer, Charles. 'Afghanistan: The 7/11 Problem,' *Washington Post*, Jun. 25, 2010, p. A19.

Krepinevich Jr., Andrew F. 'How to Win in Iraq,' *Foreign Affairs*, 84:5, 2005, pp. 87–104.

BIBLIOGRAPHY

Kurle, David. 'Lawyers Provide Operational Advice to CAOC Commanders,' USAF Central, Public Affairs, Mar. 9, 2010.

Lacan, Jacques. *Ecrits*, Alan Sheridan (trans), London: Routledge. 1977.

LaCapra, Dominick. *History and Memory after Auschwitz*, Ithaca: Cornell University Press, 1998.

LaFeber, Walter. *The Clash: A History of U.S.—Japan Relations*, New York: W. W. Norton & Company, 1997.

Lake, Eli. 'Drone Footage Overwhelms Analysts' *Washington Times*, Nov. 9, 2010.

Latifa. *My Forbidden Face: Growing Up Under the Taliban, A Young Woman's Story*, with Shékéba Hachemi, Linda Coverdale (trans), New York: Hyperion, 2001.

Lautensach, Hermann. *Korea: A Geography Based on the Author's Travels and Literature*, Katherine and Eckart Dege (trans), Berlin: Springer-Verlag, 1988 [1945].

Layton, Charles. 'Behind Bars,' *American Journalism Review*, 28:6, Dec. 2006–Jan. 2007, pp. 32–41.

Lawrence, T.E. 'The 27 Articles of T.E. Lawrence,' *The Arab Bulletin*, 60, Aug. 20,1917.

Lederer, Emil. 'On the Sociology of World War,' *European Journal of Sociology*, 47:2, 2006, pp. 241–68.

Lee, Chong-sik. 'Stalinism in the East: Communism in North Korea' in Robert Scalapino (ed), *The Communist Revolution in Asia*, Englewood Cliffs: Prentice-Hall, 1969, pp. 114–39.

Lemov, Rebecca. 'Towards a Data Base of Dreams: Assembling an Archive of Elusive Materials, C. 1947–61,' *History Workshop Journal*, 67:1, 2009, pp. 44–68.

Lendman, Stephen. 'Afghanistan's Operation Phoenix,' *Global Research*, Jun. 17, 2009. Available at http://www.globalresearch.ca/index.php?context=va&aid=13999.

Lerner, Ben. 'Citizenship as Sword,' Oct. 25, 2010. Available at http://spectator.org/archives/2010/10/25/citizenship-as-sword.

Letellier, Patrick. 'Egyptians Protest "Gay" Abuse in Iraq; LGBT Groups Hit out at "Torture" Confusion,' Gay.com/PlanetOut.com Network, May 18, 2004. Available at http://www.globalgayz.com/country/Egypt/view/EGY/gay-egypt-news-and-reports–200–7#article17.

Lévinas, Emmanuel. *Totality and Infinity*, Pittsburgh: Duquesne University Press, 1969.

Li, Darryl. 'A Universal Enemy?: "Foreign Fighters" and Legal Regimes of Exclusion and Exemption under the "Global War on Terror,"' *Columbia Human Rights Law Review*, 41:2, 2010, pp. 355–428.

Lieberman, Joe. 'Lieberman Statement on Introduction of Terrorist Expatriation Act,' May 6, 2010. Available at http://lieberman.senate.gov/index.cfm/news-events/news/2010/5/lieberman-statement-on-introduction-of-terrorist-expatriation-act.

Limpkin, John J., and Lolita Baldor. 'New Instances Of Using "Gay" As Means Of Torture,' *Associated Press*, Jul. 13, 2005.

Lindlaw, Scott. 'UAV Operators Suffer War Stress,' Associated Press, Aug. 8, 2008.

Lindqvist, Sven and Joan Tate. *Exterminate All the Brutes*, New York: New Press, 1992.

Linebaugh, Peter and Marcus Buford Rediker. *The Many-Headed Hydra: Sailors, Slaves, Commoners, and the Hidden History of the Revolutionary Atlantic*, Boston: Beacon Press, 2000.

Lockman, Zachary. *Contending Visions of the Middle East: The History and Politics of Orientalism*, Cambridge: Cambridge University Press, 2004.

Londono, Ernesto and Joshua Partlow. 'Afghan Prison an Insurgent Breeding Ground,' *Washington Post*, Mar. 6, 2011.

'Lord Brougham on Popular Education and the Mutiny in India,' *Times*, Nov. 5, 1857, p. 5.

Lord, Carnes. 'American Strategic Culture,' *Comparative Strategy*, 5:3, 1985, pp. 269–4.

Lowe, Lisa. *Critical Terrains: French and British Orientalisms*, Ithaca: Cornell University Press, 1992.

Löwenheim, Nava. 'A haunted past: requesting forgiveness for wrongdoing in international relations,' *Review of International Studies*, 35, 2009, pp. 531–55.

Luban, David. 'Torture and the Professions,' *Criminal Justice Ethics*, Summer/Fall 2, 2007, pp. 58–65.

Luhmann, Niklas. *Die Gesellschaft Der Gesellschaft I*, Frankfurt am Main: Suhrkamp, 1997.

Luik, Jüri. 'Our Duty,' *Diplomaatia*, Mar. 2008, pp. 16–8.

Lyall, Jason and Isaiah Wilson III. "Rage against the Machines: Explaining Outcomes in Counterinsurgency Wars," *International Organization* 63:1, 2009, pp. 67–106.

Lye, Colleen. *America's Asia: Racial Form and American Literature, 1893–1945*, Princeton: Princeton University Press, 2005.

MacArthur, John. *Second Front: Censorship and Propaganda in the Gulf War*, Berkeley: University of California Press, 1992.

MacDonald, Lt. Col. J.H. 'The Bengal Army,' *Times*, Aug. 20, 1857, p. 10.

——— 'The Indian Mutinies,' *Times*, Aug. 8, 1857, p. 12.

——— 'The Mahommedans in India,' *Times*, Sept. 11, 1857, p. 5.

MacKenzie, John M. *Orientalism: History, Theory and the Arts*, Manchester: Manchester University Press, 1995.

Mahmoud, Saba. 'Feminist Theory, Agency, and the Liberatory Subject' in Fereshte Nouraie-Simone (ed), *On Shifting Ground: Muslim Women in the Global Era*, New York: CUNY/Humanist Press, 2005, pp. 111–52

——— 'Feminist Theory, Embodiment, and the Docile Agent: Some Reflections on the Egyptian Islamic Revival,' *Cultural Anthropology*, 16:2, 2001, pp. 202–36.

Mamdani, Mahmood. 'Good Muslim, Bad Muslim,' Social Science Research Council, *After Sept. 11*. Available at http://essays.ssrc.org/sept11/essays/mamdani_text_only.html.

Mann, Michael. *States, War and Capitalism*, Oxford: Blackwell, 1988.

Malia, Martin. 'Foreword: The Uses of Atrocity' in S. Courtois *et al.* (eds), *The Black Book of Communism: Crimes, Terror, Repression*, J. Murphy and M. Kramer (trans), Cambridge: Harvard University Press, 1999, pp. ix-xx.

Mälksoo, Maria. 'The Memory Politics of Becoming European: The East European Subalterns and the Collective Memory of Europe,' *European Journal of International Relations*, 15:4, 2009, pp. 653–80.

———— 'Liminality and Contested Europeanness: Conflicting Memory Politics in the Baltic Space' in p. Ehin and E. Berg (eds), *Identity and Foreign Policy: Baltic-Russian Relations in the Context of European Integration*, Aldershot: Ashgate, 2009, pp. 65–83.

Malleson, G.B. *The Indian Mutiny of 1857*, New Delhi: Datta Book Center, 1977 [1891].

Mao, Zedong. *On Guerrilla Warfare*, New York: Praeger, 1961.

Maran, Rita. *Torture: The Role of Ideology in the French-Algerian War*, New York: Praeger, 1989.

Martin, Matt J. *Predator: The Remote Control Air War over Iraq and Afghanistan*, with Charles Sasser, Minneapolis: Zenith Press, 2010.

Masco, Joseph. 'Target Audience,' *Bulletin of the Atomic Scientists*, 64:3, Jul./Aug., 2008, pp. 14–21.

Massad, Joseph. *Desiring Arabs*, Chicago: University of Chicago Press, 2007.

———— 'Re-Orienting Desire: The Gay International and the Arab World,' *Public Culture*, 14:2, 2002.

Masso, Iivi Anna. 'Habras ja haavatav tõde' [Fragile and Vulnerable Truth] in S. Oksanen and I. Paju (eds), *Kõige taga oli hirm: kuidas Eesti oma ajaloost ilma jäi* [Behind Everything was the Fear: how Estonia lost its history], Tallinn: Eesti Päevalehe Kirjastus, 2010, pp. 223–31.

Masters, Cristina. 'Bodies of Technology: Cyborg Soldiers and Militarised Masculinities,' *International Feminist Journal of Politics* 7:1, 2005, pp. 112–32.

Matthews, Matt M. *We Were Caught Unprepared: The 2006 Hizballa-Israeli War*, The Long War Series, Occasional Paper 26, US Combined Arms Centre, Combat Studies Institute Press, Fort Leavenworth, Texas, 2008.

Matthews, William. 'One Sensor to do the Work of Many,' *Defense News*, Mar. 1, 2010.

Mayer, Jane. *The Dark Side: The Inside Story of How the War on Terror Turned into a War on American Ideals*, New York: Anchor Books, 2008.

———— 'The Predator War,' *New Yorker*, Oct. 26, 2009.

Mbembe, Achille. *On The Postcolony*, Berkeley: University of California Press, 2001.

BIBLIOGRAPHY

McAlister, Melani. *Epic Encounters: Culture, Media and U.S. Interests in the Middle East, 1945–2000*, Berkeley: University of California Press, 2001.

McAuliffe, Mary Sperling. *Crisis on the Left: Cold War Politics and American Liberals, 1947–1954*, Amherst: University of Massachusetts Press, 1979.

McChesney, Robert W. *The Problem of the Media*, New York: Monthly Review Press, 2004.

McClintock, Anne. *Imperial Leather: Race, Gender and Sexuality in Colonial Contest*, London: Routledge, 1995.

———— 'Paranoid Empire: Specters from Guantánamo and Abu Ghraib,' *Small Axe*, 28, 2009, pp. 50–74.

McCloskey, Megan. 'Two Worlds of a Drone Pilot,' *Stars & Stripes*, Oct. 27, 2009.

McCoy, Alfred. *A Question of Torture: CIA Interrogation, from the Cold War to the War on Terror*, New York: Metropolitan Books, 2006.

McCrystal, Stanley. 'It Takes a Network,' *Foreign Policy*, 185, Mar.-Apr. 2011, p. 66–70.

McNeill, William H. *The Pursuit of Power: Technology, Armed Force, and Society since A.D. 1000*, Chicago: University of Chicago Press, 1984.

McWilliams, Carey. *Factories in the Field: The Story of Migratory Farm Labor in California*, Berkeley: University of California Press, 1999 [1939].

Medvedev, Dmitry. 'Address of the President of the Russia Federation on the Day of the Political Prisoner in his video blog,' Oct. 30, 2009.

———— 'Go, Russia!,' Sept. 10, 2009.

———— 'Interview to Der Spiegel,' Nov. 7, 2009.

———— 'On Great Patriotic War, Historical Truth and Our Memory,' *President Medvedev in his video blog*, May 7, 2009.

———— 'Speech at Ceremony Awarding Decorations to Veterans of the Great Patriotic War,' Moscow, Dec. 4, 2009.

———— 'Remarks at the News Conference,' Bratislava, Apr. 7, 2010.

Meinshausen, Paul and Schaun Wheeler. 'Tribes and Afghanistan: Choosing More Appropriate Tools to Understand the Population,' *Small Wars Journal*, 6:6, Jun. 2010.

Mermin, Jonathan. *Debating War and Peace: Media Coverage of U.S. Intervention in the Post-Vietnam Era*, Princeton: Princeton University Press, 1999.

Metcalf, Thomas. *The Aftermath of Revolt: India, 1857–1870*, New Delhi: Manohar, 1990.

Metz, Christian. *The Imaginary Signifier: Psychoanalysis and the Signifier*, Bloomington: Indiana University Press, 1982.

Miles. 'On the Late Mutinies in India,' *Times*, Jul. 6, 1857, p. 11.

Mirzoeff, Nicholas. 'War is Culture: Global Counterinsurgency, Visuality and the Petraeus Doctrine,' *PMLA*, 124:5, 2009, pp. 1737–46.

Mitchell, Greg. *So Wrong for So Long: How the Press, the Pundits, and the President Failed on Iraq*, New York: Union Square Press, 2008.

Mitchell, Timothy. *Colonising Egypt*, Cambridge: Cambridge University Press, 1988.

———— 'Orientalism and the Exhibitionary Order' in Nicholas Dirks (ed), *Colonialism and Culture*, Ann Arbor: University of Michigan Press, 1992, pp. 289–318.

———— 'The World-as-Exhibition,' *Comparative Studies in Society and History*, 31:2, 1989, pp. 217–36.

Mitzen, Jennifer. 'Anchoring Europe's Civilizing Identity: Habits, Capabilities, and Ontological Security,' *Journal of European Public Policy*, 13:2, 2006, pp. 270–85.

———— 'Ontological Security in World Politics,' *European Journal of International Relations*, 12:6, 2006, pp. 341–70.

Moore, Patrick. 'Weapons of Mass Homophobia,' *The Advocate*, Jun. 8, 2004.

Moore, Molly. 'NATO confronts surprisingly fierce Taliban,' *Washington Post*, Feb. 26, 2008, p. A1.

Monmonier, Mark S. *How to Lie with Maps*, 2nd ed, Chicago: University of Chicago Press, 1996.

'Monument.' Available at http://dictionary.reference.com/browse/monument.

Morrillo, Stephen. *What is Military History?*, Cambridge: Polity, 2006.

Morozov, Viatcheslav. 'The Baltic States in Russian Foreign Policy Discourse: Can Russia Become a Baltic Country' in M. Lehti and D. J. Smith (eds), *Post-Cold War Identity Politics. Northern and Baltic Experiences*, London and Portland: Frank Cass, 2003, pp. 219–52.

Mowitt, John. 'The Battle of Algiers: Pentagon Edition' in Tina Mai Chen and David S. Churchill (eds), *History, Film and Cultural Citizenship: Sites of Production*, London and New York: Routledge, 2007, pp. 179–97.

Mulrine, Anna. 'Warheads on Foreheads,' *Air Force Magazine*, 91:10. Oct. 2008.

Murray, Stephen O. 'Male Homosexuality, Inheritance Rules, and the Status of Women in Medieval Egypt: The Case of the Mamluks' in Stephen O. Murray and Will Roscoe (eds) *Islamic Homosexualities: Culture, History, and Literature*, New York: New York University Press, 1997, pp. 161–73.

Myjer, Judge. *Concurring Opinion in the Kononov v. Latvia Judgement*, Strasbourg, Jul. 24, 2008.

Nagl, John. *Learning to Eat Soup with a Knife: Counterinsurgency Lessons from Malaya and Vietnam*, Chicago: University of Chicago Press, 2005.

'Napalm Jelly Bombs Prove a Blazing Success in Korea,' *All Hands*, Apr. 1951.

National Commission on Terrorist Attacks upon the United States. *The 9/11 Commission Report: Final Report of the National Commission on Terrorist Attacks Upon the United States*, New York: Norton, 2004.

Nayar, Pramod. *The Penguin 1857 Reader*, New Delhi: Penguin Books, 2007.

Ne Cede Malis. 'The Indian Rebellion,' *Times*, Aug. 3, 1857, p. 5.

Neumann, Iver B. 'Europe's post-Cold War memory of Russia: cui bono?' in J.W. Müller (ed), *Memory & Power in Post-War Europe: Studies in the Presence of the Past*, Cambridge: Cambridge University Press, 2002.

———— *Russia and the Idea of Europe: A Study in Identity and International Relations*, London and New York: Routledge, 1996.

———— 'Series Editor Preface' in Maria Mälksoo, *The Politics of Becoming European: A Study of Polish and Baltic post-Cold War Security Imaginaries*, London and New York: Routledge, 2010, pp. xi-xii.

New York Times, Mar. 13, 1950.

———— Mar. 14, 1950.

———— Mar. 22, 1950.

———— Mar. 27, 1950.

———— Mar. 31, 1950

———— Apr. 4, 1950.

———— Apr. 5, 1950.

———— Apr. 19, 1950.

———— Apr. 21, 1950.

———— May 16, 1950.

———— Jul. 14, 1950.

———— Jul. 16, 1950.

———— Jul. 19, 1950.

———— Aug. 1, 1950.

———— Aug. 21, 1950.

Ngai, Mae M. *Impossible Subjects: Illegal Aliens and the Making of Modern America*, Princeton: Princeton University Press, 2004.

Nguyên, Hương Thảo. 'Kỳ tích 'hồi sinh' cầu Long Biên trong bom đạn,' ('The Legendary Restoration of Long Bien Bridge under Bombings'), *Đất Việt Newspaper*, Apr. 13, 2009, Available at http://www.baodatviet.vn/Home/congdongviet/Ky-tich-hoi-sinh-cau-Long-Bien-trong-bom-dan/20094/37435. datviet.

Nietzsche, Friedrich. *On the Genealogy of Morals*, Douglas Smith (trans), Oxford: Oxford University Press, 1998 [1887].

Nordland, Rod. 'Ready or Not, Iraq's Military Prepares to Stand on Its Own,' *New York Times*, Jun. 27, 2009, p. 3.

———— 'Taliban Hit Back with a Campaign of Intimidation,' *New York Times*, Mar. 18, 2010, p. A1.

Norton, Anne. 'Gender, Sexuality and the Iraq of Our Imagination,' *Middle East Report*, 21:5, 173, 1991, pp. 26–8.

O'Connell, Mary Ellen. 'Unlawful Killing with Combat Drones: A Case study of Pakistan, 2004–2009,' Notre Dame Law School, Legal Studies Research Paper 09–43, 2009.

Olick, Jeffrey K. 'The Guilt of Nations?,' *Ethics and International Affairs*, 17:2, 2003.

Oppel, Richard A. 'Files for Suicide Bombers Show no Down Syndrome,' *New York Times*, Feb. 21, 2008, p. A6.

BIBLIOGRAPHY

Osborne, John. 'Report from the Orient—Guns are not Enough,' *Life*, Aug. 21, 1950, pp. 74–84.

Oshinski, David. *A Conspiracy So Immense: The World of Joe McCarthy*, New York: Free Press, 1983.

Owens, Patricia. 'Accidents Don't Just Happen: The Liberal Politics of High-Technology "Humanitarian" War,' *Millennium*, 32:3, 2003, pp. 595–616.

P. 'The Indian Mutinies,' *Times*, Aug. 5, 1857, p. 9.

Palmerston, Viscount. 'Speech to the House of Commons,' Feb. 12, 1858, *Hansard*, Vol. 148: cc 1282.

Palumbo-Liu, David. *Asian/American: Historical Crossings of a Racial Frontier*, Stanford: Stanford University Press, 1999.

Partlow, Joshua. 'Troops in Diyala Face a Skilled, Flexible Foe,' *Washington Post*, Apr. 22, 2007, p. A1.

Patai, Raphael. *The Arab Mind*, revised edition, new foreword by Norvell B. De Atkine, New York: Hatherleigh Press, 2002 [1972].

Pazira, Nelofer. *A Bed of Red Flowers: In Search of My Afghanistan*, New York: Free Press, 2005.

Pedelty, Mark. *War Stories: The Culture of War Correspondents*, New York: Routledge, 1995.

Perla, Peter P. *The Art of Wargaming: A Guide for Professionals and Hobbyists*, Annapolis: Naval Institute Press, 1990.

Perlez, Jane. 'Militant den is Penetrated by Pakistan,' *New York Times*, Oct. 19, 2009, p. A4.

Perlez, Jane and Pir Zubair Shah. 'Pakistan is Mired in Brutal Battle to Oust Taliban,' *New York Times*, Nov. 11, 2008, p. A1.

Perry, Commodore M. C. *Narrative of the Expedition to the China Seas and Japan, 1852–1854* in Francis L. Hawks (ed), Dover Publications Reprint, 2000 [1856].

Peters, Ralph. 'The Counter-Revolution in Military Affairs: Fashionable Thinking about Defense Ignores the Great Threats of our Time.' *Weekly Standard* 11:20, 2006, pp. 18–24.

Phillips, Michael. 'Civilians in Cross-Hairs Slow Troops,' *Wall Street Journal*, Feb. 21, 2010, p. A1.

Porter, Gareth. 'CIA Drone Operators Oppose Strikes as Helping al Qaeda,' Truthout, Jun. 3, 2010. Available at http://archive.truthout.org/cia-drone-operators-oppose-strikes-helping-al-qaeda60097.

Porter, Patrick. 'Culture Wars in Afghanistan: Guerrillas of the Information Age Rewrite the Rules,' *Le Monde Diplomatique*, Nov. 2009, p. 3.

———— *Military Orientalism: Eastern War through Western Eyes*, London: Hurst, 2009.

Porter, Theodore M. *The Rise of Statistical Thinking, 1820–1900*. Princeton: Princeton University Press, 1986.

Powell, Colin. 'Why Generals get Nervous,' *New York Times*, Oct. 18, 1992, p. A35.

Power, Samantha. *A Problem from Hell: America and the Age of Genocide*, New York: Harper Perennial, 2003.

Price, Jay. 'Guardsman killed Iraqi after Sex,' *North Carolina Observer*, Dec. 18, 2004.

Price, Alfred. 'Bridge Busting,' *Air Force Magazine*, 76:12, Dec. 1993. Available at http://www.airforce-magazine.com/MagazineArchive/Pages/1993/December%20 1993/1293bridge.aspx.

Princeton University. J.F. Dulles Papers, Curtis LeMay oral history, Apr. 28, 1966.

———— J.F. Dulles Papers, William Sebald oral history, Jul. 1965.

Puar, Jasbir K. *Terrorist Assemblages: Homonationalism in Queer Times*, Durham: Duke University Press, 2007.

Putin, Vladimir. 'Address on the 60th Anniversary of the Beginning of the Great Patriotic War,' Moscow, Jun. 22, 2001.

———— 'Pages of History—Reason for Mutual Complaints or Ground for Reconciliation and Partnership?,' *Gazeta Wyborcza*, Aug. 31, 2009.

———— 'Remarks at the Butovo Shooting Range,' Oct. 30, 2007.

———— 'Remarks at the Commemoration Ceremony of the Victims of Katyń,' Smolensk, Apr. 7, 2010.

Radner, Joan N. 'Preface' in Joan S. Lanser (ed), *Feminist Messages: Coding in Women's Folk Culture*, Campaign: University of Illinois, 1993, pp. vii-xiv.

Radner, Joan N., and Susan S. Lancer. 'Strategies of Coding in Women's Cultures' in Joan S. Lanser (ed), *Feminist Messages: Coding in Women's Folk Culture*, Campaign: University of Illinois, 1993, pp. 1–30.

Ray, Larry. 'Mourning, Melancholia and Violence' in D. Bell (ed), *Memory, Trauma and World Politics: Reflections on the Relationship Between Past and Present*, London: Palgrave, 2006, pp. 135–56.

Record, Jeffrey. *Beating Goliath: Why Insurgencies Win*, Washington, D.C.: Potomac Books, 2009.

Reid, Tim. 'Kandahar comes out of the closet,' *Times*, Jan. 12, 2002.

Renda, Mary. *Taking Haiti: Military Occupation and the Culture of U.S. Imperialism*, Chapel Hill: University of North Carolina Press, 2001.

Renton, James. 'Changing Languages of Empire and the Orient: Britain and the Invention of the Middle East, 1917–1918,' *Historical Journal*, 50:3, 2007, pp. 645–67.

Revel, Jean-Francois. *How Democracies Perish*, Garden City: Doubleday, 1984.

Reynolds, Maura. 'Kandahar's Lightly Veiled Homosexual Habits,' *Los Angeles Times*, Apr. 3, 2002.

Ricks, Thomas. *Fiasco: The American Military Adventure in Iraq*, New York: Penguin, 2006.

Rivera, Ray. 'Inroads by the Taliban challenge U.S. troops in Eastern Afghanistan,' *New York Times*, Dec. 26, 2010, p. A8.

BIBLIOGRAPHY

Robb, David. *Operation Hollywood: How the Pentagon Shapes and Censors the Movies*, Amherst: Prometheus Books, 2004.

Roberts, Frederick. *Letters Written During the Indian Mutiny*. New Delhi: Lal Publishers. 1979 [1857].

Roberts, Tom. *The Insurgency*. PBS Frontline, 2006. Available at http://www.pbs.org/wgbh/pages/frontline/insurgency/.

Robin, Ron. *The Making of the Cold War Enemy: Culture and Politics in the Military-Intellectual Complex*, Princeton: Princeton University Press, 2001.

Rondeaux, Candace. 'For Pakistan's Tribesmen, a Difficult, Deadly Choice,' *Washington Post*, Nov. 11, 2008, p. A14.

Rostami-Povey, Elaheh. 'Women in Afghanistan: Passive Victims of the Borqa [*sic*] or Active Social Participants?,' *Development in Practice*, 13:2–3, 2003, pp. 266–77.

Roy, Arundhati. 'Seize the Time,' *In These Times*, Jul. 2003. Available at http://www.thirdworldtraveler.com/Arundhati_Roy/Seize_the_Time.html.

Rubin, Alissa. 'Taliban Bet on Fear Over Brawn as a Tactic,' *New York Times*, Feb. 27, 2011, p. A6.

Rubin, Elizabeth. 'Battle Company is Out There,' *New York Times Magazine*, Feb. 24, 2008, pp. 38–45, 64, 82.

Rudalevige, Andrew. *The New Imperial Presidency: Renewing Presidential Power After Watergate*, Ann Arbor: University of Michigan Press, 2005.

Rusk, Dean. *As I Saw It*, with Richard Rusk and Daniel S. Papp, New York: W.W. Norton, 1990.

Said, Edward. *Covering Islam: How the Media and the Experts Determine How We See the Rest of the World*, New York: Pantheon, 1981.

——— *Orientalism*, London: Penguin, 1978.

——— *Culture and Imperialism*, London: Vintage, 1994.

——— *The Question of Palestine*, New York: Times Book, 1979.

——— *Reflections on Exile and Other Essays*, Cambridge: Harvard University Press, 2000.

Sahni, Kalpana. *Crucifying the Orient: Russian Orientalism and the Colonization of Caucasus and Central Asia*, Bangkok: White Orchid Press, 1997.

Saletan, William. 'Ghosts in the Machine: Do Remote-Control War Pilots Get Combat Stress,' *Slate*, Aug. 11, 2008.

Santora, Marc and Suadad N. Al-Salhy. 'Iraq Tribes are Upset by Sentence Given to G.I.,' *New York Times*, May 23, 2009, p. A5.

Satia, Priya. *Spies in Arabia: The Great War and the Cultural Foundations of Britain's Covert Empire in the Middle East*, Oxford: Oxford University Press, 2008.

Scales, Rebecca. 'Subversive Sound: Transnational Radio, Arabic Recordings, and the Dangers of Listening in French Colonial Algeria, 1934–1939,' *Comparative Studies in Society and History*, 52:2, 2010, pp. 384–417.

Scarry, Elaine. *The Body in Pain: the Making and Unmaking of the World*, Oxford: Oxford University Press, 1985.

Schechter, Danny. *Media Wars: News At a Time of Terror*, Lanham: Rowman and Littlefield, 2003.

Schell, Jonathan. *The Unconquerable World: Power, Nonviolence, and the Will of the People*, New York: Metropolitan Books, 2003.

Schild, Maarten. 'Islam' in Arno Schmitt and Jehoeda Sofer (eds) *Sexuality and Eroticism among Males in Moslem Societies*, Binghamton NY: Haworth Press, 1992, pp. 179–80.

Schmitt, Carl. 'Theory of the Partisan: Intermediate Commentary on the Concept of the Political (1963),' *Telos* 127 (Spring 2004): 11–78.

Sedgewick, Eve Kosofsky. *Epistemology of the Closet*, Berkeley: University of California Press, 1990 [2008].

Sengoopta, Chandak. *Imprint of the Raj: How Fingerprinting Was Born in Colonial India*, Oxford: Macmillan, 2003.

Shadid, Anthony. *Night Draws near: Iraq's People in the Shadow of America's War*, New York: Picador, 2006.

Shanker, Thom. 'Civilian Risks Curbing Strikes in Afghan War,' *New York Times*, Jul. 23, 2008, p. A1.

Shachtman, Noah. 'Army Social Scientist Set Afire in Afghanistan,' *WIRED*, Nov. 6, 2008. Available at http://www.wired.com/dangerroom/2008/11/army-social-sci/.

Shaheen, Jack G. *Guilty: Hollywood's Verdict on Arabs After 9/11*, Northampton: Olive Branch Press, 2008.

———— *Reel Bad Arabs: How Hollywood Vilifies a People*, Northampton: Olive Branch Press, 2009.

Shanker, Thom. 'Rival Factions Unite for Raids in Afghanistan,' *New York Times*, Dec. 28, 2010, p. A1.

Shanker, Thom and Alissa Rubin. 'Quest to Neutralize Taliban is Showing Glimpses of Success, NATO Says,' *New York Times*, Jun. 29, 2010, p. A10.

Sharp, Joanne P. *Condensing the Cold War: Readers Digest and American Identity*, Minneapolis: University of Minnesota Press, 2000.

Shaw, Martin. *Dialectics of War*, London: Pluto Press, 1988.

Shohat, Ella. 'On the Margins of Middle Eastern Studies: Situating Said's *Orientalism*,' *ROMES*, 43:1, 2009, pp. 18–24.

Shulman, Robin. 'Terror-Themed Game Suspended,' *Washington Post*, Mar. 8, 2008, p. A3.

Shuman, Amy. *Other People's Stories: Entitlement Claims and the Critique of Empathy*, Champaign: University of Illinois Press, 2005.

Silverman, Barry. 'Human Terrain Data—What Should We Do with It?' *Departmental Papers (ESE)*, 2007.

BIBLIOGRAPHY

Simpson, Christopher. *Blowback: America's Recruitment of Nazis and Its Effects on the Cold War*, New York: Weidenfeld & Nicholson, 1988.

Singer, Peter. 'The Soldiers Call it War Porn,' *Spiegel Online*, Mar. 12, 2010.

Singer, P.W. *Wired for War: The Robotics Revolution and Conflict in the 21st Century*, New York: Penguin Press, 2009.

Singh, Nikhil. 'The Afterlife of Fascism,' *The South Atlantic Quarterly*, 105:1, 2006, pp. 71–93.

Śmigielski, Robert. 'Commentary on the Ceremony to Mark the 70th Anniversary of the Katyń Massacre,' *Bulletin of the Polish Institute of International Affairs*, 51:127, Apr. 8, 2010.

Smith, Craig S. 'Shh, It's an Open Secret: Warlords and Pedophilia,' *New York Times*, Feb. 21, 2002, p. A4.

Smith, Jonathan Z. 'The Bare Facts of Ritual,' *History of Religions*, 20:1/2, 1980, pp. 112–27.

Smith, Roger. 'The Long History of Gaming in Military Training,' *Simulation Gaming*, 41:1, 2010, pp. 6–19.

Smith, Rupert. *The Utility of Force: The Art of War in the Modern World*, London: Penguin, 2006.

Sneider, Daniel. 'Let them Eat Rockets,' *New York Times*, Apr. 9, 2009.

Snyder, Timothy. 'Holocaust: The Ignored Reality,' *The New York Review of Books*, Jul. 16, 2009.

Solé, Robert. *Les Savants de Bonaparte*, Paris: Éd. du Seuil, 1998.

Solzhenitsyn, Aleksandr. *Cancer Ward*, London: Vintage Books, 2003 [1968].

Somaini, Antonio. 'On the Scopic Regime,' *On the Scopic Regime*, 5, 2005–6, pp. 25–38.

Spivak, Gayatri Chakravorty. 'Can the Subaltern Speak?' in Cary Nelson and Larry Grossman (eds), *Marxism and the Interpretation of Culture*, New York: MacMillan, 1988, pp. 271–313.

Springer, Chris. *North Korea Caught in Time: Images of War and Reconstruction*, with Balazs Szalontai, Berkshire: Garnet Publishing Ltd., 2010.

'Stability Operations in Iraq (Op-Telic 2–5): An Analysis from a Land Perspective,' London, Chief of the General Staff, 2006.

Stanski, Keith. '"So These Folks are Aggressive": An Orientalist Reading of "Afghan Warlords,"' *Security Dialogue*, 40:1, 2009, pp. 73–94.

Steele, Brent J. *Ontological Security in International Relations: Self-Identity and the IR State*, London and New York: Routledge, 2008.

Steiner, Jesse F. *Behind the Japanese Mask*, New York: MacMillan, 1943.

Stockman, Farah. 'Anthropologist's War Death Reverberates,' *Boston Globe*, Feb. 12, 2009.

Stoddard, Lothrop. *The Rising Tide of Colour Against White World Supremacy*, New York: Charles Scribner's Sons, 1920.

Stoler, Ann Laura. *Race and the Education of Desire: Foucault's 'History of Sexuality' and the Colonial Order*, Durham: Duke University Press, 1995.

Strachan, Hew. *Clausewitz's On War*, New York: Grove, 2007.

———— 'A General Typology of Transcultural Wars—the Modern Age' in Hans-Henning Kortüm (ed), *Transcultural Wars from the Middle Ages to the Twenty First Century*, Berlin: Akademie Verlag, 2006, pp. 85–103.

Struck, Doug. 'U.S., South Korea Gingerly Probe the Past,' *Washington Post*, Oct. 27, 1999, p. A24.

Sullivan, Andrew. 'Our War Too: Gay Heroes and Gay Necessities,' *PlanetOut*, Sept. 21, 2001. Available at http://sullivanarchives.theatlantic.com/homosexuality.php.

'Sulima' and 'Hala.' *Behind the Burqa: Our Life in Afghanistan and How We Escaped to Freedom*, with Batya Swift Yasgur, Hoboken: John Wiley, 2002.

Sultan, Masuda. *My War at Home*, New York: Washington Square Press, 2006.

Suzuki, Shogo. 'Seeking "Legitimate" Great Power Status in Post-Cold War International Society: China's and Japan's Participation in UNPKO,' *International Relations*, 22, 2008, pp. 45–63.

Sykes, Mark. 'The Future of the Near East,' *Daily News*, Sept. 18–19, 1918.

Taguba Report. 'Article 15–6 Investigation of the 800th Military Police Brigade,' 2004. Available at http://www.globalsecurity.org/intell/library/reports/2004/800-mp-bde.htm.

Tanaka, Yuki and Marilyn B. Young. *Bombing Civilians: A Twentieth-Century History*, New York: New Press, 2009.

Tannberg, Tõnu. 'Eesti saatust kujundanud välistegurid' [The external factors shaping the fate of Estonia], in *Sõja ja rahu vahel: Esimene punane aasta II* [Between War and Peace: The First Red Year II], Tallinn: S-Keskus, 2010.

Targeting, USAF DD 2–1.9, Jun. 2006.

Teitel, Ruti G. *Transitional Justice*, Oxford: Oxford University Press, 2000.

'The Indian Mutinies,' *The Times*, Aug. 8, 1857, p. 12.

'There Were Orders to Follow,' *New York Times*, Apr. 4, 2008, p. 22.

Thomas, Evan and John Barry, 'Surprising Lessons of Vietnam,' *Newsweek*, Nov. 16, 2009, p. 36.

Thompson, Reginald. *Cry Korea*, London: Macdonald & Company, 1951.

Thussu, Daya Kishan and Des Freedman (eds). *War and the Media*, Thousand Oaks: Sage, 2003.

Tilly, Charles. *Coercion, Capital, and European States, AD 990–1990*, Cambridge: Blackwell, 1990.

Tirpak, John. 'Beyond Reachback,' *Air Force Magazine*, 92:3, Mar. 2009.

Todorova, Maria. *Imagining the Balkans*, Oxford: Oxford University Press, 1997.

Townsend, J. 'They Don't Like Hell Bombs,' *Armed Forces Chemical Journal*, Jan. 1951

BIBLIOGRAPHY

'Transcript of Round Table Discussion on American Policy toward China,' State Department, Oct. 6–8, 1949, declassified in Carrolton Press, CRC 1977, item 316B.

Transition to and from Hostilities, Defense Science Board Summer Study, Department of Defense: Washington, D.C., 2004.

Trexler, Richard. *Sex and Conquest: Gendered Violence, Political Order, and the European Conquest of the Americas*, Ithaca: Cornell University Press, 1995.

'Troops in Contact: Airstrikes and civilian deaths in Afghanistan,' Washington, D.C.: Human Rights Watch, 2008.

Tucker, Judith E. 'Pensée 2: We've Come a Long Way, Baby—But We've Got a Long Way to Go,' *International Journal of Middle East Studies*, 40:1, 2008, pp. 19–21.

Turse, Nick. *The Complex: How the Military Invades our Everyday Lives*, New York: Metropolitan Books, 2009.

Tusk, Donald. 'Remarks of the Prime Minister of Poland at the Commemoration Ceremony of the Victims of the Katyń Massacre,' Apr. 7, 2010.

Tyson, Ann Scott. 'A Historic Success in Military Recruiting,' *Washington Post*, 14 Oct. 2009.

Ucko, David. *The New Counterinsurgency Era: Transforming the U.S. Military for Modern Wars*, Washington, D.C.: Georgetown University Press, 2009.

Uecker, Timothy. *Full-motion Video: The New Dimension of Imagery*, Research Report, Air Command and Staff College, Maxwell AFB, 2005.

Uldricks, Teddy J. 'War, Politics and Memory: Russian Historians Reevaluate the Origins of WWII,' *History & Memory*, 21:2, 2009, pp. 60–82.

'Unmanned Aerial System First to Fire Missiles in Combat,' Operation Iraqi Freedom. Available at http://www.mnf-iraq.com/index.php?option=com_content&task=view&id=25656&Itemid=128.

U.S. Army. 'HTS Components.' Available at http://humanterrainsystem.army.mil/components.html.

———'Welcome to the HTS Home Page,' Mar. 24, 2011. Available at http://hts.army.mil/overview.html.

U.S. Army and U.S. Marine Corps. *Field Manual 3–24: Counterinsurgency*, Washington, D.C.: Department of the Army, 2006.

United States Central Intelligence Agency. *Factbook: Afghanistan*. Available at https://www.cia.gov/library/publications/the-world-factbook.

United States Marine Corps. *Small Wars Manual*, Honolulu: University Press of the Pacific, 2005 [1940].

'United States-Viet Nam Scientific Conference on Human Health and Environmental Effects of Agent Orange/Dioxins,' March 3–6, 2002, Ha Noi, Vietnam. Available at http://www.utvet.com/agentorange.html.

Van Staaveren, Jacob. *Gradual Failure: The Air War over North Vietnam 1965–1966*, Washington, D.C.: Air Force Museums and History Program, 2002, p. 46.

BIBLIOGRAPHY

Vaughn, Jessica. 'Faisal Shahzad: So Easy, Anyone Can Do It,' Center for Immigration Studies, May 7, 2010. Available at http://www.cis.org/faisal-shahzad.

Virilio, Paul. *War and Cinema: The Logistics of Perception*, Patrick Camiller (trans), London: Verso, 1989 [1984].

Von Laue, Theodore. *Why Lenin? Why Stalin? Why Gorbachev?: The Rise and Fall of the Soviet System*, New York: Longman, 1993.

Watson, Julia and Sidonie Smith. 'Introduction' in Sidonie Smith and Julia Watson (eds), *De/Colonizing the Subject: The Politics of Gender in Women's Autobiography*, Minneapolis: University of Minnesota Press, 1992, pp. xiii-xxxi.

Wayne, Stephen J. 'Presidential Decision Making: The Influence of Personality on George W. Bush's Decisions to go to War' in George C. Edwards III (ed), *Readings in Presidential Politics*, Belmont: Thompson/Wadsworth, 2006, pp. 135–55.

Weber, Cynthia. *Imagining America at War: Morality, Politics and Film*, New York: Routledge, 2006.

Weiner, Tim. 'Robert S. McNamara, Architect of a Futile War, Dies,' *New York Times*, Jul. 6, 2009, p. 1.

Weldes, Jutta *et al.* (ed). *Cultures of Insecurity: States, Communities, and the Production of Danger*, Minneapolis: University of Minnesota Press, 1999.

White, Richard. 'Gorgon Stare Broadens UAV Surveillance,' *Aviation Week*, Nov. 3, 2010.

Whitlock, Gillian. *Soft Weapons: Autobiography in Transit*, Chicago, University of Chicago Press, 2006.

WikiLeaks. 'Collateral Murder,' Available at http://www.collateralmurder.com/.

Will, George. 'A Tet in Afghanistan?,' *Washington Post*, Dec. 16, 2010, p. A25.

Wilson, J.C. 'The Indian Mutiny,' *Times*, Mar. 24, 1858, p. 5.

Winichakul, Thongchai. *Siam Mapped: A History of the Geo-Body of a Nation*, Honolulu: University of Hawai'i Press, 1994.

Wittfogel, Karl. *Oriental Despotism*, New Haven: Yale University Press, 1957.

Wolff, Larry. *Inventing Eastern Europe: The Map of Civilization in the Mind of the Enlightenment*, Stanford: Stanford University Press, 1994.

Wright, Stephen. *Meditations in Green*, New York: Vintage, 2003.

Yoo, John. *Crisis and Command*, New York: Kaplan Publishing, 2009.

Young, Marilyn. 'Lost in the Desert: Lawrence and the Theory and Practice of Counterinsurgency' in David Ryan and Patrick Kiely (eds), *America and Iraq: Policy-making, Intervention and Regional Politics*, New York: Taylor and Francis, 2009, pp. 76–91.

Young, Robert, J.C. *Colonial Desire: Hybridity in Theory, Culture, and Race*, New York: Routledge, 1995.

Zarakol, Ayşe. 'Ontological (In)Security and State Denial of Historical Crimes: Turkey and Japan,' *International Relations*, 24:1, 2010, pp. 3–23.

Zeeland, Steven. *The Masculine Marine: Homoeroticism in the US Marine Corps*, New York: Harrington Park Press, 1996.

BIBLIOGRAPHY

Zelizer, Barbie and Stuart Allen. *Journalism After September 11*, New York: Routledge, 2002.

Zepezauer, Mark. *The CIA's Greatest Hits*, Tucson: Odonian Press, 2002.

Zhurzhenko, Tatiana. 'The Geopolitics of Memory,' *Eurozine*, May 10, 2007.

Zizek, Slavoj. 'Desire: Drive = Truth: Knowledge,' *Umbr(a)*. 1997. Available at http://www.lacan.com/zizek-desire.htm.

———— 'What Rumsfeld Doesn't Know that He Knows About Abu Ghraib,' *In These Times*, May 21, 2004. Available at http://www.inthesetimes.com/article/747/.

'Zoya.' *Zoya's Story*, with John Follain and Rita Cristofari, New York: William Morrow, 2002.

Zucchino, David. 'Drone Pilots have a Front-row Seat on War from Half a World Away,' *Los Angeles Times*, Feb. 21, 2010.

INDEX

INDEX